ROMAN

..... Under Trajan A.D. 98-117

...... Eastern Frontier under
Hadrian, A.D. 117-138

D1204339

Pontus Euxinus

Danuvius

ESIA

RACIA

BITHYNIA ET PONTUS

Ancyra

GALATIA CAPPADOCIA

ASIA

ARMENIA

PARTHIA

LYCIA ET
PAMPHYLIA

CILICIA

Athenae

ASSYRIA

MESOPOTAMIA

SYRIA

CRETA

CYPRUS

Euphrates

Tigris

JUDAEA

CA

ARABIA

AEGYPTUS

Nilus

ESSENTIALS OF LATIN

Triumph of Marcus Aurelius (emperor A.D. 161–180),
Palazzo dei Conservatori, Rome

ESSENTIALS OF LATIN

AN INTRODUCTORY COURSE

USING SELECTIONS FROM LATIN LITERATURE

JOHN F. C. RICHARDS

DEPARTMENT OF GREEK AND LATIN
COLUMBIA UNIVERSITY

NEW YORK · OXFORD UNIVERSITY PRESS · 1958

PA
Z 087
.R527
1958

LUDOVICO M. HACKER
DECANO INDULGENTISSIMO
HOC OPUS
D. D. D.

PREFACE

THIS book is intended for mature students in colleges or schools who wish to learn Latin as quickly as possible, and for those who wish to study Latin privately. Its purpose is to introduce the student to Latin literature while he is learning the language.

It consists of an Introduction and forty-one lessons, which are suitable for a course meeting three or four times a week during a session of about fourteen weeks. But those who wish to use the book more slowly may prefer to take two instead of three lessons a week.

There are three exercises in each lesson, translation from Latin into English, translation from English into Latin, and questions expressed in Latin which are to be answered in Latin.

In the first ten lessons simple Latin sentences have been written for Exercise 1. After that nearly all the sentences are taken from Latin authors. These quotations cover a wide range of authors and include poetry as well as prose. Naturally they are more difficult than the sentences in the earlier lessons, but the instructor may assign any part of Exercise 1 that he thinks is appropriate.

The sentences in Exercise 2 are based on the subject-matter of Exercise 1. Stress is laid on translating from English into Latin, not because students are expected to be good at composition, but because in the writer's opinion this will make them far more sensitive to the language and will therefore help them to read it better. If they concentrate only on reading, the results will be less satisfactory.

Stress is also laid on Exercise 3, since this gives useful practice in the oral or direct method of teaching Latin, which is an important feature of the book. The questions asked in Exercise 3 make use of the material in Exercise 1, so that there is a close relationship in each lesson between the three parts of the drill. The book has already been used in G.S. Latin 1, an elementary course in the School of General Studies at Columbia University. This course is intended partly for undergraduates in General Studies, Columbia College and Barnard College, and partly for graduate students in such fields as English Literature, Romance Languages, or Medieval

History, who may need a knowledge of Latin for the Ph.D. degree.

The writer would like to thank Professor J. Whatmough of Harvard University for his kindness in reading the manuscript of the book.   J. F. C. R.

Columbia University
  December 1957

CONTENTS

LIST OF ILLUSTRATIONS

ESSENTIALS OF LATIN

INTRODUCTION

Sect. 1. The alphabet

THE Latin alphabet consists of twenty-three letters. The letters *i* and *u* (*v*) were used as both vowels and consonants, and there was no sign for the English *w*. Consonantal *i* was written instead of *j*, but in modern texts it is customary to use the character *v* for consonantal *u*. Though *k* survives in *Kalendae* (the first day of the month), the letter *c* was generally used for the sound of *k*. In Cicero's time, *y* and *z* were borrowed from Greek to represent Greek sounds. There are five vowels (*a, e, i, o, u*), and these may be either short or long in quantity. The Greek *y* is also used as a vowel. There are six diphthongs (*ae, au, ei, eu, oe, ui*). In a diphthong, two vowel sounds are combined in the same syllable. Other combinations of vowels are pronounced as two syllables.

Sect. 2. Pronunciation

Vowels and consonants

A	ā	approximately as in father	**māter**, mother
	a	as in arise	**pater**, father
B		as in best (but before *s* and *t*, pronounced as *p*)	**bonus**, good **urbs**, city (='urps')
C		hard as in cat, *not* soft as in city	**caput**, head
D		as in dog	**dōnum**, gift
E	ē	as *a* in day[1]	**rēs**, thing
	e	as *e* in get	**ego**, I
F		as in faith	**fidēs**, faith
G		hard as in go, *not* soft as in gem	**Gallia**, Gaul[2]
H		a breathing, as in home	**homo**, man
I	ī	as in seen	**sīdus**, star
	i	as in sit	**similis**, similar
	consonantal *i*	like *y* in you	**iānua**, door

---

[1] The comparison between English and Latin sounds is not always exact. For example, Latin *e* and *o* do not correspond precisely to the vowels in English 'day' and 'gold'.

[2] The character *C* originally had the value of *G*; this has been kept in the abbreviation C. for Gāius and Cn. for Gnaeus.

K (rare)	as in kindness	**Kalendae,** Calends
L	as in long	**longus,** long
M	as in man	**manus,** hand
N	as in name	**nōmen,** name
O ō	as in gold	**ōtium,** leisure
o	as in obey	**opus,** work
P	as in peace	**pāx,** peace
Q (u)	as in quick	**quis,** who?
R	as in Rome	**Rōma,** Rome
S	as in sea and ships, *not* as in days	**sōl,** sun; **diēs,** day
T	as in time, *not* as in relation	**tempus,** time
U (V) ū	as in cool	**rūs,** the country
u	as in took	**tuba,** trumpet
consonantal *u* (= *v*) like *w* in wife		**vīta,** life
X (= cs, ks)	as in axe	**saxum,** rock
Y (= Greek upsilon), between *u* and *i* as in French *tu*, German *über*		**Syria,** Syria
Z (= Greek zeta) like z as in zone		**Amazōn,** Amazon

Diphthongs

ae	as in high	**aestās,** summer
au	as in cow	**aurum,** gold
ei (rare)	as in eight	**ei,** an exclamation
eu	like 'ehóo'	**seu,** or if
oe	as in soil	**poena,** punishment
ui	like 'oóee', as in French **huit**	**cui, huic,** *dative of* **qui,** who, *and* **hic,** this

eu and *ui* have no English equivalent.

Aspirates

ph ⎫
th ⎬ were originally pronounced like *p, t, k* followed by *h*, which is a breathing or aspiration.
ch ⎭

But *ph* may be pronounced like *f* in fill   **philosophus,** philosopher
and *th* may be pronounced like *t*   **thēsaurus,** treasure
ch is pronounced like *k* followed by *h*, as   **Acherōn,** Acheron
     in German *ach*

The *C* in *Cicerō* is pronounced like *K* and not like *Ch*, as in the Italian pronunciation of Latin. This is shown clearly by Greek authors who used the spelling *Kikerōn* for this Roman name.

Sect. 3. Syllables

Each syllable contains a vowel or a diphthong, and when a word is divided into syllables, a consonant is pronounced with the vowel that follows it, e.g. *a-mī-cī*. If two consonants occur together, the first is pronounced with the vowel that precedes it, e.g. *nūl-lī*, and both of them must be pronounced. Since a double consonant like *x* cannot be divided, it should be written with the vowel that precedes it, e.g. *māx-i-mī* (= *mac-si-mī*).

Sect. 4. Quantity of syllables

Vowels are either short or long by nature; the *a* of *amō* is short, the *o* is long. Diphthongs are always long. A syllable containing a long vowel or diphthong is long. If a syllable contains a short vowel, followed by two consonants, it is long by position. Thus the first syllable of *hasta* is long.

Another explanation is that a syllable ending with a consonant is long; thus the first syllable of *hasta* is long because it ends with *s*, and *t* belongs to the next syllable.

When the second of two consonants in a single word is a liquid (*l*, *r*), the syllable may be short or long. Thus *agrum* may be written as *a-grum* or *āg-rum*.

When a vowel stands before another vowel or *h*, it is short; thus the *i* of *diēs* is short before *e*.

When a vowel is followed by two consonants, the syllable is long, but the vowel itself may be either long or short. This is said to be a hidden quantity. For example, a vowel is long before *nf* and *ns*, as in *īnfāns*, but it is short before *nd* and *nt*, as in *amandus* and *amant*.

Sect. 5. Accent

If a word has two syllables, the accent is on the first syllable, e.g. *Rōma*. If it has more than two syllables, the accent is on the last but one (the penult) if that is long, e.g. *Rōmānī*; but it is on the last but two (the third from the end or antepenult), if the penult is short, e.g. *Horātius*. When an enclitic like *-que* is added to a word, the accent falls on the syllable to which it is attached, e.g. *Horātiúsque*.

Exercise in pronunciation

Aenēās	iūdex	optimē	uxor	cui
Cicerō	magnō	frāter	via	ei
Caesar	clārissimī	patre	Aeschylus	eī
Vergilius	hodiē	sum	zōna	audiō
Catullus	obtineō	autumnus	moenia	emō
Iūlius	Mūsa	Philippī	neu	ēmī
	dēsīderium	amat	amōre	

LESSON I

THE INDICATIVE OF THE VERB *sum*:
PRESENT, IMPERFECT, FUTURE
NOUNS OF THE FIRST DECLENSION. THE CASES:
NOMINATIVE, GENITIVE, ABLATIVE OF PLACE WHERE

Sect. 6. The Indicative of the verb sum, 'I am'; Infinitive esse, 'to be'

THE Latin verb is formed by adding the personal endings to the stem. There are six of these endings, three for the singular and three for the plural. The ending of the first person singular is either -ō or -*m*, but the other five endings are always the same in the present, imperfect, and future tenses. The verb 'to be' is irregular and the stem varies, but in the regular verbs the stem generally does not change. In English it is necessary to add the pronouns 'I', 'you', and 'he' in the singular, and 'we', 'you', and 'they' in the plural, but in Latin these meanings are expressed clearly by the endings attached to the stem. If pronouns are added, the purpose is to emphasize the meaning.

Sect. 7. Personal endings

Singular		Plural	
1st person (I)	**-ō** or **-m**	1st person (we)	**-mus**
2nd person (you)	**-s**	2nd person (you)	**-tis**
3rd person (he, she, it)	**-t**	3rd person (they)	**-nt**

Sect. 8. Conjugation of sum

	Present		Imperfect		Future	
S. 1	**sum**	I am	**eram**	I was (used to be)	**erō**	I shall be
2	**es**	you are	**erās**	you were	**eris**	you will be
3	**est**	he is	**erat**	he was	**erit**	he will be
P. 1	**sumus**	we are	**erāmus**	we were	**erimus**	we shall be
2	**estis**	you are	**erātis**	you were	**eritis**	you will be
3	**sunt**	they are	**erant**	they were	**erunt**	they will be

Any noun or adjective which is used with *sum* is always in the nominative case, when *sum* is a copulative or link verb. See Sect. 28.

Sect. 9. Nouns of the first declension

The endings of the five important cases are as follows:

	Singular	Plural
Nominative	-a	-ae
Genitive	-ae	-ārum
Dative	-ae	-īs
Accusative	-am	-ās
Ablative	-ā	-īs

The letter -a appears in all the cases of the first declension except the dative and ablative plural, which have the ending -is.

Declension of silva, a wood, forest

	Singular	Plural
Nom.	silva	silvae
Gen.	silvae	silvārum
Dat.	silvae	silvīs
Acc.	silvam	silvās
Abl.	silvā	silvīs

Sect. 10. Gender

All nouns of the first declension are feminine except words like *nauta*, 'a sailor', which clearly refer to men.

Sect. 11. Nominative, the subject, and vocative

The subject of a sentence is in the nominative case.

There is also a vocative case, which is the same as the nominative in this declension. It is used for addressing someone. Thus *Tullia* is the vocative of the name *Tullia*. Sometimes the vocative is preceded by *Ō*.

In some grammars the cases appear in the following order: nominative, vocative, accusative, genitive, dative, ablative. This is convenient, since the dative and ablative, which often have the same ending, are put together.

Sect. 12. Genitive of possession

The genitive is generally used to show possession, e.g. *agricolae silva*, 'the forest of the farmer', 'the farmer's forest'. In the vocabulary the ending of the genitive is added after the nominative.

Sect. 13. Ablative of place where

There are many uses of the ablative case. One common use is to express place where, when it follows the preposition *in* (in, on), e.g. *agricola in silvā est*, 'the farmer is in the forest'.

Here *agricola* is the subject of the sentence and is in the nominative; since the subject is singular, the verb *est* is in the third person singular. *Silvā* is in the ablative after the preposition *in* and expresses place where.

For the accusative and dative see Lesson 2.

Sect. 14. Questions

The enclitic *-ne*, attached to the first word of a sentence, shows that a question is being asked. It is omitted if an interrogative word like *ubi* (where?) is used to ask the question.

VOCABULARY

Acadēmīa, -ae, *f.*, University.[1]
Āfrica, -ae, *f.*, Africa.
agricola, -ae, *m.*, farmer.
America, -ae, *f.*, may be used for America.
crās, *adv.*, tomorrow.
et, *conj.*, and.
Eurōpa, -ae, *f.*, Europe.
fīlia, -ae, *dat. and abl. pl.* filiābus, *f.*, daughter.
Graecia, -ae, *f.*, Greece.
herī, *adv.*, yesterday.
hodiē, *adv.*, today.
in, *prep. with abl.*, in, on.

ita, *adv.*, yes; *lit.* thus, so.
Ītalia, -ae, *f.*, Italy.
minimē, *adv.*, no, not at all; *lit.* least.
nauta, -ae, *m.*, sailor.
-ne, *enclitic*, asks a question.
nōn, *adv.*, not (*used before a verb*).
nostra, our, *f. of* noster (Lesson IV).
puella, -ae, *f.*, girl.
Rōma, -ae, *f.*, Rome.
schola, -ae, *f.*, school.
silva, -ae, *f.*, wood, forest.
sum, I am (*the verb* 'to be').
ubi, *adv.*, where?
via, -ae, *f.*, road.

EXERCISE 1

TRANSLATE INTO ENGLISH:

1. Nostra Acadēmīa in Americā est. 2. Hodiē in Acadēmīa sumus. 3. Crās in Acadēmīa erimus. 4. Herī in Acadēmīa nōn erāmus. 5. Ubi est Acadēmīa nostra? In Americā est. 6. Ubi est agricola? Hodiē in silvā est. 7. Ubi sunt puellae? In silvā agricolae sunt. 8. Crās agricola in silvā nōn erit. 9. Herī agricola in silvā erat. 10. Rōma in Ītaliā est. 11. Ubi est Rōma? In Ītaliā est. 12. Ubi est Ītalia? In Eurōpā est. 13. Est-ne Graecia in Eurōpā? Ita. In Eurōpā est. 14. Erat-ne Rōma

[1] *Acadēmia* is a Greek word and refers to Plato's Academy at Athens. It is often used today for a University, e.g. *Acadēmia Harvardiāna*, 'Harvard University'. But the word *Ūniversitās* (f.) is also used, though it is not found in this sense in Classical Latin, e.g. *Ūniversitās Columbiae*, 'Columbia University', lit. 'Columbia's University'.
The *i* in *Acadēmia* is long because it represents the Greek diphthong *ei*.

in Āfricā? Minimē. In Eurōpā erat. 15. Hodiē nōn estis in Eurōpā. In Americā estis. 16. Crās in nostrā Acadēmiā eritis.

EXERCISE 2

TRANSLATE INTO LATIN:

1. Today the farmers are on the road. 2. Are the sailors on the road? 3. The girls were in the forest yesterday. 4. Italy and Greece are in Europe. 5. Is our University in America? 6. You were not in the University yesterday. 7. Our daughter will be in school tomorrow. 8. Tomorrow we shall be in the forests.

EXERCISE 3

ANSWER THE QUESTIONS IN LATIN:

1. Ubi estis hodiē? 2. Ubi est nostra Acadēmia? 3. Ubi sunt puellae? 4. Ubi erat agricola? 5. Est-ne Rōma in Eurōpā? 6. Est-ne Graecia in Āfricā? 7. Ubi crās erimus?

LESSON II

FIRST CONJUGATION, INDICATIVE ACTIVE:
PRESENT, IMPERFECT, FUTURE
NOUNS OF THE SECOND DECLENSION. GENDER
THE CASES (*cont.*): ACCUSATIVE, THE DIRECT OBJECT,
DATIVE, THE INDIRECT OBJECT,
DATIVE OF POSSESSION, VOCATIVE

Sect. 15. First Conjugation: amō, 'I love'

THE stem of all verbs of the first conjugation ends in -*ā*-. The present infinitive, *amāre*, 'to love', gives the present stem *amā*-. The personal endings (see Lesson I) are added to this stem. Thus in the present tense *amā-mus* means 'we love' or 'we are loving'. In the imperfect the syllable -*bā*- is added to the stem. Thus *amā-bā-mus* means 'we were loving' or 'we used to love' or 'we loved'. In the future the syllable -*bi*- is added to the stem. Thus *amā-bi-mus* means 'we shall love'. But there are a few variations from the pattern.

		Present		*Imperfect*
S.	1 **amō**	I love, am loving	**amā-ba-m**	I was loving, loved, used to love
	2 **amā-s**	you love	**amā-bā-s**	you were loving
	3 **ama-t**	he loves	**amā-ba-t**	he was loving
P.	1 **amā-mus**	we love	**amā-bā-mus**	we were loving
	2 **amā-tis**	you love	**amā-bā-tis**	you were loving
	3 **ama-nt**	they love	**amā-ba-nt**	they were loving

	Future	
S.	1 **amā-bō**	I shall love
	2 **amā-bi-s**	you will love
	3 **amā-bi-t**	he will love
P.	1 **amā-bi-mus**	we shall love
	2 **amā-bi-tis**	you will love
	3 **amā-bu-nt**	they will love

In the present tense the -*ā*- of the stem contracts with the personal ending -*ō* of the first person, and in the imperfect the personal ending is -*m* (as in *sum*) and not -*ō*. In the third person the -*ā*- of

the stem is shortened before -*t* and -*nt* in *amat* and *amant*, and
the -*ā*- of -*bā*- is shortened in *amābam, amābat,* and *amābant.* In the
future the -*i*- of -*bi*- does not appear in *amābō* and *amābunt.*

Principal parts

There are four principal parts of the verb:
1. **amō**, 'I love', present indicative active.
2. **amāre**, 'to love', present infinitive active.
3. **amāvī**, 'I have loved', 'I loved', perfect indicative active
(see Lesson V).
4. **amātum**, supine (see Lessons XIII, XXXVIII).

These provide the three stems *amā, amāv-,* and *amāt-* from
which all the forms of the verb are derived. Some prefer to take
amātus, the perfect participle passive, as the fourth principal part,
since the supine is used far less frequently.

Sect. 16. Nouns of the second declension

The endings of the cases are as follows:

	Singular	Plural
Nom.	-**us** (*m., f.*), -**um** (*neut.*)	-**ī** (*m., f.*), -**a** (*neut.*)
Gen.	-**ī**	-**ōrum**
Dat.	-**ō**	-**īs**
Acc.	-**um** (*m., f. and neut.*)	-**ōs** (*m., f.*), -**a** (*neut.*)
Abl.	-**ō**	-**īs**

The nominative and accusative of the neuter are the same; in
the singular they end in -*um*; in the plural they end in -*a*.

Declension of **hortus**, *m.*, garden; **dōnum**, *n.*, gift

	Singular	Plural	Singular	Plural
Nom.	hortus	hortī	dōnum	dōna
Gen.	hortī	hortōrum	dōnī	dōnōrum
Dat.	hortō	hortīs	dōnō	dōnīs
Acc.	hortum	hortōs	dōnum	dōna
Abl.	hortō	hortīs	dōnō	dōnīs

Sect. 17. Vocative and Gender

The vocative ends in -*e* in the singular. Thus *Marce* is the
vocative of the name *Marcus.* In the plural it is the same as the
nominative.

Nouns of the second declension ending in -*us* are nearly always masculine; but some nouns, such as names of cities and trees ending in *-us*, are feminine, e.g. *Corinthus*, 'Corinth'; *laurus*, 'laurel'. Nouns ending in *-um* are neuter.

'A man', 'month', 'mountain', 'river', 'wind', and 'people' are masculine; 'a woman', 'island', 'city', 'tree', and 'country' are feminine.

Sect. 18. Accusative, the direct object

The object of a transitive verb is in the accusative case.

Fīliās amat.   He loves (his) daughters.

Sect. 19. Dative, the indirect object

The word *dative* is derived from the verb *dō*, 'I give'. When one person gives a present to another, the gift is in the accusative case and the person *to* whom it is given is in the dative case. The name was then applied to other uses of the case.

Dōnum fīliae dat.   He gives a present *to* (his) daughter.

Lūnam fīliae mōnstrat.

He shows the moon *to* (his) daughter.

Here *fīliae* is in the dative case and is the indirect object; *dōnum* and *lūnam* are the direct objects.

Sect. 20. Dative of possession

The dative may also be used with the verb *sum* to express possession.

Hortus est dominō.

The master has a garden, lit. there is a garden *to* the master.

Here the word *hortus* must be in the nominative, since it is coupled with the verb 'to be'.

Sect. 21. Word order

The normal word order in Latin is subject, object, verb. If the subject is put last or the verb is put first, the effect is to emphasize them. The order in Latin can vary far more than in English, since the case endings of the nouns and the personal endings of the verbs make the meaning clear. But in English, if the order is changed, frequently the meaning is changed. *Agricola vaccās spectat* may be changed to *spectat vaccās agricola*, and this would emphasize both *spectat* and *agricola*. It may also be changed to *vaccās spectat agricola*.

VOCABULARY

amīcus, -ī, *m.*, friend.
amō, 1, love.[1]
aqua, -ae, *f.*, water.
cibus, -ī, *m.*, food.
cui, *dat. sing. of* **quis,** to whom? (Lesson XV).
dō, dare, dedī, datum, 1, give (*the* -a- *of the stem is short*).
dominus, -ī, *m.*, master (of a house), owner.[2]
dōnum, -ī, *n.*, gift.
equus, equī, *m.*, horse.[3]
errō, 1, wander, make a mistake.
exspectō, 1, wait-for (*with acc.*), wait.
hortus, -ī, *m.*, garden.
lūna, -ae, *f.*, moon.
mōnstrō, 1, show.

mox, *adv.*, soon.
patria, -ae, *f.*, country, fatherland.
pecūnia, -ae, *f.*, money.[3]
portō, 1, carry.
-que, *enclitic*, and (*attached to the second of two words, e.g.* **equī vaccaeque,** horses and cows).
quid, *nom. and acc. sing. neut. of* **quis,** what? (Lesson XV).
quis, *interrog. pron., nom. sing. m. and f.*, who? (Lesson XV).
semper, *adv.*, always.
servus, -ī, *m.*, slave, servant.
spectō, 1, look-at (*with acc.*), watch.
stella, -ae, *f.*, star.
taurus, -ī, *m.*, bull.
vacca, -ae, *f.*, cow.[3]

EXERCISE 1

1. Patriam semper amāmus. 2. Quis fīliās nōn amat? 3. Dominus pecūniam servō dat. 4. Mox lūnam fīliae mōnstrābō. 5. Nautae stellās spectābunt. 6. Agricola aquam taurō vaccīsque dabat. 7. Puellae in hortō errābant. 8. Puella amīcum in viā exspectat. 9. Hodiē cibum et aquam portābitis. 10. Sunt dōna servō. 11. Equus est agricolae.

EXERCISE 2

1. Do you love (your) country? 2. The girls love (their) friends. 3. Who was giving food to (his) servants? 4. The farmers will show the stars to (their) daughters. 5. Sailors always look-at the moon and the stars. 6. The master has water in the garden. 7. Soon the girl will wait-for (her) friends on the road.

EXERCISE 3

ANSWER IN LATIN:

1. Quid semper amātis? 2. Quid servō dat dominus? 3. Cui pecūniam dat dominus? 4. Quid fīliae mōnstrābis? 5. Cui lūnam mōnstrābis? 6. Quis stellās spectābit? 7. Quid spectābunt nautae? 8. Quid taurō dabat agricola? 9. Quis in hortō errābat? 10. Ubi errābant puellae? 11. Ubi amīcum exspectat puella? 12. Quid hodiē portābitis? 13. Cui sunt dōna? 14. Quid est servō?

[1] The numerals 1, 2, 3, and 4 will be used in the vocabulary to show the conjugation to which a verb belongs.

[2] In ecclesiastical Latin *Dominus* means 'The Lord', e.g. A.D. (*Annō Dominī*), 'in the year of Our Lord'.

[3] In Vulgar Latin a horse was not *equus* but *caballus*, 'a nag', from which the French *cheval* is derived. Compare 'cavalry' in English. *Vacca*, 'a cow', is the origin of the French *vache*. *Pecūnia*, 'money', comes from *pecus*, 'cattle', a noun of the third declension; in ancient times cattle were equivalent to wealth and were used as barter.

LESSON III

VERBS OF THE SECOND, THIRD, AND FOURTH
CONJUGATIONS, INDICATIVE ACTIVE: PRESENT,
IMPERFECT, FUTURE. NOUNS OF THE SECOND DECLENSION
(*cont.*). ACCUSATIVE OF PLACE TO WHICH. VOCATIVE (*cont.*)

**Sect. 22. Second conjugation: moneō, 'I advise', infin.
monēre, stem monē-
Third conjugation: regō, 'I rule', infin. regere,
stem rege-
Fourth conjugation: audiō, 'I hear' (listen-to),
infin. audīre, stem audī-**

THE personal endings are added in the usual way to the present
stem. Just as *amāmus*, 'we love', was formed from *amā-*, so
monēmus, 'we advise', and *audīmus*, 'we hear', are formed from
monē- and *audī-*. The stem of *regō* varies, and in the present
indicative the first person plural is *regimus*, 'we rule', with *regi-* as
the stem. The syllable *-bā-* is used in all conjugations as the sign
of the imperfect, but in the future the syllable *-bi-* is found only[1]
in the first and second conjugations. Thus *monēbimus*, 'we shall
advise', corresponds to *amābimus*, 'we shall love'; but the future
of *regō* is *regam* and the future of *audiō* is *audiam* with *-a-* in the
first person singular and *-ē-* (or *-e-*) in the other persons. Thus
regēmus, 'we shall rule', corresponds to *audiēmus*, 'we shall hear'.
In the imperfect *regēbam* the *e* of the stem is lengthened and in
audiēbam the stem ends in *-iē* instead of *-i*. For verbs of the third
conjugation ending in *-iō* see *capiō* in Lesson XIII.

Present indicative active

S.	1 **mone-ō**	I advise	**reg-ō**	I rule
	2 **monē-s**	you advise	**regi-s**	you rule
	3 **mone-t**	he advises	**regi-t**	he rules
P.	1 **monē-mus**	we advise	**regi-mus**	we rule
	2 **monē-tis**	you advise	**regi-tis**	you rule
	3 **mone-nt**	they advise	**regu-nt**	they rule

[1] It also appears in *ibō*, the future of *eō*, 'go' (Lesson XXXI).

S. 1 **audi-ō**   I hear
2 **audī-s**   you hear
3 **audi-t**   he hears
P. 1 **audī-mus**   we hear
2 **audī-tis**   you hear
3 **audiu-nt**   they hear

In the third person plural the -*i*- of the stem changes to -*u*- in
regunt, and -*u*- is added to the -*i*- of the stem in *audiunt*.

Imperfect indicative active

S. 1 **monē-ba-m**   I was advising   **regē-ba-m**   I was rul-
                       (I advised)   ing (I
                                                          ruled)
2 **monē-bā-s**   you were   **regē-bā-s**   you were
                    advising   ruling
3 **monē-ba-t**   he was   **regē-ba-t**   he was
                    advising   ruling
P. 1 **monē-bā-mus** we were   **regē-bā-mus** we were
                      advising   ruling
2 **monē-bā-tis**   you were   **regē-bā-tis**   you were
                     advising   ruling
3 **monē-ba-nt**   they were   **regē-ba-nt**   they were
                     advising   ruling

S. 1 **audiē-ba-m**   I was hearing (I heard)
2 **audiē-bā-s**   you were hearing
3 **audiē-ba-t**   he was hearing
P. 1 **audiē-bā-mus**   we were hearing
2 **audiē-bā-tis**   you were hearing
3 **audiē-ba-nt**   they were hearing

Future indicative active

S. 1 **monē-bō**   I shall advise   **rega-m**   I shall rule
2 **monē-bi-s**   you will advise   **regē-s**   you will rule
3 **monē-bi-t**   he will advise   **rege-t**   he will rule
P. 1 **monē-bi-mus**   we shall advise   **regē-mus**   we shall rule
2 **monē-bi-tis**   you will advise   **regē-tis**   you will rule
3 **monē-bu-nt**   they will advise   **rege-nt**   they will rule

S. 1 **audia-m**   I shall hear
2 **audiē-s**   you will hear
3 **audie-t**   he will hear

P. 1 **audiē-mus** we shall hear
2 **audiē-tis** you will hear
3 **audie-nt** they will hear

Principal parts

Present indicative	Present infinitive	Perfect indicative	Supine
moneō	**monēre**	**monuī**	**monitum**
regō	**regere**	**rēxī**	**rēctum**
audiō	**audīre**	**audīvī**	**audītum**

Most verbs of the second conjugation are irregular in the perfect, but some of them like *dēleō, dēlēre, dēlēvī, dēlētum* (I destroy) have a perfect ending in *-vī*, which corresponds to *amāvī* and *audīvī*. For the conjugation of the perfect see Lesson VI.

Sect. 23. Nouns of the second declension (*cont.*)

ager, *m.*, field **puer,** *m.*, boy **fīlius,** *m.*, son
praemium, *n.*, reward

Singular

Nom.	**ager**	**puer**	**fīlius**	**praemium**
Gen.	**agrī**	**puerī**	**fīlī, filii**	**praemī, praemiī**
Dat.	**agrō**	**puerō**	**fīliō**	**praemiō**
Acc.	**agrum**	**puerum**	**fīlium**	**praemium**
Abl.	**agrō**	**puerō**	**fīliō**	**praemiō**

Plural

Nom.	**agrī**	**puerī**	**fīliī**	**praemia**
Gen.	**agrōrum**	**puerōrum**	**fīliōrum**	**praemiōrum**
Dat.	**agrīs**	**puerīs**	**fīliīs**	**praemiīs**
Acc.	**agrōs**	**puerōs**	**fīliōs**	**praemia**
Abl.	**agrīs**	**puerīs**	**fīliīs**	**praemiīs**

The *e* of *puer* belongs to the stem and is retained in all the cases, but in *ager e* appears only in the nominative and vocative singular. Nouns ending in *-ius* and *-ium* have two forms of the genitive singular; during the Roman Republic the genitive of *fīlius* was contracted to *fīlī*, but the spelling *fīliī* is found in writers of the Empire.

Sect. 24. Vocative (*cont.*)

The vocative of *ager* and *puer* is the same as the nominative, but nouns ending in *-ius* have a contracted vocative in the singular, *fīlī* from *fīlius*, *Vergílī* from *Vergílius*.

Sect. 25. Accusative of place to which

The accusative is used after the prepositions *ad* (to) and *in* (into) to show the place to which or into which someone is going. The preposition is omitted before the names of towns and before *domus*, f., 'home', and *rūs*, n., 'the country'. Compare the use of 'go home' in English. See Lessons XVII and XVIII.

$$\text{Frūmentum} \begin{cases} \textbf{ad Graeciam} \\ \textbf{in Ītaliam} \\ \textbf{Rōmam} \end{cases} \textbf{portant.}$$

$$\text{They carry grain} \begin{cases} \text{to Greece} \\ \text{into Italy} \\ \text{to Rome.} \end{cases}$$

In with the accusative implies motion, *in* with the ablative does not. Compare *equus in agrōs errat*, 'the horse wanders into the fields', with *equus in agrīs errat*, 'the horse wanders in the fields'.

VOCABULARY

ad, *prep. with acc.*, to.
ager, agrī, *m.*, field.
audiō, audīre, audīvī, audītum, 4, hear, listen-to.
dūcō, dūcere, dūxī, ductum, 3, lead, conduct.
emō, emere, ēmī, emptum, 3, buy.
fīlius, fīlī (-iī), *m.*, son.
frūmentum, -ī, *n.*, grain.
in, *prep. with acc.*, into.
liber, librī, *m.*, book.
magister, magistrī, *m.*, master, teacher.
mittō, mittere, mīsī, missum, 3, send.
moneō, monēre, monuī, monitum, 2, advise, warn.
nāvigō, 1, sail.
Novum Eborācum, -ī, *n.*, New

York (*from* **Eborācum**, York, *in England*).
oppidum, -i, *n.*, town.
pōnō, pōnere, posuī, positum, 3, place, lay aside.
praemium, praemī (-iī), *n.*, reward.
puer, puerī, *m.*, boy.
quō, *interrog. adv.*, where? to what place?
regō, regere, rēxī, rēctum, 3, rule.
reperiō, reperīre, repperī, repertum, 4, find (*the* **p** *is doubled in the perfect*).
scrībō, scrībere, scrīpsī, scrīptum, 3, write.
templum, -ī, *n.*, temple.
veniō, venīre, vēnī, ventum, 4, come.
verbum, -ī, *n.*, word.
videō, vidēre, vīdī, vīsum, 2, see.

EXERCISE 1

1. Agricolae in agrōs veniunt. 2. Nautae ad Graeciam nāvigābunt. 3. Magister puerōs in scholam dūcēbat. 4. Dominus dōna ad templum mittit. 5. Magistrī fīlius dōnum in templō pōnit. 6. Puer verba in librō scrībet. 7. Agricolārum fīliī vaccās in hortō reperiunt. 8. Magister servōrum fīliōs monēbit. 9. Ubi librōs emētis? 10. Puerī-ne magistrī verba audiēbant? 11. Mox Novum Eborācum veniētis.

EXERCISE 2

1. Tomorrow we shall come to New York. 2. You will send rewards to the servants. 3. Do you see the farmers' horses? 4. They will find the cows in the field. 5. You will always advise (your) sons. 6. The boys listen-to (their) master in school. 7. The master (of the house) was buying grain in the town.

EXERCISE 3

ANSWER IN LATIN:

1. Quis in agrōs venit? 2. Quō nāvigābunt nautae? 3. Quis puerōs dūcēbat? 4. Quid ad templum mittit dominus? 5. Quis dōnum in templō pōnit? 6. Ubi est dōnum? 7. Quis verba scrībet? 8. Quis vaccās reperit? 9. Ubi sunt vaccae? 10. Quō mox veniētis?

LESSON IV

ADJECTIVES OF THE FIRST AND SECOND DECLENSIONS
AGREEMENT OF ADJECTIVES AND NOUNS
PREDICATE ADJECTIVE AND NOUN. APPOSITION

Sect. 26. Adjectives of the first and second declensions

THE feminine takes the endings of the first declension; the masculine and neuter take the endings of the second declension.

bonus, good   **liber,** free   **pulcher,** beautiful

		M.	*F.*	*N.*
S.	Nom.	bonus	bona	bonum
	Gen.	bonī	bonae	bonī
	Dat.	bonō	bonae	bonō
	Acc.	bonum	bonam	bonum
	Abl.	bonō	bonā	bonō
P.	Nom.	bonī	bonae	bona
	Gen.	bonōrum	bonārum	bonōrum
	Dat.	bonīs	bonīs	bonīs
	Acc.	bonōs	bonās	bona
	Abl.	bonīs	bonīs	bonīs

The vocative is the same as the nominative except in the masculine singular. Here the form *bone* is used.

		M.	*F.*	*N.*
S.	Nom.	liber	libera	liberum
	Gen.	liberī	liberae	liberī
	Dat.	liberō	liberae	liberō
	Acc.	liberum	liberam	liberum
	Abl.	liberō	liberā	liberō
P.	Nom.	liberī	liberae	libera
	Gen.	liberōrum	liberārum	liberōrum
	Dat.	liberīs	liberīs	liberīs
	Acc.	liberōs	liberās	libera
	Abl.	liberīs	liberīs	liberīs

Liber and *pulcher*, like the nouns *puer* and *ager*, do not have the ending -*us* in the masculine; the -*e* of the nominative masculine is

kept in the other cases of *līber*, but it is omitted in the other cases
of *pulcher*.

	M.	*F.*	*N.*
S. Nom.	pulcher	pulchra	pulchrum
Gen.	pulchrī	pulchrae	pulchrī
Dat.	pulchrō	pulchrae	pulchrō
Acc.	pulchrum	pulchram	pulchrum
Abl.	pulchrō	pulchrā	pulchrō
P. Nom.	pulchrī	pulchrae	pulchra
Gen.	pulchrōrum	pulchrārum	pulchrōrum
Dat.	pulchrīs	pulchrīs	pulchrīs
Acc.	pulchrōs	pulchrās	pulchra
Abl.	pulchrīs	pulchrīs	pulchrīs

Sect. 27. Agreement of adjectives and nouns

An adjective agrees with its noun in gender, number, and case.
Thus in *vir bonus*, 'a good man', the adjective must be masculine,
singular, and nominative; in *fēminās pulchrās*, 'beautiful women',
the adjective must be feminine, plural, and accusative.

S. Nom.	vir bonus	fēmina pulchra
Gen.	virī bonī	fēminae pulchrae
Dat.	virō bonō	fēminae pulchrae
Acc.	virum bonum	fēminam pulchram
Abl.	virō bonō	fēminā pulchrā
P. Nom.	virī bonī	fēminae pulchrae
Gen.	virōrum bonōrum	fēminārum pulchrārum
Dat.	virīs bonīs	fēminīs pulchrīs
Acc.	virōs bonōs	fēminās pulchrās
Abl.	virīs bonīs	fēminīs pulchrīs

Most adjectives follow their noun, but adjectives of quantity
usually come first, e.g. *multī virī*, 'many men'. If two adjectives
are used with a noun, they should be joined by *et* or *-que* (and),
e.g. *multī et bonī virī, multī bonīque virī*.

Sect. 28. Predicate adjectives and nouns

A noun used with the verb 'to be' may be followed by an
adjective or noun, which is known as the predicate, e.g. *nostrī virī
sunt bonī*, 'our men are good'.

The predicate adjective agrees with the subject in gender, number, and case; thus *boni* is masculine, plural, and nominative. The predicate noun agrees with the subject in case, e.g. *Tullia est puella*, 'Tullia is a girl'. Here *puella* is nominative. In these sentences *sum* is known as a copulative or link verb.

Sect. 29. Apposition

When one noun is added to another in order to explain or describe it, the second noun is said to be in apposition to the first. It must always be in the same case, e.g. *Tullia, Mārcī Tullī fīlia*, 'Tullia, the daughter of Marcus Tullius'; *Tulliam, Mārcī Tullī fīliam, vidēmus*, 'we see Tullia, the daughter of Marcus Tullius'.

Apposition is also used for geographical expressions like 'the city of Rome' or 'the island of Crete'. Here the genitive is not used to translate *of Crete*.

In īnsulā Crētā habitat. He lives on the island of Crete.

VOCABULARY

(For *meus, tuus, noster, vester*, possessive adjectives, see Lesson XIV)

Americānus, -a, -um, may be used for American.
bonus, -a, um, good.
Britannia, -ae, *f.*, Britain.
Corsica, -ae, *f.*, Corsica.
Crēta, -ae, *f.*, Crete.
dēlectō, 1, delight, please (*with acc.*).
diū, *adv.*, for a long time.
fēmina, -ae, *f.*, woman.
fīdus, -a, -um, loyal, faithful.
habeō, habēre, habuī, habitum, 2, have.
habitō, 1, live, reside.
honestus, -a, -um, honorable, virtuous.
īnsula, -ae, *f.*, island.
laudō, 1, praise.
līber, -era, -erum, free.
līberī, *m. pl.*, children.
magnus, -a, -um, great.
maneō, manēre, mānsī, mānsum, 2, remain.
Mārcus Tullius, -ī, *m.*, Marcus Tullius Cicero, 106–43 B.C., statesman and orator, consul 63 B.C.,

author of speeches, works on rhetoric and philosophy, and letters.
meus, mea, meum, my, mine.
multus, -a, -um, much.
multī, -ae, -a, many.
noster, nostra, nostrum, our, ours.
prīmus, -a, -um, first.
prōvincia, -ae, *f.*, province.[1]
pulcher, -chra, -chrum, beautiful.
quālis, *m. and f.*, of what kind? (*pl.* quālēs).
quantus, -a, -um, how great?
quōrum, *gen. pl. m. of* **quis,** of whom? whose?
Rōmānus, -a, -um, Roman.
Rōmānī, -ōrum, *m. pl.*, Romans.
Sardinia, -ae, *f.*, Sardinia.
socius, -ī (-iī), *m.*, ally, companion.
Syria, -ae, *f.*, Syria.
tuus, tua, tuum, your, yours (*sing.*).
vester, vestra, vestrum, your, yours (*pl.*).
vir, virī, *m.*, man, husband (a man in the best sense of the word).

[1] The Roman province in the south of France was known as *prōvincia* (see Caesar's *Gallic War*); this is the origin of the French word *Provence*.

EXERCISE 1

1. Mārcus Tullius, vir honestus, in Ītaliā habitābat. 2. Virōs bonōs et honestōs laudāmus. 3. Multae et pulchrae fēminae in oppidō nostrō habitant. 4. Fēminae pulchrae amīcōs dēlectant. 5. Multōs et fīdōs sociōs habētis. 6. Britannia est magna īnsula. 7. Sicilia et Corsica et Sardinia sunt īnsulae.¹ 8. Diū in īnsulā Siciliā habitābāmus. 9. Sicilia prīma Rōmānōrum prōvincia erat. 10. Graecia, Syria, Britannia prōvinciae erant Rōmānae. 11. Rōmānī erant virī līberī. 12. Līberī meī in scholā manent. 13. Mox līberōs tuōs ad scholam dūcēs. 14. Fīdī sunt amīcī vestrī.

EXERCISE 2

1. Americans are free men and have many free allies. 2. You will see many beautiful women in your town. 3. We shall always praise good men and honorable women. 4. The Romans listened-to Marcus Tullius, a good and honorable man. 5. Greece was a Roman province. 6. Did you live for a long time on the island of Corsica? 7. You will find my children in school.

EXERCISE 3

ANSWER IN LATIN:

1. Ubi habitābat Mārcus Tullius? 2. Quālis erat Mārcus Tullius? 3. Quālēs sunt fēminae nostrae? 4. Quālēs sunt sociī vestrī? 5. Quanta est īnsula Britannia? 6. Quōrum prōvincia erat Sicilia? 7. Ubi manent līberī meī?

---

¹ When several nouns are joined together, *et* (and) may be placed before each additional noun, as in sentence 7 of Exercise 1, or it may be omitted, as in sentence 10. It should not be put only before the last noun, as is usual in English.

LESSON V

VERBS OF THE FIRST CONJUGATION, INDICATIVE
ACTIVE, AND THE VERB *sum*: PERFECT, PLUPERFECT,
FUTURE PERFECT. ABLATIVE OF THE INSTRUMENT

Sect. 30. Perfect, pluperfect, and future perfect of amō, 'I love'

THE perfect and the third principal part of *amō* is *amāvī*, and the stem of *amāvī* is *amāv-*. The personal endings are not the same in the perfect as they are in the present, but they are used with the perfect stem in all the conjugations. The perfect *amāvī* means either 'I have loved' (present perfect) or 'I loved' (historic perfect).

Personal endings

Singular	Plural
1 -ī	-imus
2 -istī	-istis
3 -it	-ērunt, -ēre

In the pluperfect the endings which are added to the perfect stem are the same as the imperfect of *sum*. Thus *amāv-eram* means 'I had loved'. In the future perfect the endings are the same as the future of *sum* with the exception of the third plural, which ends in *-erint* and not in *-erunt*. Thus *amāv-erō* means 'I shall have loved'.

	Perfect		Pluperfect	
S. 1 **amāv-ī**	I have loved, I loved	**amāv-eram**	I had loved
2 **amāv-istī**	you have loved	**amāv-erās**	you had loved
3 **amāv-it**	he has loved	**amāv-erat**	he had loved
P. 1 **amāv-imus**	we have loved	**amāv-erāmus**	we had loved
2 **amāv-istis**	you have loved	**amāv-erātis**	you had loved
3 **amāv-ērunt** (**-ēre**)	they have loved	**amāv-erant**	they had loved

Future perfect

S. 1 **amāv-erō**	I shall have loved
2 **amāv-eris**	you will have loved
3 **amāv-erit**	he will have loved

P. 1 **amāv-erimus**   we shall have loved
   2 **amāv-eritis**   you will have loved
   3 **amāv-erint**   they will have loved

Sect. 31. Perfect infinitive

This is formed by adding -isse to the perfect stem: *amāvisse*,
'to have loved'.

Sect. 32. Perfect of sum, 'I am'

The perfect of *sum* is *fu-ī*, and the perfect stem is *fu-*. The
endings are the same as in the perfect of *amō*.

	Perfect		*Pluperfect*	
S. 1	**fu-ī**	I have been, I was	**fu-eram**	I had been
2	**fu-istī**		**fu-erās**	
3	**fu-it**		**fu-erat**	
P. 1	**fu-imus**		**fu-erāmus**	
2	**fu-istis**		**fu-erātis**	
3	**fu-ērunt (-ēre)**		**fu-erant**	

Future perfect

S. 1 **fu-erō**   I shall have been
   2 **fu-eris**
   3 **fu-erit**
P. 1 **fu-erimus**
   2 **fu-eritis**
   3 **fu-erint**

The perfect infinitive is *fu-isse*.

Meaning of the perfect, pluperfect, and future perfect

The historic perfect shows that an action has been completed
in the past, e.g. 'I did this yesterday'.

The imperfect is similar, but implies continuous action, e.g.
'I was doing this yesterday'.

The present perfect shows that an action has been completed
in the past but its results influence the present, e.g. 'I have done
this today in order to please you now'.

The pluperfect shows that one action was completed before another action in the past, e.g. 'I had done this before you came'. The future perfect shows that an action will have been completed at some time in the future, e.g. 'I shall have done this before you leave tomorrow'.

Sect. 33. Ablative of the instrument (means)

An ablative without a preposition is used to express the instrument with which something is done or the means by which it is done.

Taurum gladiō vulnerat.

He wounds the bull *with* a sword.

Vocabulary

Anglia, -ae, *f.*, England; **Nova Anglia,** New England.
anteā, *adv.*, formerly, before.
Apūlia, -ae, *f.*, Apulia (in the southeast of Italy).
carrus, -ī, *m.*, wagon.
castra, -trōrum, *n.*, camp[1] (*pl. of* **castrum,** fort).
cōpiae, -ārum, *f.*, troops, forces (*pl. of* **cōpia,** abundance, plenty).
Gallia, -ae, *f.*, Gaul.
gladius, -ī (-iī), *m.*, sword.
hasta, -ae, *f.*, spear.
Hispānia, -ae, *f.*, Spain.
Horātius, -ī (-iī), *m.*, Quintus Horatius Flaccus, poet, 65–8 B.C., author of *Odes, Satires,* and *Epistles.*
labōrō, 1, work.

nūper, *adv.*, recently.
poēta, -ae, *m.*, poet.
posteā, *adv.*, afterwards.
properō, 1, hasten, hurry.
pugnō, 1, fight.
quandō, *interrog. adv.*, when?
quōmodo, *interrog. adv.*, how?
Sabīnus, -a, -um, Sabine (the Sabines lived in central Italy, north-east of Rome).
saepe, *adv.*, often.
saxum, -ī, n., rock, stone.
sed, *conj.*, but.
vīlla, -ae, *f.*, country-house, villa, farm.
Virginia, -ae, *f.* may be used for Virginia.

Exercise 1

1. Līberōs tuōs semper amāvī. 2. Herī līberōs tuōs in hortō exspectāvī. 3. Nūper in Novā Angliā habitāvī, sed anteā in Virginiā habitāveram. 4. Anteā in Hispāniā fuistī, sed mox in Galliā eris. 5. Herī cōpiae nostrae ad castra properāvērunt; hodiē in castrīs labōrābunt. 6. Rōmānī gladiīs et hastīs pugnāvērunt. 7. Horātius poēta in Apūliā habitāverat; posteā in vīllā Sabīnā librōs scrīpsit. 8. Saxa ad vīllam nostram carrīs portābimus. 9. Crās cōpiās in oppidō spectābō; cōpiae ad oppidum anteā properāverint.

Exercise 2

1. Recently they were in Virginia, but formerly they had lived in New

---

[1] Names of towns like Chester and Winchester are derived from *castra.* The Roman legions in the north of Britain were stationed at Chester and York.

England. 2. We shall hurry to New York tomorrow; our friends will have waited for a long time. 3. The farmers had carried grain to the town. 4. The sailor had often fought with a sword. 5. The poet Horace loved (his) Sabine villa.

EXERCISE 3

ANSWER IN LATIN:

1. Ubi līberōs tuōs exspectāvī? 2. Ubi nūper habitāvī? 3. Ubi anteā habitāveram? 4. Ubi anteā fuistī? 5. Quis in castrīs labōrābit? 6. Quōmodo saxa portābimus? 7. Quō saxa portābimus? 8. Quandō cōpiās spectābō? 9. Quō cōpiae properāverint?

LESSON VI

VERBS OF THE SECOND, THIRD, AND FOURTH
CONJUGATIONS, INDICATIVE ACTIVE: PERFECT,
PLUPERFECT, FUTURE PERFECT. ABLATIVE OF MANNER

**Sect. 34. Verbs of the second, third, and fourth conjugations:
moneō, 'I advise'; regō, 'I rule'; audiō, 'I hear'**

THE perfect, pluperfect, and future perfect are formed like the
verbs of the first conjugation, as was explained in Lesson V.

Perfect stem: **monu-** **rēx-** **audīv-**

Perfect

S. 1	**monuī** I have advised	**rēxī** I have ruled	**audīvī** I have heard
2	**monuistī**	**rēxistī**	**audīvistī**
3	**monuit**	**rēxit**	**audīvit**
P. 1	**monuimus**	**rēximus**	**audīvimus**
2	**monuistis**	**rēxistis**	**audīvistis**
3	**monuērunt (-ēre)**	**rēxērunt (-ēre)**	**audīvērunt (-ēre)**

Pluperfect

S. 1	**monueram** I had advised	**rēxeram** I had ruled	**audīveram** I had heard
2	**monuerās**	**rēxerās**	**audīverās**
3	**monuerat**	**rēxerat**	**audīverat**
P. 1	**monuerāmus**	**rēxerāmus**	**audīverāmus**
2	**monuerātis**	**rēxerātis**	**audīverātis**
3	**monuerant**	**rēxerant**	**audīverant**

Future Perfect

S. 1	**monuerō** I shall have advised	**rēxerō** I shall have ruled	**audīverō** I shall have heard
2	**monueris**	**rēxeris**	**audīveris**
3	**monuerit**	**rēxerit**	**audīverit**
P. 1	**monuerimus**	**rēxerimus**	**audīverimus**
2	**monueritis**	**rēxeritis**	**audīveritis**
3	**monuerint**	**rēxerint**	**audīverint**

Sect. 35. Ablative of manner (modal)

A noun in the ablative case, preceded by the preposition *cum*, is used to express the manner in which something is done. If an adjective is added to the noun, *cum* may be either kept or omitted.

cum gaudiō, with joy

magnō gaudiō (magnō cum gaudiō), with great joy.

Sect. 36. Ablative with dē

The preposition *dē*, meaning about or concerning, takes the ablative case.

VOCABULARY

agricultūra, -ae, *f.*, agriculture.

Arethūsa, -ae, *f.*, Arethusa, a Greek nymph who was changed into a spring of water at Syracuse.

arma, -ōrum, *n.*, arms.

Ascraeus, -a, -um, of Ascra. Hesiod, who wrote the *Works and Days*, an early Greek poem about farming, came from Ascra in Boeotia. Vergil refers to ·him in his poem about farming called the *Georgics*.

Asia, -ae, *f.*, Asia, part of Asia Minor.

Caesar, *m.*, Gaius Iulius Caesar, Roman statesman, general, and author, 102(100)–44 B.C., conquered Gaul between 58 and 51; defeated Pompey's armies at Pharsalus in Thessaly (48), Thapsus in Africa (46), Munda in Spain (45), and won the battle of Zela in Asia Minor (47). Author of the *Gallic War* and the *Civil War*.

canō, canere, cecinī, 3, sing.

carmen, carminis, *n.*, song (Lesson XVI).

Catullus, -ī, *m.*, Gaius Valerius Catullus, Roman lyric and elegiac poet, *c.* 84–*c.* 54 B.C.

cōnsul, cōnsulis, *m.*, one of the two chief magistrates at Rome (Lesson XVI).

Corinna, -ae, *f.*, a lady mentioned in Ovid's love poetry, probably not a real person.

Cynthia, -ae, *f.*, a lady described in the love poetry of Propertius; probably her real name was Hostia.

dē, *prep. with abl.*, about, concerning.

Dēlia, -ae, *f.*, a lady described in the love poetry of Tibullus; perhaps her real name was Plania.

forma, -ae, *f.*, form, shape, beauty.

Gallī, -ōrum, the Gauls.

gaudium, -ī (-iī), *n.*, joy.

gignō, gignere, genuī, genitum, 3, beget, produce.

haec, *nom. f. sing. or nom. neut. pl. of* **hic,** this (Lesson XIV).

hostēs, *nom. and acc. pl. of* **hostis,** the enemy (*usually in pl.*) (Lesson XVII).

Lesbia, -ae, *f.*, a lady described in the love poetry of Catullus; probably her real name was Clodia. The name Lesbia suggests Sappho, the Greek poetess of Lesbos (600 B.C.).

littera, -ae, *f.*, a letter (of the alphabet); *in the plural* a letter (epistle) *or* literature.

Mantua, -ae, *f.*, Mantua in north Italy; Vergil was born at Andes near Mantua.

mūtō, 1, change; **mūtātus** (*perfect part.*) changed (Lesson XIII).

Narcissus, -ī, *m.*, a youth in Greek mythology who fell in love with his reflection and was changed into a narcissus.

nunc, *adv.*, now.

Ovidius, -ī (-iī), *m.*, Publius Ovidius Naso, Roman elegiac poet, 43 B.C.–*c.* A.D. 18, and author of the *Metamorphoses*, a poem in hexameters about transformations.

Parthenopē, -ēs, *f.* (a Greek name), the old name of Neapolis, Naples.

Some Greek nouns retain Greek forms in Latin, e.g. *nom*. **-ē**, *gen*. **-ēs**.

Pompēius, -ēī, *m*., Gnaeus Pompeius Magnus, Roman statesman and general, rival of Julius Caesar, 106–48 B.C.

Propertius, -ī (-iī), *m*., Sextus Propertius, Roman elegiac poet, *c*. 50–*c*. 16 B.C.

quem, *acc. sing. of* **quis**, whom? (Lesson XV).

Sulmō, *m*., Sulmona, Ovid's birthplace in Italy in the land of the Paeligni.

tantum, *adv*., only, merely.

teneō, tenēre, tenuī, 2, hold, keep.

Tibullus, -ī, *m*., Albius Tibullus, Roman elegiac poet, *c*. 55–19 B.C.

Tomis, -is, *f*. (a Greek name), a town on the Black Sea to which Ovid was banished in A.D. 8.

Vergilius, -ī (-iī), *m*., Publius Vergilius Maro, Roman epic poet, 70–19 B.C., author of the *Eclogues*, *Georgics*, and *Aeneid*.

Vērōna, -ae, *f*., birthplace of Catullus in north Italy (Cisalpine Gaul).

vincō, vincere, vīcī, victum, 3, conquer.

EXERCISE 1

1. Mantua Vergilium poētam genuit, tenet nunc Parthenope.[1] 2. Vērōna Catullum poētam anteā genuerat. 3. Ovidius poēta Vergilium vīdit tantum.[2] 4. Arma virumque canō.[3] 5. Catullus dē Lesbiā, Propertius dē Cynthiā cecinerat; Ovidius dē Corinnā et fēminīs Rōmānīs cecinit. 6. Vergilius Ascraeum cecinit carmen. 7. Sulmō Ovidiō patria fuerat, sed posteā Tomis poētam tenuit. 8. Ovidius dē formīs mūtātīs, dē Narcissō et Arethūsā scrīpserat. 9. Caesar ad Asiam vēnerat; mox hostēs vīdit et vīcit. 10. Haec verba in litterīs scrīpsit: vēnī, vīdī, vīcī. 11. Cōnsul Rōmānōs monuit et rēxit; verba cōnsulis audīvērunt Rōmānī. 12. Crās Rōmam veniēs; cōpiās nostrās in castrīs vīderis.

EXERCISE 2

1. The poet Ovid came to Rome and wrote about the changed forms of Narcissus and Arethusa. 2. The poet Catullus had loved Lesbia; afterwards Propertius wrote about Cynthia. 3. Vergil sang (his) song of Ascra about agriculture. 4. Tibullus had praised Delia, but Ovid wrote about Corinna. 5. Caesar had conquered the Gauls; afterwards he conquered Pompey's forces in Greece, Spain, and Africa.

EXERCISE 3

ANSWER IN LATIN:

1. Quem genuit Mantua? 2. Quem nunc tenet Parthenopē? 3. Quem anteā genuerat Vērōna? 4. Quem tantum vīdit Ovidius? 5. Quis dē Corinnā cecinit? 6. Quis dē Lesbiā cecinerat? 7. Cui patria fuerat Sulmō? 8. Quis dē Narcissō scrīpserat? 9. Quis vēnit, vīdit, vīcit? 10. Quō Caesar vēnerat? 11. Quis Rōmānōs monuit et rēxit? 12. Quid audīvērunt Rōmānī? 13. Quō crās veniēs? 14. Quid in castrīs vīderis?

---

[1] Adapted from the epitaph attributed to Vergil by Donatus.
[2] *Vergilium vīdī tantum* occurs in Ovid's autobiography (*Tristia* 4. 10).
[3] The first words of Vergil's *Aeneid*. The word *virum* (i.e. Aeneas) corresponds to the Greek accusative *andra* (the man, i.e. Odysseus), the first word in Homer's *Odyssey*.

LESSON VII

VERBS OF THE FIRST CONJUGATION, INDICATIVE PASSIVE: PRESENT, IMPERFECT, FUTURE. ABLATIVE OF THE AGENT

Sect. 37. Verbs of the first conjugation, indicative passive: amor, 'I am loved'

THE personal endings of the passive are added to the stem *amā-* in the present, to *amābā-* in the imperfect, and to *amābi-* in the future.

Personal endings

Singular	Plural
1 **-or**	**-mur**
2 **-ris (-re)**	**-minī**
3 **-tur**	**-ntur**

The present *amor* means 'I am loved' or 'I am being loved'. The imperfect *amābar* means 'I was loved' or 'I was being loved'. The future *amābor* means 'I shall be loved'.

	Present	*Imperfect*	*Future*
S. 1	**amor**	**amābar**	**amābor**
2	**amāris (-re)**	**amābāris (-re)**	**amāberis (-re)**
3	**amātur**	**amābātur**	**amābitur**
P. 1	**amāmur**	**amābāmur**	**amābimur**
2	**amāminī**	**amābāminī**	**amābiminī**
3	**amantur**	**amābantur**	**amābuntur**

The *ā* of the stem is absorbed in *amor*, it is short in *amantur*. The *ā* of the imperfect ending *bā* is shortened in *amābar* and *amābantur*. The *i* of the future ending *bi* is absorbed in *amābor*, it is changed to *e* in *amāberis* and to *u* in *amābuntur*. Instead of the *-e* of the present infinitive active, *amāre*, the letter *-ī* appears in the present infinitive passive, *amārī*, 'to be loved'.

Sect. 38. Ablative of the agent

The ablative case preceded by the preposition *ā (ab)* is used after a passive verb. It represents the person by whom something is done. It refers to persons and not to things; the ablative of the instrument is used for things (Lesson V).

Ab amīcīs amāmur. We are loved by our friends.

The form *ab* should be used before a word beginning with a vowel. Only transitive verbs, which govern an object in the accusative, are used personally in the passive. The verb *amō* is transitive, but *properō*, 'I hasten', is not. The impersonal use of the passive will be explained in Lesson XXXV.

VOCABULARY

amīcitia, -ae, *f.*, friendship.
appellō, 1, call (by name), name.
Daphnē, -ēs, *f.* (a Greek name), the daughter of the river-god Peneus, who was loved by Apollo and was turned into a laurel-tree.
dēsīderō, 1, miss, long for.
deus, -ī, *nom. pl.* **dī,** *m.*, god.

Graecus, -a, -um, Greek.
laurus, -ī, *f.*, laurel.
narcissus, -ī, *m.*, narcissus.
ōlim, *adv.*, once upon a time, once.
superō, 1, overcome.
urbs, urbis, *acc.* **urbem,** *abl.* **urbe,** *f.*, city (Lesson XVII).
vērō, *adv.*, indeed.

EXERCISE 1

1. Haec urbs Novum Eborācum[1] appellātur; nunc in urbe Novō Eborācō habitāmus. 2. Fīlius tuus ab amīcō dēsīderātur. 3. Lūna ab agricolā saepe spectātur. 4. Crās lūna ā fīliā meā spectābitur. 5. Gallī ā Rōmānīs superābantur. 6. Ōlim Daphnē in laurum, Arethūsa in aquam mūtābātur. 7. Cicerō librum dē amīcitiā scrīpsit; amīcitia vērō semper dēsīderābitur. 8. Ā līberīs vestrīs amābāminī.

EXERCISE 2

1. A Greek boy was being changed into a narcissus. 2. Once Daphne was loved by a god. 3. The stars will often be watched by your children. 4. Grain was being carried by our troops. 5. Friendship will always be praised by good men.

EXERCISE 3

ANSWER IN LATIN:

1. Quis fīlium tuum dēsīderat? 2. Quis ab amīcō dēsīderātur? 3. Quid ab agricolā spectātur? 4. Quis lūnam spectat? 5. Quid ā fīliā meā spectābitur? 6. Quis lūnam spectābit? 7. Quandō lūna spectābitur? 8. Quis in laurum mūtābātur? 9. Quid semper dēsīderābitur?

[1] The name of some other city (e.g. *Cantabrigia*, 'Cambridge') may be substituted for *Novum Eborācum*.

LESSON VIII

Sect. 39. Verbs of the second, third, and fourth conjugations: moneor, 'I am advised'; regor, 'I am ruled'; audior, 'I am heard'

THE personal endings of the passive are added to the stems of the present, imperfect, and future, as was explained in Lesson VII on the first conjugation.

Personal endings

	Singular	Plural
1	-or	-mur
2	-ris (-re)	-minī
3	-tur	-ntur

Present	*Imperfect*	*Future*
Stem: **monē-**	Stem: **monēbā-**	Stem: **monēbi-**
I am advised	I was advised	I shall be advised
S. 1 **moneor**	**monēbar**	**monēbor**
2 **monēris (-re)**	**monēbāris (-re)**	**monēberis (-re)**
3 **monētur**	**monēbātur**	**monēbitur**
P. 1 **monēmur**	**monēbāmur**	**monēbimur**
2 **monēminī**	**monēbāminī**	**monēbiminī**
3 **monentur**	**monēbantur**	**monēbuntur**
Stem: **rege-**	Stem: **regēbā-**	Stem: **regē-**
I am ruled	I was ruled	I shall be ruled
S. 1 **regor**	**regēbar**	**regar**
2 **regeris (-re)**	**regēbāris (-re)**	**regēris (-re)**
3 **regitur**	**regēbātur**	**regētur**
P. 1 **regimur**	**regēbāmur**	**regēmur**
2 **regiminī**	**regēbāminī**	**regēminī**
3 **reguntur**	**regēbantur**	**regentur**

Stem: audī-	Stem: audiēbā-	Stem: audiē-
I am heard	I was heard	I shall be heard
S. 1 audior	audiēbar	audiar
2 audīris (-re)	audiēbāris (-re)	audiēris (-re)
3 audītur	audiēbātur	audiētur
P. 1 audīmur	audiēbāmur	audiēmur
2 audīminī	audiēbāminī	audiēminī
3 audiuntur	audiēbantur	audientur

Sect. 40. Ablative of place from which

A noun in the ablative case preceded by a preposition, either *ā*, *dē*, or *ē* (*ex*), expresses the place from which someone moves, i.e. it shows motion from a place. The preposition *ā* or *ab* means 'from', 'away from', *dē* means 'from', 'down from', and *ē* means 'from', 'out of'. The preposition is omitted before names of towns and before *domus*, 'home', and *rūs*, 'country'. Compare accusative of place to which (Lesson III).

$$\text{Cōpiae nostrae} \begin{cases} \text{ē castrīs} \\ \text{dē locīs altīs} \\ \text{ab oppidō} \\ \text{Rōmā} \end{cases} \text{properābant.}$$

Our troops hastened out of the camp, down from the high places, away from the town, away from Rome.

VOCABULARY

altus, -a, -um, high, deep.
amor, -ōris, *m.*, love (Lesson XVI).
Bacchus, -ī, *m.*, Bacchus, the Greek Dionysus, god of wine.
bellum, -ī, *n.*, war.
caelum, -ī, *n.*, sky, heaven.
Cerēs, -eris, *abl.* -ere, *f.*, Ceres, the Greek Demeter, goddess of the fruits of the earth.
colō, colere, coluī, cultum, 3, worship, cultivate.
cuius, *gen. sing. of* **quis,** whose?, of whom? (Lesson XV).
Iuppiter, Iovis, *abl.* **Iove,** *m.*, Jupiter, the Greek Zeus, greatest of the Greek and Roman gods.
locus, -ī, *m.*, place; *pl.* **loca, locōrum,** *n.*
Mars, Martis, *m.*, Mars, the Greek Ares, god of war.
mūniō, mūnīre, mūnīvī, mūnītum, 4, fortify.
nuntius, -ī (-iī), *m.*, messenger.
populus, -ī, *m.*, people.
Venus, Veneris, *abl.* **Venere,** *f.*, Venus, the Greek Aphrodite, goddess of love.
vīnum, -ī, *n.*, wine.

EXERCISE 1

1. Multōs deōs colēbat populus Rōmānus. 2. Iuppiter caelum, Mars bellum regēbat. 3. Cerēs frūmentum, Bacchus vīnum regit. 4. Frūmentum ā Cerere, vīnum ā Bacchō regitur. 5. Amor ā Venere semper

regētur.   6. Ab amīcīs monēberis.   7. Vergilī poētae verba ā populō Rōmānō audiēbantur.   8. Castra ā Rōmānīs mūniuntur.   9. Nuntius ad oppidum ā castrīs mittētur.   10. Litterae Novum Eborācum ā Novā Angliā mittuntur.

EXERCISE 2

1. Many gods were worshipped by the Romans.   2. Mars has always ruled wars, but love is ruled by Venus.   3. Grain will always be ruled by Ceres (and) wine by Bacchus.   4. Bacchus was called Dionysus (nom.) by the Greeks.   5. We shall be advised by the poets.   6. Messengers were being sent from the town to the camp.   7. A letter will soon be sent to Rome from Verona.

EXERCISE 3

ANSWER IN LATIN:

1. Quis multōs deōs colēbat?   2. Quis caelum regēbat?   3. Quid ā Cerere regitur?   4. Quid ā Venere semper regētur?   5. Cuius verba ā populō Rōmānō audiēbantur?   6. Quis Vergilī verba audiēbat?   7. Quid ā Rōmānīs mūnītur?   8. Quis ā castrīs mittētur?   9. Quō nuntius mittētur? 10. Quō litterae mittuntur?

LESSON IX

VERBS OF THE FIRST CONJUGATION, INDICATIVE
PASSIVE: PERFECT, PLUPERFECT, FUTURE PERFECT
ABLATIVE OF ACCOMPANIMENT

Sect. 41. Verbs of the first conjugation: Perfect passive, amātus sum, 'I have been loved', 'I was loved'

THE perfect, pluperfect, and future perfect passive of *amō* are formed from the perfect passive participle *amātus* (loved), combined with the present, imperfect, and future of *sum*. The perfect passive is *amātus sum*, 'I have been loved', 'I was loved', the pluperfect is *amātus eram*, 'I had been loved', and the future perfect is *amātus erō*, 'I shall have been loved'. The participle *amātus* is declined like the adjective *bonus, -a, -um*, and must agree with the subject in gender, number, and case.

Perfect	*Pluperfect*
I have been (was) loved	I had been loved
S. 1 **amātus (-a, -um) sum**	**amātus (-a, -um) eram**
2 **amātus (-a, -um) es**	**amātus (-a, -um) erās**
3 **amātus (-a, -um) est**	**amātus (-a, -um) erat**
P. 1 **amātī (-ae, -a) sumus**	**amātī (-ae, -a) erāmus**
2 **amātī (-ae, -a) estis**	**amātī (-ae, -a) erātis**
3 **amātī (-ae, -a) sunt**	**amātī (-ae, -a) erant**

Future perfect

I shall have been loved

S. 1 **amātus (-a, -um) erō**
2 **amātus (-a, -um) eris**
3 **amātus (-a, -um) erit**
P. 1 **amātī (-ae, -a) erimus**
2 **amātī (-ae, -a) eritis**
3 **amātī (-ae, -a) erunt**

Fīlius tuus amātus est. Your son was loved.
Fīliae tuae dēsīderātae sunt. Your daughters were missed.

Here *amātus* is masculine, singular, and nominative in agreement with *fīlius*; *dēsīderātae* is feminine, plural, and nominative in agreement with *fīliae*.

Sect. 42. Ablative of accompaniment

The preposition *cum* followed by a noun in the ablative case expresses accompaniment.

Rōmam cum amīcō vēnī.

I have come to Rome with a friend.

For the use of *cum* with personal pronouns, see Lesson XIV.

Sect. 43. The preposition sine, 'without', governs the ablative, the prepositions ob and propter, 'on account of', govern the accusative

VOCABULARY

aedificō, 1, build.
agō, agere, ēgī, āctum, 3, drive, do; live (*with acc., e.g.* **annōs**).
annus, -ī, *m.,* year.
arbor, -oris, *acc.* **-orem,** *f.,* tree (Lesson XVI).
arō, 1, plough.
Baucis, -idis, *abl.* **-ide,** *f.,* the wife of Philemon.
beneficium, -ī (-ii), *n.,* kindness; *abl.* = by the kindness (of).
cadō, cadere, cecidī, cāsum, 3, fall.
collocō, 1, place.
concors, -cordis, harmonious (Lesson XVIII).
coniūnx, -iugis, *abl.* **-iuge,** *f.,* wife, husband (Lesson XVI).
cum, *prep. with abl.,* with.
currus, -ūs, *abl.* **currū,** *m.,* chariot (Lesson XVIII).
Daedalus, -ī, *m.,* Daedalus, who invented wings and escaped from Crete.
ē, ex, *prep. with abl.,* from, out of.

Īcarus, -ī, *m.,* Icarus, the son of Daedalus, who tried to fly but fell into the sea.
Īō, *f.,* the daughter of Inachus who was changed into a cow.
ira, -ae, *f.,* anger.
Iūnō, -nōnis, *f.,* Juno, the wife of Jupiter.
levō, 1, lift up, raise.
ob, *prep. with acc.,* on account of.
penna, -ae, *f.,* wing.
perveniō, pervenire, pervēnī, perventum, 4, arrive (*with* **ad** *and acc.*).
Phaëthōn, -ontis, *m.,* the son of Apollo who tried to drive the chariot of the sun.
Philēmōn, -onis, *m.,* an old man who prayed that he might never be separated from his wife. The gods turned them both into trees.
Phoebus, -ī, *m.,* Phoebus or Apollo, the god of the sun.
sine, *prep. with abl.,* without.
sōl, sōlis, *m.,* sun (Lesson XVI).
volō, 1, fly.

EXERCISE 1

1. Philēmōn et Baucis concordēs ēgerant annōs et Iovis beneficiō in arborēs mūtātī sunt. 2. Ā Iove amāta erat Īō; posteā Iūnōnis ob īram in vaccam mūtāta est. 3. Phaëthōn, Phoebī fīlius, ē currū Sōlis cecidit. 4. Semper ab amīcīs laudātī estis. 5. Ad īnsulam Siciliam properābis; mox vīlla tua aedificāta erit. 6. Pecūnia in templīs deōrum collocāta erat. 7. Daedalus pennīs levātus erat; cum fīliō Īcarō ab īnsulā Crētā volābat. 8. Īcarus in aquam cecidit; Daedalus sine fīliō ad Graeciam pervēnit.

Exercise 2

1. Philemon had always been loved by Baucis and had lived harmonious years. 2. By-the-kindness (abl.) of the gods he was changed into a tree. 3. Icarus has been lifted up on-wings (abl.) and is flying to Greece with Daedalus. 4. Phaethon is driving the horses of the sun, but will soon fall from the chariot. 5. Tomorrow the fields will have been ploughed by the farmers.

Exercise 3

ANSWER IN LATIN:

1. Quis in arborem mūtātus est? 2. Cuius beneficiō mūtāta est Baucis? 3. Quis concordēs ēgit annōs? 4. Quis in vaccam mūtāta est? 5. Quis ē currū Sōlis cecidit? 6. Quid in Siciliā aedificātum erit? 7. Quid in templīs collocātum erat? 8. Quis cum Īcarō volābat? 9. Quōmodo levātus erat? 10. Quis in aquam cecidit? 11. Quis sine fīliō ad Graeciam pervēnit?

VERBS OF THE SECOND, THIRD, AND FOURTH
CONJUGATIONS, INDICATIVE PASSIVE:
PERFECT, PLUPERFECT, FUTURE PERFECT
ABLATIVE OF TIME WHEN (OR WITHIN WHICH)

Sect. 44. Verbs of the second, third, and fourth conjugations: perfect passive, monitus sum, rēctus sum, audītus sum, 'I have been (was) advised, ruled, heard'

THE perfect, pluperfect, and future perfect passive in these conjugations are formed from the perfect passive participle (*monitus, rēctus, audītus*) in the way that was explained in Lesson IX on the first conjugation.

Perfect

	I have been (was) advised	I have been (was) ruled
S. 1	monitus (-a, -um) sum	rēctus (-a, -um) sum
2	monitus (-a, -um) es	rēctus (-a, -um) es
3	monitus (-a, -um) est	rēctus (-a, -um) est
P. 1	monitī (-ae, -a) sumus	rēctī (-ae, -a) sumus
2	monitī (-ae, -a) estis	rēctī (-ae, -a) estis
3	monitī (-ae, -a) sunt	rēctī (-ae, -a) sunt

I have been
(was) heard

S. 1	audītus (-a, -um) sum	
2	audītus (-a, -um) es	
3	audītus (-a, -um) est	
P. 1	audītī (-ae, -a) sumus	
2	audītī (-ae, -a) estis	
3	audītī (-ae, -a) sunt	

Pluperfect

	I had been advised	I had been ruled
S. 1	monitus (-a, -um) eram	rēctus (-a, -um) eram
2	monitus (-a, -um) erās	rēctus (-a, -um) erās
3	monitus (-a, -um) erat	rēctus (-a, -um) erat

Pluperfect (contd.)

P. 1 **monitī (-ae, -a) erāmus**   **rēctī (-ae, -a) erāmus**
   2 **monitī (-ae, -a) erātis**   **rēctī (-ae, -a) erātis**
   3 **monitī (-ae, -a) erant**   **rēctī (-ae, -a) erant**

I had been heard

S. 1 **audītus (-a, -um) eram**
   2 **audītus (-a, -um) erās**
   3 **audītus (-a, -um) erat**
P. 1 **audītī (-ae, -a) erāmus**
   2 **audītī (-ae, -a) erātis**
   3 **audītī (-ae, -a) erant**

Future Perfect

I shall have   I shall have
been advised   been ruled

S. 1 **monitus (-a, -um) erō**   **rēctus (-a, -um) erō**
   2 **monitus (-a, -um) eris**   **rēctus (-a, -um) eris**
   3 **monitus (-a, -um) erit**   **rēctus (-a, -um) erit**
P. 1 **monitī (-ae, -a) erimus**   **rēctī (-ae, -a) erimus**
   2 **monitī (-ae, -a) eritis**   **rēctī (-ae, -a) eritis**
   3 **monitī (-ae, -a) erunt**   **rēctī (-ae, -a) erunt**

I shall have
been heard

S. 1 **audītus (-a, -um) erō**
   2 **audītus (-a, -um) eris**
   3 **audītus (-a, -um) erit**
P. 1 **audītī (-ae, -a) erimus**
   2 **audītī (-ae, -a) eritis**
   3 **audītī (-ae, -a) erunt**

Sect. 45. Ablative of time

The ablative is used to show the time when or within which an act takes place.

> **Hōc annō vēnimus.**   We came this year.
> **Quattuor annīs veniēmus.**
> We shall come within four years.

VOCABULARY

Augustus, -ī, *m.,* Augustus, the first Emperor, *princeps* 27 B.C.–A.D. 14.

bis, *adv.,* twice.

Brutus, -ī, *m.,* and **Cassius, -ī (-iī),** *m.,* leaders of the conspiracy against Julius Caesar, 44 B.C.

Caesare, *abl. of* Caesar.

Carthāgō, -inis, *f.,* Carthage (Lesson XVI).

Claudius, -ī (-iī), *m.,* the Emperor Claudius, *princeps* A.D. 41–54.

condō, condere, condidī, conditum, 3, found.

cōnsulēs, *abl.* **cōnsulibus,** *pl. of* **cōnsul,** consul (Lesson XVI).

creō, 1, create, appoint.

Dācia, -ae, *f.,* Dacia, the modern Rumania, conquered by Trajan.

dēleō, dēlēre, dēlēvī, dēlētum, 2, destroy.

dēscrībō, *compound of* **scrībō,** 3, describe.

dictātor, -ōris, *m.,* dictator (Lesson XVI). Title used in emergencies and held by Julius Caesar.

dīvus, -ī, divine. Epithet for certain Roman emperors after their death.

duo, duae, duo, two (Lesson XXIX).

expellō, expellere, expulī, expulsum, 3, expel, drive out.

fābula, -ae, *f.,* story, tale.

gerō, gerere, gessī, gestum, 3, carry on, wage (war), perform.

hae, *nom. f. pl. of* **hic,** this (Lesson XIV).

hōc, *abl. m. sing. of* **hic,** this.

inscrībō, *compound of* **scrībō,** 3, inscribe.

Līvius, -ī (-iī), *m.,* Titus Livius (Livy), 59 B.C.–A.D. 17, historian of the Roman Republic. Only 35 of his 142 books survive.

Monumentum Ancyrānum, -ī, *n.,* the Monumentum Ancyranum,

containing an inscription in Latin and Greek, set up at Ancyra in Asia Minor. It is the official account of the achievements of Augustus.

nuntiō, 1, announce.

occīdō, occīdere, occīdī, occīsum, 3, *compound of* **caedō,** kill.

Octāviānus, -ī, *m.,* C. Iulius Caesar Octavianus, the grand-nephew and adopted son of Julius Caesar, who became the Emperor Augustus.[1]

Poenī, *m. pl.,* Carthaginians; **Pūnicus, -a, -um,** Punic, Carthaginian. There were three Punic Wars, 264–241 B.C., 218–202 B.C., 149–146 B.C.

princeps, principis, *abl.* **principe,** *m.,* chief (*here* = the title of the Roman emperors (Lesson XVI)).

quattuor, *numeral,* four (Lesson XXIX).

quī, quae, quod, *interrog. adj.,* which? (Lesson XV).

quot, *indecl. adj.,* how many?

rēs, reī, *f.,* thing; **rēs gestae,** achievements (Lesson XVIII).

rēx, rēgis, *pl.* **rēgēs,** *abl.* **rēgibus,** *m.,* king (Lesson XVI).

Rōmulus, -ī, *m.,* Romulus, the first Roman king. The tradition is that there were kings at Rome from 753 to 510 B.C.

septem, *numeral,* seven (Lesson XXIX).

sex, *numeral,* six (Lesson XXIX).

Sicilia, -ae, *f.,* Sicily.

tandem, *adv.,* at last, finally.

Tarquinius, -ī (-iī), *m.,* Tarquinius Superbus, Tarquin the Proud, the last Roman king.

Trāiānus, -ī, *m.,* the Roman Emperor Trajan, *princeps* A.D. 98–117.

trēs (*neuter* **tria**), *numeral,* three (Lesson XXIX).

EXERCISE 1

1. Rōmānī prīmō urbis annō ā Rōmulō rēctī sunt.   2. Septem rēgēs fuērunt; rēx prīmus fuit Rōmulus; ā Rōmulō condita est Rōma.   3. Rōma

[1] A Roman praenomen or first name was often abbreviated, e.g. A. for Aulus, C. for Gāius, Cn. for Gnaeus, D. for Decimus, L. for Lūcius, M. for Mārcus, P. for Pūblius, Q. for Quīntus, T. for Titus, Ti. for Tiberius.

ā sex rēgibus rēcta est; tandem Tarquinius Superbus Rōmā expulsus est. 4. Posteā Rōma ā cōnsulibus rēcta est; duo cōnsulēs fuērunt. 5. Multae fābulae dē rēgibus Rōmānīs ā T. Līviō et ā Vergiliō et Ovidiō poētis scrīptae sunt. 6. Sicilia et Hispānia ā Rōmānīs superātae erant; posteā Poenī in Āfricā victī sunt. 7. Tria bella Pūnica cum Poenīs gesta erant; tandem Carthāgō ā Rōmānīs dēlēta est. 8. Haec bella ā T. Līviō dēscrīpta sunt. 9. C. Iūlius Caesar dictātor creātus erat; posteā ā Brūtō Cassiōque occīsus est. 10. Tandem C. Iūlius Caesar Octaviānus prīnceps fuit et Augustus appellātus est. 11. Gallia ā C. Iūliō Caesare, Britannia ā Claudiō prīncipe, Dācia ā Trāiānō prīncipe superātae sunt. 12. Rēs gestae dīvī Augustī in Monumentō Ancyrānō īnscrīptae sunt.

EXERCISE 2

1. Rome was ruled by seven kings; in the first year it was ruled by Romulus. 2. Carthage had been destroyed and Spain had been overcome by the Romans; afterwards Gaul was conquered by C. Julius Caesar. 3. Caesar sailed to Britain twice; finally Britain was overcome by the Emperor Claudius. 4. A monument was built and the achievements of the Emperor Augustus were announced to-the-Romans (dat.). 5. These stories have often been heard.

EXERCISE 3

ANSWER IN LATIN:

1. Quot rēgēs Rōmānī fuērunt? 2. Quis fuit rēx prīmus? 3. Quis fābulās dē rēgibus Rōmānīs scrīpsit? 4. Quī rēx Rōmā expulsus est? 5. Quae urbs ā Rōmānīs dēlēta est? 6. Quae īnsula ā Claudiō superāta est? 7. Quis Augustus appellātus est? 8. Quis Galliam superāvit? 9. Quot bella cum Poenīs gesta sunt? 10. Quis bella Pūnica dēscrīpsit? 11. Quid in Monumentō Ancyrānō īnscrīptum est?

LESSON XI

IMPERATIVE MOOD IN THE FOUR CONJUGATIONS
PROHIBITION OR NEGATIVE COMMAND

Sect. 46. Imperative mood

THE imperative mood expresses a command. The name is derived from *imperō*, 'I command', and the common forms are the second person singular and the second person plural. The first of these is usually the same as the stem of the verb: thus *amā* means 'love' and *monē* means 'advise'.

The personal endings of the imperative:

	Active	Passive
2nd pers. sing.	. .	-re
2nd pers. pl.	-te	-minī

The imperative mood in the four conjugations and the verb *sum*:

Active

Sing.	amā	monē	rege	audī	es
Pl.	amāte	monēte	regite	audīte	este

Passive

Sing.	amāre	monēre	regere	audīre	. .
Pl.	amāminī	monēminī	regiminī	audīminī	. .

Dūcō, 'I lead', and *dīcō*, 'I say', have a shortened form of the imperative, *dūc* and *dīc*.

There is a third person singular and a third person plural of the imperative, e.g. *amātō*, *amantō*, 'let him love', 'let them love', but it is more common to use the subjunctive for such commands (see Lesson XXV). And there are alternative forms of the second person singular and the second person plural, e.g. *amātō* and *amātōte*, but these are not common. These forms are known as the future imperative.

Sect. 47. Prohibition (negative command)

The common form of a negative command in prose is the imperative of the verb *nōlō*, 'I am unwilling', combined with the infinitive of the verb. The second person singular is *nōlī*, and the second person plural is *nōlīte*.

Nōlī venīre.   Do not come (Be unwilling to come).

Negative commands may also be expressed by *nē* with the perfect subjunctive (see Lesson XXVII). Sometimes *nē* is used with the present imperative in poetry.

LESSONS XI–XLI

In Lessons XI–XLI most of the sentences in the first exercise are quotations from Latin authors. The meaning of common words is given in the Vocabulary, but words that are less important are explained in the Notes and need not be learned. Ten sentences of Exercise 1 in each lesson are marked with an asterisk. If a choice has to be made, these sentences are recommended.

VOCABULARY

adsum, *compound of* **sum,** am present.
ambulō, 1, walk.
aperiō, aperīre, aperuī, apertum, 4, open.
claudō, claudere, clausī, clausum, 3, shut.
cōnsīdō, cōnsīdere, cōnsēdī, cōnsessum, 3, sit down.
crēta, -ae, *f.,* chalk.
currō, currere, cucurrī, cursum, 3, run.
dīcō, dīcere, dīxī, dictum, 3, say.
faciō, facere, fēcī, factum, 3, do (Lesson XII).
fenestra, -ae, *f.,* window.
festīnō, 1, hasten.
hūc, *adv.,* to this place (hither).
iaceō, iacēre, iacuī, 2, lie down.
iam, *adv.,* now, already.
iānua, -ae, *f.,* door.
laetus, -a, -um, joyful, glad.
lateō, latēre, latuī, 2, lie hid.
mihi, *dat. of* **ego,** to me.
per, *prep. with acc.,* through.

Procris, *f.* (*voc.* **Procri**), Procris, the wife of Cephalus. In this legend she thought he was in love with 'Aura', when he was really addressing **aura** (the breeze). He mistook her for a wild beast and shot her in the forest.
procul, *adv.,* far, far away.
reddō, reddere, reddidī, redditum, 3, give back.
salvē (*imperat. of* **salveō,** am well), greetings, good-day, *lit.* be well.
sedeō, sedēre, sēdī, sessum, 2, sit, be seated.
sella, -ae, *f.,* chair.
stō, stāre, stetī, statum, 1, stand.
surgō, surgere, surrēxī, surrēctum, 3, stand up, rise.
tēlum, -ī, *n.,* weapon.
tibi, *dat. of* **tū,** to you.
valē (*imperat. of* **valeō,** am strong, healthy), farewell, good-bye (*used at the end of a letter*).

NOTES

Ex. 1.
1. **vesper,** *m.,* evening.
   iuvenēs, *voc. m. pl. of* **iuvenis,** young man.
   cōnsurgō, *compound of* **surgō,** 3, stand up, arise together.

2. **lentē,** *adv.,* slowly.
   noctis, *gen. of* **nox,** *f.,* night.
   Marlowe quotes this line in *Faustus* and adds **O lentē** at the beginning.

3. **atque**, and.
   in perpetuum, forever.
   fräter, *m.*, brother.
   avē atque valē, hail and farewell.
5. **Quīntilius Vārus**, a general
   whose legions were defeated by
   the Germans in A.D. 9 while
   Augustus was emperor.
   legiōnēs, *acc. pl. of* **legiō**, *f.*,
   legion.
6. **profānus, -a, -um**, profane,
   uninitiated.
7. **hinc**, *adv.*, from here.
   sevērus, -a, -um, strict, severe.
8. **parēns**, *m. and f.*, parent, father,
   mother.
   frūgum, *gen. of* **frūgēs**, *f. pl.*,
   fruits (of the earth).
   Sāturnius, -a, -um, of Saturn,
   an ancient king of Latium and
   afterwards the god of agriculture.
   tellūs, *f.*, land, earth.
9. **rīvus, -ī**, *m.*, stream.
   sat = **satis**, enough.
   prātum, -ī, *n.*, meadow.
   bibō, bibere, bibī, 3, drink.

10. **anxius, -a, -um**, anxious.
   solitus, -a, -um, customary,
   usual.
   ille, he (that man), *i.e.* Cephalus.
   herba, -ae, *f.*, grass.
   Zephyrus, -ī, *m.*, west wind.
   mollēs, *pl. of* **mollis**, soft.
   aura, -ae, *f.*, breeze. **Zephyrī**
   and **aura** *are voc.*
11. **īnfēlīx**, unhappy.
   fera, -ae, *f.*, wild beast.
   supprimō (*compound of* **premō**,
   press), 3, suppress, check.
   mē miserum, alas (*lit.* miserable
   me).
   iaculum, -ī, *n.*, javelin.
   fīxa est, *perf. pass. of* **fīgō**, 3, fix,
   pierce.
12. **sānctus, -a, -um**, holy.
   spīritus, -ūs, *m.*, breath, spirit;
   (*Late Latin*) the (Holy) Ghost.
   Here voc.
13. **fidēlēs**, *voc. pl. of* **fidēlis**, faithful.
   triumphantēs (*pres. part. pl. of*
   triumphō), triumphant.
   Bethlehem, *biblical name used
   without a case-ending for the
   acc.*

EXERCISE 1

*1. Vesper adest, iuvenēs, cōnsurgite.
*2. Lentē currite, Noctis equī.
*3. Atque in perpetuum, frāter, avē atque valē.
  4. Festīnā lentē.
*5. Quīntilī Vāre, legiōnēs redde.
*6. Procul, ō procul este, profānī.
  7. Procul hinc, procul este, sevērae.
*8. Salvē, magna parēns frūgum, Sāturnia tellūs.
*9. Claudite iam rīvōs, puerī; sat prāta bibērunt.
*10. Anxia, Procri, latēs; solitās iacet ille per herbās
     et 'Zephyrī mollēs auraque', dīxit, 'ades.'
*11. Quid facis, īnfēlīx? Nōn est fera, supprime tēla.
     Mē miserum, iaculō fīxa puella tuō est.
 12. Venī, Sāncte Spīritus.
*13. Adeste, fidēlēs,
     laetī triumphantēs;
     venīte, venīte in Bethlehem.

EXERCISE 2

1. Open (sing.) the door, shut the window, (and) sit down. 2. Do not shut (pl.) the door, but open the window. 3. Now your friend is sitting down, but soon he will stand up. 4. You are not standing (sing.), but you are sitting on a chair. 5. Do not walk (sing.), but sit down on (your) chair. 6. I have given you the chalk, you have given me a book.

EXERCISE 3

ANSWER IN LATIN:

1. Iānuam aperiō. Quid faciō? 2. Nunc iānuam claudō. Quid faciō? 3. Iānuam aperī. Quid facis? 4. Nunc iānuam claude. Quid facis? 5. Fenestram aperī. Quid fēcistī? 6. Nunc fenestram claude. Quid fēcistī? 7. Fenestram clausī. Quid fēcī? 8. Fenestram aperuī. Quid fēcī? 9. Amīcī tuī fenestram clausērunt. Quid fēcērunt? 10. Nunc fenestram aperīte. Quid fēcistis? 11. Nōlī fenestram aperīre, sed iānuam aperī. Quid fēcistī? 12. Crētam tibi dō. Quid tibi dedī? 13. Dā mihi crētam. Quid mihi dedistī? 14. Surgō. Quid faciō? 15. Nunc stō. Quid faciō? 16. Cōnsīdō. Quid faciō? 17. Nunc in sellā sedeō. Quid faciō? 18. Surge. Quid facis? 19. Nunc stās. Quid facis? 20. Cōnsīde. Quid facis? 21. Nunc in sellā sedēs. Quid facis? 22. Cōnsurgite. Quid facitis? 23. Cōnsīdite. Quid facitis? 24. Hūc venīte. Quid fēcistis? 25. Ad iānuam ambulāte. Quid facitis?

The Pantheon, Rome

Tellus on the *Ara Pacis*, Rome

Sect. 48. Second form of the third conjugation: capiō, 'I take'

SOME verbs end in **-iō** and seem to belong to the fourth conjugation, but their infinitive ends in *-ere* and not *-īre*, so that they really belong to the third conjugation. *Capiō* is conjugated like *regō*, but the letter *i* appears in *capiō* and *capiunt* and in the imperfect *capiēbam* and the future *capiam*.

Principal parts

	capiō	capere	cēpī	captum

Indicative

	Present	Imperfect	Future
Active			
S. 1	capiō	capiēbam	capiam
2	capis	capiēbās	capiēs
3	capit	capiēbat	capiet
P. 1	capimus	capiēbāmus	capiēmus
2	capitis	capiēbātis	capiētis
3	capiunt	capiēbant	capient
Passive			
S. 1	capior	capiēbar	capiar
2	caperis (-re)	capiēbāris (-re)	capiēris (-re)
3	capitur	capiēbātur	capiētur
P. 1	capimur	capiēbāmur	capiēmur
2	capiminī	capiēbāminī	capiēminī
3	capiuntur	capiēbantur	capientur

	Perfect	Pluperfect	Future perfect
Active	cēpī	cēperam	cēperō
Passive	captus sum	captus eram	captus erō

Imperative

Active	cape[1]	capite
Passive	capere	capiminī

[1] But the imperative of *faciō* is *fac*.

Prepositions taking the accusative and the ablative

(*a*) Prepositions taking the accusative:

ad	to	**ob**	on account of
adversus	against	**penes**	in the power of
ante	before	**per**	through
apud	at, near	**pōne**	behind
circā, circum	around	**post**	after
citrā, cis	this side	**praeter**	beyond
contrā	against	**prope**	near
ergā	towards		
(not used of place)		**propter**	on account of
extrā	outside	**secundum**	next to
infrā	below	**suprā**	above
inter	among	**trāns**	across
intrā	inside	**ultrā**	on the farther side
iūxtā	near	**versus**	towards

(*b*) Prepositions taking the ablative:

ā, ab	away from, by	**ē, ex**	out of
absque	without, but for	**prae**	in comparison with
cōram	in the presence of	**prō**	in front of, on behalf of,
cum	with		for
dē	from, down from,	**sine**	without
	concerning	**tenus**	up to, as far as

(*c*) Prepositions taking either the accusative or the ablative:

in	into, in	**sub**	under
subter	beneath	**super**	above

The accusative is used with these prepositions to express *motion to*, the ablative to express *rest in* a place.

It is not necessary to learn all these prepositions at this time. As the majority take the accusative, it is a good plan to learn the prepositions that take the ablative and those that take both cases.

For *in* with the ablative see Lesson I (place where).
For *in, ad* with the accusative see Lesson III (place to which).
For *dē* (concerning) with the ablative see Lesson VI.
For *ā, ab* with the ablative see Lesson VII (agent).

For *ā*, *ab*, *dē*, *ex*, *ē* with the ablative see Lesson VIII (place from which).

For *cum* with the ablative see Lesson IX (accompaniment).

For *sine*, *ob*, *propter* see Lesson IX.

VOCABULARY

ad, *prep. with acc.* (to, Lesson III), near.

agrestis, -e, *dat.* **agrestī,** *pl.* **agrestes, -ia,** of the country, rustic.

Alpēs, -ium, *f. pl.*, the Alps (Lesson XVII).

animus, -ī, *m.*, mind.

apud, *prep. with acc.*, in the writings of, in the house of.

Cannae, -ārum, *f. pl.*, a village in Apulia where Hannibal defeated the Romans in 216 B.C.

Cantabrigia, -ae, *f.*, Cambridge in England and in Massachusetts.

capiō, capere, cēpī, captum, 3, take, capture.

charta, -ae, *f.*, paper (cf. the Magna Carta); *may be used for* a map.

Cisalpīnus, -a, -um, Cisalpine (on the Italian side of the Alps).

doceō, docēre, docuī, doctum, 2, teach.

fluvius, -ī, *m.*, river.

fugiō, fugere, fūgī, 3, flee, flee from.

Georgia, -ae, *f.*, may be used for Georgia.

Hannibal, *m.*, Carthaginian general in the Second Punic War.

infrā, *prep. with acc.*, below.

inter, *prep. with acc.*, between.

iter, itineris, *n.*, journey (Lesson XVII); **iter faciō,** march.

iaciō, iacere, iēcī, iactum, 3, throw, cast.

legō, legere, lēgī, lēctum, 3, read.

Londinium, -ī (-iī), *n.*, London (in England); **Novum Londinium,** New London (in Connecticut).

manus, -ūs, *abl.* **-ū,** *f.*, hand; band (of men) (Lesson XVIII).

ōtium, -ī (-iī), *n.*, leisure, rest.

parvus, -a, -um, small.

prope, *prep. with acc.*, near.

Rubicō, -ōnis, *acc.* **-ōnem,** *m.*, the Rubicon, a river which was the boundary between Cisalpine Gaul and north Italy.

Suētōnius, -ī (-iī), *m.*, C. Suetonius Tranquillus, who published the *Lives of the Caesars* (Julius to Domitian) about A.D. 120.

super, *prep. with acc.*, over.

suprā, *prep. with acc.*, above.

Tamesis, -is, *acc.* **-im,** *m.*, the river Thames in England and in Connecticut.

trādūcō, trādūcere, trādūxī, trāductum, 3, lead across.

trāns, *prep. with acc.*, across.

Trasimēnus, -ī, *m.* (*used with* **lacus, -ūs,** lake), Lake Trasimene in Etruria, where Hannibal defeated the Romans in 217 B.C.

unde, *interrog. adv.*, from where? whence?

NOTES

Ex. 1.

A. 1. **captus, -a, -um,** captured.
  ferus, -a, -um, wild, rude.
  victōrem, *acc. of* **victor,** conqueror.
  artēs, *acc. pl. of* **ars,** the arts.
  intulit, *3rd sing. perf. of* **inferō,** introduce, bring in (*with acc. and dat.*).

Latium, -ī, *n.*, Latium, a part of Italy which includes Rome.

2. **parva,** *nom. neut. pl.*, little things.
  levēs, *acc. pl. of* **levis,** light.
  ūtile, *neut. of* **ūtilis,** useful.
  pulvīnus, -ī, *m.*, cushion.
  facilī, *abl. of* **facilis,** easy, ready.
  composuisse, *perf. inf. of* **compōnō,** put together, arrange.

3. **intereā,** meanwhile.
irreparābile, *neut. of* **irreparābilis,** irretrievable, that cannot
be recovered.
tempus, -oris, *n.,* time.
4. **tē,** *acc. of* **tū,** you.
vātem, *acc. of* **vātēs,** a poet,
prophet.

lascīvus, -a, -um, wanton, playful.
5. **ālea, -ae,** *f.,* a game played with
dice; *with* **iacta est,** the die is
cast.
6. **Meliboeus, -ī,** *m.,* a shepherd in
Vergil's *Eclogues.*
nōbīs, *dat. of* **nōs,** (for) us.

EXERCISE 1

A. *1. Graecia capta ferum victōrem cēpit et artēs
intulit agrestī Latiō.
*2. Parva levēs capiunt animōs; fuit ūtile multīs
pulvīnum facilī composuisse manū.
*3. Sed fugit intereā, fugit irreparābile tempus.
*4. Cynthia tē vātem fēcit, lascīve Propertī.
5. Iacta ālea est.
6. Ō Meliboee, deus nōbīs haec ōtia fēcit.
B. *1. Graecia ā Rōmānīs capta est, sed ā Graecīs captī sunt Rōmānī.
*2. Caesar cōpiās trāns fluvium Rubicōnem trādūxit et ālea iacta est.
Haec apud Suētōnium legimus.
3. Propertius ā Cynthiā poēta factus est.
4. Augustus agrōs reddidit et ōtium Vergiliō fēcit.
5. Puellārum animī parvīs beneficiīs capiuntur.
C. *1. Hannibal per Hispāniam et posteā super Alpēs in Italiam iter fēcit.
*2. Rōmānī prope lacum Trasimēnum et posteā ad Cannās ā Poenīs
victī sunt.
*3. In chartā Americae Virginiam īnfrā urbem Novum Eborācum et
suprā Georgiam vidēmus.
*4. Novum Londinium inter urbem Cantabrigiam et urbem Novum
Eborācum vidēbis.

EXERCISE 2

1. New London is near the river Thames. On the map of America I see
New London above the city (of) New York and below the city (of)
Cambridge. 2. The river Rubicon is between Italy and Cisalpine Gaul;
Caesar hastened across the river into Italy. 3. The Carthaginians marched
from Spain over the Alps. 4. The Greeks were conquered, but they taught
many (things) about literature and captured the minds of the Romans.
5. We are often charmed (captured) by a small kindness.

EXERCISE 3

ANSWER IN LATIN:

1. Quis Rōmānōs cēpit? 2. Quid docuit Graecia? 3. Quid fugit? 4.
Quis Propertium poētam fēcit? 5. Ubi ālea iacta est? 6. Quis trāns
fluvium Rubicōnem cōpiās trādūxit? 7. Quis super Alpēs iter fēcit?
8. Unde Hannibal in Italiam iter fēcit? 9. Ubi victī sunt Rōmānī?
10. Quī fluvius prope urbem Novum Londinium est? 11. Ubi Virginiam
in chartā vidēs?

REVIEW OF THE PRINCIPAL PARTS OF THE FOUR
CONJUGATIONS AND THE THREE STEMS OF THE VERB
MEANING OF THE INFINITIVES AND PARTICIPLES
REVIEW OF VERBS

Sect. 49. Principal parts

	Present indicative	Present infinitive	Perfect indicative	Supine
1st Conjugation	amō	amāre	amāvī	amātum
2nd ,,	moneō	monēre	monuī	monitum
3rd ,,	regō	regere	rēxī	rēctum
	capio	capere	cēpī	captum
4th ,,	audiō	audīre	audīvī	audītum

(For the use of the supine see Lesson XXXIX.)

The three stems

Present	Perfect	Supine
amā-	amāv-	amāt-
monē-	monu-	monit-
rege-	rēx-	rēct-
capi-	cēp-	capt-
audī-	audīv-	audīt-

Parts of the verb derived

(*a*) From the present stem:

Stem:	amā-	monē-	rege-	capi-	audī-
Active					
Pres. imperat.	amā	monē	rege	cape	audī
Pres. part.	amāns	monēns	regēns	capiēns	audiēns
Pres. infin.	amāre	monēre	regere	capere	audīre
Pres. indic.	amō	moneō	regō	capiō	audiō
Imperf. indic.	amābam	monēbam	regēbam	capiēbam	audiēbam
Future indic.	amābō	monēbō	regam	capiam	audiam
Passive					
Pres. imperat.	amāre	monēre	regere	capere	audīre
Pres. part.	. .	. .	. .	. .	
Pres. infin.	amārī	monērī	regī	capī	audīrī
Pres. indic.	amor	moneor	regor	capior	audior

Imperf. indic.	amābar	monēbar	regēbar	capiēbar	audiēbar
Future indic.	amābor	monēbor	regar	capiar	audiar
Gerundive	amandus	monendus	regendus	capiendus	audiendus

(For the use of the gerundive see Lesson XXXVIII.)

(b) From the perfect stem:

Stem:	amāv-	monu-	rēx-	cēp-	audīv-
Active					
Perf. infin.	amāvisse	monuisse	rēxisse	cēpisse	audīvisse
Perf. indic.	amāvī	monuī	rēxī	cēpī	audīvī
Plup. indic.	amāveram	monueram	rēxeram	cēperam	audīveram
Fut. perf. indic.	amāverō	monuerō	rēxerō	cēperō	audīverō

(c) From the supine stem:

Stem:	amāt-	monit-	rēct-	capt-	audīt-
Passive					
Perf. part.	amātus	monitus	rēctus	captus	audītus
Perf. infin.	amāt[us] esse	monit[us] esse	rēct[us] esse	capt[us] esse	audīt[us] esse
Perf. indic.	amātus sum	monitus sum	rēctus sum	captus sum	audītus sum
Plup. indic.	amātus eram	monitus eram	rēctus eram	captus eram	audītus eram
Fut. perf. indic.	amātus erō	monitus erō	rēctus erō	captus erō	audītus erō
Future infin.	amātum īrī	monitum īrī	rēctum īrī	captum īrī	audītum īrī

(For the use of the future infinitive passive see Lesson XXXIX.)

Active
Future part.

| amātūrus | monitūrus | rēctūrus | captūrus | audītūrus |

Future infin.

| amātūr[us] esse | monitūr[us] esse | rēctūr[us] esse | captūr[us] esse | audītūr[us] esse |

(The future infinitive active and the perfect infinitive passive are used in the *accusative* in indirect statement. See Lesson XXIV.)

Sect. 50. Meaning of the participles and infinitives

(a) Participles

	Active	Passive
Pres. part.	**amāns,** loving	..
Perf. part.	..	**amātus,** loved, having been loved
Future part.	**amātūrus,** about to love	(Gerundive) **amandus,** must be loved, ought to be loved

For the declension of *amāns* see Lesson XVIII on third declension adjectives.

The future participle of *sum* is *futūrus* and the future infinitive is *futūrus esse*.

Amātus, -a, -um, amātūrus, -a, -um, and *amandus, -a, -um* are declined like the adjective *bonus*. Just as *amātus* is combined with *sum, eram*, and *erō* to form the perfect, pluperfect, and future perfect passive, so *amātūrus* can be combined with the verb 'to be' and forms what is known as the first or active periphrastic conjugation.

Amātūrus est.   He is about to love, going to love.

So, too, the gerundive *amandus* can be combined with the verb 'to be' and forms the second or passive periphrastic conjugation.

Amanda est.   She ought to be loved, she should be loved.

As the gerundive will be explained in Lesson XXXVIII, it can be omitted at this time.

The use of the participles will be explained in Lesson XXIII.

(b) Infinitives

	Active	*Passive*
Pres. infin.	**amāre,** to love	**amārī,** to be loved
Perf. infin.	**amāvisse,** to have loved	**amāt[us] esse,** to have been loved
Future infin.	**amātūr[us] esse,** to be about to love	**amātum īrī,** to be about to be loved

The use of the infinitive is explained in Lesson XXI. It is used, for example, with verbs like *volō*, 'I wish'.

venīre volō.   I wish to come.

It is also used very frequently after verbs of saying in Indirect Statement. See Lesson XXIV.

Review of verbs
EXERCISE 1

Identify the following forms and give their meaning:

aedificātur	audiēminī	collocāta sunt
agit	canunt	condita
amārī	capiuntur	cōnsurgitis
aperīte	cecidērunt	creāti estis
appellātus	claude	dedimus
arābantur	colere	dēlectāvit

dēlēvimus	habitūrus est	properābitis
dēscrībī	iacta	pugnābant
dēsīderāta es	īnscrīptum	rēctī erātis
dīc	labōrāre	reddidisse
docēbāris	lēgistī	repperistī
ductī erant	levātus esse	scrīpta est
ēmistis	mānserō	sedētis
errābātis	monitūrī	spectātūra est
expulsus est	mōnstrāveris	stās
exspectābitis	mūnīre	tenuēre
faciēbāmus	mūtātus eris	trādūxērunt
fugiēns	nāvigābunt	veniēmus
futūrus	nuntiātum est	vīcī
genuit	pervēnērunt	vīsus esse
gessērunt	pōnēns	vulnerātus erat
habitāverās	portāvisse	

EXERCISE 2

you have built (sing.), he will take, they were being taught, you are buying (pl.), you were missed (m. pl.), it was given, they will be driven out, he is about to lead, to have changed, you had fortified (pl.), carrying (sing.), they gave back, it had been found, it will have been written, you stood (sing.), we are sitting, they have conquered, we were seen, to be held, you have done (pl.).

EXERCISE 3

Derivatives

Give the Latin word from which each of the following words is derived, or a Latin word closely related to it:

action, agriculture, altitude, amatory, aquarium, aqueduct, audience, bellicose, beneficial, captive, chart, Chester, copious, creation, demonstrate, describe, diction, docile, equestrian, expect, expulsion, fabulous, fact, feminine, filial, fugitive, gladiator, habitation, horticulture, hostile, inscribe, insular, laboratory, latent, laudable, literature, lecture, liberty, locality, lunatic, magnitude, missive, monitor, multitude, mutation, nautical, navigation, otiose, pecuniary, poetical, popular, portable, position, procrastinate, puerile, regal, scholastic, scripture, servile, silvan, solar, tenable, urban, vaccination, verbal, victor, visual, vulnerable, wine.

LESSON XIV

PERSONAL PRONOUNS, *ego, tū, nōs, vōs*. POSSESSIVE
PRONOUNS. DEMONSTRATIVE PRONOUNS, *hic, ille, is*
EMPHATIC AND REFLEXIVE PRONOUNS, *ipse, sē*
USE OF *sē* AND *suus*

Sect. 51. Personal pronouns

THERE are four personal pronouns, *ego* (I), *nōs* (we), *tū* (you), *vōs*
(you). *Nōs* and *vōs* are plural. There is no personal pronoun for
the third person, but the demonstrative pronoun *is, ea, id* may be
used. It is not necessary to use personal pronouns for the subject
of a sentence, since the meaning is shown by the personal endings
of the verbs, but the pronouns are needed in the oblique cases
(genitive, dative, accusative, and ablative) and they may be used
for emphasis in the nominative.

First person	*Singular*	*Plural*
Nom.	**ego**	**nōs**
Gen.	**meī**	**nostrum, nostrī**
Dat.	**mihi**	**nōbīs**
Acc.	**mē**	**nōs**
Abl.	**mē**	**nōbīs**
Second person		
Nom.	**tū**	**vōs**
Gen.	**tuī**	**vestrum, vestrī**
Dat.	**tibi**	**vōbīs**
Acc.	**tē**	**vōs**
Abl.	**tē**	**vōbīs**

Nostrum and *vestrum* are partitive genitives, *nostrī* and *vestrī* are
objective.

See Lesson XVI for the partitive genitive and Lesson XL for
the objective genitive.

The Romans put the first person before the second (*ego et tū*),
and the second person before the third (*tū et Gāius*). When there
are two subjects, the first prevails.

Ego et tū vēnimus. You and I came (we came).
Tū et Gāius vēnistis. You and Gaius came (you came).

Ablative of accompaniment (see Lesson IX).

When *cum* is used with the ablative of a personal or reflexive pronoun, it follows the pronoun and is attached to it.

Mēcum, with me; **nōbīscum,** with us.

Sect. 52. Possessive pronouns (adjectives)

The possessive adjectives corresponding to the four personal pronouns are:

meus, mea, meum, my, mine.
tuus, tua, tuum, your, yours (sing.).
noster, nostra, nostrum, our, ours.
vester, vestra, vestrum, your, yours (pl.).

These should be used to indicate possession instead of the genitives of *ego, tū, nōs, vōs*.

Sect. 53. Demonstrative pronouns

The important pronouns are *hic, ille,* and *is,* but *iste* is also used. *Hic* means 'this'; it is the demonstrative of the first person and means 'this thing near me', whereas *iste* is the demonstrative of the second person and means 'that near you'. Hence *iste* is sometimes derogatory, meaning 'that of yours', and is often used for an opponent in a law-court.

Ille is the demonstrative of the third person, and means 'that over there'. It is sometimes used in a complimentary sense, meaning 'distinguished', e.g. *Pompēius ille,* 'that great man, Pompey'.

Frequently *hic* means 'the latter' and *ille* means 'the former'. But sometimes when two things are mentioned, *hic* refers to the one which is more to the fore in the writer's mind.

The pronoun *is, ea, id* is less precise; it is seldom as strong in meaning as 'this' or 'that' and generally means 'he', 'she', 'it'. It is also used with the relative pronoun *quī*; thus *is quī* means 'he who', 'the one who' (see Lesson XV).

Singular	*M.*	*F.*	*N.*
Nom.	**hic**	**haec**	**hoc**[1]
Gen.	**hūius**	**hūius**	**hūius**
Dat.	**huic**	**huic**	**huic**
Acc.	**hunc**	**hanc**	**hoc**
Abl.	**hōc**	**hāc**	**hōc**

[1] The syllable is long in the neuter singular *hoc,* which represents *hocc* (from *hod-ce*).

Plural	*M.*	*F.*	*N.*
Nom.	hī	hae	haec
Gen.	hōrum	hārum	hōrum
Dat.	hīs	hīs	hīs
Acc.	hōs	hās	haec
Abl.	hīs	hīs	hīs

Singular			
Nom.	ille	illa	illud
Gen.	illīus	illīus	illīus
Dat.	illī	illī	illī
Acc.	illum	illam	illud
Abl.	illō	illā	illō

Plural			
Nom.	illī	illae	illa
Gen.	illōrum	illārum	illōrum
Dat.	illīs	illīs	illīs
Acc.	illōs	illās	illa
Abl.	illīs	illīs	illīs

Singular			
Nom.	is	ea	id
Gen.	ēius	ēius	ēius
Dat.	eī	eī	eī
Acc.	eum	eam	id
Abl.	eō	eā	eō

Plural			
Nom.	eī (iī)	eae	ea
Gen.	eōrum	eārum	eōrum
Dat.	eīs (iīs)	eīs (iīs)	eīs (iīs)
Acc.	eōs	eās	ea
Abl.	eīs (iīs)	eīs (iīs)	eīs (iīs)

Sect. 54. Emphatic and reflexive pronouns

Ipse is an emphatic or intensive pronoun meaning '(I) myself', '(you) yourself', '(he) himself'.

Ipse tē vīdī.   I saw you myself (with my own eyes).

Note also: *illō ipsō annō*, 'in that *very* year'; *benevolentiā ipsā*, 'by his *mere* goodwill'.

Singular	*M.*	*F.*	*N.*
Nom.	ipse	ipsa	ipsum
Gen.	ipsīus	ipsīus	ipsīus
Dat.	ipsī	ipsī	ipsī
Acc.	ipsum	ipsam	ipsum
Abl.	ipsō	ipsā	ipsō

Plural			
Nom.	ipsī	ipsae	ipsa
Gen.	ipsōrum	ipsārum	ipsōrum
Dat.	ipsīs	ipsīs	ipsīs
Acc.	ipsōs	ipsās	ipsa
Abl.	ipsīs	ipsīs	ipsīs

The third person reflexive pronoun is *sē* (or *sēsē*), 'himself', 'herself', 'itself', 'themselves'.

Gen.	suī
Dat.	sibi
Acc.	sē
Abl.	sē

It has no nominative. The possessive adjective which corresponds to it is *suus, -a, -um*, 'his own', 'her own', 'its own', 'their own'.

Sē and *suus* refer to the subject of the sentence in which they occur.

Gallī sē suaque Rōmānīs dēdidērunt.

The Gauls surrendered themselves and their (possessions) to the Romans.

This is the direct reflexive. There is also an indirect reflexive which looks back from a dependent clause to the subject of the verb in the main clause. This will be explained in Lesson XXIV on Indirect Statement.

For the first and second persons the oblique cases of *ego* and *tu* are used.

Mē culpō, I blame myself.
Tē culpās, you blame yourself.

Sometimes *ipse* is added for emphasis.

Tē ipsum culpās.

VOCABULARY

Aenēās, -ae, *abl.* **-ā,** *m.,* Aeneas, the hero of Vergil's *Aeneid.*

ante, *prep. with acc.,* before.

Athēnae, -ārum, *f. pl.,* Athens.

autem, *conj.,* but, however, moreover.

bene, *adv.,* well.

causa, -ae, *f.,* cause.

Creūsa, -ae, *f.,* the wife of Aeneas at Troy.

Dēmophoōn, -ontis, *m.,* a son of Theseus, king of Athens, who deserted Phyllis (Ovid, *Heroides* 2).

Dīdō, -ōnis, *dat.* **-ōnī,** *f.,* Dido, queen of Carthage, who killed herself when Aeneas sailed for Italy (Vergil, *Aeneid* 4).

ego, *pers. pron.,* I.

et, *adv.,* also, even.

etiam, *adv.,* also, even.

frangō, frangere, frēgī, fractum, 3, break.

hic, haec, hoc, *dem. pron.,* this (near me); the latter.

hīc, *adv.,* here.

hinc, *adv.,* from here, hence.

inquam, *irreg.,* say; *3rd pers. sing.* **inquit,** he said (*used after one or more words of a quotation*).

ille, illa, illud, *dem. pron.,* that (over there); the former.

ipse, ipsa, ipsum, *emph. pron.,* himself, herself, itself.

is, ea, id, *dem. pron.,* he, she, it.

iste, ista, istud, *dem. pron.,* that (near you, of yours).

lacrima, -ae, *f.,* tear.

laus, laudis, *dat.* **laudi,** *f.,* praise, glory, worth (Lesson XVI).

mors, mortis, *acc.* **-em,** *f.,* death (Lesson XVII).

nōn iam, no longer.

nōs, *pers. pron.,* we.

oculus, -ī, *m.,* eye.

Phyllis, -idis, *acc.* **-ida,** *f.,* Phyllis, a Thracian princess who was deserted by Demophoon (Ovid, *Heroides* 2).

praebeō, praebēre, praebuī, praebitum, 2, offer, supply.

quoque, *adv.,* also, too.

relinquō, relinquere, relīquī, relictum, 3, leave behind, leave.

sē, suī, *reflex. pron., sing. and pl.,* himself, herself, itself, themselves.

servō, 1, save, preserve, keep.

suus, -a, -um, *poss. adj.,* his (her, its) own, their own.

Trōiānus, -a, -um, Trojan.

tū, *pers. pron.,* you (*sing.*).

umbra, -ae, *f.,* shade, shadow; ghost (*poet.*).

uxor, -ōris, *f.,* wife (Lesson XVI).

vīvō, vīvere, vīxī, victum, 3, live.

vōs, *pers. pron.,* you (*pl.*).

NOTES

Ex. 1

2. This comes from Shakespeare's *Julius Caesar,* but in Suetonius (*Julius* 82) Caesar speaks in Greek (*Kai su, teknon,* lit. = 'you too, my child').

3. **exemplāria,** *n. pl. from* **exemplar,** models.

    nocturnus, -a, -um, by night, nightly.

    versō, 1, turn, turn over, *i.e.* read.

    diurnus, -a, -um, by day, daily.

4. **dūrō,** 1, endure, hold out.

    vōsmet = **vōs** (*acc.*).

    rēbus, *dat. pl. of* **rēs,** circumstances (*here* = good fortune).

    secundus, -a, -um, favorable.

7. **cāsus, -ūs,** *m.,* fall, misfortune.

    miseror, 1 (*deponent*), pity (Lesson XXXII). Deponent verbs are passive in form and active in meaning.

8. **Pȳthagorās,** *m.,* Greek philosopher about 550 B.C., founder of the Pythagorean philosophy.

9. **senectūs, -ūtis,** *f.,* old age (Lesson XVI).

    morbus, -ī, *m.,* disease, sickness.

10. **vīsa** = **vīsa est** (*perf. pass.*).

11. **lētum, -ī,** *n.,* death.

    hospes, hospitis, host, guest (*here* = guest).

    amāns, *acc.* **amantem,** loving, lover (Lesson XVIII).

nex, necis, *f.,* death.
12. **ēnsis, -is,** *m.,* sword.
concidō, concidere, concidī,
3, fall down.
suā manū cadere (concidere),
to fall by one's own hand =
mortem sibi cōnscīscere,
commit suicide, kill one's self
(**cōnscīscō,** *perf.* **cōnscīvī,** 3).
ūsa, *perf. part. deponent from* **ūtor**
(*which takes abl.*), having used,
using (Lesson XXXII).
13. **ēn,** look, behold (*with nom.*).

Priamus, -ī, *m.,* Priam, king of
Troy, in Vergil's *Aeneid.* He
was represented on the walls
of the temple at Carthage.
(**sculpō, -ere, sculpsī, sculptum,** 3, carve.)
sua *refers to* **laudī,** *the logical
subject of the sentence.* **Sunt
laudī** *is equivalent to* **laus habet.**
14. **superbus, -a, -um,** proud.
bona, *neut. pl. of* **bonus,** good
things, blessings, property.
15. **Sabbatum, -ī,** *n.,* Sabbath.

EXERCISE 1

1. Tū quoque.   *2. Et tū, Brūte?
*3.   . . . Vōs exemplāria Graeca
nocturnā versāte manū, versāte diurnā.
4. Dūrāte et vōsmet rēbus servāte secundīs.
*5. Hic amor, haec patria est.
6. Hinc illae lacrimae.
*7. Hī suum cāsum, illī suōrum miserābantur.
*8. 'Ipse dīxit.' 'Ipse' autem erat Pȳthagorās.
9. Senectūs ipsa est morbus.
*10. . . . Ipsius umbra Creūsae
vīsa mihi ante oculōs.
*11. Phyllida Dēmophoōn lētō dedit hospes amantem;
ille necis causam praebuit, ipsa manum.
*12. Praebuit Aenēās et causam mortis et ēnsem;
ipsa suā Dīdō concidit ūsa manū.
*13. Ēn Priamus! Sunt hīc etiam sua praemia laudī.
*14. Frangitur ipsa suīs Rōma superba bonīs.
15. Ō quanta, quālia sunt illa Sabbata!

EXERCISE 2

1. Horace advised the Romans well. You Romans, he said, always read
(imperat.) Greek literature.   2. The Romans and the Greeks have taught
us well; the latter wrote poems, the former ruled peoples.   3. Aeneas saw
the ghost of Creusa, his wife, but Creusa herself was no longer living.
4. Demophoon sailed to Athens; Phyllis was left behind and afterwards
killed herself.   5. The Trojan war was carved on the temple of the Carthaginians; even in that city glory had its own reward.

EXERCISE 3

ANSWER IN LATIN:

1. Quid ab Aenēā vīsum est?   2. Quis mortis causam Phyllidī praebuit?
3. Quis gladium Dīdōnī dedit?   4. Quis mortem sibi cōnscīvit?   5. Ubi
sculptus est rēx Troiānus?   6. Quid praemium suum habet?   7. Quae urbs
bonīs suīs fracta est?

Sect. 55. Relative pronoun

THE relative pronoun *quī, quae, quod*, meaning *who, which*, introduces a dependent clause and must agree with its antecedent in *gender* and *number*. The antecedent is the noun to which it refers; normally this precedes it, but sometimes it follows the relative clause. The *case* of the relative is determined by its own clause.

Catullus erat poēta quī Lesbiam amābat.

Catullus was the poet who loved Lesbia.

Here *quī* is masculine and singular because it agrees with its antecedent *poēta*; it is in the nominative case because it is the subject of *amābat*, the verb in the relative clause.

Catullus erat poēta quem Lesbia amābat.

Catullus was the poet whom Lesbia loved.

Here *quem* is masculine and singular, but in this sentence it is in the accusative case, since it is the object of the verb in the relative clause.

Singular	*M.*	*F.*	*N.*
Nom.	quī	quae	quod
Gen.	cūius	cūius	cūius
Dat.	cui	cui	cui
Acc.	quem	quam	quod
Abl.	quō	quā	quō

Plural			
Nom.	quī	quae	quae
Gen.	quōrum	quārum	quōrum
Dat.	quibus	quibus	quibus
Acc.	quōs	quās	quae
Abl.	quibus	quibus	quibus

The pronoun *is* is often used as the antecedent of *quī*.

Is est quī hoc fecit. He is the man who did this.

Sect. 56. Interrogative pronoun and adjective

The interrogative pronoun **quis, quid,** means 'who?', 'what?', and introduces a question.

	M. and F.	*N.*
Nom.	**quis**	**quid**
Gen.	**cūius**	**cūius**
Dat.	**cui**	**cui**
Acc.	**quem**	**quid**
Abl.	**quō**	**quō**

The plural is the same as the relative *quī*.

Quis hoc fēcit? Who did this?

Quid fēcistī? What did you do?

The interrogative adjective *quī* also introduces a question but agrees with a noun. It is declined like the relative *quī* and means 'what?'

Quem poētam vīdistī? What poet did you see?

Sect. 57. Indefinite relative pronouns

Quīcumque, quaecumque, quodcumque, 'whoever', 'whatever', is declined like *quī*, but only the first syllable changes. There is also *quisquis, quicquid,* or *quidquid,* 'whoever', 'whatever', which is generally found only in these forms. They are both indefinite relatives and normally introduce a verb in the indicative.

Quodcumque iubēs, id faciō. I do whatever you order.

The antecedent *is, ea, id* often follows the relative clause.

VOCABULARY

aevum, -ī, *n.,* life, age.

alius, alia, aliud, another (Lesson XXIX).

āra, -ae, *f.,* altar.

cēterī, -ae, -a, the others, the rest; *cf. English* 'etc.' **(et cētera).**

cōnsilium, -ī (-iī), *n.,* plan.

fātum, -ī, *n.,* fate, destiny.

fēlīx, *gen.* **fēlīcis,** happy, lucky (Lesson XVIII).

ferrum, -ī, *n.,* iron, sword.

fortūnātus, -a, -um, fortunate.

Herculēs, -is, *m.,* Hercules, the Greek Herakles, son of Jupiter and Alcmena, later the god of strength. The origin of his worship is described in Livy, Bk. 1, and Vergil, *Aeneid* 8.

iubeō, iubēre, iussī, iussum, 2, *with inf.,* order, command.

mare, maris, *n.,* the sea (Lesson XVII).

maximus, -a, -um, *superl. of* **magnus,** greatest (Lesson XIX).

miser, -era, -erum, sad, wretched; *superl.*, **miserrimus,** most wretched (Lesson XIX).

narrō, 1, relate, tell (*with dat. of person*).

nōscō, nōscere, nōvī, nōtum, 3, come to know; *perf.* **nōvī,** know.

ōra, -ae, *f.*, shore, region.

pars, partis, *acc.* **partem,** *f.*, part (Lesson XVII).

paucī, -ae, -a, few, a few.

quī, quae, quod, *rel. pron.*, who, which.

quīcumque, quaecumque, quodcumque, *indef. rel. pron.*, whoever, whatever.

quisquis, quicquid (quidquid), *indef. rel. pron.*, whoever, whatever.

rēgīna, -ae, *f.*, queen.

studium, -ī (-iī), *n.*, enthusiasm, study (*here* = partiality).

Tacitus, -ī, *m.*, Cornelius Tacitus, the historian, author of the *Annals* and *Histories, c.* A.D. 55–*c.* 117.

Tiberius, -ī (-iī), *m.*, the Emperor Tiberius, *princeps* A.D. 14–37.

trādō, trādere, trādidī, trāditum, 3, hand over, hand down, relate, transmit to posterity.

Trōia, -ae, *f.*, Troy.

vitium, -ī (-iī), *n.*, fault, defect.

NOTES

Ex. 1

1. **patrius, -a, -um,** of one's father or fathers.
   trānsigō, *perf.* **trānsēgī,** 3, *compound of* **agō,** finish, complete (*poet.*).

4. **medicus, -ī,** *m.*, doctor (*in l. 2* = as a doctor).
   vespillo, -ōnis, *m.*, *a rare word used by Martial*; a corpse-bearer. *Perhaps* undertaker.

5. **mē,** *acc. of* **ego,** *added for emphasis at the beginning of the line, depends on prep.* **in.** Nisus said this to help his friend Euryalus in Bk. 9 of Vergil's *Aeneid.*
   convertō, -ere, 3, turn, direct (towards).

6. **cōnstituō, -ere,** *perf.* **cōnstituī,** 3, set up; determine.
   sibi, *dat.*, for himself.

7. **custōdiō, -īre,** 4, guard.
   custōs, -ōdis, *pl.* **custōdēs,** *m.*, guardian, guard (Lesson XVI).

9. This refers to the *Annals* of Tacitus.

prīncipātus, -ūs, *m.*, principate, reign; chieftainship (Lesson XVIII).

procul habeō = I have far off, *i.e.* I am far from having.

10. **Ītaliam,** *used without the preposition* **ad,** to (*poet.*).
    fātō, by fate, through fate, *abl. expressing the cause. Compare* **ob** *with acc.*
    profugus, -a, -um, exiled, an exile.
    Lāvinia, *neut. pl. from* **Lāvinius,** of Lavinium, a city founded by Aeneas in honor of his Italian wife, Lavinia. *The second* **i** *of* **Lavinia** *is regarded here as consonantal.*
    lītus, -oris, *n.*, shore (Lesson XVI).

11. **īnfandus, -a, -um,** unspeakable.
    renovō, 1, renew.
    dolor, -ōris, *m.*, grief (Lesson XVI).
    quaeque = et ea quae.

EXERCISE 1

*1. Fēlīx, quī patriīs aevum trānsēgit in agrīs.

*2. Fortūnātus et ille deōs quī nōvit agrestēs.

*3. Caelum, nōn animum mūtant quī trāns mare currunt.

*4. Nūper erat medicus, nunc est vespillo Diaulus;
     quod vespillo facit, fēcerat et medicus.

5. Mē, mē, adsum quī fēcī, in mē convertite ferrum.

*6. Cōnstituitque sibī, quae Maxima dīcitur, āram.

*7. . . . Sed quis custōdiet ipsōs
custōdēs?

*8. Iuppiter est quodcumque vidēs.

*9. Cōnsilium (est) mihi pauca dē Augustō trādere, mox Tiberiī
prīncipātum et cētera, sine īrā et studiō, quōrum causās procul
habeō.

*10. Arma virumque canō, Trōiae quī prīmus ab ōrīs
Italiam fātō profugus Lāviniaque vēnit
lītora.

*11. Infandum, rēgīna, iubēs renovāre dolōrem,
. . . quaeque ipse miserrima vīdī
et quōrum pars magna fuī.

EXERCISE 2

1. He who hastens across the sea does not change the faults of his mind,
but he sees another part of the sky. 2. Those-men are fortunate who live
in the fields of-their-fathers and know the gods of-the-country. 3.
Diaulus, the undertaker, now does what he-himself had done before as-a-
doctor. 4. Hercules set-up the altar which the Romans called the Greatest
(Altar). 5. Aeneas was the man who first came from Troy to Italy on-
account-of fate. He told the queen of the Carthaginians the things he
had seen in the city of Troy.

EXERCISE 3

ANSWER IN LATIN:

1. Quis fēlīx est? 2. Quis fortūnātus est? 3. Quis animum nōn mūtat?
4. Quid nunc facit Diaulus? 5. Quis Āram Maximam cōnstituit? 6.
Custōdēs-ne ipsī custōdientur? 7. Quī deus est quodcumque vidēmus?
8. Quis est quī prīmus ab ōrīs Trōiae ad Italiam vēnit?

NOUNS OF THE THIRD DECLENSION, CONSONANT STEMS
PARTITIVE GENITIVE

Sect. 58. Nouns of the third declension

THERE are many nouns in this declension, and they have many variations. The ending of the nominative is irregular, but the stem is taken from the genitive singular, which ends in -*is*. Thus the genitive of *mīles*, 'a soldier', is *mīlitis*; the stem is *mīlit-* and all the case-endings are added to this stem.

Case-endings

	Singular		Plural	
	M. and F.	*N.*	*M. and F.*	*N.*
Nom.	(irregular)	(irregular)	**-ēs**	**-a**
Gen.	**-is**	**-is**	**-um**	**-um**
Dat.	**-ī**	**-ī**	**-ibus**	**-ibus**
Acc.	**-em**	(same as nom.)	**-ēs**	**-a**
Abl.	**-e**	**-e**	**-ibus**	**-ibus**

Most of the stems in the third declension end in a consonant, either a stop (e.g. *p, t, d, c, g*), a liquid (*l, r*), or a nasal (*n*). Thus *prīncip-* is the stem of *prīnceps*, *capit-* of *caput*, *duc-* of *dux*, *patr-* of *pater*, *nōmin-* of *nōmen*.

	prīnceps, *m.*, chief		**mīles,** *m.*, soldier	
	Singular	*Plural*	*Singular*	*Plural*
Nom.	**prīnceps**	**prīncipēs**	**mīles**	**mīlitēs**
Gen.	**prīncipis**	**prīncipum**	**mīlitis**	**mīlitum**
Dat.	**prīncipī**	**prīncipibus**	**mīlitī**	**mīlitibus**
Acc.	**prīncipem**	**prīncipēs**	**mīlitem**	**mīlitēs**
Abl.	**prīncipe**	**prīncipibus**	**mīlite**	**mīlitibus**

	dux, *m.*, leader		**caput,** *n.*, head	
	Singular	*Plural*	*Singular*	*Plural*
Nom.	**dux**	**ducēs**	**caput**	**capita**
Gen.	**ducis**	**ducum**	**capitis**	**capitum**
Dat.	**ducī**	**ducibus**	**capitī**	**capitibus**
Acc.	**ducem**	**ducēs**	**caput**	**capita**
Abl.	**duce**	**ducibus**	**capite**	**capitibus**

cōnsul, *m.*, consul

	Singular	Plural
Nom.	cōnsul	cōnsulēs
Gen.	cōnsulis	cōnsulum
Dat.	cōnsulī	cōnsulibus
Acc.	cōnsulem	cōnsulēs
Abl.	cōnsule	cōnsulibus

pater, *m.*, father

	Singular	Plural
Nom.	pater	patrēs
Gen.	patris	patrum
Dat.	patrī	patribus
Acc.	patrem	patrēs
Abl.	patre	patribus

amor, *m.*, love

	Singular	Plural
Nom.	amor	amōrēs
Gen.	amōris	amōrum
Dat.	amōrī	amōribus
Acc.	amōrem	amōrēs
Abl.	amōre	amōribus

legiō, *f.*, legion

	Singular	Plural
Nom.	legiō	legiōnēs
Gen.	legiōnis	legiōnum
Dat.	legiōnī	legiōnibus
Acc.	legiōnem	legiōnēs
Abl.	legiōne	legiōnibus

nomen, *n.*, name

	Singular	Plural
Nom.	nōmen	nōmina
Gen.	nōminis	nōminum
Dat.	nōminī	nōminibus
Acc.	nōmen	nōmina
Abl.	nōmine	nōminibus

Sect. 59. Partitive genitive (genitive of the whole)

This genitive expresses the whole to which a smaller part belongs. It is used with any word like *pars*, 'a part', which can express a part of a larger whole. It is also used with words which denote quantity or degree, such as *satis*, 'enough', *nihil*, 'nothing', *plus*, 'more', *nimis*, 'too much', *parum*, 'too little'.

 Magna pars mīlitum, a large part of the soldiers.
 Satis cibī, enough food (lit. enough of food).

The partitive genitives of *nōs* and *vōs* are *nostrum* (of us) and *vestrum* (of you).

 After numerals and words expressing number, like *nēmō*, 'no one', *multī*, 'many', *paucī*, 'few', it is usual to use the ablative with the preposition *ex* (*ē*) or *dē* instead of the partitive genitive.

 Quattuor ē mīlitibus, four of the soldiers.
 Ūna dē multīs, one (woman) out of many.

VOCABULARY

aeger, -gra, -grum, sick.
aliquis, aliquid, *pron.,* someone, something (Lesson XXX).
āter, -tra, -trum, black.
Catilīna, -ae, *m.,* Catiline, whose conspiracy was exposed by Cicero in 63 B.C.
Cerinthus, -ī, *m.,* Cerinthus, to whom Sulpicia wrote love poetry.
corpus, -oris, *n.,* body.
cūra, -ae, *f.,* care, and Care personified.
dux, ducis, *m.,* general, leader.
eques, equitis, *m.,* horseman.
homo, -inis, *m.,* man, human being.
labor, -ōris, *m.,* toil, work.
lēx, lēgis, *f.,* law.
lītus, -oris, *n.,* shore.
lūmen, -inis, *n.,* light.
lūx, lūcis, *f.,* light.
Maecēnās, -ātis, *m.,* Maecenas, a patron of Roman poets, addressed by Horace in the *Odes.*
malus, -a, -um, bad.
māter, mātris, *f.,* mother.
mīles, -itis, *m.,* soldier.

mōs, mōris, *m.,* custom; *pl.* **mōrēs,** morals, character.
nam, *conj.,* for.
Nemesis, *f.,* Nemesis, a lady mentioned in the poems of Tibullus.
nōmen, -inis, *n.,* name.
novus, -a, -um, new.
omnis, omne, *n. pl.* **omnia,** *gen. pl.* **omnium,** all, every (Lesson XVIII).
ōrātiō, -ōnis, *f.,* speech; *with* **habeō,** make a speech.
post, *prep. with acc.,* after, behind.
prīncipium, -ī (-iī), *n.,* beginning; *pl.,* first beginnings, atoms.
rūs, rūris, *n.,* the country (*opp. to* the city); *pl.* (*poet.*) fields.
saevus, -a, -um, fierce, cruel.
sīdus, -eris, *n.,* star.
sub, *prep. with acc. or abl.,* under.
tempus, -oris, *n.,* time.
ventus, -ī, *m.,* wind.
vēritās, -ātis, *f.,* truth, truthfulness.
vīta, -ae, *f.,* life.
vōx, vōcis, *f.,* voice.

NOTES

Ex. 1
A. 1. Nos. 1–5 are the mottoes of Columbia University, Columbia's School of General Studies, Harvard, Yale, and Oxford. The Columbia motto comes from Psalm xxxvi. 9 and the motto of the School of General Studies from St. John i. 5.
Lūx et vēritās in the Yale motto seems to be a translation of the two Hebrew words, *Urim* and *Thummim,* which are also included in the arms. These appear in Exodus xxviii. 30, but the words used in the Latin Bible are *doctrina* and *vēritās.* Compare Psalm xliii. 3: *ēmitte lūcem tuam et vēritātem tuam.*
The Oxford motto comes from Psalm xxvii. 1.
2. **tenebrae, -brārum,** *f. pl.,* darkness.

lūceō, 2, shine.
5. **illūminātiō, -ōnis,** *f.,* light; *lit.* a lighting up (*post-class.*).
6. Alcuin quotes this in a letter to Charlemagne, but he does not approve of it.
7. **cūriōsus, -a, -um,** painstaking, careful.
fēlicitās, -ātis, *f.,* felicity (here refers to Horace's writing).
9. **līma, -ae,** *f.,* a file (*i.e.* polishing a work of literature).
10. **pāscuum, -ī,** *n.,* a pasture (*usually in pl.*).
This refers to Vergil.
11. **cupīdō, -inis,** *m.,* desire; *also* Cupid, son of Venus (*here used in the pl.*).
Aeneadum, *gen. of* **Aeneadēs,** sons (descendants) of Aeneas.
genetrix, -trīcis, *f.,* mother.
dīvum (= **dīvōrum**), *gen. pl.,* gods.

voluptās, -ātis, *f.*, pleasure, delight.
almus, -a, -um, kindly, fostering.
12. Cicero is attacking Catiline in the senate.
senātus, -ūs, *abl.* **-ū,** *m.*, senate (Lesson XVIII).
13. **sileō, -ēre, siluī,** 2, be silent.
14. Pompey is the subject.
15. **pulvis, -eris,** *m.*, dust.
16. **geminus, -a, -um,** twin, two.
fax, facis, *f.*, torch (here refers to eyes).
18. **trāiciō,** 3, throw across (*here* = cross (*with acc.* **lītora**)); *cf.* **trānseō,** go across (Lesson XXXIX).
19. **aspiciō,** 3, look at, see.
20. **pius, -a, -um,** pious, devout, devoted.
puellae, *gen. with* **cūra,** care for your girl.
quod, because.
vexō, 1, molest, trouble.
corpora, *pl. for sing.* (*poet.*).
fessus, -a, -um, tired, weary.
calor, -ōris, *m.*, heat (*here* = a fever).
21. **nāvita, -ae,** *m.* (= **nauta**), sailor.
arātor, -ōris, *m.*, ploughman.
ēnumerō, 1, count.
vulnus, -eris, *n.*, wound.
pastor, -ōris, *m.*, shepherd.
ovis, -is, -ium, *f.*, sheep (Lesson XVII).
22. **perfringō,** *perf.* **perfrēgī,** 3, break through, violate.
ac, and.
prōsternō, *perf.* **prōstrāvī,** 3, overthrow, destroy.
cupiditās, -ātis, *f.*, desire.
furor, -ōris, *m.*, fury, madness.
pudor, -ōris, *m.*, modesty, sense of shame.

libīdō, -inis, *f.*, desire.
timor, -ōris, *m.*, fear.
audācia, -ae, *f.*, boldness.
ratiō, -ōnis, *f.*, reason, reckoning, plan.
āmentia, -ae, *f.*, madness.
B. 1. **caveō, -ēre, cāvī, cautum,** 2, beware (of).
canis, -is, -um, *m. and f.*, dog (Lesson XVII).
3. **probitās, -ātis,** *f.*, goodness, honesty.
alget, *from* **algeō,** 2, is cold (*i.e.* is neglected).
4. **atavus, -ī,** *m.*, ancestor.
ēditus, *perf. part. of* **ēdō,** sprung from.
praesidium, -ī (-ii), *n.*, guard, protection.
dulcis, -e, sweet, delightful.
decus, -oris, *n.*, glory, pride.
5. **corrigō,** *perf.* **corrēxī,** 3, correct.
cēnsor, -ōris, *m.*, censor (*here* = critic).
libellus, -ī, *m.*, *diminutive of* **liber,** book.
6. **cantō,** 1, sing.
vacuus, -a, -um, empty (*here* = empty-handed).
cōram, *prep. with abl.*, in the presence of.
latrō, -ōnis, *m.*, robber, brigand.
viātor, -ōris, *m.*, traveller.
7. **exiguus, -a, -um,** small, short, scanty.
clīnāmen, -inis, *n.*, swerve (*here* = the swerve of the falling atoms (in Lucretius, *Dē Rērum Nātūrā*), which makes free will possible).
8. **prōpōnō,** 3, propose (put forward).
dispōnō, 3, dispose (arrange).

EXERCISE 1

A.   1. In lūmine tuō vidēbimus lūmen.
     2. Lūx in tenebrīs lūcet.
     3. Vēritās.
     4. Lūx et vēritās.
     5. Dominus illūminātiō mea.
     6. Vōx populī vōx Deī.
     7. Horātiī cūriōsa fēlīcitās.

*8. Post equitem sedet ātra Cūra.
9. Līmae labor.
*10. Cecinī pāscua, rūra, ducēs.
11. (a) Māter saeva Cupīdinum.
(b) Aeneadum genetrīx, hominum dīvumque voluptās,
alma Venus.
*12. Ō tempora, ō mōrēs!
*13. Silent enim lēgēs inter arma.
14. Stat magnī nōminis umbra.
15. Pulvis et umbra sumus.
16. (a) Geminae, sīdera nostra, facēs.
(b) Oculōs, sīdera nostra, tuōs.
*17. Nōmen habet Nemesis, Cynthia nōmen habet.
*18. Trāicit et fātī lītora magnus amor.
19. Ō rūs, quandō ego tē aspiciam?
*20. Estne tibī, Cērinthe, tuae pia cūra puellae,
quod mea nunc vexat corpora fessa calor?
*21. Nāvita dē ventīs, dē taurīs narrat arātor,
ēnumerat mīles vulnera, pastor ovēs.
*22. Perfrēgit ac prōstrāvit omnia cupiditāte ac furōre; vīcit pudōrem
libīdō, timōrem audācia, ratiōnem āmentia.
23. Ex Āfricā semper aliquid novī.
*24. Plūs habet hic vītae, plūs habet ille viae.
B. (Optional)
1. Cavē canem.
2. In vīnō vēritās.
3. Probitās laudātur et alget.
4. Maecēnās atavīs ēdite rēgibus,
Ō et praesidium et dulce decus meum.
5. Saepe ego corrēxī sub tē cēnsōre libellōs.
6. Cantābit vacuus cōram latrōne viātor.
7. Id facit exiguum clīnāmen prīncipiōrum.
8. Nam homo prōpōnit, sed Deus dispōnit.

Exercise 2

1. In the light of God men will see the light. 2. In his Odes (songs) Horace
has told us about black Care, which sits behind the horseman. 3. Soldiers
tell about their wounds, shepherds about their sheep. 4. In a speech
which he made in the senate Cicero blamed the times and Catiline's
morals. 5. Vergil wrote songs about shepherds, farmers, (and) generals.

Exercise 3

ANSWER IN LATIN:

1. Quid in tenebrīs lūcet?   2. Quālis fuit Horātiī fēlīcitās?   3. Quis fuit
hominum deōrumque voluptās?   4. Ubi silent lēgēs?   5. Quōmodo
puellārum oculī ā poētīs appellantur?   6. Quid facit magnus amor?
7. Cūius puella aegra fuit?   8. Quis dē taurīs narrat?   9. Quid fēminae
malae ratiōnem vīcit?

LESSON XVII

Sect. 60. Nouns of the third declension: -i stems

THE stem of some nouns ends in the vowel -*i* and not in a consonant. Such nouns have a genitive plural ending in -*ium* instead of
-*um*. They also have an alternative form of the accusative plural
ending in -*īs*. Otherwise they are declined like nouns with consonant stems. Neuter nouns, which end in -*e*, -*al*, -*ar* in the nominative, have the ablative singular ending in -*ī* instead of -*e*, and
the nominative and accusative plural ending in -*ia*. They have
a genitive plural ending in -*ium* like the masculine and feminine
nouns.

Case-endings

	Singular		Plural	
	M. and F.	*N.*	*M. and F.*	*N.*
Nom.	**-is, -ēs,** etc.	**-e, -al, -ar**	**-ēs**	**-ia**
Gen.	**-is**	**-is**	**-ium**	**-ium**
Dat.	**-ī**	**-ī**	**-ibus**	**-ibus**
Acc.	**-em**	**-e, -al, -ar**	**-īs, -ēs**	**-ia**
Abl.	**-e**	**-ī**	**-ibus**	**-ibus**

Some pure *i*-stems, which are not neuter, like *sitis*, f., 'thirst', have
the ablative singular ending in -*ī* and the accusative singular ending
in -*im*.

	cīvis, *m. and f.*, citizen		**nūbēs,** *f.*, cloud	
	Singular	*Plural*	*Singular*	*Plural*
Nom.	**cīvis**	**cīvēs**	**nūbēs**	**nūbēs**
Gen.	**cīvis**	**cīvium**	**nūbis**	**nūbium**
Dat.	**cīvī**	**cīvibus**	**nūbī**	**nūbibus**
Acc.	**cīvem**	**cīvīs, -ēs**	**nūbem**	**nūbīs, -ēs**
Abl.	**cīve**	**cīvibus**	**nūbe**	**nūbibus**

urbs, *f.*, city   nox, *f.*, night

	Singular	*Plural*	*Singular*	*Plural*
Nom.	urbs	urbēs	nox	noctēs
Gen.	urbis	urbium	noctis	noctium
Dat.	urbī	urbibus	noctī	noctibus
Acc.	urbem	urbīs, -ēs	noctem	noctīs, -ēs
Abl.	urbe	urbibus	nocte	noctibus

mare, *n.*, sea   animal, *n.*, animal

	mare	maria	animal	animālia
Nom.	mare	maria	animal	animālia
Gen.	maris	. .	animālis	animālium
Dat.	marī	maribus	animālī	animālibus
Acc.	mare	maria	animal	animālia
Abl.	marī	maribus	animālī	animālibus

It is not easy to distinguish *i*-stems from consonant stems. Though a noun like *cīvis*, which has the same number of syllables in the genitive as it has in the nominative, has an *i*-stem, some nouns of this kind like *iuvenis*, 'a young man', and *canis*, 'a dog', have a consonant stem and a genitive plural in *-um*. For this reason the genitive plural of *i*-stem nouns will be given in the Vocabulary.[1]

Irregular nouns of the third declension

senex, *m.*, old man   vīs, *f.*, force, *pl.* strength

	Singular	*Plural*	*Singular*	*Plural*
Nom.	senex	senēs	vīs	vīrēs
Gen.	senis	senum	(vīs)	vīrium
Dat.	senī	senibus	(vī)	vīribus
Acc.	senem	senēs	vim	vīrīs, -ēs
Abl.	sene	senibus	vī	vīribus

[1] Nouns with genitive plural in *-ium*:

(1) Nouns (m. and f.) in *-is* and a few in *-er*, which have the same number of syllables in the nominative and the genitive singular (e.g. *ignis*, *imber*).

(2) Nouns (n.) in *-e*, *-al*, *-ar* (e.g. *mare*, *animal*, *calcar*).

(3) Nouns in *-ēs*, genitive *-is* (e.g. *nūbēs*).

(4) Nouns of one syllable in *-s* or *-x* (preceded by a consonant, e.g. *ars*, *arx*).

(5) Nouns of more than one syllable in *-ns* or *-rs* (e.g. *cohors*).

(6) Nouns in *-tās*, genitive *-tātis*, but usually with *-um* in genitive plural (e.g. *civitās*).

(7) Nouns like *Penātēs*, *optimātēs*, *Quirītēs*.

(8) Some nouns of one syllable in *-s* or *-x* preceded by a vowel (e.g. *dōs*, *fraus*, *mūs*, *nix*, *nox*, *vis*).

iter, *n.*, journey, march

Singular   Plural

	Singular	Plural
Nom.	**iter**	**itinera**
Gen.	**itineris**	**itinerum**
Dat.	**itinerī**	**itineribus**
Acc.	**iter**	**itinera**
Abl.	**itinere**	**itineribus**

Gender

It is difficult to give any general rules for gender in this declension. Obviously words like *pater*, 'father', are masculine and words like *māter*, 'mother', are feminine. Words like *virtūs*, 'virtue', *auctōritās*, 'authority', *multitūdō*, 'multitude', *ratiō*, 'reason', *legiō*, 'legion', are feminine; words like *iūdex*, 'judge', *mīles*, 'soldier', *imperātor*, 'general', *timor*, 'fear', are masculine; words like *mare*, 'sea', *animal*, 'animal', *calcar*, 'spur', *tempus*, 'time', *nōmen*, 'name', are neuter.

Sect. 61. Locative case

Generally the ablative expresses place where (see Lesson I), but the old locative case is still used in Latin for names of towns. In the first and second declensions it has the same ending as the genitive in the singular (-*ae* and -*ī*), and as the ablative in the plural (-*īs*).

First declension:

   Rōmae, at Rome; **Cantabrigiae,** at Cambridge; **Athēnīs,** at Athens.

Second declension:

   Tarentī, at Tarentum; **domī,** at home; **Novī Eborācī,** in New York; **Philippīs,** at Philippi.

In the third declension the ending is -*ī* or -*e* in the singular and -*ibus* in the plural:

   Carthāginī, Carthāgine, at Carthage; **rūrī** (*from* **rūs, rūris,** *n.*), in the country; **Curibus,** at Cures.

VOCABULARY

aequus, -qua, -quum, equal, impartial.
aestās, -ātis, *f.*, summer.
at, *conj.*, but, yet.
cīvis, -is, -ium, *m. and f.*, citizen.
dēbeō, -ēre, dēbuī, dēbitum, 2, owe; (*with inf.*) ought to.
domus, -ūs, *acc. pl.* **-ōs,** *f.*, home, house; **domī,** at home (Lesson XVIII).
fīnis, -is, -ium, *m.*, end; *pl.* boundaries, territory.
flōs, -ōris, *m.*, flower.
frāter, -tris, *m.*, brother.
gens, gentis, -ium, *f.*, race, clan, people.
genus, generis, *n.*, race, kind, sort.
glōria, -ae, *f.*, glory.
igitur, *conj.*, therefore.
ignis, -is, -ium, *m.*, fire.
imperium, -ī (-iī), *n.*, military power, dominion, empire.
longus, -a, -um, long.
mēns, mentis, -ium, *f.*, mind.
moenia, -ium, *n. pl.*, walls (of a city).

mōns, montis, -ium, *m.*, mountain.
moveō, -ēre, mōvī, mōtum, 2, move.
nātūra, -ae, *f.*, nature.
nāvis, -is, -ium, *f.*, ship.
nihil (nil), *n.*, *indecl.*, nothing.
odium, -ī (-iī), *n.*, hatred, dislike.
pater, patris, *m.*, father; *pl.* fathers, senators.
petō, -ere, petīvī (-iī), petītum, 3, seek, aim at, ask for; (*with ā and abl.*, Lesson XXVI), ask, request (someone).
prō, *prep. with abl.*, on behalf of, for, instead of.
rīdeō, -ēre, rīsī, rīsum, 3, laugh, smile at.
sepulcrum, -ī, *n.*, grave, tomb.
summus, -a, -um, highest, greatest.
terreō, -ēre, terruī, territum, 2, terrify.
ūnus, -a, -um, one.
vallēs (vallis), -is, -ium, *f.*, valley.
vēr, vēris, *n.*, spring.

NOTES

Ex. 1
A. 4. **potissimum,** *adv.* (*superl.*), preferably, especially.
   5. **fuga, -ae,** *f.*, flight.
     foedus, -a, -um, disgraceful, foul.
     victōria, -ae, *f.*, victory.
     glōriōsus, -a, -um, glorious.
   6. **pallidus, -a, -um,** pale.
     pulsō, 1, strike, beat.
     pēs, pedis, *m.*, foot.
     pauperum, *gen. pl. of* **pauper, -eris,** poor; a poor man.
     taberna, -ae, *f.*, hut, cottage; shop, tavern.
     turris, -is, -ium, *f.*, tower.
   7. **neque . . . hīlum** (*poet.*) = **et nihil,** and . . . not at all.
     pertineō, -ēre, pertinuī, 2, reach, concern (*with* **ad** *and acc.*).
   8. **pectora,** here *acc. in an exclamation.*
     caecus, -a, -um, blind.
   9. **dextera** *fem. of* **dexter,** right, skillful, fitting.
     praecipuē, *adv.*, especially.

     indulgentia, -ae, *f.*, indulgence, kindness.
     asperitās, -ātis, *f.*, harshness.
 10. **multa pars** = a large part.
     superstes erit = will survive.
 11. **quā,** where.
     tumidus, -a, -um, swelling, rising high.
     subsīdō, -sīdere, -sēdī, -sessum, 3, sink down, settle down.
     facilis, -e, *pl.* **-es,** easy (Lesson XVIII).
     curvus, -a, -um, curved, winding.
     vallibus, *preposition omitted* (*poet.*).
 12. **assiduus, -a, -um,** continual, perpetual.
     aliēnus, -a, -um, another's, not one's own.
     mēnsis, -is, -ium, *m.*, month.
 13. **pōmum, -ī,** *n.*, fruit, apple.
     autumnus, -ī, *m.*, autumn.
     formōsus, -a, -um, beautiful.
     messis, -is, -ium, *f.*, harvest.
     levō, 1, *here* = relieve.

hiems, hiemis, *f.*, winter.

14. **aequor, -oris,** *n.*, sea.
 vectus, *perf. part. from* **vehō,** carried.
 adveniō, 4, arrive, come.
 īnferiae, -ārum, *f. pl.*, sacrifices (in honor of the dead).

15. **gaudeō, -ēre, gāvīsus sum,** 2, semi-deponent (Lesson XXXII), rejoice, delight in (*with abl.*).
 Paelignus, -a, -um, Paelignian (*see* **Sulmo** *in* Lesson VI).

16. **dī,** *contracted nom. pl. of* **deus,** god; *abl. pl.* **dīs.**

17. **mī** = mihi.

18. **Mīsēnum, -ī,** *n.*, a town and harbor in Campania, where the Elder Pliny was admiral of the fleet. He died during the eruption of Mount Vesuvius in A.D. 79.
 classis, -is, -ium, *f.*, fleet.
 praesēns, -entis, present, in person.

19. **venustus, -a, -um,** lovely, charming.
 Sirmio, a peninsula on the Lacus Benācus in north Italy, where Catullus had a home.
 erus, -ī, *m.*, master (of a house).
 cachinnus, -ī, *m.*, laughter.

20. **strēnuus, -a, -um,** busy, strenuous.
 exerceō, 2, keep busy, drive on (*with acc.*).
 inertia, -ae, *f.*, idleness.
 quadrīgae, -ārum, *f. pl.*, four-horse team, chariot, car.
 Ulubrae, -ārum, *f. pl.*, Ulubrae, a small town in Latium, now Cisterna.
 sī, *conj.*, if.
 dēficiō, 3, fail (*with acc.*).

B. 1. **inde,** then, thereupon; thence.
 lupa, -ae, *f.*, she-wolf.
 fulvus, -a, -um, tawny.
 nūtrix, -trīcis, *f.*, nurse.

tegmen, -minis, *m.*, covering.
 excipiō, 3, take, receive.
 Māvortius, -a, -um, of Mars.

2. **Penātēs, -ium,** *m. pl.*, household gods, the Penates. Probably **dīs** is in apposition to **Penātibus.**

3. **initium, -ī (-iī),** *n.*, beginning.
 flūmen, -inis, *n.*, river.
 Rhodanus, -ī, *m.*, the river Rhone.
 contineō, 2, surround (keep together).
 Garumna, -ae, *m.*, the river Garonne.
 ōceanus, -ī, *m.*, ocean.
 Belgae, -ārum, *m. pl.*, the Belgians in the north-east of Gaul.
 attingō, 3, touch, reach.
 Rhēnus, -ī, *m.*, the river Rhine.
 vergō, 3, turn, bend.
 septentriōnēs, -um, *m.*, the seven stars of the Great Bear, *i.e.* the north.

4. **vātes, -is,** *m.*, poet, prophet.
 opus, operis, *n.*, work, task.
 tua (your) *refers to* Elegy.
 fāma, -ae, *f.*, fame, report, glory.
 ardeō, 2, burn (*intrans.*).
 exstructus, -a, -um, *perf. part.*, built up.
 inānis, -e, empty.
 rogus, -ī, *m.*, funeral pile.

5. **rōbur, -oris,** *n.*, oak; strength.
 aes, aeris, *n.*, bronze, copper.
 triplex, -icis, triple.
 circā, *prep. with acc.*, around.
 pectus, -oris, *n.*, breast, heart, mind.
 fragilis, -e, *acc.* **-em,** fragile.
 trux, trucis, *dat.* **-ī,** rough, harsh.
 committō, *perf.* **commīsī,** 3 entrust to (*with acc. and dat.*).
 pelagus, -ī, *n.*, sea.
 ratis, -is, *f.*, raft; (*poet.*) bark, boat.

EXERCISE 1

A. 1. Cīvis Rōmānus sum.
    2. Urbem Rōmam ā prīncipiō rēgēs habuēre.
    3. Imperium sine fīne dedī.

*4. Ō fortūnāta mors quae nātūrae dēbita prō patriā est potissimum
    reddita!
5. In fugā foeda mors est, in victōriā glōriōsa.
*6. Pallida Mors aequō pulsat pede pauperum tabernās
    rēgumque turrīs.
7. Nīl igitur mors est ad nōs neque pertinet hīlum.
8. Ō miserās hominum mentēs, ō pectora caeca!
*9. Dextera praecipuē capit indulgentia mentēs;
    asperitās odium saevaque bella movet.
10. Vīvam, parsque meī multa superstes erit.
*11. At vōs, quā veniet, tumidī, subsīdite, montēs,
    et facilēs curvīs vallibus este, viae.
*12. Hīc vēr assiduum, atque aliēnīs mēnsibus aestās.
*13. Pōma dat autumnus; formōsa est messibus aestās;
    vēr praebet flōrēs; igne levātur hiems.
14. Multās per gentēs et multa per aequora vectus,
    adveniō hās miserās, frāter, ad īnferiās.
*15. Mantua Vergiliō, gaudet Vērōna Catullō;
    Paelignae dīcar glōria gentis ego.
16. Dī mē terrent et Iuppiter hostis.
17. . . . Et mī genus ab Iove summō.
*18. Erat Mīsēnī classemque imperiō praesēns regēbat.
*19. Salvē, ō venusta Sirmio, atque erō gaudē.
    Rīdēte, quidquid est domī cachinnōrum.
*20. Strēnua nōs exercet inertia; nāvibus atque
    quadrīgīs petimus bene vīvere. Quod petis hīc est,
    est Ulubrīs, animus sī tē nōn dēficit aequus.

B. (Optional)
    1. Inde lupae fulvō nūtrīcis tegmine laetus
       Rōmulus excipiet gentem et Māvortia condet
       moenia Rōmānōsque suō dē nōmine dīcet.
    2. Cum patribus populōque Penātibus et magnīs dīs.
    3. Eōrum ūna pars . . . initium capit ā flūmine Rhodanō; continētur
       Garumnā flūmine, Ōceanō, fīnibus Belgārum; attingit etiam
       flūmen Rhēnum; vergit ad septentriōnēs.
    4. Ille tuī vātēs operis, tua fāma, Tibullus
       ardet in exstructō, corpus ināne, rogō.
    5. Illī rōbur et aes triplex
       circā pectus erat, quī fragilem trucī
       commīsit pelagō ratem
       prīmus. . . .

EXERCISE 2

1. The minds of men are charmed (captured) by kindness, but hatred is
caused (moved) by harshness. 2. Where a poet's girl comes, the mountains
sink down and the roads are easy in the valleys. 3. In Italy after a long
spring we see summer in many months of the year. 4. Death is impartial

and comes to the homes of all the citizens. 5. What we are seeking is here in our-own city; we find it in New York, in Cambridge, in Ulubrae.

EXERCISE 3

ANSWER IN LATIN:

1. Quī hominēs ā prīncipiō Rōmam rēxērunt? 2. Quid nātūrae dēbētur? 3. Cui potissimum redditur mors? 4. Quālis in fugā est mors? 5. Quid rēgum turrīs pulsat? 6. Quōrum mentēs miserās appellat Lucrētius? 7. Quid praecipuē mentēs nostrās capit? 8. Quid odium movet? 9. Quid pōma dat? 10. Quid flōrēs praebet? 11. Cūius ad sepulcrum vēnit Catullus? 12. Quae urbs Vergiliō gaudet? 13. Quī locus Catullō dominō suō gaudēbat? 14. Ubi Plīnius classem regēbat?

Temple of Apollo, Pompeii, and Mount Vesuvius

LESSON XVIII

ADJECTIVES OF THE THIRD DECLENSION AND
PRESENT PARTICIPLES. NOUNS OF THE FOURTH AND
FIFTH DECLENSION. GENDER. ABLATIVE OF RESPECT
(SPECIFICATION)

Sect. 62. Adjectives of the third declension and present participles

THESE adjectives are declined like *i*-stem nouns of the third declension. They have -*ī* in the ablative singular, -*ium* in the genitive plural, -*īs* or -*ēs* in the accusative plural (m. and f.), and -*ia* in the nominative and accusative plural (n.).

Some of them have two terminations like *omnis* (m. and f.), *omne* (n.); others have three terminations like *ācer, ācris, ācre*; a third group has one termination like *fēlīx* (m., f., and n.). Present participles like *amāns* (m., f., and n.) are similar to this last group.

	Singular		*Plural*	

omnis, all

	M. and F.	*N.*	*M. and F.*	*N.*
Nom.	omnis	omne	omnēs	omnia
Gen.	omnis		omnium	
Dat.	omnī		omnibus	
Acc.	omnem	omne	omnīs, -ēs	omnia
Abl.	omnī		omnibus	

ācer, keen, sharp

	M. and F.		*N.*	*M. and F.*		*N.*
Nom.	ācer	ācris	ācre	ācrēs	ācrēs	ācria
Gen.		ācris			ācrium	
Dat.		ācrī			ācribus	
Acc.		ācrem	ācre		ācrīs, -ēs	ācria
Abl.		ācrī			ācribus	

fēlīx, happy, lucky

	M. and F.	*N.*	*M. and F.*	*N.*
Nom.	fēlīx	fēlīx	fēlīcēs	fēlīcia
Gen.	fēlīcis		fēlīcium	

	Singular		*Plural*	
Dat.	**fēlīcī**		**fēlīcibus**	
Acc.	**fēlīcem**	**fēlīx**	**fēlīcīs, -ēs**	**fēlīcia**
Abl.	**fēlīcī**		**fēlīcibus**	

amāns, loving

	M. and F.	*N.*	*M. and F.*	*N.*
Nom.	**amāns**	**amāns**	**amantēs**	**amantia**
Gen.	**amantis**		**amantium**	
Dat.	**amantī**		**amantibus**	
Acc.	**amantem**	**amāns**	**amantīs, -ēs**	**amantia**
Abl.	**amantī, -e**		**amantibus**	

Participles used as adjectives have *-ī* in the ablative singular; in the ablative absolute construction they have *-e* (Lesson XXIII).

Brevis, 'short', *trīstis*, 'sad', *levis*, 'light', are declined like *omnis*; *celeber*, 'famous', *salūber*, 'healthy', *alacer*, 'brisk', are declined like *ācer*; *audāx*, 'bold', *simplex*, 'simple', *vēlōx*, 'swift', are declined like *fēlīx*; *ingēns*, 'huge', and the participles *monēns, regēns, capiēns, audiēns* are declined like *amāns*.

Names of months are masculine adjectives agreeing with *mēnsis*, which is understood. *Aprīlis* is declined like *omnis, September, October, November, December* are declined like *ācer*, and the rest, *Iānuārius, Februārius, Martius, Māius, Iūnius, Iūlius, Augustus*, are declined like *bonus*.

Sect. 63. Nouns of the fourth declension

In this declension the letter *u* appears in all the cases except the dative and ablative plural.

	Singular	*Plural*
	gradus, *m.*, step	
Nom.	**gradus**	**gradūs**
Gen.	**gradūs**	**graduum**
Dat.	**graduī**	**gradibus**
Acc.	**gradum**	**gradūs**
Abl.	**gradū**	**gradibus**

genū, *n.*, knee

Nom.	genū `	genua
Gen.	genūs	genuum
Dat.	genū	genibus
Acc.	genū	genua
Abl.	genū	genibus

Domus, f., 'house', is irregular and belongs both to the second and to the fourth declension.

	Singular	*Plural*
Nom.	domus	domūs
Gen.	domūs	domuum (domōrum)
Dat.	domuī (domō)	domibus
Acc.	domum	domōs (domūs)
Abl.	domō (domū)	domibus
Locative	domī, at home	

Manus, f., 'hand', *senātus*, m., 'senate', *passus*, m., 'pace', are declined like *gradus*; *cornū*, n., 'horn', is declined like *genū*.

Gender

Most of the nouns ending in *-us* are masculine, but *domus*, 'house', *manus*, 'hand', and *Īdūs,* 'Ides', are feminine. Nouns ending in *-ū* are neuter.

Sect. 64. Fifth declension

In this declension the letter *e* appears in all the cases.

rēs, *f.*, thing

	Singular	*Plural*
Nom.	rēs	rēs
Gen.	reī	rērum
Dat.	reī	rēbus
Acc.	rem	rēs
Abl.	rē	rēbus

Diēs, *diēī*, m., 'day', *aciēs*, f., 'line of battle', *faciēs*, f., 'face', *speciēs*, f., 'appearance', *spēs*, f., 'hope', *fidēs*, f., 'faith', are declined like *rēs*, but apart from *rēs* and *diēs* few nouns are used in the plural.

Gender

All the nouns are feminine except *diēs* and *merīdiēs*, 'noon'. But *diēs* may be feminine in the singular when it means 'an appointed day'. *Rēspūblica*, 'the state', 'republic', is declined in both its parts (*reīpūblicae, rempūblicam, rēpublicā*).

Sect. 65. Ablative of respect (specification)

This ablative shows *in what respect* a statement is true.

Hī virī mōribus sunt similēs.

These men are similar in character.

Speciē, 'in appearance', *rē ipsā*, 'in reality', *nōmine*, 'in name', *linguā*, 'in language', are other examples. Adjectives are also used with an ablative of this kind, e.g. *dignus*, 'worthy (of)'.

Dux magnō honōre dignus.

A general worthy of great honor.

The ablative is used with *praeditus*, 'endowed with', and *frētus*, 'relying on'.

Vir singulārī ingeniō praeditus.

A man endowed with remarkable ability.

VOCABULARY

adulēscēns, -entis, *m.*, youth, young man.

alō, -ere, aluī, altum, 3, nourish, sustain.

Antōnius, -ī, *m.*, Marcus Antonius (Antony), whom Cicero attacked in his *Philippics*.

apis, -is, -ium, *f.*, bee.

beātus, -a, -um, happy, blessed.

brevis, -e, short.

caelestis, -e, heavenly.

campus, -ī, *m.*, plain.

cōgō, -ere, coēgī, coāctum, 3, *compound of* **agō,** collect, compel.

cūnctī, -ae, -a, *pl. of* **cūnctus,** all, all together.

dēfendō, -ere, dēfendī, dēfēnsum, 3, defend.

diēs, -ēī, *m. and f.*, day.

dignus, -a, -um, worthy (*with abl.*).

discēdō, -ere, discessī, discessum, 3, go away, depart.

exiguus, -a, -um, small, short, scanty.

ferō, ferre, tulī, lātum, *irreg.*, bear, bring (Lesson XXXI).

fortis, -e, brave.

fortūna, -ae, *f.*, fortune.

iuvō, -āre, iūvī, iūtum, 1, help, please.

lingua, -ae, *f.*, tongue, language.

longē, *adv.*, far, by far.

medius, -a, -um, middle.

mīrus, -a, -um, wonderful.

ōdī, ōdisse, *perf. with pres. meaning*, hate, dislike.

praeter, *prep. with acc.*, beyond.

pulvis, -eris, *m.*, dust.

rēs pūblica (rēspūblica), reī pūblicae, *f.*, republic, state.

similis, -e, like, similar, (*with dat.*, Sect. 74).

soror, -ōris, *f.*, sister.

speciēs, -eī, *f.*, appearance, form.

spīritus, -ūs, *m.*, spirit, breath.

tangō, -ere, tetigī, tāctum, 3, touch.

tantus, -a, -um, so great.

terra, -ae, *f.*, earth, land; *pl.* the

whole earth, *e.g.* **orbis terrārum,**
the world.
timeō, -ēre, timuī, 2, fear.

trīstis, -e, sad.
videor, *pass. of* **videō,** 2, seem (*with
dat. of person*).

Notes

Ex. 1
A. 1. **ignōtus, -a, -um,** unknown.
   prō, for, *i.e.* is regarded as.
   magnificus, -a, -um, magnificent, splendid.
 2. **ab omnī parte,** from every point
   of view.
 3. **angulus, -ī,** *m.,* corner.
 4. **eōdem,** to the same place.
 5. **improbus, -a, -um,** bad, wicked.
   dūrus, -a, -um, hard.
   urgeō, -ēre, ursī, 2, press hard.
   egestās, -ātis, *f.,* need, want.
 6. **amāns, -antis,** loving; a lover.
   īrae, *nom. pl., used with sing. verb*
   (est).
   integrātiō, -ōnis, *f.,* a renewing.
 8. **Danai** = the Greeks.
 9. **Agamemnona,** *acc. of* **Agamemnōn.**
10. **adiuvō,** 1, help (= **iuvō**).
12. **hilaris, -e,** cheerful, gay.
   iocōsus, -a, -um, merry, humorous.
13. **intus,** within.
   tōtus, -a, -um, whole.
   īnfūsus, -a, -um, poured into.
   artūs, -uum, *m. pl.,* limbs.
   agitō, 1, move, drive.
   mōlēs, -is, *f.,* mass.
   misceō, 2, mix.
14. **tuba, -ae,** *f.,* trumpet.
   terribilis, -e, terrible.
   sonitus, -ūs, *m.,* sound.
   taratantara, the sound made by
   a trumpet.
15. **quadrupedāns, -antis,** galloping
   (on four feet).
   puter, -tris, -tre, crumbling.
   quatiō, 3, shake.
   ungula, -ae, *f.,* hoof.
16. **caecus, -a, -um,** blind (*here* =
   hidden; *with* **corpora** = atoms).
17. **rērum,** *from* **res** (*here perhaps* =
   the world, *i.e.* the tears that
   haunt the world).
   mortālis, -e, mortal. **mortālia,**

n. pl., i.e. human sorrows or
   fortunes.
18. **ēventus, -ūs,** *m.,* result, end.
   mediae rēs, *i.e.* the middle of
   the subject or story (*e.g.* of an
   epic).
   auditor, -ōris, *m.,* hearer.
   rapiō, 3, seize (*here* = hurry).
19. Here Vergil refers to bees.
   mōtus, -ūs, *m.,* motion; *also*
   emotion, passion.
   certāmen, -inis, *n.,* contest,
   struggle.
   iactus, -ūs, m., throwing.
   compressus, *perf. part of* **comprimō,** compress, crush, *i.e.*
   curb.
   quiēscō, 3, rest, keep quiet.
20. **mīlitia, -ae,** *f.,* warfare, military
   service.
   sēgnis, -e, lazy, slack.
21. **summus, -a, -um,** *here* = last.
   inēluctābilis, -e, inevitable, unavoidable.
22. **dēserō,** 3, desert, abandon.
   senex, senis, *m.,* old man.
   contemnō, *perf.* **contempsī,** 3,
   despise.
   pertimēscō, 3, fear (greatly).
23. **institūtum, -ī,** *n.,* custom, practice.
   differō, *irreg.,* differ; **inter sē,**
   among themselves, *i.e.* from one
   another.
24. **vel,** even.
25. **habitus, -ūs,** *m.,* appearance,
   condition.
   obēsus, -a, -um, fat.
B. 1. **semel,** *numeral,* once.
   īnsāniō, 4, be mad.
 2. **ergō,** therefore.
   vīvidus, -a, -um, lively.
   vīs, (vīs), vīrium, *f.,* force; *pl.,*
   strength.
   pervincō, 3, conquer, prevail.
   extrā, *prep. with acc.* **(moenia),**
   outside.

prōcēdō, *perf.* **prōcessī,** 3, advance.

flammāns, -antis, fiery, flaming.

mundus, -ī, *m.,* the universe, world.

3. **multitūdō, -inis,** *f.,* large number, crowd.

multitūdō, *here used with a plural verb.* This refers to the Christians at the time of Nero.

ingēns, ingentis, huge.

haud proinde . . . quam, not so much . . . as.

crīmen, -inis, *n.,* charge; *with* **in,** on the charge of (arson).

incendium, -ī (-iī), *n.,* fire, conflagration.

hūmānus, -a, -um, human, humane.

convincō, *perf. part.* **convictus,** 3, convict (of crime).

4. **ollī,** *old form of* **illī.**

quiēs, -ētis, 3, rest, sleep.

ferreus, -a, -um, iron, made of

somnus, -ī, *m.,* sleep.   [iron.

aeternus, -a, -um, eternal.

lūmina (*poet.*) = eyes.

nox, noctis, -ium, *f.,* night.

5. **reprehendō,** 3, blame, rebuke.

multa diēs, many a day.

litūra, -ae, *f.,* erasure, correction.

coerceō, *perf.* **coercuī,** 2, restrain, curb.

6. **carpō, -ere,** 3, gather, pluck (*here* = pluck (the blossom of) the day).

7. **sponte suā,** of its own accord.

numerī, *m. pl.,* numbers, *i.e.* poetry.

aptus, -a, -um, suitable.

temptō, 1 (*with infin.*), try to.

versus, -ūs, *m.,* verse (*poetry*).

8. **procul,** far from (*with abl.*).

negōtium, -ī (-iī), *n.,* business.

ut, like.

priscus, -a, -um, old, ancient.

paternus, -a, -um, of one's father.

bōs, *abl. pl.* **bōbus,** *m. and f.,* ox, cow.

exerceō, 2, keep busy (*here* = work, till).

10. **elegīa, elegeia, -ae,** *f.,* elegy.

prōvocō, 1, challenge.

EXERCISE 1

A. 1. Omne ignōtum prō magnificō est.

*2. Nihil est ab omnī
      parte beātum.

3. Ille terrārum mihi praeter omnīs
      angulus rīdet.

4. Omnēs eōdem cōgimur.

5. . . . Labor omnia vīcit
      improbus et durīs urgēns in rēbus egestās.

6. Amantium īrae amōris integrātiō est.

7. . . . Sed cūncta timēmus amantēs.

*8. Quidquid id est, timeō Danaōs et dōna ferentīs.

9. Vīxēre fortēs ante Agamemnona.

10. Fortīs fortūna adiuvat.

11. Tantaene animīs caelestibus īrae?

*12. Ōdērunt hilarem tristēs tristemque iocōsī.

*13. Spīritus intus alit tōtamque īnfūsa per artūs
      mēns agitat mōlem et magnō sē corpore miscet.

14. At tuba terribilī sonitū taratantara dīxit.

*15. Quadrupedante putrem sonitū quatit ungula campum.

*16. Corporibus caecīs igitur nātūra gerit rēs.
*17. Sunt lacrimae rērum et mentem mortālia tangunt.
18. Semper ad ēventum festīnat et in mediās rēs
   . . . audītōrem rapit.
*19. Hī mōtūs animōrum atque haec certāmina tanta,
   pulveris exiguī iactū compressa quiēscent.
20. Mīlitiae speciēs amor est; discēdite, sēgnēs.
21. Vēnit summa diēs et inēluctābile tempus.
*22. Dēfendī rem pūblicam adulēscēns, nōn deseram senex; contempsī
   Catilīnae gladiōs, nōn pertimescam tuōs.
*23. Hī omnēs linguā, īnstitūtīs, lēgibus inter sē differunt.
24. Vel Iove digna soror.
25. (Horātius) habitū corporis fuit brevis atque obēsus.

B. (Optional)
1. . . . Semel īnsānīvimus omnēs.
2. Ergō vīvida vīs animī pervīcit, et extrā
   prōcessit longē flammantia moenia mundī.
3. Multitūdō ingēns haud proinde in crīmine incendiī quam odiō
   hūmānī generis convictī sunt.
4. Ollī dūra quiēs oculōs et ferreus urget
   somnus, in aeternam clauduntur lūmina noctem.
5. . . . Carmen reprehendite quod nōn
   multa diēs et multa litūra coercuit. . . .
6. Carpe diem.
7. Sponte suā carmen numerōs veniēbat ad aptōs,
   et quod temptābam dīcere versus erat.
8. Beātus ille quī procul negōtiīs,
   ut prīsca gēns mortālium,
   paterna rūra bōbus exercet suīs.
9. Diēs īrae, diēs illa.
10. Elegīā quoque Graecōs prōvocāmus.

EXERCISE 2

1. Cicero, who had defended the republic (as) consul, did not fear Antony
(as) an old man.· 2. All things which are unknown seem wonderful to us.
3. The Greeks (though) bringing gifts terrified one of the Trojans. 4. The
universe is sustained by a spirit and moved by a mind. 5. All those-men
are alike in appearance, language, (and) laws.

EXERCISE 3

ANSWER IN LATIN:

1. Quid est ab omnī parte beātum? 2. Quid omnia vīcit? 3. Quid
timēmus amantēs? 4. Quandō vīxērunt virī fortēs? 5. Quid virōs fortīs
iuvat? 6. Quālēs hominēs ōdit homo trīstis? 7. Quid sonitū quadrupedante campum quatit? 8. Quid corporibus caecīs rēs gerit? 9. Quōmodo
quiēscunt apēs? 10. Quid mīlitiae speciēs est? 11. Quālis habitū
corporis fuit Horātius?

Sect. 66. Comparison of adjectives

Adjectives are compared in three degrees:

1.	Positive	**dūrus,**	hard
2.	Comparative	**dūrior,**	harder
3.	Superlative	**dūrissimus,**	hardest.

The comparative and superlative are formed by adding *-ior* and *-issimus* to the stem of the positive.

longus,	long	**longior**	**longissimus**
brevis,	short	**brevior**	**brevissimus**
audāx,	bold	**audācior**	**audācissimus**

Adjectives like *ācer* have a superlative ending in *-rimus*.

ācer,	keen	**ācrior**	**ācerrimus**
pulcher,	beautiful	**pulchrior**	**pulcherrimus**
miser,	miserable	**miserior**	**miserrimus**

Adjectives like *similis* have a superlative ending in *-limus*.

similis,	like	**similior**	**simillimus**

There are five other adjectives of this kind: *facilis*, 'easy', *difficilis*, 'difficult', *dissimilis*, 'unlike', *gracilis*, 'slender', *humilis*, 'lowly'.

Sect. 67. Irregular comparison of adjectives

In these adjectives the stems of the comparative and superlative are not the same as the stem of the positive.

bonus,	good	**melior,**	better	**optimus,**	best
malus,	bad	**pēior,**	worse	**pessimus,**	worst
magnus,	great	**māior,**	greater	**maximus,**	greatest
parvus,	small	**minor,**	smaller	**minimus,**	smallest
multus,	much	**plūs,**	more	**plūrimus,**	most

Some comparatives and superlatives correspond to adverbs derived from the same stem.

extrā, outside	**exterior,** outer	**extrēmus,** outermost
īnfrā, below	**īnferior,** lower	**īnfimus,** lowest
suprā, above	**superior,** higher	**suprēmus,**
		summus, highest
post, after	**posterior,** latter	**postrēmus,** last
intrā, within	**interior,** inner	**intimus,** inmost
prae, before	**prior,** former	**prīmus,** first
prope, near	**propior,** nearer	**proximus,** next
ultrā, beyond	**ulterior,** farther	**ultimus,** farthest

The first four do have positive adjectives, but they are rare and are more common in the plural, e.g. *superī*, 'the gods above'.

Adjectives ending in *-eus* and *-ius* form the comparative by adding *magis*, 'more', and the superlative by adding *maximē*, 'most'.

idōneus, fit	**magis idōneus**	**maximē idōneus**
dubius, doubtful	**magis dubius**	**maximē dubius**

Sect. 68. Declension of the comparative

The comparative ending in *-ior* is declined like a third declension adjective of two terminations, but the ablative singular ends in *-e* and the genitive plural in *-um*.

	Singular		*Plural*	
	M. and F.	*N.*	*M. and F.*	*N.*
	melior, better			
Nom.	**melior**	**melius**	**meliōrēs**	**meliōra**
Gen.		**meliōris**		**meliōrum**
Dat.		**meliōrī**		**meliōribus**
Acc.	**meliōrem**	**melius**	**meliōrēs (-īs)**	**meliōra**
Abl.		**meliōre**		**meliōribus**
	plūs, more			
Nom.	..	**plūs**	**plūrēs**	**plūra**
Gen.	..	**plūris**		**plūrium**
Dat.	..	..		**plūribus**
Acc.	..	**plūs**	**plūrēs (-īs)**	**plūra**
Abl.	..	**plūre**		**plūribus**

The genitive plural of *plūs* ends in *-ium*.

Sect. 69. Ablative of comparison and use of quam

After a comparative an ablative of comparison may be used. The meaning 'than' is implied.

O mātre pulchrā fīlia pulchrior.
O daughter fairer than your mother fair.

Here *mātre* is ablative of comparison with *pulchrior* and means 'than (your) mother'.

Quam also means 'than'. It would be possible to write *quam māter* instead of the ablative *mātre*; here *māter* must be in the same case as *fīlia*, which precedes *quam*.

O fīlia pulchrior quam māter pulchra.

The comparative and superlative have more than one meaning. *Dūrior* can mean either 'harder', or 'rather hard', 'too hard'; *dūrissimus* can mean 'hardest' or 'very hard'.

When the superlative is preceded by *quam*, the meaning 'as possible' is implied.

Quam maximus.   As great as possible.

Sect. 70. Ablative and genitive of quality (description)

A noun in the ablative case *combined with an adjective* is used to describe the quality of a person or thing. The genitive may be used in the same way, but is not as common as the ablative. The genitive is usual if a measurement is described, such as the height of a wall.

Vir magnā sapientiā.   A man of great wisdom
Mūrus decem pedum.   A wall of 10 feet, a wall 10 feet high.

The case-endings of the five declensions
Singular

	I	II	III	IV	V
Nom.	-a	-us	irreg.[1]	-us	-ēs
(neut.)		-um	irreg.	-ū	

[1] Endings of the nominative in the third declension:

(1) Usually masculine: *-or, -ōs, -er, -es* (gen. *-itis*), *-ex* (gen. *-icis*).
(2) Usually feminine: *-ō, -ās, -ēs, -is, -ūs, -x,* and *-s* (preceded by a consonant).
(3) Usually neuter: *-a, -e, -l, -n, -ar, -ur, -us.*
Examples of (1): *amor* (love), *flōs* (flower), *pater* (father), *miles* (soldier), *iūdex*

	I	II	III	IV	V
Gen.	-ae	-ī	-is	-ūs	-eī
Dat.	-ae	-ō	-ī	-uī (-ū)	-eī
(neut.)				-ū	
Acc.	-am	-um	-em	-um	-em
(neut.)		-um	irreg.	-ū	
Abl.	-ā	-ō	-e (-ī)	-ū	-ē
(neut.)			-ī		
Loc.	-ae	-ī	-e (-ī)		
Voc.		-e (-ī)			

Plural

	I	II	III	IV	V
Nom.	-ae	-ī	-ēs	-ūs	-ēs
(neut.)		-a	-a, -ia	-ua	
Gen.	-ārum	-ōrum	-um, -ium	-uum	-ērum
Dat.	-īs	-īs	-ibus	-ibus	-ēbus
Acc.	-ās	-ōs	-ēs, -īs	-ūs	-ēs
(neut.)		-a	-a, -ia	-ua	
Abl.	-īs	-īs	-ibus	-ibus	-ēbus
Loc.	-īs	-īs	-ibus		

Uses of the cases

Nom.　Subject (Lesson 1).

Gen.　Possession (1), Partitive (16), Quality (19), Objective (40), with verbs (40), Value (40).

Dat.　Indirect object (2), Possession (2), with adjectives (20), with verbs (35), Purpose and Reference (35), Agent (38).

Acc.　Direct object (2), Place to which (3), Accusative and Infinitive (24), Extent of space and time (29).

(judge); but *arbor* (tree) is feminine and *cor* (heart), *ōs* (mouth), *iter* (journey) and others are neuter.

Examples of (2): *multitūdō* (multitude), *legiō* (legion), *civitās* (state), *nūbēs* (cloud), *avis* (bird), *virtūs* (virtue), *nox* (night), *urbs* (city); but *sermō* (talk), *pēs* (foot), *ignis* (fire), *mēnsis* (month), *mūs* (mouse), *grex* (flock), *mōns* (mountain), and others are masculine and *rūs* (country) is neuter.

Examples of (3): *poēma* (poem), *mare* (sea), *animal* (animal), *nōmen* (name), *calcar* (spur), *rōbur* (strength), *corpus* (body), also *lac* (milk), *caput* (head); but *sōl* (sun) and others are masculine.

The adjective is often the key to the gender; thus the phrase *rāra avis* reminds us that *avis* is feminine.

Abl. Place where (1), Instrument (5), Manner (6), Agent (7), Place from which (8), Accompaniment (9), Time when (10), Respect (18), Comparison (19), Quality (19), Degree of difference (20), Ablative absolute (23), with verbs (32), Separation (32).

Loc. Locative (17).

Vocabulary

aes, aeris, *n.,* bronze, copper.
avis, -is, -ium, *f.,* bird.
decem, *numeral,* ten.
dulcis, -e, sweet, delightful.
dūrus, -a, -um, hard.
fessus, -a, -um, tired, weary.
flamma, -ae, *f.,* flame.
fōns, fontis, *m.,* spring, fountain.
grātia, -ae, *f.,* favor, charm, gratitude; *pl.* thanks; **grātiās agō,** give thanks, thank (*with dat.*).
hōra, -ae, *f.,* hour.
interim, meanwhile.
inveniō, -īre, invēnī, inventum, 4, find, find out.
iterum, again.
iuvenis, -is, -um, *m.,* young man (usually from twenty to forty years old).
lātus, -a, -um, broad.
levis, -e, light.
māior, māius, greater.

melior, melius, better.
nefās, *n., indecl.,* wrong (contrary to divine law).
nōbilis, -e, noble.
pēior, -ius, worse.
pessimus, -a, -um, worst, very bad.
philosophus, -ī, *m.,* philosopher.
plūs, plūris, *n.,* more; *pl.* **plūres, -a,** more, many.
probō, 1, approve.
propior, propius, nearer.
quam, than.
rīpa, -ae, *f.,* bank.
salūs, -ūtis, *f.,* safety, welfare.
sapiēns, -entis, wise, wise man.
sapientia, -ae, *f.,* wisdom.
sentiō, -īre, sēnsī, sēnsum, 4, feel, perceive, think.
spēs, -eī, *f.,* hope, promise.
suprēmus, -a, -um, highest, last.
turpis, -e, base, disgraceful.
unda, -ae, *f.,* wave, water.

Notes

1. **Bandusia,** a spring mentioned by Horace in the *Odes.*
   splendidus, -a, -um, bright, splendid.
   vitrum, -ī, *n.,* glass.
2. **exēgī,** *perf. of* **exigō** (*here =* complete, finish).
   perennis, -e, lasting, enduring.
3. **dēterior, -ius,** worse.
   sequor, 3, follow, *deponent* (Lesson XXXII). Here Medea is speaking.
4. **optātior, -ius,** *comp. of* **optātus** (*perf. part. of* **optō**), desired.
5. **fit,** *from* **fīō,** *irreg.,* become (Lesson XXXI).
   patientia, -ae, *f.,* patience.
   patientiā, *abl.* = by patience.

   corrigō, -ere, *perf.* **corrēxī,** 3, correct.
8. **Thūlē, -ēs,** *f.,* an island in the extreme north of Europe.
9. **reverentia, -ae,** *f.,* reverence.
10. **Helvētiī,** *m. pl.,* the Helvetians. Their territory is now Switzerland.
12. **rārus, -a, -um,** rare, scarce.
    niger, -gra, -grum, black.
    cycnus, -ī, *m.,* swan.
13. **expendō, -ere,** 3, weigh (*i.e.* in the scales).
    Hannibal, the Carthaginian general who invaded Italy in 218 B.C.
    libra, -ae, *f.,* (the Roman) pound.
15. **repente,** suddenly.
16. **bene** *with* **mūnīta,** well fortified.

ēdita (*perf. part. of* ēdō), raised up, lofty.

doctrīna, -ae, *f.* teaching, learning; *abl.* by the teaching.

sapientum = sapientium.

templa, *n. pl.*, sanctuaries, high places.

serēnus, -a, -um, serene, calm.

17. solūtīs (*from* solvō, loose) *with* cūrīs, than to be free from cares (*lit.* than cares set free).

onus, -eris, *n.*, burden.

repōnō, -ere, 3, lay aside (replace).

peregrīnus, -a, -um, foreign. Catullus had come from Bithynia to Sirmio.

lar, laris, *m.*, home; Larēs (*pl.*) household gods.

acquiēscō, -ere, 3, rest.

lectus, -ī, *m.*, bed.

18. Vesūvius, -ī (-iī), *m.*, a volcano in Campania, Italy.

relūceō, -ēre, 2, shine.

19. ēgregius, -a, -um, excellent.

spēs, *f.*, *here* = promise.

dēspondeō, -ēre, *perf.* dēspondī, 2, promise in marriage, betroth.

20. nescio quod, *acc. n. s.*, some (*lit.* I don't know what).

gurges, -itis, *m.*, gulf, waters (*here* = stream).

murmur, -uris, *n.,*, murmur, roar.

insistō, -ere, 3, stand upon.

margō, -inis, *m. and f.*, edge.

Alphēus, -ī, *m.*, Alpheus, a river in Greece (personified).

raucus, -a, -um, harsh.

ōs, ōris, *n.*, face, mouth.

EXERCISE 1

*1. Ō fōns Bandusiae splendidior vitrō.

*2. Exēgī monumentum aere perennius.

*3. . . . Videō meliōra probōque, dēteriōra sequor.

4. Quid datur ā dīvīs fēlīcī optātius hōrā?

*5. Dūrum; sed levius fit patientiā quidquid corrigere est nefās.

6. Ad māiōrem Deī glōriam.

7. Summum bonum.

8. Ultima Thūlē.

*9. Maxima dēbētur puerō reverentia.

10. Apud Helvētiōs longē nōbilissimus fuit Orgetorīx.

11. Salūs populī suprēma est lēx.

*12. Rāra avis in terrīs nigrōque simillima cycnō.

13. Expende Hannibalem: quot librās in duce summō inveniēs?

14. Grātiās tibi maximās Catullus agit pessimus omnium poēta.

*15. Nēmō repente fuit turpissimus.

*16. Sed nīl dulcius est, bene quam mūnīta tenēre ēdita doctrīnā sapientum templa serēna.

*17. Ō quid solūtīs est beātius cūrīs cum mēns onus repōnit, ac peregrīnō labōre fessī vēnimus larem ad nostrum dēsīderātōque acquiēscimus lectō?

18. Interim ē Vesūviō monte plūribus locīs lātissimae flammae altaque incendia relūcēbant.

*19. Cōnsul ēgregiae tum speī fīliam iuvenī mihi dēspondit.
20. Nescio quod mediō sēnsī sub gurgite murmur
    territaque īnsistō propiōris margine rīpae.
    'Quō properās, Arethūsa?' suīs Alphēus ab undīs,
    'quō properās?' iterum raucō mihi dīxerat ōre.

EXERCISE 2

1. Medea sees what is better but does what is worse.   2. Philosophers seek-for the highest good.   3. Nothing is sweeter than the serene sanctuaries of the philosophers.   4. Who is happier than the-man who comes home at-last without cares?   5. The wife of Tacitus was a woman of great promise.

EXERCISE 3

Review of nouns, pronouns, and adjectives

1. (nom. plur.)   those journeys; your names; the best books.
2. (gen. sing.)   a happy woman; the first step; this republic.
3. (gen. plur.)   all men; these animals; many nights.
4. (dat. sing.)   the Roman senate; a good father; a tired soldier.
5. (dat. plur.)   high mountains; our camp; my children.
6. (acc. sing.)   the greatest river; a very beautiful daughter; black care.
7. (acc. plur.)   better roads; American citizens; all the rewards.
8. (abl. sing.)   a shorter sword; a small garden; which sea?
9. (abl. plur.)   good character (morals); which days?; great strength.
10. (locative)   at home; in New York; at Rome.

Sect. 71. Adverbs and comparison of adverbs

ADVERBS are formed from adjectives.

(a) In the first and second declensions the ending is generally -ē, sometimes -ō.

dignus, worthy   **dignē,** worthily

(b) In the third declension, the ending is generally -ter, sometimes -e (the neuter accusative)

fortis, brave   **fortiter,** bravely
facilis, easy   **facile,** easily

The endings of the comparative and superlative are -ius and -issimē.

fortiter, bravely   **fortius,** more bravely   **fortissimē,** most bravely

Sect. 72. Irregular comparison of adverbs

bene,	well	**melius,**	better	**optimē,**	best
male,	badly	**pēius,**	worse	**pessimē,**	worst
magnopere,	greatly	**magis,**	more	**maximē,**	most, especially
parum,	too little	**minus,**	less	**minimē,**	least
multum,	much	**plūs,**	more	**plūrimum,**	most

These adverbs correspond to the adjectives *bonus, malus, magnus, parvus, multus.* Note that *magis* means 'more' (in degree) and *plūs* 'more' (in quantity).

diū,	long, for a long time	**diūtius**	**diūtissimē**	
saepe,	often	**saepius**	**saepissimē**	
prope,	near	**propius**	**proximē**	
..		**prius,** before	**prīmum,**	first

Sect. 73. Ablative of degree of difference

An ablative may be used with a comparative to indicate the degree or measure of difference.

Multō mē sapientior est.   He is far wiser than I.

Here *multō* is an ablative meaning 'by much', and *mē* is ablative of comparison corresponding to *quam ego*.

Sect. 74. Dative with adjectives

The dative is used with certain adjectives, such as

amīcus, -a, -um, friendly (to)
fīnitimus, -a, -um,   neighboring (to)
grātus, -a, -um,   pleasing (to)

Gallīs amīcī sumus.   We are friendly to the Gauls.
Germānīs fīnitimī sunt.
They are neighbors to the Germans.

VOCABULARY

amīcus, -a, -um, friendly (to), *with dat.*
audāx, -ācis, bold.
Canada, -ae, *f.,* may be used for Canada.
color, -ōris, *m.,* color.
cōnficio, -ficere, -fēcī, -fectum, 3, complete, finish, exhaust.
crēdō, -ere, crēdidī, crēditum, 3, believe (*with dat. of person*).
dignitās, -ātis, *f.,* dignity, rank.
equidem, indeed (*usually with the first person*).
exercitus, -ūs, *m.,* army.
faciēs, -eī, *f.,* face.
fidēs, -eī, *f.,* faith, belief, trust, loyalty.
fīnitimus, -a, -um, neighboring (to); neighbor.
hūmānitās, -ātis, *f.,* humanity, kindliness, culture.
idōneus, -a, -um, suitable.
imperātor, -ōris, *m.,* general, commander-in-chief.
incolō, incolere, incoluī, 3, inhabit, live.
ingenium, -ī (-iī), *n.,* nature, ability, natural capacity, genius.

innocentia, -ae, *f.,* innocence, integrity.
magis, *adv.,* more (in degree).
maximē, *adv.,* most (in degree).
mollis, -e, soft.
orbis, -is, *m.,* circle, the world (*usually with* **terrārum**).
pār, paris, equal (*with dat.*).
plēnus, -a, -um, full (*with gen.*).
prīmum, *adv.,* first.
prius, *adv.,* before, previously, formerly.
proximus, -a, -um, next, the nearest (*with dat.*).
rēligiō, -ōnis, *f.,* religion, religious scruple.
respondeō, -ēre, respondī, respōnsum, 2, reply, answer.
Rhēnus, -ī, *m.,* the river Rhine.
sānus, -a, -um, healthy, sane.
singulāris, -e, singular, remarkable.
varius, -a, -um, various, varied.
victor, -ōris, *m.,* victor, conqueror, victorious.
virtūs, -ūtis, *f.,* virtue, courage, excellence.
vīvus, -a, -um, living, alive.

Notes

1. **ēloquēns, -entis,** eloquent.
2. This refers to one of the daughters of Danaus, Hypermnestra, who disobeyed her father and saved her husband's life.
   mendāx, -ācis, lying, false.
   splendidē, *adv.,* nobly; *with* **mendāx** = nobly false.
   virgō, -inis, *f.,* maiden.
3. This refers to Rome.
4. **continenter,** *adv.,* continuously.
5. **virtūtī,** *dat. depending on* **pār.**
   potest, *3 sing. from* **possum,** is able, can (Lesson XXI).
6. **mīlitō, 1,** *lit.* serve as a soldier.
7. **nātiō, -ōnis,** *f.,* clan, people.
   admodum, very.
   dēditus, -a, -um, devoted to (*with dat.*).
8. **aliī,** *i.e.* the Greeks, whom Vergil praises for their sculpture, oratory, and astronomy; but Quintilian compares Cicero favorably with the Greek orator Demosthenes.
   excūdō, 3, beat out, mould.
   spīrō, 1, breathe.
   aera, *n. pl. from* **aes,** bronzes.

vultus (voltus), -ūs, *m.,* face, expression.
marmor, -oris, *n.,* marble.
ōrō, 1, beg; *with* **causas** = plead causes.
meātus, -ūs, *m.,* motion.
radius, -ī, *m.,* rod (for measuring).
9. **īnsurgō, 3,** rise up, *i.e.* become sublime.
   aliquandō, *adv.,* sometimes.
   iūcunditās, -ātis, *f.,* charm, *lit.* pleasantness.
   figūra, -ae, *f.,* figure, form.
10. **praestāns, -antis,** superior, excellent.
    optābilis, -e, desirable.
    omnibus, *dat. and m.*
11. **statūra, -ae,** *f.,* height, stature.
    grandis, -e, large.
    aquilus, -a, -um, dark.
    rusticānus, -a, -um, rustic.
12. **gravitās, -ātis,** *f.,* seriousness.
    dēportō, 1, *here* = bring home.
13. **deinde,** *adv.,* then, next.
    temperantia, -ae, *f.,* moderation, temperance.
    facilitās, -ātis, *f.,* affability.

Exercise 1

*1. Respondit Cornēlius Tacitus ēloquentissimē.

*2. Splendidē mendāx et in omne virgō
    nōbilis aevum.

*3. Urbem fēcistī quod prius orbis erat.

*4. (Belgae) proximī sunt Germānīs, quī trāns Rhēnum incolunt, quibus-
    cum continenter bellum gerunt.

*5. Iam vērō virtūtī Cn. Pompēī quae potest ōrātiō pār invenīrī?

*6. Vīxī puellīs nūper idōneus
    et mīlitāvī nōn sine glōriā.

*7. Nātiō est omnis Gallōrum admodum dēdita rēligiōnibus.

*8. Excūdent aliī spīrantia mollius aera
    (crēdō equidem), vīvōs dūcent dē marmore vultūs,
    ōrābunt causās melius, caelīque meātūs
    dēscrībent radiō et surgentia sīdera dīcent.

9. (Horātius) īnsurgit aliquandō et plēnus est iūcunditātis et grātiae et
    variīs figūrīs et verbīs fēlīcissimē audāx.

10. Id quod est praestantissimum maximēque optābile omnibus sānīs
    et bonīs et beātīs, cum dignitāte ōtium.

(For 11–13 see Lessons XVIII–XIX.)

*11. (Vergilius) corpore et statūrā fuit grandī, aquilō colōre, faciē rusticānā.

*12. Fuit in hīs prōvinciīs singulārī innocentiā, gravitāte, virtūte, bellum in Āfricā maximum cōnfēcit, victōrem exercitum dēportāvit.

13. Ac prīmum quantā innocentiā dēbent esse imperātōrēs, quantā deinde in omnibus rēbus temperantiā, quantā fidē, quantā facilitāte, quantō ingeniō, quantā hūmānitāte!

EXERCISE 2

1. What was formerly the world the Romans made a city. 2. The Greeks did many things better than the Romans. 3. Hypermnestra was far braver than her sisters. 4. The Americans are friendly to their neighbors, who live in Canada. 5. Pompey was a general of remarkable integrity.

EXERCISE 3

ANSWER IN LATIN

1. Quis ēloquentissimē respondit? 2. Quis fuit splendidē mendāx? 3. Quid fēcit Rōma? 4. Quibus nūper idōneus fuit Horātius? 5. Quī hominēs causās melius quam Rōmānī ōrābant? 6. Quis fuit fēlīcissimē audāx? 7. Quibus proximī sunt Belgae? 8. Quālī corpore fuit Vergilius? 9. Quālis in prōvinciīs fuit Pompēius?

LESSON XXI

THE INFINITIVE USED AS THE SUBJECT. INFINITIVE
WITH IMPERSONAL VERBS (*oportet*) AND WITH A
PREDICATE GENITIVE. COMPLEMENTARY INFINITIVE
WITH *possum, volō, nōlō, mālō, dēbeō, videor.* CONJUGATION
IN THE INDICATIVE OF *possum, volō, nōlō, mālō*

Sect. 75. Infinitive as subject

THE infinitive is a verbal noun and it is neuter in gender; it may
be used in two cases, the nominative and the accusative.

Labōrāre est ōrāre. To work is to pray (work is prayer).

Here *labōrāre* is the subject of *est* and *ōrāre* is the predicate noun.
But though the infinitive is used as a noun, it may govern a case,
since it is a verb, and may be modified by an adverb.

Honestum est hoc rectē facere.
It is honorable to do this correctly.

Here *facere* is the subject and *honestum*, a neuter adjective, is the
predicate adjective; *rectē*, 'rightly', is an adverb modifying *facere*.

Sect. 76. Infinitive with impersonal verbs

The infinitive may also be the subject of an impersonal verb like
oportet, 'it is necessary (one ought)'.

Hoc facere oportet.
It is necessary to do this.
Tē hoc facere oportet.
You ought to do this (it is necessary for you to do this).

Here *tē* is in the accusative case and is the subject of *facere*.

For the use of the accusative as the subject of an infinitive see
Lesson XXIV.

Other impersonal verbs are *licet*, 'it is lawful (permitted)', *placet*,
'it is pleasing', which are used with the dative case:

Placet-ne tibi venīre? Does it please you to come?

When a predicate genitive is used with the infinitive, the meaning
is '*it is the part of*'. This is called the genitive of characteristic.

Sapientis est vēra dīcere.

It is the part of a wise (man) to tell the truth.

Here *sapientis*, the genitive of the adjective *sapiēns*, 'wise', is the predicate.

Sect. 77. Complementary infinitive

The infinitive may be used as the object of a number of verbs.

(*a*) *possum*, I am able.

(*b*) *dēbeō*, I ought; *soleō*, I am accustomed.

(*c*) *volō*, I wish; *nōlō*, I am unwilling; *mālō*, I prefer; *cupiō*, I desire.

(*d*) *incipiō*, I begin; *dēsinō*, I cease.

(*e*) *properō*, I hasten; *dubitō*, I hesitate.

(*f*) *discō*, learn (how); *sciō*, know (how).

	possum.	I am able to do this, I can do it.
	dēbeō.	I ought to do this.
Hoc facere	**volō.**	I wish to do this.
	sciō.	I know *how* to do this.

Labōrāre mālō quam ōtiōsus esse.

I would rather work than be at leisure (I prefer to work).

If a predicate noun or adjective is used with the infinitive, it must be in the nominative case.

Cīvis Rōmānus esse cupit.

He wants to be a Roman citizen.

The accusative may be used as the subject of the infinitive with *volō* or *cupiō*. The predicate noun is also in the accusative.

Cīvem Rōmānum tē esse vult.

He wants you to be a Roman citizen.

The following verbs may also be used with an infinitive which has its subject in the accusative:

iubeō, I order; **prohibeō**, I prevent; **sinō**, I allow; **vetō**, I forbid.

	iubeō.	I order you to come.
Tē venīre	**prohibēbō.**	I shall prevent you from coming (lit. to come).

For other verbs of commanding and preventing see Lessons XXVI and XLI.

Sect. 78. Conjugation of possum, volō, nōlō, mālō

Principal parts:

possum,	posse,	potuī,	..	I am able, I can
volō,	velle,	voluī,	..	I wish
nōlō,	nōlle,	nōluī,	..	I am unwilling
mālō,	mālle,	māluī,	..	I prefer

Present indic.	possum	volō	nōlō	mālō
	potes	vīs	nōn vīs	māvīs
	potest	vult	nōn vult	māvult
	possumus	volumus	nōlumus	mālumus
	potestis	vultis	nōn vultis	māvultis
	possunt	volunt	nōlunt	mālunt
Imperf.	poteram	volēbam	nōlēbam	mālēbam
Future	poterō	volam	nōlam	mālam
	poteris	volēs	nōlēs	mālēs, etc.
Perfect	potuī	voluī	nōluī	māluī
Pluperf.	potueram	volueram	nōlueram	mālueram
Future perf.	potuerō	voluerō	nōluerō	māluerō
Pres. inf.	posse	velle	nōlle	mālle
Perf. inf.	potuisse	voluisse	nōluisse	māluisse
Pres. part.	potēns	volēns	nōlēns	..
	(powerful)			
Imperat.	..	..	nōlī, nōlīte	..

Possum is formed from *sum* and the adjective *potis* or *pote*, 'able'.
Nōlō is formed from *volō* and a negative, *mālō* from *volō* and *mage*
(= *magis*), 'more'.

VOCABULARY

amāns, -antis, loving; a lover.
Britannus, -a, -um, British; *m. pl.* the Britons.
careō, -ēre, caruī, 2, lack, be without (*with abl.*).
certē, *adv.,* at any rate.
cognōscō, -ere, cognōvī, cognitum, 3, get to know, learn, understand.
cupidus, -a, -um, eager.
cupiō, -ere, cupīvī, cupītum, 3, desire, wish.
difficilis, -e, difficult.
discō, -ere, didicī, 3, learn, learn (how).

Hadriānus, -ī, *m.,* the Emperor Hadrian, *princeps* A.D. 117–38.
īdem, eadem, idem, *pron.,* the same (Lesson XXX).
iūstitia, -ae, *f.,* justice.
iuvat, *impers.,* 1, it pleases (*with inf.*).
licet, -uit, *impers.,* 2, it is allowed, lawful (*with dat. and inf.*).
mālō, mālle, māluī, *irreg.,* prefer.
Martiālis, -is, *m.,* M. Valerius Martialis, the Roman poet Martial, A.D. *c.* 40–*c.* 104.
meminī, -isse, *irreg.,* remember (Lesson XXXI).
mulier, -eris, *f.,* woman.

neco, 1, kill.

nisi, *conj.*, unless.

nōlō, nōlle, nōluī, *irreg.*, be unwilling.

officium, -ī (-iī), *n.*, duty.

oportet, -uit, *impers.*, 2, it is necessary, one must, ought (*with inf.*).

patior, patī, passus sum, 3, *deponent*, suffer, endure, allow (Lesson XXXII).

placet, -uit, *impers.*, 2, it pleases, seems good (*with dat. and inf.*).

Platō, Platōn, -ōnis, *m.*, the Greek philosopher, Plato, founder of the Academic philosophy, *c.* 429–347 B.C.

possum, posse, potuī, *irreg.*, be able, can.

prope, *adv.*, almost.

quārē, why.

sapiō, sapere, 3, be wise, have sense.

scelus, -eris, *n.*, crime.

sciō, scīre, scīvī, 4, know, know (how).

sērus, -a, -um, late.

stultus, -a, -um, foolish.

subitō, *adv.*, suddenly.

taberna, -ae, *f.*, hut, cottage; shop, tavern.

valeō, -ēre, valuī, 2, be strong, well (in health).

verberō, 1, beat, flog.

vērus, -a, -um, true; vērum, *n.*, the truth.

volō, velle, voluī, *irreg.*, be willing, wish.

NOTES

1. Here Vergil is thinking of Lucretius, who had written about the philosophy of Epicurus and the theory that matter consists of atoms.

2. **tantum**, so much, *with gen.* **malōrum**.

   rēligiō, *here perhaps* = superstition.

   suādeō, 2, advise, urge.

   mala, *n. pl.*, evils, wickedness.

3. **Sabidī**, *voc. of* **Sabidius**. Compare 'I do not love thee, Dr. Fell', a translation of Martial's poem by an Oxford undergraduate of the seventeenth century, in which the Dean of Christ Church takes the place of Sabidius.

5. **nimis** *with* **sēra**, too late.

   crāstinus, -a, -um, tomorrow's.

6. **Postume**, *voc. of* Postumus.

7. **dēpōnō**, 3, lay aside.

8. **facinus**, -oris, *n.*, misdeed, outrage.

   vinciō, -īre, vīnxī, vīnctum, 4, bind.

   **parricīdium, -ī, *n.*, parricide. Killing a Roman citizen is as bad as killing one's father.

9. **misceō, -ēre, miscuī, mixtum**, 2, mix; mix with (*with abl.*).

   **stultitia, -ae, *f.*, folly.

   dēsipiō, -ere, 3, *compound of* **sapiō**, be foolish.

   in locō, at the right place or time.

10. **mōlēs, -is, *f.*, mass (*here* = trouble (so vast a task)).

12. **Caesar**, the Emperor Hadrian.

    Scythicus, -a, -um, Scythian.

    pruīna, -ae, *f.*, frost.

    Flōrus, -ī, *m.*, Roman writer who lived in the time of Hadrian.

    latitō, 1, = **lateō**, lie hid.

    popīna, -ae, *f.*, cookshop.

13. **istīs**, *i.e.* the Pythagoreans.

14. **patrēs cōnscrīptī**, senators (**patrēs** = fathers).

    clēmēns, -entis, gentle, merciful. Cicero means that he wants to be regarded as merciful.

15. **dēsiliō, -īre**, 4, leap, jump down.

    aquila, -ae, *f.*, eagle; the eagle or standard of a Roman legion.

    prōdō, -ere, prōdidī, prōditum, 3, betray; give forth, hand down.

    praestō, -āre, praestitī, 1, be superior (to), surpass; perform, show.

16. **monitī**, *part.*, (having been) warned.

    temnō, -ere, 3, despise.

    dīvī, *m. pl.*, the gods (= **dī**).

17. **dēmum**, *adv.*, at last; *with* **ea** = precisely, indeed.

    firmus, -a, -um, firm, steadfast.

18. **forsan**, perhaps.
    ōlim, *here* = one day, hereafter.
19. **potēns, -entis**, powerful; *(with gen.)* master of.

dēgō, -ere, 3, spend, pass (time) *(here* = live).
in diem, *here* = daily.
20. **rapidus, -a, -um**, rapid *(here* = running (water)).

EXERCISE 1

*1. Fēlīx quī potuit rērum cognōscere causās.
 2. Tantum rēligiō potuit suādēre malōrum.
*3. Nōn amo tē, Sabidī, nec possum dīcere quārē;
     hoc tantum possum dīcere, nōn amo tē.
 4. Nōn est vīvere, sed valēre vīta est.
*5. Nōn est, crēde mihī, sapientis dīcere 'Vīvam';
     sēra nimis vīta est crāstina, vīve hodiē.
 6. Crās vīvēs? Hodiē iam vīvere, Postume, sērum est;
     ille sapit quisquis, Postume, vīxit herī.
 7. Difficile est longum subitō dēpōnere amōrem.
*8. Facinus est vincīre cīvem Rōmānum, scelus verberāre, prope parri-
     cīdium necāre.
*9. Miscē stultitiam cōnsiliīs brevem;
     dulce est dēsipere in locō.
*10. Tantae mōlis erat Rōmānam condere gentem.
 11. Virtūs est vitium fugere, et sapientia prīma
     stultitiā caruisse.
 12. Ego nōlō Caesar esse,   Ego nōlō Flōrus esse,
     ambulāre per Britannōs,   ambulāre per tabernās,
     Scythicās patī pruīnās.   latitāre per popīnās.
*13. Errāre mālō cum Platōne quam cum istīs vēra sentīre.
 14. Cupiō, patrēs cōnscrīptī, mē esse clēmentem.
*15. 'Dēsilīte', inquit, 'mīlitēs, nisi vultis aquilam hostibus prōdere; ego
     certē meum reī pūblicae atque imperātōrī officium praestiterō.'
 16. Discite iūstitiam monitī et nōn temnere dīvōs.
 17. Idem velle atque idem nōlle, ea dēmum firma amīcitia est.
*18. . . . Forsan et haec ōlim meminisse iuvābit.
 19.   Ille potēns suī
     laetusque dēget, cui licet in diem
     dīxisse 'vīxī'.
*20. . . . Sed mulier cupidō quod dīcit amantī
     in ventō et rapidā scrībere oportet aquā.

EXERCISE 2

1. Happy is the-man who is able to understand the nature of things.
2. It is the-part-of a wise-man to live today (and) of a foolish-man to live
tomorrow. 3. It is a crime to beat an American citizen, (it is) a far greater
crime to kill (him). 4. Florus did not wish to be Hadrian; the emperor
preferred to walk with the Britons (rather) than to hide with Florus in the
taverns at Rome. 5. Must (we) write the words of lovers on the winds
and rivers?

EXERCISE 3

ANSWER IN LATIN:

1. Quis fēlīx fuit? 2. Quem nōn amāvit Martiālis? 3. Quandō nōs vīvere oportet? 4. Quid nōn subitō dēpōnitur? 5. Quem nōn licet vincīre? 6. Quid cōnsiliīs miscēre nōs iubet Horātius? 7. Quid tempore idōneō dulce est? 8. Quam gentem difficile erat condere? 9. Quid virtūs est fugere?

CONJUNCTIONS TAKING THE INDICATIVE MOOD:
TEMPORAL, *ubi, postquam, simul ac; dum, donec, antequam*;
CONCESSIVE, *quamquam*; CAUSAL, *quod, quia* (BUT SEE
LESSON XXXVI)

SUBORDINATE clauses may be introduced by a number of conjunctions. These clauses may be temporal, concessive, or causal. For conditional sentences with *sī*, 'if', see Lesson XXXIV.

Sect. 79. Conjunctions taking the indicative mood

1. Temporal, *ubi*, 'when'; *postquam*, 'after'; *simul ac* (*atque*), 'as soon as'; sometimes *ut*, 'when'

Ubi	
Postquam	**Rōmānōs vīdērunt, lēgātōs ad Caesarem**
Simul ac	**mīsērunt.**
When	
After	they saw (had seen) the Romans, they sent
As soon as	envoys to Caesar.

In past time, the perfect is usual after these conjunctions, even though it is common in English to say 'after they had seen'.

2. Temporal, *dum*, 'while'

(*a*) When *dum* means 'at some time while, (in the course of the time while)', it always takes the present indicative, even when the main verb is in past time.

Dum nostrī iter faciunt, lēgātī ad Caesarem vēnērunt.
While our men were marching, the envoys came to Caesar.

(*b*) When *dum* means 'all the time while', it is followed by a verb in the same tense as the verb in the main clause.

Dum vīxit, honestus fuit.
He was honorable throughout his life (while he lived).

3. Temporal, *dum*, *dōnec*, 'until'

When *dum* means 'until', it takes the indicative if it does not express anything more than time (but see Lesson XXXVI).

Caesar exspectāvit dum lēgātī ad castra vēnērunt.
Caesar waited until the envoys came to the camp.

4. Temporal, *antequam, priusquam,* 'before'

Antequam takes the indicative if it does not express anything more than time (but see Lesson XXXVI). *Ante* and *prius* may be separated from *quam.*

Antequam lēgātī ad castra vēnērunt, legiōnēs ēdūxit.
He led out his legions before the envoys came to the camp.

5. Concessive, *quamquam,* 'although', and *etsī*

Quamquam, although, takes the indicative (but see Lesson XXXIII for *cum,* 'although', and Lesson XXXVI for *quamvīs,* 'although').

Quamquam Caesar diū exspectāvit, lēgātī ad castra nōn vēnērunt.
Although Caesar waited a long time, the envoys did not come to the camp.

6. Causal, *quod, quia* (sometimes *proptereā quod*), 'because'

Quod, 'because', takes the indicative when the reason given is stated as a fact (but see Lesson XXXVI).

Caesar, quod lēgātī ad castra nōn vēnerant, legiōnēs ēdūxit.
Because the envoys had not come to the camp, Caesar led out his legions.

Quoniam, 'since', takes the indicative (but see Lesson XXXIII for *cum,* 'since').

Note also *quod,* 'that', 'the fact that', and *ut,* 'as'. Both take the indicative.

Quod frāter meus tūtus est, mīrum vidētur.
The fact that my brother is safe seems wonderful.
Ut suprā dīxī, frāter meus tūtus est.
As I have said above, my brother is safe.

VOCABULARY

absum, *compound of* **sum,** be away; *with* **longē,** be far from.
antequam, before.
appropinquō (adp-), 1, approach (*with dat.*).

ars, artis, *f.,* art; *pl.* the arts.
colloquium (conl-), -ī (-iī), *n.,* conference.
commoveō, -movēre, -mōvī, -mōtum, 2, move deeply.

cōnferō, *compound of* **ferō,** *irreg.,* collect, compare (Lesson XXXI).

contendō, -ere, contendī, contentum, 3, hasten, fight, struggle.

cultus, -ūs, *m.,* civilization, culture.

cūr, why.

dōnec, until (*sometimes* = while).

dum, while, until.

eō, to that place.

ferus, -a, -um, wild, rude, uncivilized.

fidēlis, -e, faithful; *adv.,* **fidēliter,** faithfully.

grātus, -a, -um, pleasing.

īnfēlīx, -īcis, unlucky, unhappy.

ingenuus, -a, -um, free-born; worthy of a freeman; (*with* **artēs**) liberal.

iūdex, -icis, *m.,* judge.

Lēander, -rī, *m.,* Leander (in Ovid's *Heroides*), who swam the Hellespont to visit Hero.

lēgātus, -ī, *m.,* envoy, ambassador; legion-commander, lieutenant-general.

nō, 1, swim.

obses, -idis, *m. and f.,* hostage.

paupertās, -ātis, *f.,* poverty.

pāx, pācis, *f.,* peace.

poscō, -ere, poposcī, 3, demand, request.

postquam, after.

proelium, -ī (-ii), *n.,* battle.

proptereā (*lit.* on that account) **quod,** because.

quamquam, although.

quod, because; the fact that.

reliquus, -a, -um, remaining, rest of.

turris, -is, -ium, *acc.* **-im,** *f.,* tower.

ubi, when.

ut, as (*sometimes* = when).

NOTES

1. Tacitus makes a Caledonian chief say this about the Romans in the *Agricola.*
   sōlitūdō, -inis, *f.,* loneliness, desert.
2. **damnō,** 1, condemn.
   nocēns, guilty (*here* = a guilty man).
   absolvō, 3, acquit.
3. **turrim movērī vīdērunt,** saw the tower to be moving, saw that it was being moved. *This is the accusative and infinitive construction.* See Lesson XXIV.
6. **Persae, -ārum,** *m.,* the Persians.
   vigeō, -ēre, viguī, 2, be vigorous, flourish (*here* = live).

7. **prōvincia,** *i.e.* the Roman province in the south of France.
8. **praecēdō,** 3, surpass.
   ferē, almost.
   cottīdiānus, -a, -um, daily.
9. **aspiciō, -ere, aspexī, aspectum,** 3, look at.
   ignis, -is, *m., here* = a flame, lover (*poet.*). Leander is speaking about Hero.
10. **addō, -ere, addidī, additum,** 3, add.
    ēmolliō, 4, soften, make mild.
    sinō, -ere, sīvī, 3, allow.
11. **rīdiculus, -a, -um,** laughable, funny, ridiculous.

EXERCISE 1

*1. Ubi sōlitūdinem faciunt, pācem appellant.

2. Iūdex damnātur ubi nocēns absolvitur.

*3. Ubi vērō (turrim) movērī et appropinquāre moenibus vīdērunt, novā . . . speciē commōtī lēgātōs ad Caesarem dē pāce mīsērunt.

*4. Eō postquam pervēnit, obsidēs, arma, servōs . . . poposcit.

*5. Dum ea . . . cōnferuntur, (Helvētiī) . . . ad Rhēnum fīnēsque Germānōrum contendērunt.

6. Dōnēc grātus eram tibi . . .
   Persārum viguī rēge beātior.

*7. Hōrum omnium fortissimī sunt Belgae, proptereā quod ā cultū
atque hūmānitāte prōvinciae longissimē absunt.

*8. Helvētiī ... reliquōs Gallōs virtūte praecēdunt, quod ferē cottīdiānīs
proeliīs cum Germānīs contendunt.

*9. Ut procul aspexī lūmen, 'meus ignis in illō est;
illa meum', dīxī, 'lītora lūmen habent.'

*10. Adde quod ingenuās didicisse fidēliter artēs
ēmollit mōrēs nec sinit esse ferōs.¹

*11. Nīl habet īnfēlīx paupertās dūrius in sē
quam quod rīdiculōs hominēs facit.

*12. Eō, ut erat dictum, ad colloquium vēnērunt.

EXERCISE 2

1. When the tower approached the walls, envoys were sent to Caesar by
the Gauls. 2. After the Romans had arrived at the camp of the Helvetians,
they demanded hostages. 3. While (their) leaders were collecting the
arms, many of the Helvetians fled from the camp. 4. The Helvetians
were braver than the rest (of the) Gauls because they often fought with
the Germans. 5. Although Leander was far away, he was willing to swim
through the sea to his girl.

EXERCISE 3

ANSWER IN LATIN:

1. Quid moenibus appropinquābat? 2. Quōs hominēs ad Caesarem
mīsērunt Gallī? 3. Quandō damnātur iūdex? 4. Quandō arma poposcit
Caesar? 5. Quandō Helvētiī ad Rhēnum contendērunt? 6. Quandō
Persārum rēge beātior fuit poēta? 7. Cūr fortissimī sunt Belgae? 8. Cūr
magnā virtūte sunt Helvētiī? 9. Quid procul aspexit Lēander? 10. Quid
mōrēs ēmollit?

---

¹ No. 10, l. 2, is the motto of the University of South Carolina.

LESSON XXIII

USES OF THE PARTICIPLES. ABLATIVE ABSOLUTE

Sect. 80. Uses of the participles (for the forms of the participles see Lesson XIII)

PARTICIPLES are verbal adjectives, which are inflected and may be attached to a noun. As verbs they express both tense and voice (e.g. present tense and active voice) and sometimes they govern a case. When they stand in apposition to a noun, they take the place of a subordinate clause.

Mīles clāmāns discessit. The soldier went away shouting.

Here the present participle *clāmāns* is equivalent to the subordinate clause *dum clāmat*, 'while he was shouting' (lit. 'while he is shouting').

1. The present participle is always active in meaning and describes action that takes place *at the same time* as the action of the main verb. The example given above (*mīles clāmāns discessit*) shows that the soldier was shouting while he was going away. It does not mean 'having shouted, he went away', which would be equivalent to *postquam clāmāvit*, 'after he had shouted'. There is no perfect participle active, which would give this meaning. But there is a useful perfect participle of deponent verbs, which is active in meaning (see Lesson XXXII).

The oblique cases of the present participle, especially the genitive and dative, describe a class of people.

Pugnantium clāmōrem audīvī.
I heard the shouts (shouting) of those who were fighting.

Here *pugnantium*, 'of the fighters', is equivalent to *eōrum quī pugnābant*. But the nominative *pugnantēs* would not mean 'those who were fighting', but 'while they were fighting'.

Pugnantēs clāmābant.
They shouted while they were fighting.

2. The perfect participle is passive in meaning and describes action which took place *before* the action of the main verb.

Arch of Trajan at Beneventum (A.D. 114)

Imp[erātōrī] Caesarī dīvī Nervae fīliō
Nervae Trāiānō optimō Aug[ustō]
Germānicō Dācicō pontif[icī] max[imō] trib[ūniciā]
potest[āte] XVIII imp[erātōrī] VII cō[n]s[ulī] VI p[atrī] p[atriae]
fortissimō prīncipī senātus p[opulus] q[ue] R[ōmānus].

The Senate and the Roman people dedicated this arch to the Emperor Trajan,
the son of Nerva and conqueror of Dacia (*Dācicus*). His authority depended
on the military *imperium* and on the tribunician power (*tribūnicia potestās*),
which he had held for 18 years. He had been hailed as *imperātor* 7 times and
had been *cōnsul* 6 times. He was chief priest (*pontifex maximus*) and father of
his country (*pater patriae*).

Graecia capta ferum victōrem cēpit.
Captured Greece captured her fierce conqueror (i.e. the Romans).

Here *capta* means 'having been captured', 'after she had been captured', or even 'although she was captured'.
Thus it is equivalent to *postquam capta est* or *quamquam capta est*.

3. The future participle is always active in meaning and refers to an action which takes place *after* the action of the main verb.

Iamque volātūrus parvō dedit oscula nātō.
And now, as he was about to fly, he kissed (gave kisses to) his little son.

Here *volātūrus*, 'about to fly', is in apposition to the subject of *dedit*, namely, Daedalus, the father of Icarus. But the future participle is generally combined with the verb *sum*.

Daedalus volātūrus erat.   Daedalus was about to fly.

For the gerundive, which is passive in meaning, see Lesson XXXVIII.

Sect. 81. Ablative absolute

The present and perfect participles are constantly used in an important construction called the ablative absolute. A noun or pronoun in the ablative case is combined with a participle which agrees with it.

Hōc audītō discessit.
When he had heard this, he went away (lit. this having been heard).

Tē audiente carmen recitāvit.
He recited the poem while you were listening (lit. you listening; compare 'God willing').

Since the verb *sum* has no present participle like the English 'being', a noun or a pronoun in the ablative may be combined with a predicate adjective or noun without a participle.

Tē duce.
Under your leadership, with you as leader (lit. you being leader).

Cōnsule Plancō.

In the consulship of Plancus, when Plancus was consul (lit. Plancus being consul).

The ablative absolute should not be used if the person concerned is the subject or object of the main verb. The participle should agree with the subject or object and should not be in the ablative.

Ducem captum līberāvit.

He set the captured general free, he released the general who had been captured.

It would not be correct to write *duce captō eum līberāvit.*

An ablative absolute like *hōc audītō* should never be translated literally as 'this having been heard'. According to the context it might mean 'having heard this', 'when he had heard this', 'since he had heard this', 'although he had heard this'.

VOCABULARY

adversus, *adv.*, opposite; *prep. with acc.*, toward, against.
albus, -a, -um, white.
celer, -eris, -ere, swift; *adv.* **celeriter,** swiftly.
cupiditās, -ātis, *f.*, desire.
dēdūcō, 3, lead down, lead away.
domina, -ae, *f.*, mistress of a house, lady, sweetheart.
ēdūcō, 3, lead out.
extrēmus, -a, -um, outermost, last.
facilis, -e, easy; *adv.* **facile,** easily.
fās, *n., indecl.*, right, divine law.
folium, -ī (-ii), *n.*, leaf.
fuga, -ae, *f.*, flight.
hīberna, -ōrum, *n. pl.*, winter quarters.
inopia, -ae, *f.*, lack, want.
invītus, -a, -um, unwilling.
iuxtā, *adv.*, close by; *prep. with acc.*, near to.
laedō, -ere, laesī, laesum, 3, hurt (*with acc.*).
loquor, loquī, locūtus sum, 3, *deponent*, speak, talk (Lesson XXXII).
metus, -ūs, *m.*, fear.

Minerva, -ae, *f.*, goddess of wisdom, called Pallas Athene by the Greeks.
modo, only.
nusquam, nowhere.
opus, operis, *n.*, work, task.
opus est (*with abl.*), there is need of.
ōs, ōris, *n.*, face, mouth.
pīlum, -ī, *n.*, javelin.
possideō, -ēre, possēdī, possessum, possess.
prohibeō, -ēre, prohibuī, prohibitum, 2, keep off, restrain, prevent.
putō, 1, think.
quidem, indeed.
recipiō, -ere, recēpī, receptum, 3, take back, recover; **sē recipere,** retreat, recover (oneself).
rēctus, -a, -um, right, correct; *adv.*, **rēctē,** rightly.
rēgnum, -ī, *n.*, kingdom, kingship.
rogō, 1, ask.
salvus, -a, -um, sound in health, safe and sound.
scūtum, -ī, *n.*, shield.
superior, -ius, higher.
vel, -ve, or; **vel . . . vel,** either . . . or.
vigilia, -ae, *f.*, watch.
vocō, 1, call, summon, name.

Notes

1. **dulce** *with* **rīdentem,** laughing, smiling sweetly (smiling a sweet smile).
   Lalagē, -ēs, *f.,* a girl's name in Horace's *Odes* (from a Greek word meaning 'to prattle').
2. **excēdō, -ere, excessī, excessum,** 3, go out, go away.
   vestīgium, -ī (-iī), *n.,* footstep, footprint.
3. This refers to Icarus who fell into the sea and to his father, Daedalus (Lesson IX).
   dēcidō, -ere, dēcidī, 3, fall down.
   auferō, *compound of* **ferō,** *irreg.,* carry off.
   viridis, -e, green.
   ōra, *acc. pl. of* **ōs;** *pl. for sing.* (*poet.*).
   loquentis, *gen. of pres. part. of* **loquor.**
4. Here Catullus is translating a poem by Sappho.
   mi = mihi.
   identidem, again and again.
7. **scītor, -ārī,** 1, *deponent,* ask (*poet.*), *pres. part.* **scītāns** (Lesson XXXII).
   Atalanta, -ae, *f.,* a girl in Ovid's *Metamorphoses,* famous for her speed in running, who was beaten by Hippomenes and married him.
8. **vitiōsus, -a, -um,** faulty, bad.
   ēmendō, 1, free from faults, correct.
9. **addūcō,** 3, lead to, induce.
   dēditiō, -ōnis, *f.,* surrender.

10. **phalanx, -angis,** *f.,* phalanx.
    perfringō, -fringere, -frēgī, -fractum, 3, break through.
11. **expōnō,** 3, put out, disembark, expound.
    vigilia, the twelve hours of the night were divided into four watches.
13. **Is = Orgetorīx.**
    Messalla, -ae, *m.,* Messalla, consul in 61 B.C.
    Pīsō, -ōnis, *m.,* M. Piso, consul in 61 B.C.
    indūcō, 3, lead in, induce.
    coniūrātiō, -ōnis, *f.,* conspiracy.
16. **furō, -ere,** 3, be mad (*here* = play the fool).
17. **Philippī, -ōrum,** *m. pl.,* a town in Macedonia where Octavian and Antony defeated Brutus and Cassius in 42 B.C.
    sēnsī = I experienced.
    nōn *modifies* **bene.**
    parmula, -ae, *f.,* a (small) shield.
18. *Here* **proximus** *is used with* **ā** *and the abl. and not with the dat.*
    nūllō *is used instead of the abl. of* **nēmō,** no one.
    sedētō, *2nd pers. sing. imperat.* (= **sedē**).
19. **croceus, -a, -um,** yellow (saffron-colored).
    medium, the middle.
    cingō, 3, surround.
    This refers to Narcissus who was changed into a flower (Lesson VI).

Exercise 1

*1. Dulce rīdentem Lalagēn amābō,
    dulce loquentem.

2.   . . . Extrēma per illōs
   Iūstitia excēdēns terrīs vestīgia fēcit.

3. Dēcidit, atque cadēns, 'pater, ō pater, auferor', inquit;
   clausērunt viridēs ōra loquentis aquae.

*4. Ille mī pār esse deō vidētur,
    ille, sī fās est, superāre dīvōs,
    quī sedēns adversus identidem tē
         spectat et audit
    dulce rīdentem.

5. Pōne metum, Cērinthe; deus nōn laedit amantēs.
   Tū modo semper amā; salva puella tibi est.
*6. Nōn possidentem multa vocāveris
   rēctē beātum.
7. Scītantī deus huic dē coniuge 'Coniuge', dīxit,
   'nīl opus est, Atalanta, tibī.'
*8. Multa quidem scrīpsī, sed quae vitiōsa putāvī
   ēmendātūrīs ignibus ipse dedī.
9. Helvētiī omnium rērum inopiā adductī lēgātōs dē dēditiōne ad eum
   mīsērunt.
10. Mīlitēs ē locō superiōre pīlīs missīs facile hostium phalangem per-
    frēgērunt.
11. Caesar, expositō exercitū et locō castrīs idōneō captō . . . dē tertiā
    vigiliā ad hostēs contendit.
*12. Caesar ūnā aestāte duōbus maximīs bellīs cōnfectīs . . . in hīberna . . .
    exercitum dēdūxit.
*13. Is M. Messallā et M. Pīsōne cōnsulibus rēgnī cupiditāte inductus
    coniūrātiōnem . . . fēcit.
14. . . . Mūtātō nōmine dē tē
    fābula narrātur.
*15. Tū nihil invītā dīcēs faciēsve Minervā.
*16. . . . receptō
    dulce mihī furere est amīcō.
*17. Tēcum Philippōs et celerem fugam
    sēnsī relictā nōn bene parmulā.
*18. Proximus ā dominā, nūllō prohibente, sedētō.
19. Nusquam corpus erat; croceum prō corpore flōrem
    inveniunt foliīs medium cingentibus albīs.

Exercise 2

1. The-man who sat close by, while-he-listened to Lesbia laughing, seemed to be like a god. 2. We do not always call those-who-possess many-things happy men. 3. Ovid gave all his poems which seemed to be faulty to the fire that-would-destroy-them. 4. You ought to write nothing (if) Minerva is-unwilling. 5. After-he-had-captured the camp of the enemy and finished the war, Caesar led his army into winter quarters.

Exercise 3

Answer in Latin:

1. Quis rīdēns amābitur? 2. Quis Īcarī cadentis verba audīvit? 3. Quis amantēs nōn laedit? 4. Quis Atalantam dē coniuge rogantem monuit? 5. Quī hominēs inopiā adductī lēgātōs ad Caesarem mīsērunt? 6. Quid pīlīs missīs frēgērunt mīlitēs? 7. Quot bella ūnā aestāte cōnfēcit Caesar? 8. Quandō coniūrātiō facta est? 9. Quandō dulce est Horātiō furere? 10. Quid Philippīs relīquit Horātius? 11. Quālis est narcissī color?

LESSON XXIV

INDIRECT STATEMENT: THE ACCUSATIVE AND INFINITIVE
(PRESENT, PERFECT, OR FUTURE INFINITIVE) AFTER
VERBS OF SAYING, THINKING, KNOWING, PERCEIVING,
REMEMBERING, e.g. *dīcō, putō, sciō, sentiō, meminī*
USE OF REFLEXIVE (*sē*). FUTURE INFINITIVE WITH *spērō*

Sect. 82. Indirect statement: accusative and infinitive

DIRECT speech (*ōrātiō rēcta*) is used when the exact words of a
speaker are quoted. The verb *inquit* (he says, he said) is added
after the first or second word of the quotation.

Nūper, inquit, in Ītaliā fuistī.
Recently, he said, you were in Italy.

Indirect speech (*ōrātiō oblīqua*) is used very frequently in Latin
to express what the speaker said. It is used after a verb of 'saying'
like *dixit*, 'he said', or *respondit*, 'he answered'.

The main clause in indirect statement is always in the accusative
and infinitive. The accusative is the subject of the infinitive, and
either the present, perfect, or future infinitive is used.

(*a*) The present infinitive refers to action that takes place at the
same time as that of the verb of saying.

Dīcit tē in Ītaliā esse.
He says that you are in Italy.
Dīxit tē in Ītaliā esse.
He said that you were in Italy (i.e. when he spoke).

(*b*) The perfect infinitive refers to action that took place *before*
that of the verb of saying.

Dīcit tē in Ītaliā fuisse.
He says that you were (have been) in Italy.
Dīxit tē in Ītaliā fuisse.
He said that you were (had been) in Italy.

(*c*) The future infinitive refers to action that takes place *after*
that of the verb of saying.

Dīcit tē in Ītaliā futūrum esse.
He says that you will be in Italy.
Dīxit tē in Ītaliā futūrum esse.
He said that you would be in Italy.

In the future infinitive (*futūrum esse*) the participle *futūrum* must agree with the subject (here *tē*) in gender, number, and case. In this sentence, it is masculine, singular, and accusative.

Sect. 83. Use of the reflexive

When the subject of the infinitive refers to the subject of a verb of saying in the third person, the reflexive *sē* is used.

Dīxit sē in Ītaliā fuisse.
He said that he (the speaker) had been in Italy.

But if the word *he* refers to someone else and not to the speaker, *eum* should be used instead of *sē*.

Dīxit eum in Ītaliā fuisse.
He said that he (someone else) had been in Italy.

Sect. 84. Indirect statement may be introduced by several kinds of verbs

(1) Verbs of saying: *dīcō*, I say; *negō*, I deny; *nuntiō*, I report; *certiōrem faciō*, I inform (I make someone more certain).
(2) Verbs of thinking: *putō*, or *exīstimō*, I think; *crēdō*, I believe.
(3) Verbs of knowing: *sciō*, I know; *nesciō*, I do not know; *intellegō*, I understand.
(4) Verbs of perceiving: *sentiō*, I feel, am aware; *videō*, I see; *audiō*, I hear.
(5) Verbs of remembering: *meminī*, or *memoriā teneō*, I remember.

Note that the word 'that', which is used in English after 'he said', is not translated in Latin.

Sect. 85. Dīcō should not be followed by a negative like nōn, 'not', or numquam, 'never'; negō ('I say that not') should be used and may be followed by a word like umquam, 'ever'

Negat sē umquam in Ītaliā fuisse.
He says that he was never in Italy.
(He denies that he was ever in Italy.)

Sect. 86. Some verbs like spērō, I hope, prōmittō, I promise, iūrō, I swear, take the accusative and the future infinitive

Spērat sē in Ītaliā futūrum esse.

He hopes he will be in Italy.

The infinitive of *possum*, 'I am able', may be used with a future meaning.

Spērat sē in Ītaliā habitāre posse.

He hopes he will be able to live in Italy.

For subordinate clauses in indirect statement see Lesson XXXI. For commands and questions in indirect statement see Lesson XLI.

Personal use of **dīcitur**

When a verb of 'saying' or 'thinking' is in the passive, it is better to use it personally.

Dīcitur honestus esse.   He is said to be honorable.

Here the nominative is used and not the accusative. The impersonal use of *dīcitur* would not be correct (e.g. *dīcitur eum honestum esse*, 'it is said that he is honorable'), but this could be expressed by a verb in the active.

Dīcunt eum honestum esse.   They say that he is honorable.

VOCABULARY

accipiō, -ere, accēpī, acceptum, 3, receive.
Apollō, -inis, *m.,* Apollo (*see* **Phoebus** (Lesson IX)).
armō, 1, arm.
auctōritās, -ātis, *f.,* authority, influence.
comes, -itis, *m. and f.,* companion.
condūcō, 3, collect, lead together.
cōnfirmō, 1, confirm, establish, prove.
cōnsuētūdō, -inis, *f.,* custom.
dēpellō, -ere, dēpulī, dēpulsum, 3, drive away.
eō, īre, iī, itum, *irreg.,* go (Lesson XXXI).
ferē, nearly, almost, about.
illūc, to that place.
initium, -ī (-iī), n., beginning.
Ītalicus, -a, -um, Italian.

iūrō, 1, swear.
lyricus, -a, -um, lyric.
modus, -ī, *m.,* measure, limit, way; meter, rhythm.
morbus, -ī, *m.,* disease.
negō, 1, say no, deny, say that . . . not.
nēmō, *acc.* **neminem,** no one.
nihilum (nīlum, *poet.***) -ī,** *n.,* nothing, = **nihil (nil),** *indecl.*
nōn modo . . . sed etiam, not only . . . but also.
numerus, -ī, *m.,* number.
opīniō, -ōnis, *f.,* opinion, reputation.
plūrimus, -a, -um, most, very much; *adv.* **plūrimum.**
polliceor, -ērī, pollicitus sum, 2, *deponent,* promise (Lesson XXXII).
prōmittō, -ere, prōmīsī, prōmissum, 3, promise.

quisquam (*acc.* **quemquam**), **quid-quam, quicquam,** *pron.,* anyone (*after a negative*).
quoniam, since.
redeō, -īre, rediī, *irreg.,* return (Lesson XXXI).

senex, senis, *m.,* old man.
senior, *comp. of* **senex,** older (man).
simul ac (atque), as soon as.
spērō, 1, hope.
statim, immediately.
vidētur, *impers.,* it seems good.

NOTES

1. **condiciō, -ōnis,** *f.,* agreement, terms.
3. The subject is the Helvetian Orgetorix.
   conciliō, 1, obtain, win over.
5. **Bellovacī,** *m. pl.,* a tribe of the Belgae in Gaul.
6. **age,** *imperat.,* come.
7. **quī** *refers to* **passer,** Lesbia's pet sparrow.
   tenebricōsus, -a, -um, shadowy.
8. **tumulus, -ī,** *m.,* mound (*here* = tomb, monument).
   scelerātus, -a, -um, wicked.
   vir, *here* = husband.
   fēcisse ('she did it') *is ambiguous.* One meaning is that she made or erected the monuments.
   Chloē, -es, *f.,* Chloe.
   pote = **potest,** can.   [honest.
   simplex, -icis, simple, frank,
9. **dīlūcēscō, -lūxī,** 3, shine.

superveniō, 4, come upon, arrive.
10. Baucis and Philemon were turned into trees (Lesson IX).
    frondeō, -ēre, 2, put forth leaves.
    cōnspiciō, -ere, conspexī, conspectum, 3, look at, catch sight of.
11. **princeps** = **prīmus,** first.
    Aeolius, -a, -um, Aeolian; refers to the Greek odes of Sappho and Alcaeus.
    Ītalus, -a, -um, Italian (= **Ītalicus**).
12. **artificium, -ī (-iī),** *n.,* handicraft.
    caelestēs, *pl.,* the gods.
13. **iūrārās** = **iūrāverās. iūrō** *with* **per** = to swear by.
    ūsque, always.
    cadūcus, -a, -um, falling.
    irritus (inr-), -a, -um, vain, useless.
    quā, where.

EXERCISE 1

*1. Cicerō . . . respondit nōn esse cōnsuetūdinem populī Rōmānī accipere ab hoste armātō condiciōnem.
2. Hī . . . omnēs nuntiāvērunt manūs cōgī, exercitum in ūnum locum condūcī.
*3. Sē suīs copiīs suōque exercitū illīs rēgna conciliātūrum (esse) cōnfirmat.
*4. Hostēs proeliō superātī, simul atque sē ex fugā recēpērunt, statim ad Caesarem lēgātōs dē pāce mīsērunt; obsidēs (sē) datūrōs . . . pollicitī sunt.
*5. (Dīcēbant) . . . plūrimum inter eōs Bellovacōs et virtūte et auctōritāte et hominum numerō valēre.
6. Nunc age, rēs quoniam docuī nōn posse creārī dē nīlō . . .
*7. Quī nunc it per iter tenebricōsum illūc, unde negant redīre quemquam.
*8. Īnscrīpsit tumulīs septem scelerāta virōrum sē fēcisse Chloē. Quid pote simplicius?

*9. Omnem crēde diem tibi dīlūxisse suprēmum.
Grāta superveniet quae nōn spērābitur hōra.

*10.   ... Frondēre Philēmona Baucis,
Baucida cōnspexit senior frondēre Philēmōn.

*11. Dīcar ...
prīnceps Aeolium carmen ad Ītalōs
dēdūxisse modōs.

12. Dē hīs eandem ferē, quam reliquae gentēs, habent opīniōnem:
Apollinem morbōs dēpellere, Minervam operum atque artificiōrum
initia trādere, Iovem imperium caelestium tenēre, Martem bella
regere.

*13. At mihi tē comitem iūrārās ūsque futūram—
per mē perque oculōs, sīdera nostra, tuōs.
Verba puellārum, foliīs leviōra cadūcīs,
irrita, quā vīsum est, ventus et unda ferunt.

EXERCISE 2

1. The soldiers reported that the enemy were collecting an army (and) had
already left their camp (and) would soon come to the river. 2. As soon as
the Gauls had been conquered, they sent envoys, who promised that (their)
leaders would come to Caesar. 3. Lucretius teaches not only that nothing
is created from nothing, but also that nothing returns to nothing. 4. We
all believe that no one returns from that place. 5. Horace says that he
was-the-first-to write the lyric poems of the Greeks in Italian rhythms.

EXERCISE 3

ANSWER IN LATIN:

1. Quid ab hostibus armātīs nōn accipiunt Rōmānī? 2. Quid in ūnum
locum condūcēbātur? 3. Quid sē amīcīs conciliātūrum dīxit Orgetorīx?
4. Quōmodo haec factūrus erat? 5. Quid hostēs pollicitī sunt? 6. Quī
hominēs auctōritāte valēbant? 7. Quō nunc it Lesbiae passer? 8. Quid
in sepulcrīs septem virōrum īnscrīpsit Chloē? 9. Quae hōra grāta nōbīs
veniet? 10. Quem frondēre vīdit Baucis? 11. Quī deus morbōs dēpellit?
12. Quī deus bella regere dīcitur? 13. Quid iūrāverat Ovidiī puella?
14. Quālia puellārum verba esse dīcit poēta?

LESSON XXV

THE SUBJUNCTIVE MOOD. PRESENT SUBJUNCTIVE OF
THE FOUR CONJUGATIONS, ACTIVE AND PASSIVE, AND
OF THE VERB *sum*. JUSSIVE AND HORTATORY
SUBJUNCTIVES, DELIBERATIVE SUBJUNCTIVE, OPTATIVE
SUBJUNCTIVE (POSSIBLE WISHES FOR THE FUTURE)

Sect. 87. The subjunctive mood

THIS mood describes action that is willed or desired or conditional.
It is generally represented in English by auxiliary words like may,
might, should, would, though the subjunctive still survives in
expressions like 'if this be so'. It is used either independently in
simple sentences or in subordinate clauses. This lesson describes
some of the independent uses, and some important uses of the
subjunctive in subordinate clauses are described in Lessons XXVI,
XXVII, and XXVIII.

There are four forms of the subjunctive, the present, the imperfect, the perfect, and the pluperfect. This lesson deals with
the present subjunctive.

Sect. 88. Present subjunctive of the four conjugations and the verb sum

Active

		I	II	III (*a*)
S.	1	amem	moneam	regam
	2	amēs	moneās	regās
	3	amet	moneat	regat
P.	1	amēmus	moneāmus	regāmus
	2	amētis	moneātis	regātis
	3	ament	moneant	regant

		III (*b*)	IV	Sum
S.	1	capiam	audiam	sim
	2	capiās	audiās	sīs
	3	capiat	audiat	sit
P.	1	capiāmus	audiāmus	sīmus
	2	capiātis	audiātis	sītis
	3	capiant	audiant	sint

Passive

	I	II	III (a)
S. 1	amer	monear	regar
2	améris (-re)	moneáris (-re)	regáris (-re)
3	amétur	moneátur	regátur
P. 1	amémur	moneámur	regámur
2	amémini	moneámini	regámini
3	amentur	moneantur	regantur

	III (b)	IV
S. 1	capiar	audiar
2	capiáris (-re)	audiáris (-re)
3	capiátur	audiátur
P. 1	capiámur	audiámur
2	capiámini	audiámini
3	capiantur	audiantur

The vowel *a* appears everywhere in the second, third, and fourth conjugations, but *e* appears in the first conjugation, in which *a* is used for the present indicative. In the third and fourth conjugations there is no difference in the first person singular between the present subjunctive and the future indicative (*regam, capiam, audiam*), but the other persons have *a* in the subjunctive and *e* in the future.

Sect. 89. Jussive and hortatory subjunctives (the subjunctive of will)

The present subjunctive is used to express a command and is generally in the third person. In the first person it expresses an exhortation. The name *jussive* is derived from *iubeō*, 'I command', and *hortatory* is derived from *hortor*, 'I encourage'.

In the second person the jussive subjunctive may be used, but the imperative is more common.

The negative is *né*.

For prohibitions *né* with the perfect subjunctive may be used (see Lesson XXVII).

> **Caveat emptor.** Let the buyer beware.
> **Né veniant.** Let them not come.
> **Né hoc faciámus.** Let us not do this.
> **Hoc faciás.** You should do this.

Sect. 90. Deliberative subjunctive (the subjunctive of will)

This subjunctive is used to express what ought to be done. The command is put in the form of a question and the negative is *nōn*.

Quid faciam?   What am I to do?

Sect. 91. Optative subjunctive (the subjunctive of desire)

This subjunctive expresses a wish. The present subjunctive expresses a possible wish for the future. It may be introduced by *utinam*, and the negative is *nē* or *utinam nē*.

For other uses of the optative subjunctive see Lesson XXVII.

Utinam tē mox videam.
May I see you soon! (I wish I could see you soon.)
Utinam nē hoc faciās.   May you not do this!

VOCABULARY

cantō, 1, sing.
carpō, -ere, carpsī, carptum, 3, gather, pluck.
cēdō, -ere, cessī, cessum, 3, withdraw; (*with dat.*) yield to.
clārus, -a, -um, bright, clear, famous.
cōram, *prep. with acc.*, in the presence of.
dēsinō, -ere, (desii), 3, cease.
dēsum, deesse, dēfuī, *irreg.*, be lacking; fail (*with dat.*).
ēdō, -ere, ēdidī, ēditum, 3, give forth, produce, publish.
enim, for.
epistula, -ae, *f.*, letter.
expedit, *impers.*, it is expedient.
fēstus, -a, -um, festal, joyful; **fēstus diēs,** festival, holiday.
flūmen, -inis, *n.*, river.
gaudeō, -ēre, gāvīsus sum, 2, *semi-deponent* (Lesson XXXII), rejoice; delight in (*with abl.*).
humus, -ī, *f.*, earth, ground.
ignōtus, -a, -um, unknown.
Iuvenālis, -is, *m.*, Decimus Iunius Iuvenalis, Juvenal, the author of sixteen *Satires, c.* A.D. 60–130.
libenter, *adv.*, willingly.
Mūsae, -ārum, *f.*, the nine Muses.

nōnus, -a, -um, ninth.
novissimus, -a, -um, last.
optō, 1, desire, long for.
os, ossis, *n.*, bone.
pectus, -oris, *n.*, breast, heart, mind.
pereō, -īre, periī, *irreg.*, perish.
pēs, pedis, *m.*, foot.
placeō, -ēre, placuī, placitum, 2, please (*with dat.*).
premō, -ere, pressī, pressum, 3, press, press hard on, repress.
prōficiō, -ere, prōfēcī, prōfectum, 3, make progress.
prūdēns, -entis, prudent, sensible.
Quintiliānus, -i, *m.*, M. Fabius Quintilianus, Quintilian, author of twelve books on the *Training of the Orator, c.* A.D. 35–before 100.
quis, quid, *pron.*, anyone, anything; *used after* sī, nisi, num, nē.
ratiō, -ōnis, *f.*, reason, reckoning, plan.
senectūs, -ūtis, *f.*, old age.
sevērus, -a, -um, strict, severe.
sīc, *adv.*, thus.
tum, tunc, *adv.*, then.
utinam, would that (*introduces a wish in the subjunctive*).
valdē, exceedingly, very.
voluntās, -ātis, *f.*, will, wish, choice.

NOTES

1. *The last syllable of* **Amor** *is short before* **et**, *but it is regarded here as long. The ictus falls on it and it comes before a pause marked by a colon.*
3. **Prōtesilāus, -ī,** *m.*, the first Greek to be killed in the Trojan War.
4. **amīca, -ae,** *f.*, friend.
   sonus, -ī, *m.*, sound.
5. **probātō,** *2nd pers. sing. imperat.,* = **probā.**
6. **rūre** = **rūrī,** in the country.
   iners, -ertis, idle, inactive.
   rota, -ae, *f.*, wheel (*here poet. for* **currus,** a car).
   viam carpō = take one's way.
7. **rūmor, -ōris,** *m.*, rumor, gossip.
   aestimō, 1, value, reckon.
   as, assis, *m.*, the *as*, a Roman coin.
   assis, *gen. with* **aestimō,** at the value of an *as*; *cf.* **nihilī,** *gen.*, at no value.
8. **ineptiō, -īre,** 4, play the fool.
9. **coluisse,** *perf. infin. used in poetry instead of the pres. infin. Here* = to have cultivated (once and for all).
   linguae duae, *i.e.* Greek and Latin.
   ēdiscō, -ere, 3, *compound of* **discō,** learn (thoroughly).
13. **Tībur, -uris,** *n.*, a town in Latium, now Tivoli.
   sēdes, -is, *f.*, seat.
   senecta, -ae, *f.*, old age (= **senectūs**).

15. **premō,** *here* = suppress, keep back (the manuscript of a book). Horace warns writers not to publish a book too soon.
16. **Mēdēa, -ae,** *f.*, Medea, who killed her own children in the tragedy written by Euripides.
   trucīdō, 1, kill, slaughter.
17. **exorior,** *compound of* **orior, ortus sum,** 4, *deponent,* arise (Lesson XXXII).
   ultor, -ōris, *m.*, avenger, i.e. of Dido.
21. **riguus, -a, -um,** that waters (*here* = running).
   amnis, -is, *m.*, stream, river.
   inglōrius, -a, -um, inglorious, without glory.
22. **compositus, -a, -um,** composed, calm.
   epistula, here refers to Ovid's *Heroides* or *Epistulae,* 'letters of heroines'.
   novō, 1, make new, invent.
24. **vigilō,** 1, watch, be wakeful.
   ecce, behold, look.
   mināciter, *adv.*, with threats.
   immineō, 2, hang over, threaten, be near at hand.
   arbiter, -trī, *m.*, judge.
25. **iūcundus, -a, -um,** delightful, pleasant.
   iuventūs, -ūtis, *f.*, youth.
   molestus, -a, -um, troublesome.

EXERCISE 1

*1. Omnia vincit Amor: et nōs cēdāmus Amōrī.
*2. Crās amet quī numquam amāvit, quīque amāvit crās amet.
3. Bella gerant aliī; Prōtesilāus amet.
4. Audiat optātōs semper amīca sonōs.
5. . . . Quicquid probat illa, probātō;
      quod dīcet, dīcās; quod negat illa, negēs.
*6. Rūre erit et dīcet 'veniās'; Amor ōdit inertēs;
      sī rota dēfuerit, tū pede carpe viam.
*7. Vīvāmus, mea Lesbia, atque amēmus,
      rūmōrēsque senum sevēriōrum
      omnēs ūnius aestimēmus assis.

8. Miser Catulle, dēsinās ineptīre.
*9. Nec levis ingenuās pectus coluisse per artēs
    cūra sit et linguās ēdidicisse duās.
10. Ad clāras Asiae volēmus urbēs.
*11. Ille sē prōfēcisse sciat cui Cicerō valdē placēbit.
12. Quid agam, iūdicēs?
13. Tībur . . .
    sit meae sēdēs utinam senectae.
*14. Expedit esse deōs; et, ut expedit, esse putēmus.
*15. Nōnumque premātur in annum.
*16. Nē puerōs cōram populō Mēdēa trucīdet.
17. Exoriāre aliquis nostrīs ex ossibus ultor.
18. Hoc volo, sīc iubeō, sit prō ratiōne voluntās.
19. Sit tibi terra levis.
20. Mē vērō prīmum dulcēs ante omnia Mūsae . . .
    accipiant caelīque viās et sīdera mōnstrent.
21. Rūra mihi et riguī placeant in vallibus amnēs,
    flūmina amem silvāsque inglorius. . . .
22. Vel tibi compositā cantētur epistula vōce;
    ignōtum hoc aliīs ille novāvit opus.
*23. Pereant, inquit, quī ante nōs nostra dīxērunt.
24. Hōra novissima, tempora pessima sunt, vigilēmus.
   Ecce mināciter imminet arbiter ille suprēmus.
25. Gaudeāmus igitur,
    iuvenēs dum sumus;
    post iūcundam iuventūtem,
    post molestam senectūtem
    nōs habēbit humus.

EXERCISE 2

1. On the festival of Venus, as an unknown poet commands, let those love who have never loved before. 2. If (his) girl has written[1] in a letter 'you should come to the country' and there is[1] no car, a young man should walk to her. 3. Let no one publish his book immediately, but if Horace advises correctly, let him suppress it until the ninth year. 4. I-wish-that Cicero's books would soon please you; for then, as Quintilian says, you will have made progress. 5. What are you to do, (you) unlucky young man, if anyone has published[1] your dissertation (book) before you?

EXERCISE 3

ANSWER IN LATIN:

1. Cui nōs cēdere oportet? 2. Quid facere dēbet Prōtesilāus? 3. Quālēs sonōs libenter audiunt puellae? 4. Sī quid puella probat, quid facit iuvenis prūdēns? 5. Quālēs iuvenēs ōdit Amor? 6. Quid Lesbiae suae dīcit Catullus? 7. Quōrum rūmōrēs nihilī aestimant iuvenēs? 8. Quid

---

[1] Future perfect.

sibi dīcit Catullus? 9. Quot linguās discere dēbent iuvenēs? 10. Quō properāre voluit Catullus? 11. Quī locus erit Horātiō senī grātus? 12. Cūr deōs esse putat Ovidius? 13. Oportet-ne nōs Mēdēam puerōs in fābulā occīdentem vidēre? 14. Quālis homo ex ossibus Dīdōnis oriētur? 15. Quid uxor mala dē voluntāte suā apud Iuvenālem dīcit? 16. Quālis dēbet esse in sepulcrō terra? 17. Quid dē Mūsīs dīxit Vergilius? 18. Quid amāre vult Vergilius? 19. Quod opus novum scrīpsit Ovidius?

LESSON XXVI

IMPERFECT SUBJUNCTIVE OF THE FOUR CONJUGATIONS,
ACTIVE AND PASSIVE, AND OF THE VERB *sum*
SUBJUNCTIVE IN PURPOSE OR FINAL CLAUSES
(ADVERBIAL CLAUSES OF PURPOSE). USE OF *ut* AND *nē*
(*nē quis*). SUBJUNCTIVE AFTER VERBS OF ASKING,
ADVISING, PERSUADING, COMMANDING, e.g. *rogō, moneō,
persuādeō, imperō* (SUBSTANTIVE CLAUSES OF PURPOSE)
BUT *iubeō* WITH THE INFINITIVE. INDIRECT REFLEXIVE

Sect. 92. Imperfect subjunctive of the four conjugations and of the verb sum

Active

		I	II	III (*a*)
S.	1	amārem	monērem	regerem
	2	amārēs	monērēs	regerēs
	3	amāret	monēret	regeret
P.	1	amārēmus	monērēmus	regerēmus
	2	amārētis	monērētis	regerētis
	3	amārent	monērent	regerent

		III (*b*)	IV	Sum
S.	1	caperem	audīrem	essem
	2	caperēs	audīrēs	essēs
	3	caperet	audīret	esset
P.	1	caperēmus	audīrēmus	essēmus
	2	caperētis	audīrētis	essētis
	3	caperent	audīrent	essent

Passive

		I	II	III (*a*)
S.	1	amārer	monērer	regerer
	2	amārēris (-re)	monērēris (-re)	regerēris (-re)
	3	amārētur	monērētur	regerētur
P.	1	amārēmur	monērēmur	regerēmur
	2	amārēminī	monērēminī	regerēminī
	3	amārentur	monērentur	regerentur

	III (*b*)	IV
S.	1 **caperer**	**audīrer**
	2 **caperēris (-re)**	**audīrēris (-re)**
	3 **caperētur**	**audīrētur**
P.	1 **caperēmur**	**audīrēmur**
	2 **caperēminī**	**audīrēminī**
	3 **caperentur**	**audīrentur**

The suffix *-rem, -rēs*, etc., is added to the present stem (e.g. *amā-*). The imperfect subjunctive resembles the present infinitive (e.g. *amāre*) followed by the usual personal endings (*-m, -s, -t*, etc.).

Sect. 93. Subjunctive in purpose or final clauses (adverbial clauses of purpose). Use of ut and nē (nē quis)

Purpose or final clauses express the purpose or end in view; the name final is derived from *fīnis*, 'end'. They are introduced by the conjunction *ut*, 'in order that', or by the negative *nē*, 'in order that . . . not'.

In English it is possible to say 'I came in order *to* do this', but in Latin prose the infinitive must not be used to express purpose.

The subjunctive in a final clause is either present or imperfect. If the main verb is primary, the present subjunctive is used; if the main verb is secondary (or historic), the imperfect subjunctive is used.

Sequence of tenses

	Indicative		*Subjunctive*
Primary	Present Future Perfect (e.g. I have done) Future perfect	followed by	Present
Secondary	Imperfect Perfect (e.g. I did) Pluperfect	followed by	Imperfect

Crās veniēs, ut mē videās.
You will come tomorrow in order to see me (in order that you may see me).

Hodiē vēnī, ut tē videam.
I have come today in order to see you (in order that I may see you).

Herī vēnī, ut tē vidērem.
I came yesterday in order to see you (in order that I might see you).

The negative is always *nē*, which may be followed by *quis*, 'anyone' (see Lesson XXX), or *umquam*, 'ever'.

> Do not write *ut nōn*, or use *nēmō* ('no one') or *numquam* ('never') after *ut*.
>
> *Nē quis* means 'lest anyone', 'in order that no one'.

If there are two negative clauses, the first is introduced by *nē*, the second by *nēve* or *neu*.

Herī discessī, nē quis mē vidēret.

I went away yesterday in order that no one might see me.

Sect. 94. Relative clauses of purpose

The relative *quī* may be used instead of *ut* in a purpose clause. Here *quī* is equivalent to *ut is* ('in order that he').

Lēgātum mīsit, quī haec nuntiāret.

He sent an envoy to announce this (who should announce these things).

Here *quī* refers to *lēgātum*, the object of *mīsit*.

Sect. 95. Purpose clauses containing a comparative

When a purpose clause contains a comparative, *quō* must be used instead of *ut*. Here *quō* is equivalent to *ut eō*, 'in order that by that amount'; *eō* is an ablative of degree of difference.

Lēgātum mīsit, quō celerius haec nuntiāret.

He sent an envoy in order to announce this more quickly (lit. by that amount more quickly).

Sect. 96. Subjunctive after verbs of asking, advising, persuading, commanding (substantive clauses of purpose)

Verbs like *rogō*, 'I ask', are followed by a clause of purpose introduced by *ut* or *nē*. This is a substantive or noun clause and is really an indirect command. In English it is possible to say 'I ask you *to* do this', but in Latin the infinitive must not be used. It is necessary to say 'I ask that you should do this'.

Like the adverbial clauses of purpose, these clauses use either the present or the imperfect subjunctive.

Tē rogō ut hoc faciās.   I ask you to do this.
Tē rogāvī ut hoc facerēs.
I asked you to do this (lit. I asked that you should do this).

The following list contains some of the verbs that take *ut* with the subjunctive.

1. Verbs of asking: *rogō* (with acc.) or *petō* (with *ā* and abl.), 'I ask', 'request'; *ōrō* (with acc.), 'I beg'.
2. Verbs of advising: *moneō*, 'I advise'; *hortor*, 'I encourage' (with acc.).
3. Verbs of persuading: *persuādeō* (with dat.), 'I persuade'.
4. Verbs of commanding: *imperō* (with dat.), 'I command'.

Sect. 97. Iubeō with the infinitive

Iubeō, 'I command', does not take *ut* with the subjunctive, but is followed by the infinitive (see Lesson XXI).

Tibi imperō ut veniās.
Tē venīre iubeō. } I order you to come.

Vetō, I forbid, is also used with the infinitive.

Sect. 98. Indirect reflexive

In substantive clauses of purpose, e.g. after verbs of asking and encouraging, the reflexive *sē* and the adjective *suus* may refer to the subject of the main verb and not to the subject of the dependent clause in which they occur. This is an indirect rather than a direct reflexive.

Lēgātī Caesarem ōrābant ut sē ex perīculō servāret.
The envoys begged Caesar to save them from danger.

Here *sē* refers to *lēgātī* and not to *Caesar*, the subject of *servāret*. They are not asking Caesar to save himself. Usually the context makes the meaning clear, but sometimes *sē* may be ambiguous. If it is ambiguous, the sentence ought to be written in another way.

VOCABULARY

adventus, -ūs, *m.,* arrival.
almus, -a, -um, kindly, fostering.
amābilis, -e, lovable.
avunculus, -ī, *m.,* uncle.
certus, -a, -um, certain, sure.
certiōrem faciō, make someone more certain, inform (*with acc.*).
certior fīō, become more certain, be informed.
cīvitās, -ātis, *f.,* state; citizenship.
committō (proelium), -mittere,

-mīsī, -missum, 3, engage in, join (battle).
cōnor, -ārī, cōnātus sum, 1, *deponent,* try (Lesson XXXII).
exeō, -īre, -iī, -itum, *irreg.,* go out.
fīō, fierī, factus sum, *irreg., passive of* **faciō,** become, be made (Lesson XXXI).
hortor, -ārī, hortātus sum, 1, *deponent,* encourage (Lesson XXXII).
immortālis, -e, immortal.

impetrō, 1, gain a request, obtain (by asking).
in animō esse (*with dat.*), have it in mind, intend.
intrā, *prep. with acc.*, inside, within.
nē, in order that . . . not, lest.
nēve, neu, and that . . . not, and lest.
nox, noctis, -ium, *f.*, night.
obtineō, -ēre, obtinuī, obtentum, 2, obtain, hold.
occupō, 1, seize, occupy.
oppugnō, 1, attack.
orior, orīrī, ortus sum, 4, *deponent,* arise; (*with abl.*), spring from, be born (Lesson XXXII).
perīculum, -ī, *n.*, danger, risk.
persuādeō, -ēre, persuāsī, persuāsum, 2, persuade (*with dat.*).
pōns, pontis, -ium, *m.*, bridge.
possim, -īs, -it, . . . -int, *pres. subjve. of* **possum** (Lesson XXXI).

posterus, -a, -um, next; **posterī,** *m. pl.*, posterity.
principātus, -ūs, *m.*, chieftainship, principate.
proficīscor, -īscī, profectus sum, 3, *deponent,* set out (Lesson XXXII).
quidam, quaedam, quiddam, *pron.,* a certain (Lesson XXX).
quō (= **ut eō**), in order that (*with a comp.*).
quōndam, once, formerly.
rapiō, -ere, rapuī, raptum, 3, seize, snatch, hurry away.
removeō, -ēre, remōvī, remōtum, 2, remove, move back.
sōlus, -a, -um, alone, only (Lesson XXIX).
tempestās, -ātis, *f.*, storm, weather.
theātrum, -ī, *n.*, theatre.
ūllus, -a, -um, any (*after a negative*) (Lesson XXIX).
ut (utī), in order that, so that.

NOTES

1. **cōnspectus, -ūs,** *m.*, sight, view.
   aequō, 1, make equal.
   tollō, -ere, sustulī, sublātum, *irreg.*, lift, remove, take away.
2. **cōnscribō,** *compound of* **scrībō,** 3, write together, enroll (*here =* write).
   intercipiō, -cipere, -cēpī, -ceptum, 3, cut off, intercept.
3. **estō** = **es,** *2nd pers. imperat. of* **sum.**
4. **spectātum,** *supine of* **spectō,** here used to express purpose = **ut spectent** (Lesson XXXIX).
5. **maleficium, -ī (-ii),** *n.*, evil deed, harm, wrong.
6. **coorior,** *compound of* **orior,** *deponent,* arise.
   adflīgō, -flīgere, -flīxī, -flictum, 3, shatter.
   ēiciō, -icere, -iēcī, -iectum, 3, cast out, cast ashore.
7. **nimis**; *here Terence translates the Greek phrase* **mēden agān,** 'nothing in excess'. *A verb should be understood with* **nē,** *e.g.* **agās.**
8. **exitus, -ūs,** *m.*, departure, end, result.

9. **dēcernō, -ere, dēcrēvī, dēcrētum,** 3, decide, decree.
   dētrīmentum, -ī, *n.*, loss; *with* **capiō** = suffer harm.
10. **almus, -a, -um,** *here perhaps* = sunny.
11. **trāgula, -ae,** *f.*, javelin.
    āmentum, -ī, *n.*, thong.
    dēligō, 1, tie together, bind fast.
    mūnitiō, -ōnis, *f.*, fortification.
    abiciō, -icere, -iēcī, -iectum, 3, throw away.
12. **Sēquanus, -a, -um,** *pl.* **Sēquanī, -ōrum,** *m.*, a tribe in Gaul (**Sēquana** = the Seine).
13. Quintus Cicero's camp is being attacked by the Gauls.
    prīstinus, -a, -um, former, original.
    retineō, -ēre, retinuī, retentum, 2, retain, keep.
16. **Dumnorīx, -igis,** *m.*, Dumnorix, an Aeduan.
    Aeduus, -a, -um, Aeduan; *pl.,* **Aeduī (Haeduī), -ōrum,** *m.*, a tribe in Gaul between the Loire and the Saône.

17. **dēferō,** *compound of* **ferō,** *irreg.,* bring down, deliver.
18. **proficīscentēs,** *acc. m. pl. of the pres. part., the object of* **implōrābant.**

implōrō, 1, beg, entreat.
servitūs, -ūtis, *f.,* slavery.
19. **Genāva, -ae,** *f.,* Geneva.
rescindō, -ere, 3, break down.

EXERCISE 1

*1. Caesar . . . omnium ex cōnspectū remōtīs equīs, ut aequātō omnium perīculō spem fugae tolleret . . . proelium commīsit.
*2. Hanc Graecīs cōnscrīptam litterīs mittit, nē interceptā epistulā nostra ab hostibus cōnsilia cognōscantur.
*3. Sit procul omne nefās; ut amēris, amābilis estō:
  quod tibi nōn faciēs sōlave fōrma dabit.
*4. Spectātum veniunt, veniunt spectentur ut ipsae.
*5. Ubi dē ēius adventū Helvētiī certiōrēs factī sunt, lēgātōs ad eum mittunt . . . quī dīcerent sibi esse in animō sine ūllō maleficiō iter per prōvinciam facere.[1]
6. Equitēs . . . ad Caesarem vēnērunt, quī nuntiārent superiōre nocte maximā coortā tempestāte prope omnēs nāvēs adflictās atque in lītore ēiectās esse.
7. Nē quid nimis.
*8. Petis, ut tibi avunculī meī exitum scrībam, quō vērius trādere posterīs possīs.
*9. Dēcrēvit quōndam senātus utī L. Opimius cōnsul vidēret nē quid rēs pūblica dētrīmentī caperet.
*10. Immortālia nē spērēs, monet annus et almum
  quae rapit hōra diem.
11. Monet ut trāgulam cum epistulā ad āmentum dēligātā intrā mūnitiōnem castrōrum abiciat.
12. (Dumnorīx) ā Sēquanīs impetrat ut per fīnēs suōs Helvētiōs īre patiantur.
13. (Caesar Cicerōnem) hortātur ut prīstinam virtūtem retineat.
*14. Cīvitātī persuāsit ut dē fīnibus suīs cum omnibus cōpiīs exīrent.
15. In eō itinere persuādet Casticō . . . Sēquanō . . . ut rēgnum in cīvitāte suā occupāret.
16. Dumnorīgī Aeduō . . . quī eō tempore prīncipātum in cīvitāte obtinēbat . . . ut idem cōnārētur persuādet.
*17. Tum cuidam ex equitibus Gallīs magnīs praemiīs persuādet utī ad Cicerōnem epistulam dēferat.
18. Mulierēs . . . in proelium proficīscentēs . . . implōrābant, nē sē in servitūtem Rōmānīs trāderent.
19. Pontem quī erat ad Genāvam iubet rescindī.

EXERCISE 2

1. No one is loved because his face alone is beautiful; a young man ought

[1] Caesar often uses the vivid (historic) present when he is referring to past time. Thus in sentence 5 the main verb *mittunt* is present, but it is followed by *dīcerent,* an imperfect subjunctive in secondary sequence. Compare *persuādet* in sentences 15 and 16.

to be lovable in order to be loved. 2. Roman women not only came to the theatre to look at everything, but also to be seen themselves. 3. The Greeks advise those who wish to be happy not to do anything in excess (too much). 4. Tacitus asked Pliny to tell (him) everything about the death of his uncle, in order that he might describe (it) better himself. 5. Caesar persuaded one of the horsemen to carry a letter to Quintus Cicero, because he had heard that the Gauls had attacked (his) camp.

Exercise 3

ANSWER IN LATIN:

1. Cūr equōs ex cōnspectū remōvit Caesar? 2. Cūr epistulam Graecīs litterīs scrīpsit Caesar? 3. Quid lēgātōs dīcere iussērunt Helvētiī? 4. Quid Caesarī nuntiāvērunt equitēs? 5. Quid vidēre dēbet cōnsul? 6. Quid apud Horātium tē monet annus? 7. Quid equitem monuit Caesar? 8. Quid ā Sēquanīs impetrāvit Dumnorīx? 9. Quem hortātus est Caesar ut virtūtem retinēret? 10. Cui persuāsit Orgetorīx ut rēgnum occupāret?

LESSON XXVII

PERFECT AND PLUPERFECT SUBJUNCTIVE OF THE FOUR
CONJUGATIONS, ACTIVE AND PASSIVE, AND OF THE
VERB *sum*. OPTATIVE SUBJUNCTIVE (IMPOSSIBLE WISHES,
PRESENT AND PAST TIME). SUBJUNCTIVE IN RESULT OR
CONSECUTIVE CLAUSES: USE OF *ut* AND *ut nōn* (*ut nēmō*).
nē WITH THE PERFECT SUBJUNCTIVE (PROHIBITIONS)

**Sect. 99. Perfect and pluperfect subjunctive of the four
conjugations and the verb sum**

Perfect active

	I	II	III (*a*)
S. 1	amāverim	monuerim	rēxerim
2	amāverīs	monuerīs	rēxerīs
3	amāverit	monuerit	rēxerit
P. 1	amāverīmus	monuerīmus	rēxerīmus
2	amāverītis	monuerītis	rēxerītis
3	amāverint	monuerint	rēxerint

	III (*b*)	IV	Sum
S. 1	cēperim	audīverim	fuerim
2	cēperīs	audīverīs	fuerīs
3	cēperit	audīverit	fuerit
P. 1	cēperīmus	audīverīmus	fuerīmus
2	cēperītis	audīverītis	fuerītis
3	cēperint	audīverint	fuerint

Pluperfect active

	I	II	III (*a*)
S. 1	amāvissem	monuissem	rēxissem
2	amāvissēs	monuissēs	rēxissēs
3	amāvisset	monuisset	rēxisset
P. 1	amāvissēmus	monuissēmus	rēxissēmus
2	amāvissētis	monuissētis	rēxissētis
3	amāvissent	monuissent	rēxissent

Sometimes contracted forms are used, e.g. *amārit* for *amā(ve)rit*,
amāsset for *amā(vi)sset*.

	III (b)	IV	Sum
S. 1	cēpissem	audīvissem	fuissem
2	cēpissēs	audīvissēs	fuissēs
3	cēpisset	audīvisset	fuisset
P. 1	cēpissēmus	audīvissēmus	fuissēmus
2	cēpissētis	audīvissētis	fuissētis
3	cēpissent	audīvissent	fuissent

Perfect passive

	I	II	III (a)
S. 1	amātus sim	monitus sim	rēctus sim
2	amātus sīs	monitus sīs	rēctus sīs
3	amātus sit	monitus sit	rēctus sit
P. 1	amātī sīmus	monitī sīmus	rēctī sīmus
2	amātī sītis	monitī sītis	rēctī sītis
3	amātī sint	monitī sint	rēctī sint

	III (b)	IV
S. 1	captus sim	audītus sim
2	captus sīs	audītus sīs
3	captus sit	audītus sit
P. 1	captī sīmus	audītī sīmus
2	captī sītis	audītī sītis
3	capti sint	audītī sint

Pluperfect passive

	I	II	III (a)
S. 1	amātus essem	monitus essem	rēctus essem
2	amātus essēs	monitus essēs	rēctus essēs
3	amātus esset	monitus esset	rēctus esset
P. 1	amātī essēmus	monitī essēmus	rēctī essēmus
2	amātī essētis	monitī essētis	rēctī essētis
3	amātī essent	monitī essent	rēctī essent

	III (b)	IV
S. 1	captus essem	audītus essem
2	captus essēs	audītus essēs
3	captus esset	audītus esset
P. 1	captī essēmus	audītī essēmus
2	captī essētis	audītī essētis
3	captī essent	audītī essent

In the perfect subjunctive active the endings *-erim*, *-erīs*, etc., are added to the perfect stem (e.g. *amāv-*). Apart from the first person singular the perfect subjunctive looks like the future perfect and is often mistaken for it. But it is distinguished by the long *i* in *amāverīs*, *amāverīmus*, and *amāverītis*. This vowel is short in the same forms of the future perfect. In the pluperfect subjunctive active the endings *-issem*, *-issēs*, etc., are added to the perfect stem. This subjunctive resembles the perfect infinitive (e.g. *amāvisse*) followed by the usual personal endings (*-m*, *-s*, *-t*, etc.).

In the perfect and pluperfect subjunctive passive the perfect participle passive (e.g. *amātus*) is combined with *sim* and *essem* (the present and the imperfect subjunctive of *sum*), and the participles must be changed to indicate gender (e.g. *amātus*, *-a*, *-um*, and *amatī*, *-ae*, *-a*).

Sect. 100. Optative subjunctive (impossible wishes, present and past time)

The subjunctive, usually introduced by *utinam*, or *utinam nē*, may express impossible or unfulfilled wishes. The imperfect subjunctive expresses a wish referring to present time and the pluperfect subjunctive a wish referring to past time.

Utinam adessēs.
I wish you were here (now) (*sc.* but you are not here).
Utinam herī vēnissēs.
I wish you had come yesterday (*sc.* but you did not come).

Sect. 101. Subjunctive in result or consecutive clauses. Use of ut and ut nōn (ut nēmō)

A result or consecutive clause expresses the result of the action of the main verb. It is introduced by *ut* or *ut nōn*, followed in primary sequence by the present subjunctive and in secondary sequence by the imperfect subjunctive. (Sometimes the perfect subjunctive instead of the imperfect is used to show that the result is something completed.) The clause is usually preceded by some word like *ita*, 'in such a way', *tam*, 'so' (with an adjective or adverb), *tālis*, 'such', 'of such a character', *tantus*, 'so great'.

Purpose clauses stress an intention or motive and are sometimes preceded by *eō cōnsiliō*, 'with the intention (that)', but result clauses stress only the result of an action. Purpose clauses take *ut* or *nē* (*nē quis*); result clauses take *ut* or *ut nōn* (*ut nēmō*). The infinitive must not be used in a result clause, even though in English it is possible to say 'He is not so foolish as to do this'.

Nōn est tam stultus ut hoc faciat.
He is not so foolish as to do this.
Nōn fuit tam stultus ut hoc faceret.
He was not so foolish as to do this (that he should do it).
Tanta fuit mīlitum virtūs ut nēmō vāllum relinqueret.
So great was the courage of the soldiers that no one left the rampart.

Sect. 102. When faciō or efficiō are used to mean 'bring it about', they may be followed by a subjunctive clause introduced by ut or nē

Effēcit ut manērent.
He made them stay (brought it about that they stayed).

Sometimes the subjunctive is used without *ut*.

Fac domī maneās.
See that you stay at home, be sure to stay.

Here the two clauses (*fac* and *maneās*) are co-ordinate.

Sect. 103

After verbs of will like *rogō* and the impersonal verb *necesse est*, 'it is necessary', and the subjunctives of *volō*, *nōlō*, *mālō* (see Lesson XXXI), a subjunctive clause may be added without *ut*.

Hoc faciās necesse est.   You must do this.
Maneās velim.
I want you to stay (I should like you to stay).

The subjunctive without *ut* is common when the verb is in the second person singular.

Sect. 104

Impersonal verbs like *accidit*, 'it happens', 'it happened', *fierī potest*, 'it is possible (it can happen)', may have a noun clause as their subject. This is in the subjunctive and is introduced by *ut*.

Accidit ut domī manērēs.
It happened that you stayed at home.

Sect. 105. Nē with the perfect subjunctive (prohibitions)

A negative command may be expressed by *nē* with the perfect subjunctive. The alternative, *nōlī* with the infinitive, was described in Lesson XI.

Nē haec fēcerīs.   Do not do this.

This command is peremptory.

VOCABULARY

abeō, -īre, -iī, -itum, *irreg.,* go away.

accidit ut (*with subjve.*), it happened that, *from* **accidō,** 3, happen, occur.

aeternus, -a, -um, eternal, immortal.

anima, -ae, *f.,* soul.

augeō, -ēre, auxī, auctum, 2, increase.

celeritās, -ātis, *f.,* swiftness, speed.

commodē, *adv.,* properly, well; completely.

cōnstitūtus, -a, -um, appointed.

cūrō, 1, attend to, care for, take care that (**ut**).

efficiō, -ere, effēcī, effectum, 3, effect, accomplish, bring it about that (**ut**).

effugiō, -ere, effūgī, 3, escape.

exemplum, -ī, *n.,* example, precedent.

fac, *imperat. of* **faciō,** see that, bring it about that.

fōrmōsus, -a, -um, beautiful.

honōs (honor), -ōris, *m.,* honor, repute, public office.

incrēdibilis, -e, incredible, unbelievable.

inops, -opis, resourceless, needy, poor.

īrāscor, īrāscī, īrātus sum, 3, *deponent,* be angry; (*with dat.*) be angry with (Lesson XXXII).

Lucrētius, -ī, *m.,* T. Lucretius Carus, author of the *De Rerum Natura* on the philosophy of Epicurus, 99 (94)–55 B.C.

mātūrus, -a, -um, early, timely; *adv.* **mātūrē.**

necesse est, *impers.,* it is necessary, one must (*with subjve.*).

nisi, *after interrog. or neg. clause,* except, save, only.

paene, almost.

plācābilis, -e, easily appeased.

plācō, 1, appease, reconcile.

possem, -ēs, -et, . . . -ent, *imperf. subjve. of* **possum.**

potuissem, -ēs, -et, . . . -ent, *pluperf. subjve. of* **possum** (Lesson XXXI).

prōdō, -ere, prōdidī, prōditum, 3, betray; give forth, hand down.

recordor, -ārī, recordātus sum, 1, *deponent,* recollect, remember (Lesson XXXII).

saeculum, -ī, *n.,* generation, age, century.

Sōcratēs, -is, *m.,* famous Greek philosopher, 469–399 B.C., who appears in the works of Plato.

tam, so (*with adjs.*).

tamen, however, yet.

tenebrae, -brārum, *f. pl.,* darkness.

terror, -ōris, *m.* terror, fright.

tot, so many.

vigeō, -ēre, viguī, 2, be vigorous, flourish.

NOTES

1. **sēcēdō, -ere,** 3, withdraw.

2. **cervīx, -īcis,** *f.* (*usually pl.*), neck.

4. **commūtātiō, -ōnis,** *f.,* change.

    redintegrō, 1, renew.

5. **angustus, -a, -um,** narrow, contracted, difficult.

    contineō, -ēre, continuī, contentum, 2, keep together, enclose, check.

adigō, -igere, -ēgī, -āctum, 3, bring to; (of weapons) drive home, send to.

6. **pellō, -ere, pepulī, pulsum,** 3, drive, repel, banish.
   decurro, -ere, 3, run down.
7. **pācō,** 1, pacify, make peaceful.
   barbarus, -a, -um, foreign; a foreigner, native.
   perferō, -ferre, -tulī, -lātum, *irreg.*, carry through, announce, endure.
8. **suī,** *gen.*, of their own, belonging to them.
   dēperdō, -ere, 3, lose.
   auctiōrēs, *comp. of* **auctus,** increased, greater.
   velit, *pres. subjve. of* **volō** (Lesson XXXI).
9. **adeō,** so, to such an extent.
   sterilis, -e, barren; (*with gen.*) destitute of.
10. **loquēris,** you will say; Horace is addressing his book (*liber*).
   praecānus, -a, -um, grey before one's time.
   sōlēs, *pl. of* **sōl,** the heat of the sun (*poet.*).
   īrāscī, *inf. with* **celer,** quick to get angry.

11. **forum, -ī,** *n.*, forum, market-place.
   forō, used without a preposition, = in the forum.
12. Cicero is writing to Tiro, his secretary.
   convalēscō, -ere, convaluī, 3, recover, grow strong.
13. **recordārī,** *inf. used as a noun* = recollection.
15. **radius, -ī,** *m.*, ray (of the sun).
   lūcida tēla, bright shafts.
   discutiō, -ere, 3, scatter, dispel.
17. **quae portāret,** *subjve. in a relative clause of characteristic,* i.e. no ship of the kind which carried (Lesson XXX).
18. **ne . . . quidem,** not even.
19. **Vespasian** (*prīnceps* A.D. 69-79) and his sons, Titus (A.D. 79-81) and Domitian (A.D. 81-96), were the three Flavian emperors. Tacitus began his public career under Vespasian.
   incohō, 1, begin.
   prōvehō, -vehere, -vexī, -vectum, 3, carry forward, advance.
   abnuō, -ere, abnuī, 3, deny, refuse.
   nōn abnuerim, *perf. subjve.,* I would not deny.

EXERCISE 1

*1. Quod cupiō mēcum est; inopem mē cōpia fēcit.
   Ō utinam ā nostrō sēcēdere corpore possem!
2. Utinam populus Rōmānus ūnam cervīcem habēret!
3. Tot tibi tamque dabit fōrmōsās Rōma puellās,
   'Haec habet', ut dīcās, 'quicquid in orbe fuit'.
*4. Hōrum adventū tanta rērum commūtātiō est facta, ut nostrī . . . proelium redintegrārent.
*5. Cūius locī haec erat nātūra, atque ita montibus angustīs mare continēbātur, utī ex locīs superiōribus in lītus tēlum adigī posset.
*6. Hīs facile pulsīs . . . incrēdibilī celeritāte ad flūmen dēcucurrērunt, ut paene ūnō tempore et ad silvās et in flūmine et iam in manibus nostrīs hostēs vidērentur.
*7. Omnī Galliā pācātā tanta hūius bellī ad barbarōs opīniō perlāta est, utī ab eīs quī trāns Rhēnum incolerent mitterentur lēgātī.
8. (Dīxit) populī Rōmānī hanc esse cōnsuētūdinem, ut sociōs atque amīcōs nōn modo suī nihil dēperdere, sed gratiā, dignitāte, honōre auctiōrēs velit esse.
9. Nōn tamen adeō virtūtum sterile (fuit) saeculum, ut nōn et bona exempla prōdiderit.

*10. (. . . loquēris mē . . .)
corporis exiguī, praecānum, sōlibus aptum,
īrāscī celerem, tamen ut plācābilis essem.

*11. Iussus adesse forō, iussā mātūrius hōrā
fac semper veniās, nec nisi sērus abī.

12. Modo fac . . . nē quid aliud cūrēs hōc tempore nisi ut quam com-
modissimē convalēscās.

*13. Efficī vult Sōcratēs, ut discere nihil aliud sit nisi recordārī.

14. Quidquid est illud, quod sentit, quod sapit, quod vīvit, quod viget,
caeleste et dīvinum ob eamque rem aeternum sit necesse est.

15. Hunc igitur terrōrem animī tenebrāsque necesse est
nōn radiī sōlis neque lūcida tēla diēī
discutiant, sed nātūrae speciēs ratiōque.

16. Eādem nocte accidit ut esset lūna plēna.

*17. Ac sīc accidit utī ex tanto nāvium numerō . . . neque hōc neque
superiōre annō ūlla . . . nāvis, quae mīlitēs portāret, dēsīderārētur.

*18. Nē vōs quidem, iūdicēs, . . . mortem timuerītis.

19. Dignitātem nostram ā Vespasiānō incohātam, ā Titō auctam, ā
Domitiānō longius prōvectam nōn abnuerim.

EXERCISE 2

1. Narcissus said that he was poor on account of plenty. Would that he
had been able to escape from himself! 2. When Caesar sailed to Britain,
the cliffs (mountains) were so high that the Britons could easily throw
javelins onto the shore. 3. If you must be angry, Horace can advise you.
For it is better to be angry in such a way that you are easily-appeased.
4. In order to please a girl, see that you come earlier than the appointed
hour. 5. Do not fear death, (my) friend. If learning is recollection, the
soul must be immortal.

EXERCISE 3

ANSWER IN LATIN:

1. Quis apud Ovidium ā corpore sēcēdere voluit? 2. Quid dē populō
Rōmānō apud Suētōnium dīxit Caligula? 3. Quae urbs tot et tam
fōrmōsās habuit puellās? 4. Quid rērum commūtātiōne factā redinte-
grāvērunt Rōmānī? 5. Quō Gallī incrēdibilī celeritāte dēcucurrērunt?
6. Quid omnī Galliā pācātā fēcērunt Germānī? 7. Quōs hominēs honōre
auctiōrēs esse vult populus Rōmānus? 8. Quis fuit plācābilis? 9. Ubi
puella tē properāre iubet, quandō venīre dēbēs? 10. Quid Tīrōnem
aegrum cūrāre iubet Cicerō? 11. Quid aeternum sit necesse est? 12.
Quid efficī vult Sōcratēs? 13. Quid apud Lucrētium animī terrōrem
dēpellit? 14. Quid apud Platōnem iūdicibus dīxit Sōcratēs? 15. Quis
Tacitī dignitātem prōvexit?

Sect. 106. Direct questions

(*a*) DIRECT questions may be introduced by an interrogative word like *ubi*, 'where?', or *quis*, 'who?', and also by *-ne*, *nōnne*, and *num*.

The enclitic *-ne*, attached to the first word of a sentence, merely asks a question; *nōnne* expects the answer 'yes', and *num* expects the answer 'no'.

Nōnne haec fēcistī?　You did this, didn't you?
Num haec fēcistī?
You didn't do this, did you? (Surely you didn't do it?)

(*b*) Double direct questions are introduced by *utrum* or *-ne* followed by *an* or *annōn* (or, or not).

Utrum haec fēcistī annōn?　Did you do this or not?

Sect. 107. Indirect questions. Sequence of tenses

An indirect question is a noun clause depending on a verb of asking, telling, or knowing, or on a verb which suggests a question. It may be introduced by an interrogative word like *cūr*, 'why?', *quid*, 'what?', or *quandō*, 'when?' A single indirect question is usually introduced by *num*, 'whether', but here this does not imply an answer in the negative; a double question is introduced by *utrum* or *-ne* (whether) followed by *an* or *necne* (or, or not). *Necne* corresponds to *annōn*, which is used in a double direct question. Sometimes a single indirect question is introduced by *-ne* and occasionally by *nōnne* (after *quaerō*).

The verb of an indirect question is always in the subjunctive. It is present or perfect subjunctive after a primary tense in the main clause, and imperfect or pluperfect subjunctive after a secondary tense.

Sequence of tenses

	Indicative	Subjunctive
Primary sequence	Present Future Perfect (e.g. I have asked) Future Perfect	Present Perfect
Secondary sequence	Imperfect Perfect (e.g. I asked) Pluperfect	Imperfect Pluperfect

(*a*) In primary sequence the present subjunctive refers to action which takes place at the *same* time as that of the main verb.

Tē rogō { **quid faciās.**
{ **num haec faciās.**

I ask you { what you are doing.
{ whether you are doing this.

The perfect subjunctive refers to time *before* the action of the main verb.

Tē rogō { **quid herī fēcerīs.**
{ **num haec fēcerīs.**

I ask you { what you did yesterday.
{ whether you did this.

(*b*) In secondary sequence the imperfect subjunctive refers to action which took place at the *same* time as that of the main verb.

Tē rogāvī { **quid facerēs.**
{ **num haec facerēs.**

I asked you { what you were doing.
{ whether you were doing this (i.e. at the time when I asked the question).

The pluperfect subjunctive refers to time *before* the action of the main verb.

Tē rogāvī { **quid herī fēcissēs.**
{ **num haec fecissēs.**

I asked you { what you had done yesterday.
{ whether you had done this.

(*c*) When an indirect question refers to future time, i.e. *after* the action of the main verb, the future participle must be used in combination with the subjunctive of the verb *sum*. The present subjunctive *sim* is used in primary sequence.

Tē rogō quid crās factūrus sīs.
I ask you what you will do tomorrow.

The imperfect subjunctive *essem* is used in secondary sequence.

Tē rogāvī quid factūrūs essēs.
I asked you what you would do (were going to do).

In double indirect questions two subjunctives are used, or *necne* is substituted for the second.

Tē rogō {**utrum haec fēcerīs an factūrus sīs.**
{**utrum haec fēcerīs necne.**

I ask you {whether you have done this or are going to do it.
{whether you have done this or not.

Sometimes it is difficult to understand why a clause should be an indirect question in Latin when it does not seem to be a question in English. But if the English sentence contains any word like 'who?', 'what?', 'why?', 'when?', it is generally easy to see what the corresponding direct question would be. In *dīc mihi quid fēcerīs*, 'tell me what you did', the direct question would be *quid fēcistī?*, 'what did you do?' And when this is introduced by *dīc* and *quid*, the indicative *fēcistī* must be changed to the subjunctive *fēcerīs*. Though the imperative *dīc* is a verb of saying, it would not be followed by the accusative and infinitive unless it meant 'tell me that you did this', *dīc mihi tē hoc fēcisse*.

Often an indirect question in Latin is the best way of translating an abstract noun in English, such as nature or character.

Quāle et quantum sit perīculum nesciō.
I am ignorant of the nature and extent of the danger. (I do not know of what kind and how great the danger is.)

Sect. 108

Distinguish carefully between *num*, 'whether', and *sī*, 'if'. *Sī* is used in conditions (see Lesson XXXVI) and should not be used for *whether* in an indirect question. The same is true of *sīve* (*seu*), even though these words are often translated in English as *whether . . . or*.

An exception is found after verbs like *exspectō*, 'wait', and *cōnor*, 'try', where *si* means 'in the hope that'.

Sect. 109. Both direct and indirect questions are introduced by interrogative pronouns:

> **quis, quid,** who, what?; **quālis,** of what kind?; **quantus,** how great; **quot,** how many?

or by interrogative adverbs:

> **ubi,** where?; **unde,** whence?; **quō,** whither?; **quandō,** when?; **quotiēns,** how often?; **quōmodo,** how?; **cūr,** why?

VOCABULARY

an, or, *introduces second half of a double question.*

annōn, or not (*in direct questions*).

arbitror, -ārī, arbitrātus sum, 1, *deponent,* think, consider (Lesson XXXII).

aut, or; **aut . . . aut,** either . . . or.

avus, -ī, *m.,* grandfather.

candidus, -a, -um, white, dazzling white, beautiful.

centum, *numeral,* a hundred.

cōnsulō, -ere, cōnsuluī, cōnsultum, 3, consult; *with dat.,* consult the interests of.

cruciō, 1, torture, torment.

fluō, -ere, fluxī, fluxum, 3, flow.

forsitan (*with subjve.*), perhaps.

fortasse, perhaps.

ignōrō, 1, not to know, be ignorant of.

intereā, meanwhile.

iūdicō, 1, judge, pass judgment, decide.

iūstus, -a, -um, just, upright.

Lupercal, -ālis, *n.,* grotto on the Palatine Hill at Rome, sacred to Lycean Pan. His festival, the Lupercalia, was in February.

mercātor, -ōris, *m.,* merchant, trader.

mōtus, -ūs, *m.,* motion, movement.

nāscor, nāscī, nātus sum, 3, *deponent,* be born (Lesson XXXII).

nātiō, -ōnis, *f.,* clan, people.

-ne, *used instead of* **utrum,** whether.

nec (neque) . . . nec (neque), neither . . . nor.

necne, or not (*in indirect questions*).

nesciō, -īre, nescīvī (-iī), 4, not to know, to be ignorant.

nix, nivis, *f.,* snow.

nōnne, *introduces a question expecting the answer* yes.

nōtus, -a, -um, well-known.

num, *introduces a question expecting the answer* no.

num, whether (*in single indirect questions*).

ostendō, -ere, ostendī, ostentum, 3, show.

precor, -ārī, precātus sum, 1, *deponent,* pray, beg, request.

quaerō, -ere, quaesīvī (-iī), quaesītum, 3, seek, ask, inquire (*with ā and abl.*).

quam, how (*with adjs. and advs.*); as (*with* **tam,** so).

quotus, -a, -um, which in number, e.g. **quota hōra est?,** what time is it?

requīrō, -quīrere, -quīsīvī (-iī), -quīsītum, 3, ask, ask for, search for (*see* **quaerō**).

reservō, 1, keep back, retain.

signum, -ī, *n.,* sign, standard, statue, seal.

sīve . . . sīve (seu), whether (= if) . . . or.

sors, sortis, *f.,* lot, casting of lots, fate.

ter, three times.

undique, from all sides, everywhere.

uter, utra, utrum, *pron.,* which of two (Lesson XXIX).

utrum . . . an . . . (necne), whether . . . or . . . (or not) (*in double indirect questions*).

utrum . . . an . . . (annōn) (*in double direct questions*).

NOTES

1. **excrucio**, 1, torment greatly; *pass.*, be in agony.
3. **Varius, -ī**, *m.*, L. Varius, a tragic poet, contemporary with Vergil and Horace.
5. **Arar, -is**, *abl.* **Ararī**, *m.*, a river in Gaul, the Arar, now the Saône.
   influō, 3, flow into.
   lēnitās, -ātis, *f.*, gentleness (*here* = slowness).
   partem, *here* = direction.
7. **Hērō, -ūs**, *f.*, Hero of Sestos, who was loved by Leander of Abydos.
8. **praedor**, 1, *deponent*, plunder; **praedāta est** = has caught me.
10. **eat**, *3rd sing. pres. subjve. of* **eō**, to go (Lesson XXXI).
    quō with **cōnsule**, *abl. abs.*
    nec . . . require, *poet. use of imperat. in neg. command.* = **nē rogāverīs quō cōnsule nāta sit.**
11. **fuge quaerere** = **nōlī quaerere.**
12. **nefās**, *sc.* **est**, it is wrong.
    Leuconoē, -ēs, Greek name of a girl in Horace's *Odes*.
13. **ut**, how.
    Sōracte, a mountain in Etruria mentioned in Horace's *Odes*.
14. **diurna**, daily records (*sc.* **ācta**).
    cūrātius, *comp. of adv.* **cūrātē**, carefully.
    Thrasea, -ae, *m.*, Thrasea Paetus, Stoic philosopher put to death by Nero. His death occurs in the last surviving chapter of the *Annals* of Tacitus.
15. **quem nostrum**, which one of us? **quem ignōrāre**, *accus. and infin. after a verb of thinking* (*indirect statement*).
16. **cōnsīderō**, 1, consider, reflect.
17. **nōris** = **nōveris**, *fut. perf. of* **nōscō.**
    quam (how) *with* **curta.**
    curtus, -a, -um, broken, short (here of an ill-furnished mind).
    supellex, -ectilis, *f.*, furniture (here the furniture of the mind).
18. **sortibus cōnsultum (esse)**, *perf. inf. pass.* (*impers.*) *from* **cōnsulō**, consult = that lots were drawn to decide . . . .
    ignī, *abl.*, by fire.
    necārētur, *imp. subjve.*, was to be killed, not 'was killed'.
19. **genitālis, -e**, causing birth, generative.
    māteria, -ae, *f.*, matter, materials, timber.
    materiāī, *old form of gen. used by Lucretius.*
    resolvō, 3, unbind, loose.
    expediō, 4, *here* = explain, relate.
20. **tabella, -ae**, *f.*, writing-tablet; *pl.*, letter.
    Lentulus, -ī, *m.*, one of the conspirators supporting Catiline.
    -ne, whether.
    adnuō, 3, nod, give assent.
    imāgō, -inis, *f.*, image, picture.
    ūnicē, *adv.*, especially.

EXERCISE 1

*1. Ōdī et amō: quārē id faciam, fortasse requīris.
   Nescio, sed fierī sentiō et excrucior.

2. Nunc scio quid sit Amor.

3.   . . . Optimus ōlim
   Vergilius, post hunc Varius dīxēre quid essem.

*4. Centum sunt causae cūr ego semper amem.

*5. Flūmen est Arar quod . . . in Rhodanum īnfluit, incrēdibilī lēnitāte, ita ut oculīs, in utram partem fluat, iūdicārī nōn possit.

*6. Itaque vocātīs ad sē undique mercātōribus neque quanta esset īnsulae magnitūdō, neque quae aut quantae nātiōnēs incolerent . . . reperīre poterat.

7. Quid loquar intereā tam longō tempore, quaeris?
    Nīl nisi Lēandrī nōmen in ōre meō est.
8. Iusta precor: quae mē nūper praedāta puella est,
    aut amet aut faciat cūr ego semper amem.
9. Forsitan et quaerās, cūr sit locus ille Lupercal?
*10. Nec quotus annus eat, nec quō sit nāta, requīre,
    cōnsule . . .
11. Quid sit futūrum crās, fuge quaerere.
*12. Tū nē quaesierīs (scīre nefās) quem mihi, quem tibi
    fīnem dī dederint, Leuconoē . . .
13. Vidēs ut altā stet nive candidum
    Sōracte . . .
*14. Diurna populī Rōmānī per prōvinciās, per exercitūs cūrātius legun-
    tur, ut nōscātur quid Thrasea nōn fēcerit.
*15. Quid proximā, quid superiōre nocte ēgerīs, . . . quem nostrum
    ignōrāre arbitrāris?
16. Quibus ortus sīs, nōn quibuscum vīvās cōnsīderā.
17. Tēcum habitā: nōris quam sit tibi curta supellex.
*18. Is . . . dē sē ter sortibus cōnsultum dīcēbat utrum ignī statim
    necārētur an in aliud tempus reservārētur.
19. Nunc age, quō mōtū genitālia māteriāī
    corpora rēs variās gignant genitāsque resolvant, . . .
    expediam.
*20. Tum ostendī tabellās Lentulō et quaesīvī cognōsceret-ne signum.
    Adnuit. 'Est vērō', inquam, 'nōtum quidem signum, imāgō avī
    tuī, clārissimī virī, quī amāvit ūnicē patriam et cīvēs suōs.'

EXERCISE 2

1. Catullus does not know why he hates and loves, but says that he is
being tormented. 2. Before Caesar sailed to Britain, he asked many
merchants what-kind-of an island it was and what peoples they had seen.
3. Do not ask, Horace says to all (of) you, what you will do tomorrow, (and)
what fate the gods have given to you. 4. Cicero then asks Lentulus
whether he recognizes the seal or not. 5. This-man did not know whether
the Gauls wished to kill the soldiers immediately or would keep (them)
until another time.

EXERCISE 3

ANSWER IN LATIN:

1. Cūr excruciātur Catullus? 2. Quis Maecēnātī dīxit quālis esset
Horātius? 3. Quot causae sunt cūr semper amet poēta? 4. Quid dē
flūmine Ararī nōn potest iūdicārī? 5. Quid dē magnitūdine Britanniae
reperīre nōn poterat Caesar? 6. Dē quō semper loquitur Hērō? 7. Quid
fēminās rogāre dēbet nēmō? 8. Cūr populī Rōmānī diurna in prōvinciīs
leguntur? 9. Quid dē Catilīnā nēmō ignōrat? 10. Sī quis sēcum habitat,
quid dē sē discit? 11. Quid dē corporibus māteriae docet Lucrētius?

Part of the title of the Monumentum Ancyranum and the first three lines of the Latin text, which describes the events in the reign of the Emperor Augustus up to A.D. 14.

Rērum gestārum dīvī Aug[ustī, quibus orbem terrārum imperiō populī Rōm.] subiēcit, et inpēnsārum, quās [in rem pūblicam populumque Rōmānum fēcit, incīsārum] in duābus ahēneīs pīlīs, quae sunt Rōm[ae positae, exemplar subiectum.]

Annōs ūndēvīgintī nātus exercitum prīvātō cōnsiliō et prīvātā impēnsā comparāvī, per quem rem pūblicam domīnātiōne factiōnis oppressam in lībertātem vindicāvī. . . .

Vergil, *Aeneid* 6, 688–94, manuscript in capitals at St. Gall, No. 1394, fourth century

'Vīcit iter dūrum pietās? Datur ōra tuērī,
nāte, tua et nōtās audīre et reddere vōcēs?
Sīc equidem dūcēbam animō rēbarque futūrum,
tempora dīnumerāns, nec mē mea cūra fefellit.
Quās ego tē terrās et quanta per aequora vectum
accipiō! quantīs iactātum, nāte, perīclīs!
Quam metuī, nē quit (= quid) Libyae tibi rēgna nocērent!'

(Anchises is speaking to his son Aeneas, who is visiting him in the Lower World.)

LESSON XXIX

NUMERALS. DECLENSION OF NUMERALS
DECLENSION OF ADJECTIVES WITH GENITIVE IN *-īus*
(*tōtus, sōlus, ūllus, nūllus, alius, alter, uter, neuter, uterque*)
USES OF *alius, alter*. ACCUSATIVE OF EXTENT OF
SPACE AND DURATION OF TIME

Sect. 110. Numerals

MOST numerals are adjectives or adverbs.

(*a*) Cardinal numerals, e.g. *ūnus, duo, trēs*, one, two, three.

(*b*) Ordinal numerals, e.g. *prīmus, secundus, tertius*, first, second, third.

(*c*) Distributive numerals, e.g. *singulī, bīnī, ternī*, one each (at a time), two each, three each.

(*d*) Numeral adverbs, e.g. *semel, bis, ter*, once, twice, thrice.

Only the cardinal and ordinal numerals are listed here. It is not necessary to learn them all, but at least the common numbers (1–10, 20, 30, 50, 100, 200, 1,000, 2,000) should be learned, and the rest can be taken from the list when they are needed.

Most of the cardinal numerals are indeclinable, but *ūnus, duo, trēs, ducentī, -ae, -a*, and the other multiples of a hundred, and *mīlia*, the plural of *mīlle*, 'a thousand', are declined.

After *vīgintī*, 'twenty', the other multiples of ten from *trīgintā* to *nōnāgintā* all end in *-gintā*. The multiples of *centum*, 'a hundred', from *ducentī* to *nōngentī* all end in *-centī* or *-gentī*. *Ducentī, -ae, -a* and ordinal numerals like *prīmus, -a, -um* are all declined like *bonus*.

Sect. 111. Roman numerals

The following symbols are used for numerals:

I (= 1), V (= 5), X (= 10), L (= 50), C (= 100),
D (= 500), M (= 1,000).

If a smaller number comes before a larger one, it must be subtracted:

CM = 1,000 − 100, i.e. 900.   MCMLIV = 1954.

Sect. 112. Cardinals and ordinals

	Cardinals	Ordinals	Roman numerals
1	ūnus, -a, -um	prīmus, -a, -um	I
2	duo, duae, duo	secundus (alter)	II
3	trēs, tria	tertius	III
4	quattuor	quārtus	IIII, IV
5	quīnque	quīntus	V
6	sex	sextus	VI
7	septem	septimus	VII
8	octō	octāvus	VIII
9	novem	nōnus	VIIII, IX
10	decem	decimus	X
11	ūndecim	ūndecimus	XI
12	duodecim	duodecimus	XII
13	tredecim	tertius decimus	XIII
14	quattuordecim	quārtus decimus	XIIII, XIV
15	quīndecim	quīntus decimus	XV
16	sēdecim	sextus decimus	XVI
17	septendecim	septimus decimus	XVII
18	duodēvīgintī	duodēvīcēsimus	XVIII
19	ūndēvīgintī	ūndēvīcēsimus	XVIIII, XIX
20	vīgintī	vīcēsimus	XX
21	vīgintī ūnus / ūnus et vīgintī	vīcēsimus prīmus / ūnus et vicesimus	XXI
22	vīgintī duo / duo et vīgintī	vīcēsimus secundus / alter et vīcēsimus	XXII
30	trīgintā	trīcēsimus	XXX
40	quadrāgintā	quadrāgēsimus	XXXX, XL
50	quīnquāgintā	quīnquāgēsimus	L
60	sexāgintā	sexāgēsimus	LX
70	septuāgintā	septuāgēsimus	LXX
80	octōgintā	octōgēsimus	LXXX
90	nōnāgintā	nōnāgēsimus	LXXXX, XC
100	centum	centēsimus	C
200	ducentī, -ae, -a	ducentēsimus	CC
300	trecentī	trecentēsimus	CCC
400	quadringentī	quadringentēsimus	CCCC
500	quīngentī	quīngentēsimus	D
600	sescentī	sescentēsimus	DC

700	**septingentī**	**septingentēsimus**	DCC
800	**octingentī**	**octingentēsimus**	DCCC
900	**nōngentī**	**nōngentēsimus**	DCCCC, CM
1,000	**mīlle**	**mīllēsimus**	M
2,000	**duo mīlia**	**bis mīllēsimus**	MM

Duodēvīgintī and *ūndēvīgintī* are more common than *octōdecim*, *novendecim*. Either *vīgintī ūnus* or *ūnus et vīgintī* may be used. Ordinals ending in *-ēsimus* may also end in *-ēnsimus*, e.g. *vīcēsimus* or *vīcēnsimus*, 'twentieth'.

Sect. 113. Declension of numerals

| | **unus,** one | | | **duo,** two | | |
	M.	*F.*	*N.*	*M.*	*F.*	*N.*
Nom.	**ūnus**	**ūna**	**ūnum**	**duo**	**duae**	**duo**
Gen.	**ūnīus**	**ūnīus**	**ūnīus**	**duōrum**	**duārum**	**duōrum**
Dat.	**ūnī**	**ūnī**	**ūnī**	**duōbus**	**duābus**	**duōbus**
Acc.	**ūnum**	**ūnam**	**ūnum**	**duōs (duo)**	**duās**	**duo**
Abl.	**ūnō**	**ūnā**	**ūnō**	**duōbus**	**duābus**	**duōbus**

| | **tres,** three | | **mīlle,** a thousand |
	M. and F.	*N.*	(in the plural)
Nom.	**trēs**	**tria**	**mīlia**
Gen.	**trium**	**trium**	**mīlium**
Dat.	**tribus**	**tribus**	**mīlibus**
Acc.	**trēs (trīs)**	**tria**	**mīlia**
Abl.	**tribus**	**tribus**	**mīlibus**

Mīlle passūs, 'a thousand paces', is the Latin for 'a mile'. Here *mīlle* is an adjective, but the plural *mīlia* is a noun and is followed by the genitive *passuum*.

Duo mīlia passuum, two miles, *lit.* two thousands of paces.

Sect. 114

The following adjectives have a genitive ending in *-īus* and are declined like *ūnus*:

tōtus, -a, -um, whole   **alter, altera, alterum,** the other (of two)

sōlus, -a, um, alone   **uter, utra, utrum,** which (of two)

ūllus, -a, -um, any   **neuter, neutra, neutrum,** neither
nūllus, -a, -um, no, none   **uterque, utraque, utrumque,** both,
alius, alia, aliud, another   each (of two)

Uterque is used in apposition to a noun, but with the genitive of a pronoun.

Uterque cōnsul, each consul.
Uterque nostrum, each of us.

	M.	*F.*	*N.*	*M.*	*F.*	*N.*
Nom.	**alter**	**altera**	**alterum**	**alius**	**alia**	**aliud**
Gen.	**alterīus**	**alterīus**	**alterīus**	. .	. .	. .
Dat.	**alterī**	**alterī**	**alterī**	**aliī**	**aliī**	**aliī**
Acc.	**alterum**	**alteram**	**alterum**	**alium**	**aliam**	**aliud**
Abl.	**alterō**	**alterā**	**alterō**	**aliō**	**aliā**	**aliō**

The genitive *alterīus* is used instead of *alīus*. The plural of these adjectives is like the plural of *bonus*. The prepositions *ex* or *dē* with the ablative should be used with cardinal numerals instead of the partitive genitive, as was explained in Lesson XVI.

Sect. 115. Alius and alter

Alius means 'another' (of any number), but *alter* means 'the other of two', 'one of two', or 'second'.

Duōrum frātrum alter Rōmae, alter Athēnīs habitat.
One of the two brothers lives in Rome, the other in Athens.

When *alius* is repeated, it may be used in several ways.

Aliī Rōmae, aliī Athēnīs habitant.
Some live in Rome, others in Athens.
Aliud dīcunt, aliud faciunt.
They say one thing and do something else.
Aliī alia dīcunt. Some say one thing and some another (lit. others say other things, i.e. they all say different things).

Sect. 116. Dates

Dates are calculated from 753 B.C., the year when Rome is supposed to have been founded, and ordinal numbers are used.

Annō $\begin{cases} \textbf{ab urbe conditā} \\ \textbf{urbis conditae} \end{cases}$ **septingentēsimō** (=A.U.C.**DCC**).

In the 700th year after the foundation of the city.

Compare

Annō Dominī (A.D.)   } **millēsimō nōngentēsimō**
Annō Salūtis (A.S.)   } **quinquāgēsimō quartō**
Annō post Christum nātum } (= A.D. **MCMLIV).**
In the year of Our Lord 1954.

(*Post Christum nātum* = 'after the birth of Christ'. *Nātum* is from *nāscor*, 'I am born'. See Lesson XXXII.) For the Roman Calendar see Appendix I.

Sect. 117. Accusative of extent

The accusative is used to express both extent of space and duration of time.

Duo mīlia passuum prōcessit.
He advanced for two miles.
Quattuor annōs Athēnīs habitābat.
He lived at Athens for four years.

Abhinc is used with the accusative to show how long ago something occurred.

Abhinc quattuor annōs Athēnās vēnit.
He came to Athens four years ago.

VOCABULARY

ācer, ācris, ācre, keen, sharp.
adversus, -a, -um, opposite, unfavorable; **rēs adversae,** adversity.
alter, -era, -erum, the other (of two); **alter . . . alter,** the one . . . the other.
auctor, -ōris, *m.,* author, originator.
crīmen, -inis, *n.,* charge, accusation.
deinde, *adv.,* then, next.
dīvidō, -ere, dīvīsī, dīvīsum, 3, divide.
doctus, -a, -um, learned.
explōrātor, -ōris, *m.,* scout.
inferus, -a, -um, lower; **inferī,** *pl.,* the inhabitants of the lower world, the dead.
inūtilis, -e, useless.
libellus, -ī, *m., diminutive of* **liber,** book.
metuō, -ere, metuī, 3, fear.

mīlle, *numeral, indecl. in sing.,* thousand; *pl.* **milia,** thousands.
nūllus, -a, -um, no, none.
opēs, *pl. of* **(ops)**,*f.,* wealth, resources.
pāgus, -ī, *m.,* country district, canton.
parēns, -entis, *m. or f.,* parent.
passus, -ūs, *m.,* pace.
plēbs, -bis, *f.,* the common people.
prōpōnō, -pōnere, -posuī, -positum, 3, put forward, offer.
pugnātum est, *pass. impers.,* a battle was fought.
quīndecim, *numeral,* fifteen.
quīnque, *numeral,* five.
recēns, -entis, recent, new.
satura, -ae, *f.,* satire.
secundus, -a, -um, second, favorable; **rēs secundae,** prosperity, good fortune.
septimus, -a, -um, seventh.

temptō, 1, attempt, try.
tertius, -a, -um, third.
tōtus, -a, -um, whole.
turba, -ae, *f.*, crowd, throng.

uterque, utraque, utrumque, both,
each (of two).
vīgintī, *numeral,* twenty.

NOTES

1. **dīversus, -a, -um,** in different
directions, different.
2. These words which appear on
United States coins may have
been adapted from **ē plūribus
ūnus** in the *Moretum,* a minor
poem attributed to Vergil.
3. **anxius, -a, -um,** anxious (*here* =
anxiously).
pānis, -is, *m.,* bread.
circensēs, the games in the
Circus, *sc.* **lūdī,** games.
4. **omnis,** *here* = as a whole.
Belgae, Aquitānī, Celtae were
the three groups of people in
Gaul.
6. **circiter,** *adv.,* about.
7. **Ariovistus, -ī,** *m.,* Ariovistus,
leader of the Germans who
fought against Caesar in Gaul.
mīlibus, *abl. with* **abesse,** by the
extent of so many miles. *The
accus. of extent of space might
also be used.*
8. **infernī,** *here* = **inferī.**
9. **bāsium, -ī,** *n.,* kiss.
11. **ocellus, -ī,** *m., diminutive of*
oculus, eye.
12. **druidēs, -um,** *m.,* druids, the
priestly class in Gaul.
13. **sīc,** thus.

15. This refers to 43 B.C., the year
when Ovid was born.
16. **cursus, -ūs,** *m.,* running, course.
This refers to chariot races.
Here **uterque** (*sing.*) *is in apposition to the subject of* **spectēmus**
(*pl.*).
17. **ācriter,** *adv. of* **ācer,** keen.
utrīque, *pl.* = both sides.
18. Pliny is writing to the Emperor
Trajan about the Christians in
Bithynia; cf. Lessons XXXII
and XXXVIII.
superstitiō, -ōnis, f., superstition.
prāvus, -a, -um, bad, depraved.
immodicus, -a, -um, excessive.
Christiānī, -ōrum, *pl.,* Christians.
20. **infestus,** hostile (*here* = **adversus**); **infestīs . . . secundīs** =
**in rēbus infestīs, in rēbus
secundīs.**
praeparō, 1, prepare beforehand.
22. **quid,** why?
Maeonidēs = **Homērus, -ī,** *m.,*
Homer.
23. Here Trajan is writing to Pliny.
sine auctōre = anonymous.
libellus, *here* = accusation.
nec nostrī saeculī (*gen.*), and not
in accordance with the spirit of
our age.

EXERCISE 1

*1. Fēcistī patriam dīversīs gentibus ūnam.
2. Ē plūribus ūnum.
3. . . . Duās tantum rēs anxius optat,
pānem et circensēs.
*4. Gallia est omnis dīvīsa in partēs trēs, quārum ūnam incolunt Belgae,
aliam Aquitānī, tertiam quī ipsōrum linguā Celtae, nostrā Gallī
appellantur.
5. Omnis cīvitās Helvētia in quattuor pāgōs dīvīsa est.
*6. Castra movet diēbusque circiter quīndecim ad fīnēs Belgārum
pervēnit.
*7. Septimō diē . . . ab explōrātōribus certior factus est Ariovistī cōpiās
ā nostrīs mīlibus passuum quattuor et vīgintī abesse.

*8. Sunt apud īnfernōs tot mīlia fōrmōsārum.
  9. Dā mī bāsia mīlle, deinde centum.
10. Beneficium inopī bis dat, quī dat celeriter.
11. (a) Cynthia prīma suīs miserum mē cēpit ocellīs.
    (b) Cynthia prīma fuit, Cynthia fīnis erit.
12. Dē hīs duōbus generibus alterum est druidum, alterum equitum.
*13. Sīc Nemesis longum, sīc Dēlia nōmen habēbunt,
    altera cūra recēns, altera prīmus amor.
*14. Sunt tamen et doctae, rārissima turba, puellae,
    altera nōn doctae turba, sed esse volunt.
15. . . . cum cecidit fātō cōnsul uterque parī.
*16. Tū cursūs spectās, ego tē; spectēmus uterque
    quod iuvat . . .
17. Pugnātum est ab utrīsque ācriter.
18. Nihil aliud invēnī quam superstitiōnem prāvam, immodicam.
19. Aliī parentēs, aliī līberōs, aliī coniugēs vōcibus requīrēbant . . .
20. Spērat īnfestīs, metuit secundīs
    alteram sortem bene praeparātum
    pectus . . .
*21. Satura quidem tōta nostra est.
*22. Saepe pater dīxit 'Studium quid inūtile temptās?
    Maeonidēs nūllās ipse relīquit opēs.'
23. Sine auctōre vērō prōpositī libellī in nūllō crīmine locum habēre
    dēbent. Nam et pessimī exemplī nec nostrī saeculī est.

EXERCISE 2

1. America is one country, but it has been divided into forty-eight states.
2. In five hours our men marched for fifteen miles, until they were ten
miles away from the enemy's camp. 3. Tibullus wrote poems about two
women; one was called Delia, the other Nemesis. 4. The girl (looks at)
the chariots, the young man looks at his girl; let them both look at[1] what
they wish[1] to see. 5. Some hope for another lot in adversity, others fear
(it) in prosperity; those who are wise, as Horace says, do both.[2]

EXERCISE 3

ANSWER IN LATIN:

1. Quid ē dīversīs gentibus fēcit Rōma? 2. Quae patria ē plūribus ūna
facta est? 3. Quid apud Iuvenālem optat plēbs Rōmāna? 4. Quot partēs
habuit Gallia? 5. Quot diēbus ad fīnēs Belgārum pervēnit Caesar? 6.
Quot mīlibus passuum ā Rōmānīs aberant Germānī? 7. Quot fēminās
fōrmōsās apud īnferōs esse dīcit Propertius? 8. Quotiēns is dat quī dat
celeriter? 9. Quis Propertium oculīs suīs cēpit? 10. Quid fuit alterum
Gallōrum genus? 11. Utra puellārum turba carminibus laudārī dēbet?
12. Quālī fātō cecidit uterque cōnsul? 13. Quōmodo pugnāvērunt
utrīque? 14. Quid Christiānōrum fidem esse putāvit Plīnius? 15. Quid
dē saturā dīcit Quintiliānus? 16. Quid dē Homērō dīxit Ovidiī pater?
17. Quālēs libellī nec prīncipis Trāiānī nec nostrī saeculī sunt?

[1] 3rd person singular.   [2] Accusative neuter singular.

LESSON XXX

THE PRONOUNS *īdem, quis, quisquam, quīvīs, aliquis, quīdam, quisque*
USE OF *nēmō, nūllus,* AND *quisquam, ūllus*
CORRELATIVES: *tālis . . . quālis, tantus . . . quantus, tot . . . quot*
SUBJUNCTIVE IN RELATIVE CLAUSES OF CHARACTERISTIC

Sect. 118. The pronoun īdem

īdem, the same

	Singular			*Plural*	
M.	*F.*	*N.*	*M.*	*F.*	*N.*
Nom. **īdem**	**eadem**	**idem**	**eīdem**	**eaedem**	**eadem**
Gen. **ēiusdem**	**ēiusdem**	**ēiusdem**	**eōrundem**	**eārundem**	**eōrundem**
Dat. **eīdem**	**eīdem**	**eīdem**	**eīsdem**	**eīsdem**	**eīsdem**
Acc. **eundem**	**eandem**	**idem**	**eōsdem**	**eāsdem**	**eadem**
Abl. **eōdem**	**eādem**	**eōdem**	**eīsdem**	**eīsdem**	**eīsdem**

The *i* of *īdem* is long in the masculine and short in the neuter.
Īdem quī, īdem atque, or *īdem ac* means 'the same as'.

> **Īdem est quī anteā fuit.** He is the same *as* he was before.
> **Eōdem diē vēnērunt.** They came on the same day.
> **Vir benignus erat, īdem poēta clārissimus.**
> He was a kindly man and *also* a famous poet.

Sect. 119. Indefinite pronouns, quis, quisquam, quīvīs, aliquis, quīdam, quisque

Indefinite pronouns correspond either to 'any' or to 'some' in English.

1.	**quis,** anyone		**quī,** any		
Nom.	**quis**	**quid**	**quī**	**qua (quae)**	**quod**

The indefinite *quis* and *quī* are declined like the interrogative *quis* (who?) and *quī*, but *qua* is often used instead of *quae* (except in the nominative feminine plural).

Quis is generally used after *sī* (if), *nisi* (unless), *num* (whether), or *nē* (lest). This use has already been mentioned in Lesson XXVI on purpose clauses.

> **Rōmam vēnistī, nē quis tē vidēret.**
> You came to Rome, in order that no one (lest anyone) might see you.

Num (whether) was mentioned in Lesson XXVIII on indirect questions.

Rogāvī num quis tē vīdisset.
I asked whether anyone had seen you.

2 (*a*). **quisquam,** any at all; *adjective* **ūllus, -a, -um**
Nom.   **quisquam   quidquam (quicquam)**   No plural

Quisquam and *ūllus* are used after a negative (*nec*, 'and not') or a virtual negative (*vix*, 'scarcely'), or in a question, or in comparisons (e.g. better than anyone).

Note that *nec quisquam* must be used for 'and no one', instead of *et nēmō*. Since the ablative of *quisquam* is very rare, the ablative of *ūllus* may be used instead of *quōquam*.

2 (*b*). **nēmō,** no one; *adjective* **nūllus, -a, -um**

Nom.	**nēmō**
Gen.	. .
Dat.	**nēminī**
Acc.	**nēminem**
Abl.	. .

In the genitive and ablative *nūllus* must be used instead of *nēmō*.

Nēmō tē vīdit.   No one saw you.
A nūllō vīsus es.   You were seen by no one.

But compare

Negat quemquam tē vīdisse.   He says that no one saw you (he denies that anyone saw you).

3.   **quīvīs** or **quīlibet,** anyone you like
   quīvīs quaevis quidvis; *adj.*, **quīvis quaevis quodvis**

These are used in affirmative sentences, e.g. Send anyone you like.

4 (*a*).   **aliquis,** someone   *adjective* **aliquī**
Nom.   **aliquis   aliquid   aliquī   aliqua   aliquod**

They are declined like *quis* (anyone) and *quī*.

Dīxerit aliquis.   Someone will say (will have said).

4 (*b*).   **nōnnūllī,** some few
     nōn nūllī (the plural of *nūllus*)

5 (*a*).   **quīdam,** a certain one (pronoun or adjective)

Singular

	M.	F.	N.
Nom.	quīdam	quaedam	quiddam
			quoddam, *adj.*
Gen.	cūiusdam	cūiusdam	cūiusdam
Dat.	cuidam	cuidam	cuidam
Acc.	quendam	quandam	quiddam
Abl.	quōdam	quādam	quōdam

Plural

	M.	F.	N.
Nom.	quīdam	quaedam	quaedam
Gen.	quōrundam	quārundam	quōrundam
Dat.	quibusdam	quibusdam	quibusdam
Acc.	quōsdam	quāsdam	quaedam
Abl.	quibusdam	quibusdam	quibusdam

Quōdam tempore, at a certain time; **dux quīdam,** a certain general; **quīdam ex mīlitibus,** certain of the soldiers.

5 (*b*).   **nescio quis,** somebody or other (lit. I don't know who);
adjective, **nescio quī**

6.   **quisque,** each one

Nom.   **quisque quaeque quidque;**
adj.,   **quisque quaeque quodque**

Quisque is frequently used after the adjective *suus*.

Suum quisque dōnum capiat.
Let each man take his own gift.

It is nearly always used in the singular, but it may be used in apposition to a plural subject, e.g. 'they all went away, each one with his own gift'.

Quisque is also used with a superlative adjective, nearly always in the singular, and means *all*.

Optimus quisque.   All the best men (each best man).

Sect. 120. Correlatives

A relative pronoun like *quālis* corresponds to the demonstrative *tālis*, of such a kind, and is frequently translated by the English 'as'.

Tālis es quālis anteā fuistī.

You are the same kind of man as you were before (your
character is such as it always was).

In the same way *quantus* corresponds to *tantus*, 'so great', and *quot*
and *quotiēns* correspond to *tot*, 'so many', and *totiēns*, 'so often'.

The equivalent interrogatives are *quālis?*, 'of what kind?';
quantus?, 'how great?'; *quot?*, 'how many?'; *quotiēns?*, 'how often?'

Tot sunt sententiae quot sunt hominēs.

There are as many opinions as there are men.

This is expressed briefly as follows:

Quot hominēs, tot sententiae.

Sect. 121. Subjunctive in relative clauses of characteristic (consecutive quī-clauses)

A relative clause may be used to describe the sort of person a
man is. Here the verb is in the subjunctive, and the antecedent of
quī is a demonstrative, usually *is*.

Is est quī haec faciat.

He is the sort of man to do this (who would do this).

But the indicative must be used if the relative states a fact.

Is est quī haec fēcit.　He is the man who did this.

Here *is* means the actual man who did it, not the sort of man who
might do it. One common mistake is to assume that all relative
clauses are clauses of characteristic, but most of them state facts
and have their verb in the indicative.

The subjunctive is frequently used after:

nēmō est quī,　there is no one who
quis est quī?,　who is there who?
sunt quī,　there are some who
dignus est quī,　he deserves to (he is worthy who).

Nēmō est quī haec faciat.

There is no one who would do this.

Dignus est quī amētur.　He deserves to be loved.

The reason for this is that the subjunctive incorporates the ideas
of (1) natural likelihood, or (2) ideal certainty, as well as (3) will,
intent, and (4) command.

VOCABULARY

adeō, -īre, -iī, -itum, *irreg.,* go to, approach.

āiō, *def., 3 sing.* **ait,** say.

aliquis, aliquid, *pron.,* someone; *adj.,* **aliquī, aliqua, aliquod.**

ante, *adv.,* before.

atomus, -ī, ƒ., atom (= indivisible).

auris, -is, -ium, ƒ., ear.

cēnseō, -ēre, cēnsuī, cēnsum, 2, think, propose.

Cinara, -ae, ƒ., Cinara, a lady mentioned by Horace who seems to have been a real person.

contingō, -ere, contigī, 3, happen; **contingit,** *impers.,* it happens.

Corinthus, -ī, ƒ., Corinth.

decet, *impers.,* it befits, it suits.

Dēmocritus, -ī, m., Democritus, the Greek philosopher who introduced the atomic theory of Leucippus, *c.* 460–*c.* 370 B.C.

ēligō, -ere, ēlēgī, ēlēctum, 3, choose.

Epicūrus, -ī, m., Greek philosopher, founder of the Epicurean philosophy based on the theory of atoms 342/1–271/70 B.C.

Epicūrēus, -a, -um, Epicurean; **Epicūrēī,** Epicureans, followers of the Epicurean philosophy.

ēveniō, -īre, ēvēnī, ēventum, 4, happen, turn out.

exstinguō, -ere, exstīnxī, exstīnctum, 3, extinguish, wipe out.

fēlīcitās, -ātis, ƒ., good luck, happiness.

hūmānus, -a, -um, human, humane.

mānēs, -ium, *m. pl.,* departed spirits.

morior, morī, *fut. part.* **moritūrus,** 3, *deponent,* die (Lesson XXXII).

mortuus, -a, -um, dead, dead man.

neglegō, -ere, neglēxī, neglēctum, 3, neglect.

nescio quis, nescio quid, *pron.,* someone (I don't know who).

occidō, -ere, occidī, occāsum, 3, *compound of* **cadō,** sink (of the sun), perish.

omittō, -ere, omīsī, omissum, 3, omit, lay aside, say nothing of.

quālis, -e, as (*after* **tālis,** such).

queror, querī, questus sum, 3, *deponent,* complain (Lesson XXXII).

quisque, quaeque, quidque, *pron.,* each; *adj.,* **quisque, quaeque, quodque.**

quīvīs, quaevīs, quidvīs, *pron.,* anyone you like; *adj.,* **quīvīs, quaevīs, quodvīs.**

quot, as (*after* **tot,** so many).

rārus, -a, -um, rare, scarce.

rotundus, -a, -um, round.

Stoicus, -a, -um, Stoic; **Stoicī,** the Stoics, followers of the Stoic philosophy.

tālis, -e, such, of such a character.

umquam, *adv.,* ever.

ūnā, *adv.,* together.

usquam, *adv.,* anywhere.

ūtilis, -e, useful.

NOTES

2. **lētum, -ī,** *n.,* death.
  fīniō, 4, put an end to, limit.
3. **restō,** 1, stand firm, remain.
  Ēlysius, -a, -um, refers to **Ēlysium, -ī,** *n.,* Elysium, the home of the blest.
5. Sallust is quoting a saying of Appius.
  faber, -rī, *m.,* smith, artisan; *here* = maker.
6. **ornātus, -ūs,** *m.,* adornment, ornament, dress (*here* = head-dress).

quaeque, each woman, is the subject of **ēligat.**
  speculum, -ī, *n.,* mirror.
7. **impūne,** *adv.,* with impunity.
  lacessō, -ere, lacessīvī, lacessītum, 3, provoke.
8–9. Socrates is speaking; the story is told in Plato's *Apology.*
  vītam agō, live.
10. **cui,** i.e. Socrates.
  assēnsī sunt, *perf. of* **assentior,** 4, *deponent,* agree with.

esset, *subjve. in a subordinate clause in indirect statement* (Lesson XXXI).

12. **sum**; the poet Horace is speaking. **sub rēgnō,** *i.e.* when Cinara ruled my heart. **Cinara**; this name is used in a poem by Ernest Dowson, though it appears there as Cynara.

15. **proprius,** one's own; **proprium est,** it is characteristic of (*with gen.*). **laeserīs,** *perf. subjve., 2nd pers.* = you have hurt, one has hurt.

16. **absurdē,** *adv.,* absurdly.

17. **rārā fēlīcitāte,** *abl.,* in the rare happiness (good fortune). **velīs,** *pres. subjve. of* **volō,** *subjve. in clause of characteristic.*

18. **discessus, -ūs,** *m.,* departure. **animus,** *here used like* **anima,** soul. **dissipō,** 1, scatter, disperse.

permaneō, 2, remain, last, persist.

19. **corpusculum, -ī,** *n., diminutive of* **corpus,** a little body. **concursus, -ūs,** *m.,* running together, meeting. **fortuitus, -a, -um,** accidental.

20. **praeter ... ,** *i.e.* **praeter murmur aquae corpore dīmōtae.** **dīmōtus,** *from* **dimoveō,** part, divide. **corpore,** refers to Leander. **murmur, -uris,** *n.,* murmur, sound. **Alcyonē,** the wife of Ceyx, who threw herself into the sea and was changed into a halcyon or kingfisher. **alcyonēs,** the halcyons. **memor, -oris,** mindful of (*with gen.*). **Cēyx, -ȳcis,** *m.,* Ceyx, who suffered shipwreck and was changed into a kingfisher.

Exercise 1

1. ... Rēx Iuppiter omnibus īdem;
   fāta viam invenient.

2. Sunt aliquid Mānēs; lētum nōn omnia fīnit.

*3. Sī tamen ē nōbīs aliquid nisi nōmen et umbra
   restat, in Ēlysiā valle Tibullus erit.

*4. Nōn cuivīs hominī contingit adīre Corinthum.

*5. Sed rēs docuit id vērum esse, quod in carminibus Appius ait, fabrum
   esse suae quemque fortūnae.

6. Nec genus ornatūs ūnum est; quod quamque decēbit
   ēligat, et speculum cōnsulat ante suum.

7. Nēmō mē impūne lacessit.

*8. 'Sed tempus est', inquit, 'iam hinc abīre, mē, ut moriar, vōs, ut
   vītam agātis. Utrum autem sit melius, dī immortālēs sciunt,
   hominem quidem scīre arbitror nēminem.'

*9. Nec enim cuiquam bonō malī quicquam ēvenīre potest nec vīvō nec
   mortuō, nec umquam eius rēs ā dīs immortālibus neglegentur.

*10. Cui quidem ita sunt Stoicī assēnsī, ut et quicquid honestum esset, id
    ūtile esse cēnsērent, nec ūtile quicquam quod nōn honestum.

*11. Quot caelum stellās, tot habet tua Rōma puellās.

12. Nōn sum quālis eram bonae
    sub rēgnō Cinarae.

13. Sunt quibus in saturā videar nimis ācer.

14. Erant quī metū mortis mortem precārentur.

15. Proprium hūmānī ingeniī est ōdisse quem laeserīs.

16. Nihil tam absurdē dīcī potest, quod nōn dīcātur ab aliquō philo-
sophōrum.

*17. . . . Rārā temporum fēlīcitāte ubi sentīre quae velīs et quae sentiās
dīcere licet.

*18. Sunt enim quī discessum animī a corpore putent esse mortem; sunt
quī nūllum cēnseant fierī discessum, sed ūnā animum et corpus
occidere animumque in corpore exstinguī. Quī discēdere animum
cēnsent, aliī statim dissipārī, aliī diū permanēre, aliī semper.

19. Dēmocritum . . . levibus et rotundīs corpusculīs efficientem animum
concursū quōdam fortuitō, omittāmus; nihil est enim apud istōs,
quod nōn atomōrum turba cōnficiat.

*20. Nūllaque vōx usquam, nūllum veniēbat ad aurēs
praeter dīmōtae corpore murmur aquae.
Alcyonēs sōlae, memorēs Cēȳcis amātī
nescio quid vīsae sunt mihi dulce querī.

EXERCISE 2

1. He always says the same things; although he tells us something good,[1]
he is not the kind (of man) that[2] he seems to be. 2. If Appius speaks the
truth, each (man) makes his own fortune. 3. Neither Socrates nor the
Stoics believe that anything is expedient (useful) which is not honorable.
4. No one is happy in any state who is not allowed to think what he likes
and say what he thinks. 5. There are (some) who believe that the soul
goes away from the body after death; some think it lasts for a long time,
others (think) it is immortal.

EXERCISE 3

ANSWER IN LATIN:

1. Quis omnibus īdem est? 2. Quid dē Mānibus dīcit Propertius? 3.
Quō nōn adit quīvīs homo? 4. Quis est suae fortūnae faber? 5. Quis
speculum suum cōnsulere dēbet? 6. Quis scit utrum morī melius sit an
vīvere? 7. Quis nōn crēdit virō bonō malī quicquam ēvenīre posse?
8. Quī hominēs cēnsēbant, quicquid honestum esset, id esse ūtile? 9.
Quae urbs tot puellās habuit, quot caelum stellās? 10. Quis tālis nōn
fuit, quālis Cinārā vīvente fuerat? 11. Quālis nōnnūllīs vidētur Horātius?
12. Quid ob metum mortis aliquī precābantur? 13. Quālem hominem
hūmānī ingeniī est ōdisse? 14. Quid est quod apud Dēmocritum et
Epicūrum atomōrum turba nōn faciat? 15. Quid Lēandrō querentēs
dīcere vīsae sunt Alcyonēs?

[1] Partitive genitive. [2] Such . . . as.

LESSON XXXI

CONJUGATION OF THE IRREGULAR VERBS
eō, fīō, ferō, meminī, INDICATIVE AND SUBJUNCTIVE.
SUBJUNCTIVE OF *possum, volō, nōlō, mālō*. SUBJUNCTIVE IN
SUBORDINATE CLAUSES IN INDIRECT STATEMENT

Sect. 122. Conjugation of eō, fīō, ferō, meminī

1. eō, go, īre, iī (īvī), itum

Indicative

	Present	Imperfect	Future	Perfect	Pluperfect	Future perfect
S. 1	eō	ībam	ībō	iī (īvī)	ieram	ierō
2	is	ībās	ībis		(īveram)	(īverō)
3	it	ībat	ībit			
P. 1	īmus	ībāmus	ībimus		*Imperative*	
2	ītis	ībātis	ībitis	S. 2 ī	P. 2 īte	
3	eunt	ībant	ībunt			

Subjunctive

	Present	Imperfect	Perfect	Pluperfect
S. 1	eam	īrem	ierim	īssem
2	eās	īrēs	(īverim)	(īvissem)
3	eat	īret		
P. 1	eāmus	īrēmus		
2	eātis	īrētis		
3	eant	īrent		

Infinitive
Pres. **īre**
Perf. **īsse (īvisse)**
Fut. **itūrus esse**

Participles
Pres. **iēns**
Gen. **euntis**
Fut. **itūrus**
Gerundive **eundum**

2. fīō, become, fierī, factus sum (the passive of facīō, I make)

Indicative

	Present	Imperfect	Future	Perfect	Pluperfect	Future perfect
S. 1	fīō	fīēbam	fīam	factus sum	factus eram	factus erō
2	fīs	fīēbās	fīēs			
3	fit	fīēbat	fīet		*Imperative (rare)*	
P. 1	..	fīēbāmus	fīēmus			
2	..	fīēbātis	fīētis		*Infinitive*	
3	fīunt	fīēbant	fīent		Pres. **fierī**	

Perf. **factus esse**
Fut. **factum īrī**

Subjunctive

	Present	Imperfect	Perfect	Pluperfect
S. 1	fīam	fierem	factus sim	factus essem
2	fīās	fierēs		
3	fīat	fieret		
P. 1	fīāmus	fierēmus		
2	fīātis	fierētis		
3	fīant	fierent		

Participle
Perf. **factus**
Gerundive **faciendus**

The *i* of *fīō* is long, but it is short before *-er* in *fierī, fierem.*

3. ferō, bear, ferre, tulī, lātum

Indicative

Act. Present	Imperfect	Future	Perfect	Pluperfect	Future perfect
S. 1 ferō	ferēbam	feram	tulī	tuleram	tulerō
2 fers	ferēbās	ferēs			
3 fert	ferēbat	feret			
P. 1 ferimus	ferēbāmus	ferēmus			
2 fertis	ferēbātis	ferētis			
3 ferunt	ferēbant	ferent			

Pass. Present	Imperfect	Future	Perfect	Pluperf.	Fut. perf.
S. 1 feror	ferēbar	ferar	lātus sum	lātus	lātus
2 ferris (-re)	ferēbāris (-re)	ferēris (-re)		eram	erō
3 fertur	ferēbātur	ferētur			
P. 1 ferimur	ferēbāmur	ferēmur			
2 feriminī	ferēbāminī	ferēminī			
3 feruntur	ferēbantur	ferentur			

Imperative

	S. 2	P. 2
Act.	fer	ferte
Pass.	ferre	feriminī

Subjunctive

	Present	Imperfect	Perfect	Pluperfect
Act.	feram	ferrem	tulerim	tulissem
Pass.	ferar	ferrer	lātus sim	lātus essem

Participles

	Present	Perfect	Future
Act.	ferēns	..	lātūrus
Pass.	..	lātus	ferendus (Gerundive)

Infinitive

Active
Pres.   ferre
Perf.   tulisse
Fut.   lātūrus esse

Passive
Pres.   ferrī
Perf.   lātus esse
Fut.   lātum īrī

4. meminī, remember

This verb has no present tense, but the perfect has the meaning of the present.

Indicative			Subjunctive	
Perfect	Pluperfect	Fut. Perf.	Perfect	Pluperfect
meminī	memineram	meminerō	meminerim	meminissem

Imperative		Infinitive
mementō	mementōte	meminisse

Compare ōdī, 'I hate'.

Sect. 123. Subjunctive of possum, volō, nōlō, mālō

	possum,	volō,	nōlō,	mālō,
Pres.	am able	wish	am unwilling	prefer
S. 1.	possim	velim	nōlim	mālim
2.	possīs	velīs	nōlīs	mālīs
3.	possit	velit	nōlit	mālit

P. 1	possīmus	velīmus	nōlīmus	mālīmus
2	possītis	velītis	nōlītis	mālītis
3	possint	velint	nōlint	mālint
Imp.				
S. 1	possem	vellem	nōllem	māllem
2	possēs	vellēs	nōllēs	māllēs
3	posset	vellet	nōllet	māllet
P. 1	possēmus	vellēmus	nōllēmus	māllēmus
2	possētis	vellētis	nōllētis	māllētis
3	possent	vellent	nōllent	māllent
Perf.	potuerim	voluerim	nōluerim	māluerim
Plupf.	potuissem	voluissem	nōluissem	māluissem

Sect. 124. Subjunctive in subordinate clauses in indirect statement

The main clause in an indirect statement is in the accusative and infinitive (see Lesson XXIV). The verb in all subordinate clauses must be in the subjunctive, even though it would not have been in the subjunctive in direct statement. Thus the subjunctive is used even in a relative clause. (An exception is found when a statement is added by the writer which is not part of the reported speech, but as a general rule all the dependent verbs are in the subjunctive.)

Direct statement:

> **Gallī cum Germānīs, quī trāns Rhēnum incolunt, bellum gerunt.**

> The Gauls wage war against (lit. with) the Germans who live across the Rhine.

Indirect statement:

> (*a*) **Dīcit Gallōs cum Germānīs, quī trāns Rhēnum incolant, bellum gerere.**

> He says that the Gauls wage war with the Germans who live across the Rhine.

> (*b*) **Dīxit Gallōs cum Germānīs, quī trāns Rhēnum incolerent, bellum gerere.**

> He said that the Gauls waged war with the Germans who lived across the Rhine.

Here *incolant* is present subjunctive after *dīcit*, and *incolerent* is imperfect subjunctive after *dīxit*.

Vocabulary

admīror, -ārī, admīrātus sum, 1, *deponent,* marvel at, wonder at (*here* = to be brought by anything into a state of desire or longing).

arduus, -a, -um, steep, difficult.

arx, arcis, *f.,* citadel.

aureus, -a, -um, golden.

aurum, -ī, *n.,* gold.

blandus, -a, -um, pleasant, charming.

breviter, *adv.,* briefly.

commeātus, -ūs, *m.,* provisions, supplies (*sing. and pl.*).

culpa, -ae, *f.,* fault.

cupīdō, -inis, *m.,* desire; *also* Cupid, son of Venus.

dēmēns, -entis, mad.

dēsistō, -ere, destitī, 3, cease.

dīligēns, -entis, diligent, careful; *adv.,* **dīligenter.**

dulcēdō, -inis, *f.,* sweetness, charm.

ergō, therefore.

excēdō, -ere, excessī, excessum, 3, go out, go away.

fallō, -ere, fefellī, falsum, 3, deceive, escape the notice of.

ferreus, -a, -um, made of iron, hard-hearted.

haud, not.

inter sē, among themselves, together.

mītis, -e, gentle, mild.

nitidus, -a, -um, shining.

perferō, -ferre, -tulī, -lātum, *irreg.,* carry through, announce, endure.

pōmum, -ī, *n.,* fruit, apple.

praetereō, -īre, -iī, -itum, *irreg.,* go past, pass by, pass away.

prōferō, -ferre, -tulī, -lātum, *irreg.,* bring forth, bring to light, invent.

prūdentia, -ae, *f.,* knowledge, intelligence, prudence, discretion.

quia, because.

referō, -ferre, rettulī, relātum, *irreg.,* bring back, report.

salūtem, *acc. of* **salūs,** *used at the beginning of a letter,* (sends) greetings (to).

S. = Salūtem, S.D. = Salūtem dīcit, S.P.D. (*or* **S.D.P.**) **= Salūtem plūrimam dīcit.**

satis, enough.

strepō, -ere, strepuī, 3, make a noise.

taceō, -ēre, tacuī, tacitum, 2, be silent.

valetūdō, -inis, *f.,* health, good or bad health.

vēlōx, -ōcis, swift.

virgō, -inis, *f.,* maiden.

Notes

1. Cicero is speaking of Catiline.
   ēvādō, -ere, ēvāsī, ēvāsum, 3, go out, escape, turn out.
   ērumpō, -ere, ērūpī, ēruptum, 3, break out, burst forth.

2. **diffugiō, -ere, diffūgī,** 3, flee (in different directions), scatter.
   grāmen, -inis, *n.,* grass.
   coma, -ae, *f.,* hair, foliage (*poet.*).

3. This refers to Hannibal.
   dēclāmātiō, -ōnis, *f.,* declamation, exercise in speaking.

4. **Graeculus, -a, -um,** *diminutive of* **Graecus,** Greekling.
   ēsuriō, -īre, be hungry.
   Compare 'All sciences a fasting Monsieur knows' (Johnson).
   mīseris, *fut. perf., equivalent to* **sī mīseris,** if you send.

5. **ēgelidus, -a, -um,** warm, balmy (*opposite of* **gelidus,** cold).
   tepor, -ōris, *m.,* warmth.

6. **horrendus, -a, -um,** dreadful, horrible.
   ēnsis, -is, *m.,* sword.
   vērē, *adv.,* truly.

7. **cōmis, -e,** affable, kind, friendly.
   obdūrō, 1, endure, hold out.
   postmodo, *poet. for* **posteā,** afterwards.

8. **labōrō,** 1 (*with infin.*), strive to.
   obscūrus, -a, -um, obscure.

9. **utī = ut,** like.
   chelīdōn, -onis, *f.,* swallow.

10. **mementō,** *imperat. of* **meminī** (*with infin.*), remember to.
   arduus, *here used like* **adversus.**

11. **Oebalius, -a, -um,** Oebalian, *i.e.*
    Spartan.
    Cōrycius, -a, -um, Corycian,
    from Cilicia.
12. **dolus, -ī,** *m.*, deceit, guile.
    possit, *pres. subj.*, would be able,
    could.
    praesentiō, -īre, 4, feel, perceive
    beforehand.
13. **Numīcī,** *voc. of* **Numīcius.**
    The object of **facere** *is* 'a man'.
14. **Rēmī,** a tribe in Gaul.
15. **obstipēscō (obstupēscō) -ere,**
    obstipui, 3, be amazed.
    dēclīnat cursūs, turns-aside-
    from her course.

volūbilis, -e, rolling, turning.
Hippomenēs, -ae, *m.*, the youth
who raced against Atalanta.
17. **Terentia, -ae,** *f.*, the wife of
Cicero.
18. **quod,** that, the fact that.
19. **manet,** it is established that,
regarded as settled that.
20. Birds cannot foretell the weather,
but are naturally sensitive to
any change in the atmosphere.
strepitō, 1, make a noise (*poet.*) =
strepō; *perhaps* chatter.
strepitant, *i.e.* **corvī,** rooks.
crēdō, *sc.* **eōs strepitāre.**
dīvīnitus, *adv.*, by divine power.

EXERCISE 1

1. Abiit, excessit, ēvāsit, ērūpit.
*2. Diffūgēre nivēs, redeunt iam grāmina campīs
      arboribusque comae.
*3. ... Ī dēmēns et saevās curre per Alpēs,
      ut puerīs placeās et dēclāmātiō fīās.
*4. ... Omnia nōvit
      Graeculus ēsuriēns; in caelum mīseris, ībit.
5. Iam vēr ēgelidōs refert tepōrēs.
6. Quis fuit horrendōs prīmus quī prōtulit ēnsēs?
   quam ferus et vērē ferreus ille fuit!
*7. Sī nec blanda satis nec erit tibi cōmis amantī,
      perfer et obdūrā; postmodo mītis erit.
8. ... Brevis esse labōrō,
   obscūrus fīō.
*9. Illa cantat, nōs tacēmus; quando vēr venit meum?
     Quando fīam utī chelīdōn, ut tacēre dēsinam?
*10. Aequam mementō rēbus in arduīs
      servāre mentem.
11. Namque sub Oebaliae meminī mē turribus arcis
    Cōrycium vīdisse senem.
12. At rēgīna dolōs (quis fallere possit amantem?)
    praesēnsit.
*13. Nīl admīrārī prope rēs est ūna, Numīcī,
      sōlaque quae possit facere et servāre beātum.
14. Commeātus ab Rēmīs ... ut sine perīculō ad eum portārī posset
    efficiēbat.
15. Obstipuit virgō nitidīque cupīdine pōmī
    dēclīnat cursūs aurumque volūbile tollit.
    Praeterit Hippomenēs.

*16. Sed nōn culpa mea est. Utinam dēsistere vellēs,
   aut, quoniam es dēmēns, utinam vēlōcior essēs!
17. Tullius Terentiae suae S. Sī valēs, bene est. Ego valeō. Valetudinem
   tuam velim cūrēs dīligentissimē.
*18. Magna mē, inquit, spēs tenet, iūdicēs, bene mihi ēvenīre, quod
   mittar ad mortem.
19. Maneat ergō, quod turpe sit, id numquam esse ūtile.
*20. Nescio quā praeter solitum dulcēdine laetī
   inter sē in foliīs strepitant. . . .
   haud equidem crēdō, quia sit dīvīnitus illīs
   ingenium aut rērum fātō prūdentia māior.

EXERCISE 2

1. Let Hannibal go over the Alps in order to become the-kind-of-man
boys can describe in speeches. 2. Horace thinks that those men are happy
who do not marvel at anything too much. 3. While Atalanta was taking
the golden apples, Hippomenes went past (her). 4. Socrates, who thought
that the soul was immortal, said it had turned out well for him that he
was being sent to his death. 5. Vergil does not believe that birds make a
noise at a certain time because the gods have given them a great intelligence. But he does not often tell us the same things as Lucretius.

EXERCISE 3

ANSWER IN LATIN:

1. Quid fēcit Catilīna? 2. Quid ad arborēs redit? 3. Quem ducem per
Alpēs īre iubet Iuvenālis? 4. Quō Graeculus ībit? 5. Quid tepōrem
refert? 6. Quālis is fuit quī prīmus gladiōs prōtulit? 7. Quālis saepe fīs,
dum breviter scrībere cōnāris? 8. Quālis fierī vult poēta, ut tacēre
dēsinat? 9. Quid tē beātum facere potest? 10. Quālem esse iuvenem vult
Atalanta? 11. Quid Terentiam cūrāre vult Cicerō? 12. Quid bene
Sōcratī ēvenit? 13. Quid numquam esse ūtile putāmus?

LESSON XXXII

Sect. 125. Deponent verbs of the four conjugations

DEPONENT verbs are passive in form but active in meaning. A
few active forms occur. Thus *ūtor*, 'I use', has the present active
participle *ūtēns*, the future participle active *ūsūrus*, the future
infinitive active *ūsūrus esse*, the supine *ūsum*, the gerund *ūtendī*, in
addition to its regular passive forms. The gerundive, e.g. *ūtendus*,
is found in deponent verbs which govern an object or in intransitive verbs which are used impersonally (see Lesson XXXVII).
The first conjugation contains more than half of the deponent
verbs, but examples occur in all the conjugations.

The Latin deponent is in origin a medio-passive. Greek has
a middle as well as a passive voice; thus *luomai* in Greek means
'I loose myself' (middle) and 'I am loosed' (passive). Similar con-
structions are found in Latin; *cingitur gladiō* means 'he is girded
with a sword' or 'he girds himself with a sword'. And in poetry
such a verb may be used with a Greek accusative, or accusative of
specification, instead of an ablative, e.g. *ferrum cingitur*, 'he is
girded in respect to the sword', 'he girds the sword on himself',
'he girds on the sword'.

The English phrase 'a gun fires' is equivalent to 'a gun is fired'.
The Latin deponent is like 'is fired' in form, but it has the active
meaning 'fires', i.e. 'the gun fires (a shot)'.

Conjugation I.	**mīror**	**mīrārī**	**mīrātus sum**	admire (wonder at)
II.	**vereor**	**verērī**	**veritus sum**	fear
III.	**ūtor**	**ūtī**	**ūsus sum**	use
IV.	**partior**	**partīrī**	**partītus sum**	share

Indicative

Pres.	mīror	vereor	ūtor	partior
	mīrāris, etc.	verēris, etc.	ūteris, etc.	partīris, etc.
Imperf.	mīrābar	verēbar	ūtēbar	partiēbar
Fut.	mīrābor	verēbor	ūtar	partiar

Perf.	mīrātus sum	veritus sum	ūsus sum	partītus sum
Pluperf.	mīrātus eram	veritus eram	ūsus eram	partītus eram
Fut. perf.	mīrātus erō	veritus erō	ūsus erō	partītus erō

Subjunctive

Pres.	mīrer	verear	ūtar	partiar
Imperf.	mīrārer	verērer	ūterer	partīrer
Perf.	mīrātus sim	veritus sim	ūsus sim	partītus sim
Pluperf.	mīrātus essem	veritus essem	ūsus essem	partītus essem

Imperative

	mīrāre	verēre	ūtere	partīre

Infinitive

Pres.	mīrārī	verērī	ūtī	partīrī
Perf.	mīrātus esse	veritus esse	ūsus esse	partītus esse
Fut.	mīrātūrus esse	veritūrus esse	ūsūrus esse	partītūrus esse

Participles

Pres.	mīrāns	verēns	ūtēns	partiēns
Fut.	mīrātūrus	veritūrus	ūsūrus	partītūrus
Perf.	mīrātus	veritus	ūsus	partītus
Gerund.	mīrandus	verendus	ūtendus	partiendus

Gerund

	mīrandī, etc.	verendī, etc.	ūtendī, etc.	partiendī, etc.

Supine

	mīrātum	veritum	ūsum	partītum

The perfect participle of deponent verbs generally has an active sense, e.g. *profectus*, 'having set out', from *proficīscor*. This is a very useful participle, since there is no perfect participle active in regular verbs of the four conjugations; *audītus* means 'having been heard' and cannot mean 'having heard'.

Sect. 126. Semi-deponent verbs

A few semi-deponent verbs have active forms in the present stem and passive forms in the perfect stem, but they are active in meaning.

audeō	dare	**audēre**	**ausus sum**
gaudeō	rejoice	**gaudēre**	**gāvīsus sum**
soleō	am accustomed	**solēre**	**solitus sum**

Note that some verbs have an active form with a passive meaning, e.g. *vapulō*, 1, 'am beaten'. Compare **fīō,** the passive of **faciō** (see Lesson XXXI).

Sect. 127. Deponent verbs governing the ablative

Five deponent verbs govern the ablative case instead of the accusative.

fungor	perform	**fungī**	**fūnctus sum**
fruor	enjoy	**fruī**	**frūctus sum**
vēscor	feed on	**vēscī**	..
ūtor	use	**ūtī**	**ūsus sum**
potior	get possession of	**potīrī**	**potītus sum**

The ablative is really instrumental and is used to complete the sense of the verb. Thus *vēscor* means 'I feed myself with (something)'.

Rōmānī castrīs potītī sunt.
The Romans got possession of the camp.

But note that *potior* may also govern the genitive.

Sect. 128. Ablative of separation

Verbs like *careō*, 'I lack', *egeō*, 'I want', *līberō*, 'I set free from', *abstineō*, 'I abstain from', *dēsistō*, 'I cease from', are followed by an ablative of separation.

Voluptātibus carent.   They lack pleasures.
Mortis metū līberantur.
They are freed from the fear of death.
Cōnātū dēsistunt.
They give up (cease from) their attempt.

Sometimes *līberō* takes the preposition *ā*, and prepositions generally are used with verbs implying actual separation.

Ex civitāte excēdunt.   They depart from the state.

The verb *abhorreō*, 'I shrink away from', may take the preposition *ā* (*ab*).

Ab hōc scelere abhorrent.
They shrink from (are remote from, averse to) this crime.

And adjectives implying 'freedom from' or 'want' may also take an ablative of separation, generally with the preposition *ā*, e.g. *aliēnus*, 'foreign to (removed from)'.

Ab hōc scelere aliēnī sunt.
They are incapable of (foreign to) this crime.

VOCABULARY

addō, -ere, addidī, additum, 3, add.

aetās, -ātis, *f.*, life, age; an age, generation.

aptus, -a, -um, fit, suitable (*with ad and acc., or dat.*).

Aristotelēs, -is, *m.*, Aristotle, Greek philosopher, founder of the Peripatetic School, 384–322 B.C.

audeō, -ēre, ausus sum, 2, *semideponent,* dare.

Christiānus, -a, -um, Christian; *pl.* the Christians.

Christus, -ī, *m.*, Christ (*lit.* the Anointed).

cōnstāns, -antis, constant, steadfast.

cōnstantia, -ae, *f.*, constancy, steadfastness.

contrā, *adv.*, opposite, in opposition; *prep. with acc.,* against.

conveniō, -īre, convēnī, conventum, 4, meet, assemble.

decōrus, -a, -um, fitting, suitable, proper.

dīvīnus, -a, -um, divine.

dīvitiae, -ārum, *f.*, riches, wealth.

egeō, -ēre, eguī, 2, be in want of, need (*with abl.*).

error, -ōris, *m.*, wandering, mistake, error.

hospes, -itis, *m.*, host, guest.

iaculum, -ī, *n.*, javelin.

lūx (prīma), *f.*, daylight, dawn.

mediocritās, -ātis, *f.*, a middle state, the mean (Aristotle's *mesotēs*).

mereor, -ērī, meritus sum, 2,

deponent, deserve; **bene mereor dē** (*with abl.*), deserve well of.

mīror, -ārī, mīrātus sum, 1, *deponent,* marvel at, wonder at.

mortālis, -e, mortal.

mūnus, -eris, *n.*, duty, function; gift.

patientia, -ae, *f.*, patience.

Plīnius, -ī (-iī), *m.*, the younger Pliny, C. Plinius Caecilius Secundus, A.D. 61/2–before 114, author of *Letters.*

prīscus, -a, -um, old, ancient.

pudor, -ōris, *m.*, modesty, sense of shame.

pūrus, -a, -um, pure, chaste.

quasi, as if, as it were.

revertor, -vertī, 3, *deponent,* return; *perf. usually active,* **revertī.**

rīdiculus, -a, -um, laughable, funny, ridiculous.

senātor, -ōris, *m.*, senator.

sequor, sequī, secūtus sum, 3, *deponent,* follow.

soleō, -ēre, solitus sum, 2, *semideponent,* be accustomed.

tandem, *in interrog. clauses,* pray, now, then.

tollō, -ere, sustulī, sublātum, *irreg.*, lift, raise, take away.

tūtus, -a, -um, safe.

ūtor, ūtī, ūsus sum, 3, *deponent,* use (*with abl.*).

venustus, -a, -um, lovely, charming, graceful.

NOTES

2. **lūgeō, -ēre, lūxī,** 2, mourn.
   Venerēs, *voc., poetical use of the pl. of* **Venus** (Loves).
   quantum est (*with gen.*), as many as there are of, *i.e.* all you men (of any grace).
   passer, -eris, *m.*, sparrow.
   dēliciae, -ārum, *f.*, the delight (*in apposition to* **passer**).
3. **parturiō, -īre,** 4, to be in labor.
   mūs, mūris, *m.*, mouse (here used of an anti-climax in literature).

4. This refers to Vergil's *Aeneid.*
   scriptor, -ōris, *m.*, writer.
   Grāius (Grāus), -a, -um, Greek (= **Graecus**).
   Īlias, -adis, *f.*, the *Iliad* of Homer.
5. **lībō,** 1, pour out a libation (*i.e.* Thrasea's own blood).
   līberātor, -ōris, *m.*, the deliverer (i.e. Jupiter).
   firmō, 1, make firm, strengthen.
   cōnstantibus, *adj. used instead of noun in the gen.* (**cōnstantiae**).

6. **dēnique,** *adv.*, at last, finally.
nātum, *perf. infin., sc.* **esse.**
grātulor, 1, *deponent*, congratulate (*here* = congratulate myself).

7. **dōs, dōtis,** *f.*, dowry, endowment, talent (*here pl.* = endowments).
bonīs, *dat. pl. of the neuter* **(bona).**

8. Tacitus is speaking of the Emperor Tiberius. This statement seems to be unfair.

9. **quoūsque,** *adv.*, how long?
abūtor, -ūtī, 3, *deponent*, abuse (*with abl.*).
nostrā, refers to Cicero and the other senators.

10. **tulerit,** *perf. subjve.*, would endure.
Gracchī, Tiberius and Gaius Gracchus, tribunes in 133 and 123 B.C., who lost their lives in trying to bring about reforms.
sēditiō, -ōnis, *f.*, sedition, mutiny, insurrection.

11. **nōn ēdideris,** *fut. perf.*, you will not have published, have not published.
missa, *i.e.* when it has once gone forth (been published).

12. **contrā,** *i.e.* against superstition.
ausus *with* **est,** *perf. of* **audeō.**

13. Pliny is writing about the Christians.
adfirmō (aff-), 1, affirm, declare.
summa, -ae, *f.*, main part, sum, total.

15. **status, -a, -um,** appointed, regular.

15. **spatium, -ī (-iī),** *n.*, room, space, space of time (*here* = length (of life)).

16. **integer, -gra, -grum,** untouched, whole, blameless, pure.
vītae, *gen. with* **integer,** pure in his life.
sceleris, *gen. with* **pūrus,** free from crime.
Maurus, -a, -um, Moorish.
arcus, -ūs, *m.*, bow.

17. **dīligō, -ere, dīlēxī, dīlēctum,** 3, esteem, love.
obsolētus, -a, -um, old, worn out.
sordēs, -is, -ium, *f.*, dirt, squalor (*especially in pl.*).
tēctum, -ī, *n.*, roof, house.
invidendus, -a, -um, enviable.
sōbrius, -a, -um, sober, moderate, prudent, cautious.
aula, -ae, *f.*, hall, palace.

18. **haustus, -ūs,** *m.*, a drink, draught.
aetherius, -a, -um, ethereal, heavenly, *i.e.* (draughts) of heavenly ether.

20. The Emperor Hadrian is addressing his own soul.
animula, vagulus, blandulus, *diminutives of* **anima, vagus, blandus.**
vagus, -a, -um, wandering.
iocus, -ī, *m.*, joke, jest.

EXERCISE 1

*1. Dulce et decōrum est prō patriā morī.

*2. Lūgēte, ō Venerēs Cupīdinēsque,
et quantum est hominum venustiōrum.
Passer mortuus est meae puellae,
passer, dēliciae meae puellae.

*3. Parturient montēs, nāscētur rīdiculus mūs.

4. Cēdite, Rōmānī scriptōrēs, cēdite, Grāī!
Nescio quid māius nāscitur Īliade.

5. 'Lībāmus, inquit, Iovī līberātōrī. Spectā, iuvenis; . . . in ea tempora
nātus es, quibus firmāre animum expediat cōnstantibus exemplīs.

6. Prīsca iuvent aliōs; ego mē nunc dēnique nātum
grātulor; haec aetās mōribus apta meīs.

*7. Ut dominam teneās nec tē mīrēre relictum,
ingeniī dōtēs corporis adde bonīs.

8. ... Remōtō pudōre et metū suō tantum ingeniō ūtēbātur.
9. Quoūsque tandem abūtēre, Catilīna, patientiā nostrā?
10. Quis tulerit Gracchōs dē sēditiōne querentēs?
*11.   ... Dēlēre licēbit
    quod nōn ēdideris; nescit vōx missa revertī.
12. Prīmum Grāius homō mortālīs tollere contrā
    est oculōs ausus.
*13. Adfirmābant autem hanc fuisse summam vel culpae suae vel errōris,
    quod essent solitī statō diē ante lūcem convenīre carmenque
    Christō quasi deō dīcere. . . .
14. Aut suīs fīnibus eōs prohibent, aut ipsī in eōrum fīnibus bellum
    gerunt.
*15. Fortem posce animum mortis terrōre carentem,
    quī spatium vītae extrēmum inter mūnera pōnat
    nātūrae.
16. Integer vītae scelerisque pūrus
    nōn eget Maurīs iaculīs neque arcū.
*17. Auream quisquis mediocritātem
    dīligit, tūtus caret obsolētī
    sordibus tectī, caret invidendā
    sōbrius aulā.
*18. Hīs quīdam signīs atque haec exempla secūtī
    esse apibus partem dīvīnae mentis et haustūs
    aetheriōs dīxēre.
19. Duo modo haec optō, ūnum ut moriēns populum Rōmānum līberum
    relinquam . . ., alterum ut ita cuique ēveniat ut dē rēpūblicā
    quisque mereātur.
*20. Animula vagula blandula,
    hospes comesque corporis,
    quae nunc abībis in loca . . .
    nec, ut solēs, dabis iocōs!

Exercise 2

1. Thrasea, (as he was) about to die, said that the young man (who had been) sent by the senators had been born into times, in-which he ought to strengthen his spirit (mind) with examples of courage (constancy). 2. The Christians told Pliny that they had been accustomed to assemble before dawn, in order to sing hymns (songs) to Christ. 3. Those who approve of the golden mean ought to be free-from (lack) poverty and wealth. Here Horace uses the wisdom of Aristotle. 4. Certain men believe that a part of the divine intelligence has been given to the bees. Here Vergil seems to follow the Stoics. 5. The Emperor Hadrian talks to (with) his own soul, the companion of his body, which will soon set out to other places.

Exercise 3

ANSWER IN LATIN:

1. Quid dulce et decōrum est? 2. Cūr Venerem lūgēre iubet Catullus?

3. Quid saepe nāscitur, ubi montēs parturiunt? 4. Cūr scriptōrēs cēdere iubet Propertius? 5. Cui lībāvit Thrasea? 6. Cūr sē illō tempore nātum esse gaudēbat Ovidius? 7. Quid corporis bonīs addere dēbēs, nē tē ā puellā relictum mīrēris? 8. Quid est quō Tiberius, nisi Tacitus errat, senex ūtēbātur? 9. Quōrum patientiā abūsus est Catilīna? 10. Quā dē rē querī nōn dēbet Gracchus? 11. Quid revertī nescit? 12. Quid est quō caret virī fortis animus? 13. Quid est quō nōn eget vir honestus? 14. Quālis est Aristotelis mediocritās? 15. Quid prīmum optat Cicerō?

LESSON XXXIII

THE CONJUNCTION *cum* IN TEMPORAL, CIRCUMSTANTIAL, CAUSAL, AND CONCESSIVE CLAUSES

Sect. 129. The conjunction cum

THE conjunction *cum* means 'when', if the clause is temporal or circumstantial; it means 'since' if the clause is causal, and 'although' if it is concessive. It takes the subjunctive if it means 'since' or 'although' and if it is circumstantial; it takes the indicative if it is purely temporal.

Sect. 130. Cum in temporal and circumstantial clauses

(*a*) When it refers to *present* or *future* time, *cum* takes the indicative.

Cum Rōmam $\left\{ \begin{array}{l} \textbf{veniam} \\ \textbf{vēnerō} \end{array} \right\}$ tē vidēbō.

When I come (shall have come) to Rome, I shall see you.

(*b*) When it refers to *past* time, it takes the indicative if it simply expresses a relation of time. Generally the time of the main verb is exactly the same as that of the temporal clause, and this is often indicated by the use of *tum* (then) in the main clause.

Cum Rōmam vēnī, tum Athēnās abiistī.

Just at the time when I came to Rome, you went away to Athens.

But in past time, *cum* in a circumstantial clause is much more common.

(*c*) In a circumstantial clause referring to *past* time *cum* takes the pluperfect or the imperfect subjunctive. Here *cum* not only expresses a relation of time but also the circumstances which brought about the action of the main verb. The distinction between a circumstantial clause and a purely temporal clause is not always clear, but generally *cum* in past time takes the subjunctive.

Cum hoc vīdissem, Athēnās abiī.

When (after) I had seen this, I went away to Athens.

Cum Rōmae habitārēs, Athēnās abiī.

When you were living in Rome, I went away to Athens.

(*d*) If *cum* means 'whenever', it takes the pluperfect indicative when the main verb is in the imperfect, and the perfect indicative when the main verb is in the present.

Cum Rōmam vēneram, tē vidēbam.
Whenever I came to Rome, I used to see you.

Sect. 131. Cum in causal and concessive clauses

When *cum* means 'since', it always takes the subjunctive.

Cum Rōmae habitēs, mox tē vidēbō.
Since you are living in Rome, I shall see you soon.

Quae cum ita essent, Rōmam rediī.
Since this was so, I returned to Rome.

When *cum* means 'although', it always takes the subjunctive. Sometimes the main clause is introduced by *tamen* (yet), and this clearly shows that *cum* means 'although'.

Cum Rōmae habitēs, (tamen) tē nōn vidēbō.
Although you are living in Rome, I shall not see you.

Cum Rōmam vēnissēs, (tamen) tē nōn vīdī.
Although you had come to Rome, I did not see you.

VOCABULARY

caput, -itis, *n.,* head.
coepī (*used as perf. of* **incipiō,** begin), 3, *def.,* began.
dēcēdō, -ere, dēcessī, dēcessum, 3, retire, withdraw.
dēficiō, -ere, dēfēcī, dēfectum, 3, fail, be wanting.
doleō, -ēre, doluī, 2, feel pain, grieve.
dōnō, 1, present, give.
ēgredior, ēgredī, ēgressus sum, 3, *deponent,* go out, depart.
forte, *adv.,* by chance.
impedīmentum, -ī, *n.,* hindrance; (*pl.*) baggage.
lūdus, -ī, *m.,* game.
mātūrō, 1, hasten.
multitūdō, -inis, *f.,* large number, crowd.
nāsus, -ī, *m.,* nose.
nē . . . quidem, not even.
olfaciō, -facere, -fēcī, -factum, 3, smell.
pāreō, -ēre, pāruī, 2, obey (*with dat.*).

pateō, -ēre, patuī, 2, lie open; be manifest; **patet,** it is clear (that).
pauper, -eris, poor.
perdō, -ere, perdidī, perditum, 3, destroy, ruin, lose.
perfacilis, -e, very easy.
pinguis, -e, fat.
plērīque, *pl.* (*rare in sing.*), very many, most.
porta, -ae, *f.,* gate.
potior, -īrī, potītus sum, get possession of (*with abl., sometimes gen.*).
praestō, -āre, praestitī, 1, be superior (to), surpass; perform, show.
respiciō, -ere, respexī, respectum, 3, look back.
sagitta, -ae, *f.,* arrow.
tribuō, -ere, tribuī, tribūtum, 3, allot, grant, attribute.
vāllum, -ī, *n.,* rampart.
vātēs, -is, *m.,* poet, prophet.
velut, velutī, *adv.,* even as, like.
vulnus, -eris, *n.,* wound.

Notes

1. **sollicitus, -a, -um,** anxious.
viduus, -a, -um, widowed; *here*
= unmarried (without wives).
Sabīna, *sing. for pl.,* the Sabine
women.
2. **sublīmis, -e,** high, exalted, sublime.
exitium, -ī (-iī), *n.,* destruction.
3. **unguentum, -ī,** *n.,* perfume.
Fabullus, -ī, Fabullus, a friend
of Catullus.
4. Ovid uses part of line 2 in his
poem about Tibullus; see Lesson XXXV, Ex. 1, 11.
5. **cutis, -is,** *f.,* skin.
vīsō, -ere, vīsī, vīsum, 3, look
at, view, go to see.
grex, gregis, *m.,* herd, flock.
porcus, -ī, *m.,* pig, hog.
8. **torreō, -ēre, torruī, tostum,** 2,
scorch, burn.
9. **quid . . . possent,** what they could
do (**possum** = have power).
10. **castus, -a, -um,** chaste.
Arria, -ae, *f.,* Arria, the wife of
Caecina Paetus; she chose to
die with her husband, when he
was condemned to death.
vīscera, -um, *n. pl.,* the inner
parts (of the body), flesh.
stringo, -ere, strīnxi, strictum,
3, draw tight, draw (a sword).
nōn dolet, does not hurt.
11. **nāvī** = **nāve,** *abl. of* **nāvis.**
prōiēcit, *perf. of* **prōiciō,** throw
forward.
12. **suppliciter,** *adv. from* **supplex,**
humbly.

15. **Persēs, -ae,** *m.,* a Persian;
Persae, -ārum, *m.,* the Persians.
glōrior, 1, *deponent,* boast.
prae, *prep. with abl.,* for, because
of; before, in front of; compared
with.
16. **pergō, -ere, perrēxī, perrēctum,** 3, proceed, go on, continue.
aliquandō, *adv., here* = now at
last.
17. **error,** mistake. It is not known
what Ovid did to offend the
Emperor Augustus. He was
ordered to live at Tomis on the
Black Sea.
Here **cum** *means* although. He
goes on to say that he must keep
silent about the **error.** The
carmen is the *Ars Amatoria.*
19. **omnibus,** *dat. with* **praestō.**
See Lesson XXXV.
20. **purpureus, -a, -um,** purple.
succīsus, *perf. part. pass. from*
succīdō, 3, cut down.
arātrum, -trī, *n.,* plough.
languēscō, -ere, languī, 3,
become faint, weak (*here* =
droop).
lassus, -a, -um, weary.
papāver, -eris, *n.,* poppy.
collum, -ī, *n.,* neck.
dēmīsēre, *3rd pl., perf. of*
dēmittō, send down, lower.
pluvia, -ae, *f.,* rain.
gravō, 1, weigh down.

Exercise 1

1. Prīmus sollicitōs fēcistī, Rōmule, lūdōs
cum iūvit viduōs rapta Sabīna virōs.
*2. Carmina sublīmis tunc sunt peritūra Lucrētī,
exitiō terrās cum dabit ūna diēs.
*3. Nam unguentum dabo, quod meae puellae
dōnārunt Venerēs Cupīdinēsque,
quod tū cum olfaciēs, deōs rogābis
tōtum ut tē faciant, Fabulle, nāsum.
*4. Tē spectem, suprēma mihī cum vēnerit hōra,
tē teneam moriēns dēficiente manū.

*5. Mē pinguem et nitidum bene cūrātā cute vīsēs,
    cum rīdēre volēs, Epicūrī dē grege porcum.
*6. Hūmānitās vocābātur, cum pars servitūtis esset.
 7. Pauperibus vātēs ego sum, quia pauper amāvī;
    cum dare nōn possem mūnera, verba dabam.
*8. At tanta mīlitum virtūs . . . fuit, ut, cum undique flammā torrē-
    rentur . . . nōn modo dē vāllō dēcēderet nēmō, sed paene nē
    respiceret quidem quisquam.
 9. Cum ab hīs quaereret, quae cīvitātēs quantaeque in armīs essent et
    quid in bellō possent, sīc reperiēbat: plērōsque Belgās esse ortōs
    ab Germānīs. . . .
*10. Casta suō gladium cum trāderet Arria Paetō
    quem dē vīsceribus strīnxerat ipsa suīs,
    'Sī qua fidēs, vulnus quod fēcī nōn dolet', inquit,
    'sed quod tū faciēs, hoc mihi, Paete, dolet.'
11. Hoc cum vōce magnā dīxisset, sē ex nāvī prōiēcit atque in hostēs
    aquilam ferre coepit.
*12. Quī cum eum in itinere convēnissent . . . suppliciterque locūtī . . .
    pācem petissent atque eōs . . . suum adventum exspectāre iussisset,
    pāruērunt.
13. Caesarī cum id nuntiātum esset, eōs per prōvinciam nostram iter
    facere cōnārī, mātūrat ab urbe proficīscī.
14. Diū cum esset pugnātum, impedīmentīs castrīsque nostrī potītī sunt.
*15. Ē quibus ūnus, cum Persēs hostis in colloquiō dīxisset glōriāns,
    'Sōlem prae iaculōrum multitūdine et sagittārum nōn vidēbitis',
    'In umbrā igitur', inquit, 'pugnābimus'.
16. Quae cum ita sint, Catilīna, perge quō coepistī, ēgredere aliquandō
    ex urbe; patent portae; proficīscere.
17. Perdiderint cum mē duo crīmina, carmen et error . . . .
*18. Cum pateat igitur aeternum id esse quod ā sē ipsō moveātur, quis
    est quī hanc nātūram animīs esse tribūtam neget?
19. (Dīxit) perfacile esse, cum virtūte omnibus praestārent, tōtīus
    Galliae imperiō potīrī.
20. . . . Purpureus velutī cum flōs, succīsus arātrō,
    languēscit moriēns, lassō-ve papāvera collō
    dēmīsēre caput, pluviā cum forte gravantur.

Exercise 2

1. When Fabullus smells Lesbia's perfume, he will ask Jupiter to make
him all nose. 2. Horace says he is one of the pigs of Epicurus. 'When
you want to laugh', he says, 'you will look at me.' 3. Although the soldiers
are being scorched by the flames, no one withdraws from the rampart.
4. When Arria had handed the sword to her husband, she said that her
wound did not hurt. 5. Plato believed that, since things which were
moved by themselves were immortal, the souls of men had the same
nature.

EXERCISE 3

ANSWER IN LATIN:

1. Quandō lūdōs sollicitōs fēcit Rōmulus? 2. Quandō peritūra sunt
Lucrētī carmina? 3. Quandō puellam suam manū dēficiente tenēbit
Tibullus? 4. Quid est quod, cum mūnera dare nōn posset, dabat
Ovidius? 5. Quid dē Belgīs reperiēbat Caesar? 6. Quandō Arria Paetō,
'Nōn dolet', inquit? 7. Quid is fēcit quī aquilam ferēbat? 8. Quandō
hostēs suum adventum exspectāre iussit Caesar? 9. Quandō Caesar ab
urbe proficīscī mātūrāvit? 10. Quando nostrī castrīs potītī sunt? 11.
Quid Persīs respondērunt Graecī? 12. Quid Catilīnam facere iubet
Cicerō? 13. Quot crīmina Ovidium perdidērunt? 14. Cui similis est
iuvenis apud Vergilium moriēns?

LESSON XXXIV

CONDITIONAL SENTENCES

Sect. 132. Conditional sentences

IN a conditional sentence the subordinate clause (called the Protasis) is introduced by the conjunction *sī*, 'if', or by *nisi*, 'unless (if not)'. The main clause (called the Apodosis) states what happens if the condition is fulfilled.

Conditions are of three kinds:

(1) *Open* conditions, including the *more vivid future* condition, in which both verbs are in the indicative.

(2) *Ideal* conditions or the *less vivid future*, in which both verbs are in the present subjunctive.

(3) *Contrary to fact* or *unreal* conditions, in which both verbs are in the imperfect subjunctive (present contrary to fact) or the pluperfect subjunctive (past contrary to fact).

In (1) nothing is implied; in (2) 'may yet be' is implied; in (3) 'might have been' is implied.

1. *Open conditions*

(*a*) Present time:

Sī hoc facis, peccās. (Present indicative in both clauses.)
If you are doing this, you are doing wrong.

(*b*) Past time:

Sī hoc fēcistī, peccāvistī. (Perfect indicative in both clauses.)
If you did this, you did wrong.

(*c*) More vivid future:

Sī hoc fēceris (faciēs), peccābis. (Future perfect or future followed by the future indicative.)
If you do this, you will do wrong.

Note that in (*c*) Latin uses the future perfect or future after *sī*, whereas English simply says 'if you do this'.

Sometimes an imperative or a jussive or hortatory subjunctive is used in the main clause of (*a*) instead of the present indicative.

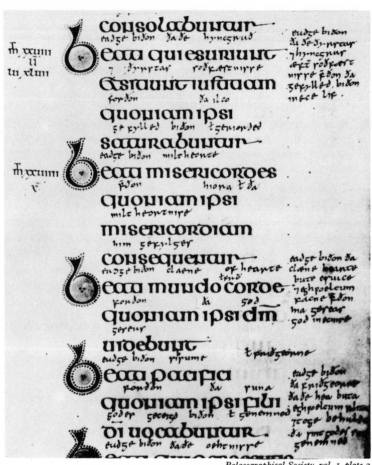

The Lindisfarne Gospels, manuscript in half-uncials in the British Museum (Cotton MS. Nero D. iv) with glosses in the Northumbrian dialect, about A.D. 700

Beātī quī ēsuriunt et sitiunt iūstitiam, quoniam ipsī saturābuntur. Beātī misericordēs, quoniam ipsī misericordiam cōnsequentur. Beātī mundō corde, quoniam ipsī Deum vidēbunt. Beātī pācificī, quoniam ipsī fīliī Deī vocābuntur.

(See Appendix 4, St. Matthew, ch. v)

2. *Ideal conditions*

Less vivid future:

Sī hoc faciās, peccēs. (Present subjunctive in both clauses.)
If you were to do this, you would do wrong.

Here it is not certain whether the condition will be fulfilled. It is less vivid than the more vivid future condition in (*c*) above.

3. *Unreal conditions*

(*a*) Present contrary to fact:

Sī hoc facerēs, peccārēs. (Imperfect subjunctive in both clauses.)
If you were doing this (now), you would be doing wrong.

(*b*) Past contrary to fact:

Sī hoc fēcissēs, peccāvissēs. (Pluperfect subjunctive in both clauses.)
If you had done this (then), you would have done wrong.

Both these conditions are impossible and can never be fulfilled. The implication in (*a*) is 'but you are not doing it', and in (*b*) 'but you didn't do it'.

It is also possible to have the pluperfect subjunctive in one clause and the imperfect in the other.

Sī hoc fecissēs, dolērēs.
If you had done this, you would be sorry (now).

The following sections may be omitted at the discretion of the instructor.

Sect. 133. Use of possum in conditions

Verbs like *possum*, 'I am able', or *dēbeō*, 'I ought', may be used in the indicative in the main clause of a condition.

Sī hoc fēcissēs, culpārī potuistī.
If you had done this, you might have been blamed.

Here the perfect indicative *potuistī* is used instead of *potuissēs*.

Sect. 134. Conditions in indirect statement

In indirect statement the verb in the main clause of a condition must be changed to the infinitive and the subjunctive must be used after *sī* in the subordinate clause.

Direct statement	*Indirect statement*
1. (*a*) Sī illud facit, peccat.	(Dīxit) eum, sī illud faceret, peccāre.
If he is doing that, he is doing wrong.	(He said that) if he was doing that, he was doing wrong.
(*b*) Sī illud fēcit, peccāvit.	(Dīxit) eum, sī illud fēcisset, peccāvisse.
(*c*) Sī illud faciēt (fēcerit), peccābit.	(Dīxit) eum, sī illud faceret (fēcisset), peccātūrum esse.
2. Sī illud faciat, peccet.	(Dīxit) eum, sī illud faceret, peccātūrum esse.
3. (*a*) Sī illud faceret, peccāret.	(Dīxit) eum, sī illud faceret, peccātūrum fuisse.
(*b*) Sī illud fēcisset, peccāvisset.	(Dīxit) eum, sī illud fēcisset, peccātūrum fuisse.

In 1 (*c*) the future *faciet* becomes the imperfect subjunctive *faceret* and the future perfect *fēcerit* becomes the pluperfect subjunctive *fēcisset*. The future *peccābit* becomes the future infinitive *peccātūrum esse*. But in 3 (*a*) and 3 (*b*) the infinitive must be changed to *peccātūrum fuisse*.

Conditions may also be introduced by *sīn* or *quod sī*, 'but if', or by words like *etiamsī*, 'even if'. Two alternative conditions may be introduced by *sīve . . . sīve* (*seu*), but these words must not be used instead of *utrum . . . an*, 'whether . . . or', which introduce indirect questions.

VOCABULARY

abhinc, ago (*usually with acc.*).
adferō (aff-), -ferre, attulī, adlātum (all-), *irreg.*, bring to.
cēna, -ae, *f.*, dinner.
cēnō, 1, dine.
commodum, -ī, *n.*, advantage, profit.
cōnsēnsus, -ūs, *m.*, agreement.
cōnstituō, cōnstituere, cōnstituī, cōnstitutum, 3, set up, determine; establish, settle.
cōnsulāris, -e, consular; one who has been consul.
contemnō, -ere, contempsī, contemptum, 3, despise.
dea, -ae, *f.*, goddess.

dēserō, -ere, dēseruī, dēsertum, 3, desert, abandon.
expōnō, 3, put out, disembark, expound.
faveō, -ēre, fāvī, fautum, 2, favor (*with dat.*).
gravis, -e, heavy; serious.
ibi, there.
immātūrus, -a, -um, untimely.
imperō, 1, command (*with acc. of thing, dat. of person*).
inānis, -e, empty; **ināne,** *n.*, the void.
incidō, -ere, incidī, incāsum, 3, fall into, meet; happen.

locō, 1, place.
lūdō, -ere, lūsī, lūsum, 3, play.
minus, *adv.*, less; (*after* sī) not at all.
molestus, -a, -um, troublesome.
multō, *adv.*, by far.
nimium, *adv.*, too much.
nūmen, -inis, *n.*, divinity, divine will or power.
omnīnō, *adv.*, altogether.
pius, -a, -um, pious, devout, devoted.

poena, -ae, *f.*, punishment.
prīvātus, -a, -um, private, a private person, not holding office.
quiēscō, -ere, quiēvī, quiētum, 3, rest, keep quiet.
sal, salis, *m.*, salt; wit.
sīn, *conj.*, but if.
versus, -ūs, *m.*, verse (poetry).
vīs, (vīs), vīrium, *f.*, force; *pl.*, strength.

NOTES

1. indignātiō, -ōnis, *f.*, indignation.
3. remaneō, -manēre, -mānsī, mānsum, 2, stay behind, remain.
4. migrātiō, -ōnis, *f.*, migration, removal.
ē vītā excēdō, -cēdere, -cessī, -cessum, 3, depart from life, die.
5. placidē, *adv.*, peacefully, calmly.
6. etenim, *conj.*, for, and indeed.
quantō, *adv.*, (by) how much; *with comp.* vērius.
7. scīstī = scīvistī, *from* scio.
8. cachinnus, -ī, *m.*, laughter.
9. percurrō, -ere, 3, run through, mention (cursorily).
10. deus, *i.e.* the deus ex māchinā, the 'god from the machine', who intervenes in some of the plays of Euripides.
intersum, -esse, -fuī, be between, be present (at).
vindex, -icis, *m.*, deliverer, liberator, avenger.
nōdus, -ī, *m.*, knot (*here* = difficulty).
11. nūmen; *compare the motto of Princeton University,* Deī sub nūmine viget.
habēs, *vivid use of the present*

indicative instead of the subj. habeās.
13. foret = esset.
14. dēclīnō, 1, swerve.
deorsum, downwards (*here* two syllables*).
imber, -bris, *m.*, rain, shower.
gutta, -ae, *f.*, drop.
profundus, -a, -um, deep, profound.
15. parvulus, *diminutive of* parvus, little.
aula, -ae, *f.*, hall, palace.
referret, *from* referō, bring back, *i.e.* would remind me of you.
16. Line 1 is from a poem by Cicero.
Rōmam *is the exclamatory accusative.*
Antonius was responsible for Cicero's death.
17. Tacitus is speaking of the Emperor Galba.
vīsus, *from* videor, *i.e.* he seemed.
capāx, -ācis, capacious; (*with gen.*) capable of.
18. agō cum (*with abl.*), negotiate, confer with.
eōs cōnstituisset, should settle them.
19. vim faciō, *i.e.* use force.

EXERCISE 1

1. Sī nātūra negat, facit indignātiō versum.
2. Aestāte puerī sī valent, satis discunt.
*3. Expōne igitur, nisi molestum est, prīmum, sī potes, animōs remanēre post mortem, tum, sī minus id obtinēbis — est enim arduum —, docēbis carēre omnī malō mortem.
*4. Sīn vēra sunt quae dīcuntur, migrātiōnem esse mortem in eās ōrās, quās quī ē vītā excessērunt incolunt, id multō iam beātius est.

*5. Sī quis piōrum mānibus locus, sī, ut sapientibus placet, nōn cum corpore exstinguuntur magnae animae, placidē quiēscās.

*6. Etenim sī abhinc annōs prope vīgintī hōc ipsō in templō negāvī posse mortem immātūram esse cōnsulārī, quantō vērius nunc negābō senī?

7. Rōmule, mīlitibus scīstī dare commoda sōlus.
Haec mihi sī dederis commoda, mīles erō.

*8. Cēnābis bene, mī Fabulle, apud mē
paucīs, sī tibi dī favent, diēbus,
sī tēcum attuleris bonam atque magnam
cēnam, nōn sine candidā puellā
et vīnō et sale et omnibus cachinnīs.

9. Nōn, mihi sī linguae centum sint ōraque centum . . .
omnia poenārum percurrere nōmina possim.

10. Nec deus intersit, nisi dignus vindice nōdus
inciderit.

11. Nūllum nūmen habēs, sī sit prūdentia; nōs tē,
nōs facimus, Fortūna, deam caelōque locāmus.

*12. Ō fortūnātōs nimium, sua sī bona nōrint,
agricolās!

13. Sī foret in terrīs, rīdēret Dēmocritus . . .

*14. Quod nisi dēclīnāre solērent, omnia deorsum,
imbris utī guttae, caderent per ināne profundum.

15. . . . Sī quis mihi parvulus aulā
lūderet Aenēās, quī tē tamen ōre referret,
nōn equidem omnīnō capta ac dēserta vidērer.

*16. 'Ō fortūnātam nātam mē cōnsule Rōmam!'
Antōnī gladiōs potuit contemnere, sī sīc
omnia dīxisset.

*17. Māior prīvātō vīsus, dum prīvātus fuit, et omnium cōnsēnsū capāx
imperiī, nisi imperāsset.

*18. Is ita cum Caesare ēgit: Sī pācem populus Rōmānus cum Helvētiīs
faceret, in eam partem itūrōs atque ibi futūrōs Helvētiōs, ubi eōs
Caesar cōnstituisset atque esse voluisset.

19. Ubi . . . lēgātī ad eum revertērunt, negat sē . . . posse iter ūllī per
prōvinciam dare et, sī vim facere cōnentur, prohibitūrum ostendit.

20. (Dīxit) sē et annīs et corpore gravem bene moritūram, sī mihi causa
mortis nōn fuisset.

EXERCISE 2

1. If Cicero dies (as) an old man, the death of one-who-has-been-consul
will not seem to be untimely.   2. If Fabullus were to bring a good dinner
with him, he would dine well at-the-house-of Catullus.   3. If Cicero's
speeches had been like his poems, Antony would not have killed him.
4. All men would (now) think that Galba would have been a good emperor,
if he had not ruled.   5. Caesar said that if the Helvetians wished to go
away, he would make peace with them.

Exercise 3

Answer in Latin:

1. Quid saturam facit? 2. Quandō puerī, sī valent, satis discunt? 3. Quid prīmum dē animīs expōnere dēbēmus? 4. Sī magnae animae cum corpore nōn exstinguuntur, quid Agricolae mortuō dīcit Tacitus? 5. Quis cum Fabullō, sī apud Catullum cēnābit, ad cēnam ībit? 6. Quandō deōrum auxiliō in fābulīs ūtī dēbent poētae? 7. Quid, sī nōbīs prūdentia sit, nōn habeat Fortūna? 8. Quālēs sint agricolae, sī bona sua nōrint? 9. Quis rīdēret, sī in terrīs esset? 10. Quid facerent atomī, nisi dēclīnārent? 11. Cūius gladiōs, sī carmina tantum scrīpsisset, contemnere potuit Cicerō? 12. Quālis, nisi imperāvisset, omnium cōnsēnsū fuisset Galba? 13. Quō ībunt Helvētiī, sī populus Rōmānus pācem faciet? 14. Quid Caesar sē factūrum (esse) dīcit, sī hostēs vim facere cōnentur?

THE DATIVE WITH INTRANSITIVE VERBS AND WITH
VERBS COMPOUNDED WITH A PREPOSITION.
IMPERSONAL USE IN THE PASSIVE.
DATIVE OF PURPOSE AND REFERENCE

Sect. 135. The dative with intransitive verbs

MANY verbs which are transitive in English are intransitive in
Latin and are used with a dative instead of an accusative. The
dative represents the person who is *interested* in the action described
by the verb.

The dative is used after verbs of helping, favoring, obeying,
pleasing, serving, injuring, opposing, displeasing, commanding,
persuading, trusting, distrusting, sparing, pardoning, envying, and
being angry.

The following are some of the verbs that take the dative:

faveō	favor	**favēre, fāvī, fautum**
imperō	command	**imperāre, imperāvī, imperātum**
īrāscor	am angry with	**īrāscī, īrātus sum**
noceō	hurt	**nocēre, nocuī, nocitum**
parcō	spare	**parcere, pepercī, parsum**
pāreō	obey	**pārēre, pāruī**
placeō	please	**placēre, placuī, placitum**
serviō	serve	**servīre, servīvī, servītum**
studeō	am eager for	**studēre, studuī**

From *suādeō, suādēre, suāsī, suāsum* comes the compound verb
persuādeō, 'I persuade', and from *fīdō, fīdere, fīsus sum* come the
compounds *cōnfīdō*, 'I trust', and *diffīdō*, 'I distrust'.

Sect. 136. Verbs compounded with a preposition

Verbs compounded with a preposition (and with certain adverbs
like *satis*) frequently take the dative, but no exact rule can be given,
since some compound verbs take the accusative. The compounds
of *sum* are intransitive and may take the dative.

The following verbs take the dative:

obstō, 1, resist	**dēsum,** fail, be lacking
satisfaciō, 3, satisfy	**intersum,** take part in
subveniō, 4, come to the help of	**praesum,** am in command of

Rōmānīs subvēnit.　He came to the help of the Romans.
Exercituī praefuit.　He was in command of the army.

But verbs like *interficiō*, 'I kill', take the accusative.

Some compound verbs like *praeficiō*, 'place in command of', take the accusative of the direct object as well as the dative:

Illum exercituī praefēcērunt.
They placed him in command of the army.
Exercituī praefectus est.
He was placed in command of the army.

The verb *nūbō, nūbere, nūpsī, nūptum*, 3, 'marry', is the verb used of a woman and takes the dative; *dūcō*, 3, 'marry (lead into marriage)' is the verb used of a man and takes the accusative.

Virō nūbit.　She marries a husband.
Uxōrem dūcit.　He marries a wife.

Crēdō, crēdere, crēdidī, crēditum, 'believe', takes the dative.

Nēmō tibi crēdit.　No one believes you.

But it also takes the accusative and infinitive.

Nēmō crēdit tē illud fēcisse.
No one believes that you did that.

Though *imperō*, 'command', *placeō*, 'please', *noceō*, 'hurt', take the dative, *iubeō*, 'command', *dēlectō*, 'please', and *laedō*, 'hurt', take the accusative. *Imperō* may take the accusative of the direct object as well as the dative, e.g. *frūmentum Gallīs imperat*, 'he orders grain from the Gauls'.

Sect. 137. Impersonal use of intransitive verbs in the passive

Intransitive verbs like *pugnō*, 'I fight', *veniō*, 'I come', and all verbs that govern the dative must not be used in the passive with the subject in the nominative. Latin uses an impersonal construction, which seems strange in English.

Tibi persuādeō. I persuade you.
Tibi persuādētur.
You are persuaded (lit. it is persuaded to you).
Pugnāvērunt. They fought.
Pugnātum est.
A battle was fought, they fought (lit. it was fought).

Sect. 138. Dative of purpose and reference

The dative is used to express a purpose or an end in view, and it is frequently combined with another dative of the person interested. This is often called the Double Dative construction. The verb is usually *sum*. The noun expressing the end is usually an abstract noun, it is in the singular, and it is normally modified only by an adjective of degree like *magnus*, 'great'.

Hoc magnō ūsuī nostrīs fuit.
This was of great use to our men.

Here *ūsuī* is the Dative of Purpose, and *nostrīs* is the Dative of Reference.

Sometimes it is used with a verb like *mittō*.

Tertiam aciem nostrīs subsidiō mīsit.
He sent the third line to help our men (lit. for a reinforcement to our men).

Other examples of the dative of purpose, which is also called the predicative dative:

Hoc tibi dōnō dō.
I give this to you as a present (for a gift).
Hoc magnō fuit dēdecorī.
This was very disgraceful (for a disgrace, **dēdecus**).
Hoc nostrīs impedīmentō fuit.
This was a hindrance to our men (for a hindrance).
Hoc tibi dolōrī est.
This causes you pain (is for a grief to you).

VOCABULARY

addūcō, 3, lead to, induce.
adprobō (app-), 1, approve of; prove, establish.
adulēscēns, -entis, *m.*, young man.
agmen, -inis, *n.*, column, army (on the march).

angustus, -a, -um, narrow, contracted, difficult.
collis, -is, *m.*, hill.
cōnsistō, -ere, cōnstitī, 3, halt, take one's stand.
cōnspiciō, -ere, cōnspexī, cōn-

spectum, 3, look at, catch sight of, observe.

convalēscō, -ere, convaluī, 3, recover, grow strong.

dēscendō, -ere, dēscendī, dēscēnsum, 3, come down, descend.

difficultās, -ātis, *f.*, difficulty.

dolor, -ōris, *m.*, pain, grief.

fera, -ae, *f.*, wild beast.

fore, *fut. infin. of* **sum,** it would be (= **futūrum esse**).

legiō, -ōnis, *f.*, legion.

Lūcānus, -ī, *m.*, M. Annaeus Lucanus, the poet Lucan, author of the *Pharsalia,* a poem about the war between Caesar and Pompey; he was condemned to death by Nero in A.D. 65.

medeor, -ērī, 2, *deponent,* heal, cure, relieve (*with dat.*).

mora, -ae, *f.*, delay.

noceō, -ēre, nocuī, nocitum, 2, hurt (*with dat.*).

novae rēs, *f. pl.,* revolution.

novissimum agmen, rear-guard.

nūbō, -ere, nūpsī, nūptum, 3, marry (*with dat.*); used of a woman.

obstō, -āre, obstitī, 1, hinder, oppose (*with dat.*).

parcō, -ere, pepercī, parsum, 3, spare (*with dat.*).

parō, 1, get ready, prepare; (*with inf.*), prepare (to).

portus, -ūs, *m.*, harbor.

potius, rather.

praeficiō, -ficere, -fēcī, -fectum, 3, place in command of (*with acc. and dat.*).

praesidium, -ī (-iī), *n.*, guard, protection.

praesum, *irreg.*, be in command of (*with dat.*).

quam (*with superl.*) . . . as possible; **quam plūrimī** = as many as possible.

sērō, *adv.*, late, too late.

serviō, -īre, servīvī, servitum, 4, serve (*with dat.*).

studeō, -ēre, studuī, 2, be eager for, favor (*with dat.*).

subsidium, -ī (-iī), *n.*, support, assistance.

superbus, -a, -um, proud.

ūsus, -ūs, *m.*, use, experience, custom, utility, need.

NOTES

1. **bonō,** *dat. sing. neut.,* (for an) advantage. **(Rogō) cui bonō fuerit,** *i.e.* Who benefits by this?

2. **victrīx,** *f. of* **victor,** victorious. **Catō, -ōnis,** *m.*, M. Porcius Catō (the younger), who killed himself after the battle of Thapsus, 46 B.C.

6. **scientia, -ae,** *f.*, knowledge, skill.

7. **singulī, -ae, -a** (*pl.*), one to each, single. **singulīs . . . singulōs,** *i.e.* one **lēgātus** was in command of each legion. **testis, -is,** *m. and f.,* witness.

8. **aditus, -ūs,** approach, entrance.

9. **obstrictās** *from* **obstringō,** bound (to him).

11. **amāta sum tibi;** *in prose* **ā tē** *would be usual instead of* **tibi. damnum, -ī,** *n.,* loss.

12. **sēcūritās, -ātis,** *f.*, freedom from care (*here* = safety). **ultiō, -ōnis,** *f.*, taking vengeance (*here* = punishment).

13. **rēs,** *pl., here* = activity, business; **rēs agō** = keep busy.

14. **medicīna, -ae,** *f.*, medicine, remedy.

15. Pyramus and Thisbe are the two lovers in a Babylonian story told by Ovid in the *Metamorphoses* and used by Shakespeare in *A Midsummer Night's Dream.* **illinc,** *lit.* from that side (*here* = on that side). **invidus, -a, -um,** envious, jealous. **pariēs, -ietis,** *m.*, wall (of a house).

16. **ēmergō, -ere,** 3, emerge, raise one's self up. *The subject is* **eī,** *the antecedent of* **quōrum.**

rēs angusta *refers to* poverty;
angustus = narrow.

17. mīrum, *an exclamation,* how
wonderful!

lupa, -ae (*f. of* lupus, -ī, *m.*),
she-wolf.

fētus, -a, -um, *here* = newly delivered. The wolf had recently
given birth to cubs.

gemellōs *from the diminutive*
gemellus, the little twins. This
refers to Romulus and Remus.

18. mementō, *imperat.,* remember
to.

impōnō, -ere, 3, place on; *here* =
impose upon (them).

mōs, mōris, *m., here* = law, rule.

subiectīs, the conquered, *from*
subiciō, put under, subdue.

dēbellō, 1, overthrow, vanquish.

19. adulēscentulus, *diminutive of*
adulēscēns, young man.

exercitum cōnficiō, raise an
army.

rem (*with* gerō) *here* = a campaign.

optimē, *superlative of* bene.

ductus, -ūs, *m.,* leadership, command.

20. cīvīlis, -e, civil.

discordia, -ae, *f.,* discord, strife.

certus, -a, -um, *here* = certain
(*like* quīdam).

Exercise 1

1. Cui bonō?
*2. Victrīx causa deīs placuit, sed victa Catōnī.
*3. Nescit Amor magnīs cēdere dīvitiīs.
4. Quīnque tibī potuī servīre fidēliter annōs.
*5. Nūllī sē dīcit mulier mea nūbere mālle
    quam mihi, nōn sī sē Iuppiter ipse petat.
6. Hīs difficultātibus duae rēs erant subsidiō, scientia atque ūsus mīlitum.
7. Caesar singulīs legiōnibus singulōs lēgātōs ... praefēcit, utī eōs testēs
    suae quisque virtūtis habēret.
*8. Magnō sibi ūsuī fore arbitrābātur, sī modo īnsulam adīsset et ...
    loca, portūs, aditūs cognōvisset.
9. Dumnorīx ... cupiditāte rēgnī adductus novīs rēbus studēbat et
    quam plūrimās cīvitātēs suō beneficiō habēre obstrictās volēbat.
10. Interim mīlitēs legiōnum duārum, quae in novissimō agmine prae-
    sidiō impedīmentīs fuerant, ... in summō colle ab hostibus
    cōnspiciēbantur.
*11. Dēlia dēscendēns 'Fēlīcius', inquit, 'amāta
    sum tibi; vīxistī, dum tuus ignis eram.'
    Cui Nemesis, 'Quid', ait, 'tibi sunt mea damna dolōrī?
    Mē tenuit moriēns dēficiente manū.'
*12. Adprobātum est nōn esse cūrae deīs sēcūritātem nostram, esse
    ultiōnem.
*13. ... Quī fīnem quaeris amōris,
    (cēdit amor rēbus), rēs age, tūtus eris.
14. Prīncipiīs obstā; sērō medicīna parātur
    cum mala per longās convaluēre morās.
*15. Saepe, ubi cōnstiterant hinc Thisbē, Pȳramus illinc, ..
    'Invide', dīcēbant, 'pariēs, quid amantibus obstās?'
16. Haud facile ēmergunt quōrum virtūtibus obstat
    rēs angusta domī.

17. Vēnit ad expositōs (mīrum!) lupa fēta gemellōs.
Quis crēdat puerīs nōn nocuisse feram?

*18. Tū regere imperiō populōs, Rōmāne, mementō
(hae tibi erunt artēs), pācisque impōnere mōrem,
parcere subiectīs et dēbellāre superbōs.

19. Quid tam novum quam adulēscentulum prīvātum exercitum difficilī
reī pūblicae tempore cōnficere? Cōnfēcit. Huic praeesse? Praefuit. Rem optimē ductū suō gerere? Gessit.

*20. Sed incidī in ipsam flammam cīvīlis discordiae vel potius bellī, cui
cum cuperem medērī et, ut arbitror, possem, cupiditātēs certōrum
hominum (nam ex utrāque parte sunt quī pugnāre cupiant) impedīmentō mihi fuērunt.

EXERCISE 2

1. Lucan said that, when Caesar had conquered Pompey's army in Africa,
the victorious cause pleased the gods, (but) the defeated cause (pleased)
Cato. 2. Caesar sent the cavalry to support the tenth legion and placed a
general in command of the legion which was the guard for the baggage.
3. If we can believe Ovid, Nemesis asked, (when) Tibullus was-dead, why
her loss caused pain to Delia. 4. Ovid says that, since love yields to
business, those who wish to cure their love will be safe, if they keep busy
(do things). 5. Vergil thinks that the Romans, who are able to rule many
peoples well, ought to spare the conquered and to give peace to all men.

EXERCISE 3

ANSWER IN LATIN:

1. Sī quid malī factum est, quid iūdex rogāre dēbet? 2. Quae causa
Catōnī placuit? 3. Quibus rēbus numquam cēdit Amor? 4. Quot annōs
Cynthiae fidēliter servīvit Propertius? 5. Cui sē nūbere mālle dīcit
Catullī puella? 6. Quae rēs difficultātibus erant subsidiō? 7. Quot
lēgātōs legiōnibus praefēcit Caesar? 8. Quālibus rēbus studēbat Dumnorīx? 9. Quibus rēbus praesidiō fuerant duae legiōnēs? 10. Quid deīs
esse cūrae dīcit Tacitus? 11. Quid Pyramō obstābat? 12. Quid domī
virīs bonīs obstat? 13. Quae fera Rōmulō et Remō nōn nocuit? 14.
Quid est cui Pompēius adulēscēns praefuit? 15. Quid est cui Cicerō
medērī cupiēbat?

CONJUNCTIONS TAKING THE INDICATIVE OR THE
SUBJUNCTIVE (TEMPORAL, *dum, dōnec, antequam*;
CAUSAL, *quod, quia*). SUBJUNCTIVE WITH *dum* (PROVIDED
THAT). SUBJUNCTIVE WITH *quamvīs* (ALTHOUGH):
FOR *quamquam* AND *cum* IN CONCESSIVE CLAUSES SEE
LESSONS XXII AND XXXIII

Sect. 139. Conjunctions taking the indicative or the subjunctive

1. *Temporal,* **dum** *or* **dōnec,** until

WHEN *dum* means 'until', it takes the indicative if it does not
express anything more than time (see Lesson XXII). But if some
idea of purpose is involved, it takes the subjunctive.

Caesar exspectāvit dum lēgātī ad castra venīrent.

Caesar waited for the envoys to come to the camp (until they
should come, i.e. in order that they might have time to
come).

This does not say that they came. It looks forward to the time of
their coming. The indicative *venērunt* would mean that they
actually came.

2. *Temporal,* **antequam, priusquam,** before

Antequam takes the indicative if it does not express anything
more than time (see Lesson XXII). But if some idea of purpose
(or result prevented) is added, it takes the subjunctive.

Antequam lēgātī ad castra venīrent, legiōnēs ēdūxit.

He led out his legions before the envoys could come to the
camp (i.e. he acted before they had time to come).

The indicative *venērunt* would mean that they actually came.

3. (*a*) *Causal,* **quod, quia,** because

Quod, 'because', takes the indicative when the reason given is
stated as an actual fact (see Lesson XXII). But if it introduces an
alleged reason, which is not stated on the authority of the writer,
it takes the subjunctive. Such a clause is virtual Indirect Statement, and is often used after verbs implying praise or blame.

Caesar lēgātōs laudāvit, quod ad castra vēnissent.

Caesar praised the envoys because (as he said) they had come to the camp (on the ground that they had come).

This may not be the real reason. The subjunctive shows that the writer is not sure whether it is true.

When there are two alternatives, *non quod* (not because) is followed by the subjunctive, and *sed quod* (*sed quia*), which gives the true reason, is followed by the indicative.

Caesar lēgātōs laudāvit, nōn quod ad castra vēnissent, sed quia legiōnēs exspectābat.

Caesar praised the envoys, not because they had come to the camp, but because he was waiting for his legions.

Sometimes *nōn quod* takes the indicative, when the clause states something that is true, although it is not the real reason.

(*b*) *Causal*, **quī,** since

The relative *quī* (or *quippe quī, utpote quī*) may introduce a causal clause.

Lēgātōs laudāvit, quippe quī sociī fidēlēs essent.

He praised the envoys since (inasmuch as) they were faithful allies.

4. *Subjunctive with* **dum** (*or* **dummodo** *or* **modo**), provided that

When *dum* means 'provided that', it takes the subjunctive.

Lūdant, dum labōrent.

Let them play, provided that they work.

5. (*a*) *Concessive*, **quamvīs** *or* **licet**, although

When *quamvīs* means 'although', it takes the subjunctive. Sometimes it is followed by *tamen* in the main clause.

Quamvīs ad castra vēnissent, (tamen) Caesarem nōn vīdērunt.

Although they had come to the camp, (yet) they did not see Caesar.

But *quamvīs* may also be combined with an adjective.

Quamvīs beātus, however happy.

(*b*) *Concessive*, **quī,** although

The relative *quī* may also be used to introduce a concessive clause. If it is followed by *tamen*, it is clear that the meaning is 'although'.

Caesar, quī diū exspectāvisset, tamen abīre cōnstituit.
Although Caesar had waited for a long time, yet he determined
to go away.

Note that *quamquam*, 'although', takes the indicative and *cum*, 'although', takes the subjunctive. See Lessons XXII and XXXIII.

VOCABULARY

accēdō, -cēdere, -cessī, -cessum, 3, approach; be added.
aciēs, -eī, *f.*, line of battle.
adulēscentia, -ae, *f.*, (the time of) youth.
caedēs, -is, -ium, *f.*, slaughter, murder.
dēcernō, -ere, dēcrēvī, dēcrētum, 3, decide, decree.
dextra, -ae, *f.* (*sc.* **manus**), right hand; the right (side).
doctrīna, -ae, *f.*, teaching, learning.
dummodo, dum, modo, *conj.*, provided that (*with subjve.*).
exīstimō, 1, think, consider.
fateor, -ērī, fassus sum, 2, *deponent*, confess.
forīs, *adv.*, out of doors, outside, abroad; **forās** *with verb of motion.*
habitus, -ūs, *m.*, condition, appearance; dress.
impediō, -īre, impedīvī, impedītum, 4, hinder, prevent (*with* **quōminus,** Lesson XLI).
incendium, -ī (-iī), *n.*, fire, conflagration.
iners, -ertis, idle, inactive.

itaque, *conj.*, and so, therefore.
lacus, -ūs, *m.*, lake, pond.
līberō, 1, set free; *with abl.*, set free from.
obvius, -a, -um, in the way, so as to meet; **obviam eō** (*with dat.*), meet.
(ops), opis, *f.*, help (*plu. in* Lesson XXIX).
ornō, 1, equip, adorn, honor.
peccō, 1, do wrong, sin.
praeclārus, -a, -um, distinguished, famous.
priusquam, *conj.*, before.
propius, *comp. adv.*, nearer.
quamvīs, *conj.*, although (*with subjve.*).
sēgnis, -e, lazy, slack.
spatium, -ī (-iī), *n.*, room, space, length of time.
sūmō, -ere, sūmpsī, sūmptum, 3, take, assume, exact (punishment).
Terentius, -ī, *m.*, P. Terentius Afer, *c.* 195–159 B.C., author of Comedies.
tergum, -ī, *n.*, back.
vertō, -ere, vertī, versum, 3, turn, change.
vērum, *conj.*, but in truth, but.

NOTES

1. **ancora, -ae,** *f.*, anchor.
2. **intercēdō, cēdere, -cessī, -cessum,** 3, come between, intervene.
   diēs, *here* = time.
   dēlīberō, 1, discuss, deliberate.
   ad dēlīberandum, for deliberation. *This is the gerund expressing purpose. See* Lesson XXXVIII.
3. **Vārus, -ī,** *m.*, P. Attius Varus, Pompeian commander in Africa (Caesar's *Civil War*).
4. **ītō** (= **ī**), *imperat. of* **eō,** go.
   pistrilla, -ae, *f.* (*diminutive*), mill.

6. **supplicātiō, -ōnis,** *f.*, public prayer or thanksgiving.
7. **mediterrāneus, -a, -um,** inland, remote from the sea (*here neut. pl.*).
   Rōmānum, *sing. for pl.*
9. **altitūdō, -inis,** *f.*, height.
   machinātiō, -ōnis, *f., here used like* **māchina,** engine, machine.
   prōmoveō, -movēre, -mōvī, -mōtum, 2, move forward.
10. **egomet** = **ego,** *emphasized by suffix* **-met.**

attingō, -ere, attigī, 3, touch,
reach, apply one's self to.
prō cōnsule (prōcōnsul, -is, *m.*),
a proconsul, governor of a province (after the consulship).
Cilicia, -ae, *f.*, Cilicia in Asia
Minor, where Cicero was
governor.
complūrēs, -ium, *pl.*, several.
commoror, 1, *deponent,* stay.
11. quaesō (*old form of* quaerō), 3, I
pray, beg (*used parenthetically*).
14. adsentātiō (ass-), -ōnis, *f.*,
flattery.
perniciōsus, -a, -um, destructive, ruinous, pernicious.
16. terminus, -ī, *m.*, limit, end.
excipiō, -ere, excēpī, exceptum, 3, take, receive.
plūs, *used without* quam (than).
genus, the race, *i.e.* the bees.
17. adripiō (arr-), -ripere, -ripuī,
-reptum, 3, seize.
hauriō, -īre, hausī, haustum, 4,
draw (water), drink in.
exprimō, -primere, -pressī,
-pressum, 3, press out, extort,
wrest.

īnstituō, -ere, īnstituī, īnstitū-
tum, 3, set up, establish, train.
imbuō, -ere, imbuī, imbūtum,
3, imbue, inspire, inure.
18. excellēns, -entis, distinguished,
excellent.
moderātus, -a, -um, observing
moderation, moderate.
exsistō, -sistere, -stitī, -stitum,
3, come forth, arise, exist.
19. adiungō, -ere, 3, add, join (to).
contendō, -ere, 3, *here* = assert,
contend.
eximius, -a, -um, extraordinary,
excellent.
20. haec studia, *i.e.* literature.
acuō, -ere, acuī, acūtum, 3,
sharpen, improve.
oblectō, 1, delight.
perfugium, -ī (-iī), *n.*, refuge.
sōlācium, -ī (-iī), *n.*, comfort,
solace.
pernoctō, 1, pass the night.
peregrinor, 1, *deponent,* go
abroad.
rusticor, 1, *deponent,* live in the
country.

EXERCISE 1

*1. Dum reliquae nāvēs eō convenīrent, ad hōram nōnam in ancorīs
exspectāvit.

2. Ut spatium intercēdere posset, dum mīlitēs . . . convenīrent, lēgātīs
respondit diem sē ad dēlīberandum sumptūrum.

*3. Itaque priusquam tēlum abicī posset aut nostrī propius accēderent,
omnis Vārī aciēs terga vertit sēque in castra recēpit.

4. Ītō ad dextram; priu(s) quam ad portam veniās, apud ipsum lacum
est pistrilla.

*5.　　　　Nunc mea māter īrāta est mihi,
quia nōn redierim domum ad sē.

*6. Supplicātiō . . . hīs dēcrēta verbīs est: quod urbem incendiīs, caede
cīvēs, Ītaliam bellō līberāssem.[1]

7. (Hannibal) . . . mediterrānea Galliae petit, nōn quia rēctior ad
Alpēs via esset, sed . . . minus obvium fore Rōmānum crēdēns.

*8. Peccāsse mihi videor, quī ā tē discesserim.

*9. Locūtī (sunt) (sē) nōn exīstimāre Rōmānōs sine ope dīvīnā bellum

---

[1] This sentence contains a good example of *Chiasmus* (a:b::b:a); *urbem*
corresponds to *cīvēs* and *incendiīs* to *caede*. And the same arrangement of words
is seen in *Ītaliam bellō* (a:b).

gerere, quī tantae altitūdinis māchinātiōnēs tantā celeritāte prōmovēre possent.

*10. Namque egomet, quī sērō . . . Graecās litterās attigissem, tamen cum prō cōnsule in Ciliciam proficīscēns vēnissem Athēnās, complūrēs tum ibi diēs sum . . . commorātus.

*11. Nōn ego laudārī cūrō, mea Dēlia; tēcum dummodo sim, quaesō sēgnis inersque vocer.

12. Oderint, dum metuant.

13. Modo liceat vīvere, est spēs.

*14. . . . Ista adsentātiō, quamvīs perniciōsa sit, nocēre tamen nēminī potest nisi eī, quī eam recipit atque eā delectātur.

15. Itaque ad quemvīs numerum . . . equitum quamvīs paucī adīre audent.

*16. Ergō ipsās quamvīs angustī terminus aevī excipiat (neque enim plūs septima dūcitur aestās), at genus immortāle manet, multōsque per annōs stat fortūna domūs. . . .

(For 17–19 see Lessons XXXII and XXXIII.)

17. Est igitur haec, iūdicēs, nōn scrīpta sed nāta lēx, quam nōn didicimus, accēpimus, lēgimus, vērum ex nātūrā ipsā adripuimus, hausimus, expressimus, ad quam nōn doctī sed factī, nōn īnstitūtī sed imbūtī sumus.[1]

18. Ego multōs hominēs excellentī animō ac virtūte fuisse sine doctrīnā, et nātūrae ipsīus habitū prope dīvīnō per sē ipsōs et moderātōs et gravīs exstitisse fateor.

19. Etiam illud adiungō, saepius ad laudem atque virtūtem nātūram sine doctrīnā quam sine nātūrā valuisse doctrīnam. Atque īdem ego hoc contendō, cum ad nātūram eximiam . . . accesserit ratiō quaedam . . . doctrīnae, tum illud nescio quid praeclārum ac singulāre solēre exsistere.

20. Haec studia adulēscentiam acuunt, senectūtem oblectant, secundās rēs ornant, adversīs perfugium ac sōlācium praebent, dēlectant domī, nōn impediunt forīs, pernoctant nōbīscum, peregrīnantur, rusticantur.

Exercise 2

1. Caesar is waiting for the cavalry to assemble (until they assemble).
2. Varus retreated to the camp before Caesar's soldiers could-come nearer.
3. Cicero is praised by the senators because (as they say) he has delivered the Romans from slaughter (and) Italy from war. 4. Tibullus was willing to be called lazy, provided that he remained with Delia. 5. Although the bees do not live for a long time, yet the race is immortal.

[1] In this sentence Cicero shows how prose becomes rhythmical by the deliberate use of antithesis; *scripta* is contrasted with *nāta, docti* with *facti*. The verbs are arranged either in pairs or in groups of three; thus *didicimus, accēpimus, lēgimus* are contrasted with *adripuimus, hausimus, expressimus*.

Exercise 3

Answer in Latin:

1. Cūr ad hōram nōnam exspectāvit Caesar?   2. Cūr Caesar diem sē sumptūrum respondit?   3. Quid fēcit Vārī aciēs, priusquam tēlum iacī posset?   4. Cūr puellae māter apud Plautum īrāta est?   5. Cūr Cicerō supplicātiōnem dēcrētam esse dīxit?   6. Cūr mediterrāneam Galliae partem petīvit Hannibal?   7. Cur Tīrōnī sē peccāvisse dīxit Cicerō? 8. Cūr Gallī Rōmānōs sine ope deōrum bellum gerere nōn existimābant? 9. Ubi complūrēs diēs commorātus est Cicerō, quamvīs sērō Graecās litterās attigisset?   10. Quid Dēliae dīcit Tibullus?   11. Cui nocet adsentātiō?   12. Quid immortāle manet?   13. Quālis est lēx, quam nōn didicimus, accēpimus, lēgimus?   14. Quid Cicerō solēre exsistere dīcit, cum ratiō quaedam doctrīnae ad nātūram eximiam accesserit?   15. Quid domī dēlectat, nōbīscum peregrīnatur, rusticātur?

Sect. 140. Subjunctive with verbs of fearing

A VERB of fearing like *timeō* or *vereor* is followed by a subordinate clause in the subjunctive. This is introduced by *nē*, 'lest', if it is affirmative, and by *ut* (= *nē nōn*), 'lest not', if it is negative.

Primary sequence:

Vereor nē hoc faciās.	(Present
I fear that (lest) you will do this.	subjunctive)
Vereor ut hoc faciās.	
I fear that (lest) you will *not* do this.	

Secondary sequence:

Veritus sum nē hoc facerēs.	(Imperfect
I feared that (lest) you would do this.	subjunctive)

Occasionally *nē . . . nōn* is used instead of *ut*. After verbs of fearing the present and imperfect subjunctive refer to future time, but the future participle and the verb *sum* may be used if the idea of future time is stressed.

Veritus sum ut hoc factūrus essēs.
I feared that you were not going to do this.

It is confusing that *ut* is used in a negative clause and *nē* in an affirmative clause, since the opposite is true in purpose and result clauses.

	Affirmative	*Negative*
Purposes clauses	**ut**	**nē**
Result clauses	**ut**	**ut nōn**
After verbs of fearing	**nē**	**ut** (= **nē nōn**)

The explanation is that a subordinate clause after a verb of fearing was originally a wish, and the subject of the main verb fears that the opposite of his wish will happen.

May you do this (*ut*), but I fear you will not.

May you not do this (*nē*), but I fear you will.

A verb of fearing may govern an accusative.

Poenōs timēbant. They feared the Carthaginians.

Sometimes it is used with the infinitive.

Proelium committere timēbant.

They feared to join battle.

The following sections may be omitted at the discretion of the instructor.

Sect. 141. Comparative clauses

There are two kinds of comparative clause:

1. Those where the comparison is stated as an actual fact.

2. Those where it is regarded as something imaginary.

In (1) the verb of the subordinate clause is in the indicative; in (2) it is in the subjunctive.

(Ita ut, perinde ac)

Hoc ita fēcit ut iusseram. (Indicative.)

He did this just as I had ordered.

(Quasi, tamquam sī, ut sī)

Hoc fēcit quasi iussissem. (Subjunctive.)

He did this just as if I had ordered it.

There are a number of demonstrative adverbs and conjunctions which introduce such clauses.

Ita and *ut* indicate 'likeness', but *aliter* (otherwise) and *ac* or *atque* (than) indicate 'difference'.

Aliter ac iusseram, hoc fēcit.

He did not do this as I had ordered. (He did this in a different way and not as I had ordered.)

'Difference' may also be indicated by a comparative adjective followed by *quam*.

Prūdentior es quam fuit pater tuus.

You are wiser than your father was.

A comparative may also be followed by *quam ut* or *quam quī* with the subjunctive.

Prūdentior es quam quī hoc faciās.

You are too wise to do this (wiser than one who would do it).

It is also possible to use *quasi*, *tamquam*, or *velut* with a single noun, and the verb can be understood from the context. These words are frequently used to introduce a metaphor and seem to apologize for the phrase, if it is not a metaphor natural to the Latin language. The meaning is 'as it were', and they correspond to *ut ita dīcam*, so to speak (lit. that I may speak thus, if I may say so). It is also possible to use *quīdam*, 'a kind of', for the same purpose.

Thus Cicero can speak of 'philosophy' as *omnium laudātārum artium . . . quasi parentem*.

Sect. 142. Double result clauses

A double result clause may be introduced by *tantum abest*. This is followed by two *ut* clauses. The first is a substantive clause and is the subject of *abest*, the second is adverbial and looks back to *tantum*.

Tantum abest ut hoc faciās ut abīre velīs.

Far from doing this you want to go away. (It is so far from being true that you are doing this that actually you wish to go away.)

In this construction the first *ut* clause is rejected in favor of the second.

VOCABULARY

antīquus, -a, -um, old, ancient, former.

caedō, -ere, cecīdī, caesum, 3, cut down, kill.

circumveniō, -venīre, -vēnī, -ventum, 3, surround.

commūnis, -e, common.

concēdō, -cēdere, -cessī, -cessum, 3, withdraw, yield, grant, allow.

concordia, -ae, *f.,* concord, harmony.

contineō, -ēre, continuī, contentum, 2, keep together, enclose, check.

dīligō, -ere, dīlēxī, dīlēctum, 3, esteem, love.

expleō, -plēre, -plēvī, -plētum, 2, fill up, satisfy.

impetus, -ūs, *m.,* attack.

inimīcus, -a, -um; unfriendly; an enemy (personal enemy).

intellegō, -ere, intellēxī, intellēctum, 3, understand.

iudicium, -ī (-iī), *n.,* trial, court, judgment.

līberālis, -e, befitting a free man, noble, honorable, liberal.

libertās, -ātis, *f.,* freedom, liberty.

magistrātus, -ūs, *m.,* civil office, magistrate.

magnitūdō, -inis, *f.,* greatness, size.

malefactum (male factum), -ī, *n.,* (= **maleficium**), evil deed, crime.

opīnor, 1, *deponent,* suppose, think.

pertineō, -ēre, pertinuī, 2, reach, concern (*with* **ad** *and acc.*).

Plautus, -ī, *m.,* T. Maccius Plautus, author of Comedies, 254–184 B.C.

quippe, *adv.,* certainly, to be sure; *with relative* **quī,** seeing that, since.

quod sī, *conj.,* but if.

salūtō, 1, greet, pay one's respects to.
sententia, -ae, f., opinion.
sitis, -is, acc. -im, f., thirst.
sōlitūdō, -inis, f., loneliness, desert.
tamquam, adv., just as, as if, as it were; tamquam sī (with subjve.), just as if.
tantum abest ut ... ut ... (with two subjunctives), far from ... (lit. so

far is it absent that ... that ...).
timidus, -a, -um, afraid, fearful.
tueor, -ērī, 2, deponent, look at, guard, protect.
vereor, -ērī, veritus sum, 2, deponent, fear, revere; fear that (with nē and subjve.), that not (with ut).
vinculum (vinclum), -ī, n., bond, fetter; pl., prison.

NOTES

2. praecipiō, -ere, 3, advise, instruct.
4. Here Scaevola is talking to Crassus.
5. angustiae, -ārum, f., narrow pass, defile; difficulties.
   frūmentārius, -a, -um, of grain; (with res), grain-supply.
   supportō, 1, bring up.
6. Labiēnus, -ī, m., one of Caesar's generals in Gaul.
   sustineō, -ēre, sustinuī, sustentum, 2, hold out against, withstand.
   remittō, -mittere, -mīsī, -missum, 3, send back.
7. tē refers to Cicero's wife, Terentia.
   superiōrēs (litterae), your previous letter.
8. Quirītēs, -ium, m. pl., citizens.
9. Anagnīnī, -ōrum, the people of Anagnia, a town in Latium.
   istum refers to M. Antonius.
10. hospitium, -ī (-iī), n., hospitality (here = inn, lodging).
11. Ephesus, -ī, f., Ephesus in Asia Minor.
12. avidē, adv., eagerly.
    arripiō (adr-), -ripere, -ripuī, -reptum, 3, seize; learn quickly.
    diūturnus, -a, -um, long, lasting.
    cupiēns; here the subjunctive might have been used.
13. cognātiō, -ōnis, f., relationship, association.
15. quīn = quī (quō) nōn. See Lesson XLI. Here it corresponds to ut nōn after efficī nōn possit.
    tam ... quam, as much ... as.
16. tantum absum ab istā sententiā = tantum abest ut ista sentiam.

in, prep. governing the abl. multitūdine.
cōnsultum, the supine of cōnsulō, expressing purpose after veniunt = to consult, for consultation. See Lesson XXXIX.
pōnendum, gerundive of pōnō, must be placed, should depend (on). See Lesson XXXVIII.
17. vetustus, -a, -um, old.
    plebēius, -a, -um, plebeian (belonging to the common people).
    patricius, -a, -um, patrician (belonging to the patricians).
    Latīnus, -a, -um, Latin (belonging to Latium).
    inveterāscō, -ere, inveterāvī, 3, grow old, become established.
    The Emperor Claudius is proposing that the chiefs of the Aeduan Gauls should be allowed to hold office at Rome.
18. profectō, adv., assuredly, certainly.
    fructus, -ūs, m., fruit, profit, reward.
    delectātiō, -ōnis, f., delight, pleasure.
    remissiō, -ōnis, f., relaxation.
19. convīvium, -ī (-iī), n., meal, banquet.
    ineō, -īre, -iī, -itum, irreg., go into, enter.
    perrārō, adv., very seldom.
    The subject is Roscius, whom Cicero defended on a charge of murder.
20. Lucius was the brother of M. Antonius.

utpote (*with* **quī**), seeing that, since.

peregrē, abroad. He had acted as a gladiator in Asia Minor.

dēpugnō, 1, fight (violently).

familiam dūcit, leads the company (gang); (**familia, -ae,** *f.*, *lit.* a household establishment).

EXERCISE 1

*1. Timeō nē male facta antīqua mea sint inventa omnia.

2. Sed vereor . . ., nē . . . quasi praecipientis cūiusdam et docentis . . . esse videātur ōrātiō mea.

*3. Cum alius aliī subsidium ferret neque timērent nē . . . ab hoste circumvenīrentur, . . . fortius pugnāre coepērunt.

4. Sed illa duo, Crasse, vereor ut tibi possim concēdere.

*5. Quī sē ex hīs minus timidōs exīstimārī volēbant, nōn sē hostem verērī sed angustiās itineris et magnitūdinem silvārum . . ., aut rem frumentāriam, ut satis commodē supportārī posset, timēre dīcēbant.

6. Labiēnus . . . veritus nē . . . hostium impetum sustinēre nōn posset . . . litterās Caesarī remittit.

*7. Accēpī tuās litterās, quibus intellēxī tē verērī nē superiōrēs mihi redditae nōn essent.

*8. Ita vērō, Quirītēs, eī, ut precāminī, ēveniat.

9. (Anagnīnī) . . . dēscendērunt, ut istum, tamquam sī esset cōnsul, salūtārent.

*10. Ex vītā ita discēdō tamquam ex hospitiō, nōn tamquam ē domō.

11. Apud eum ego sīc Ephesī fuī . . . tamquam domī meae.

*12. Graecās litterās senex didicī; quās quidem sīc avidē arripuī quasi diūturnam sitim explēre cupiēns.

13. Omnēs artēs quae ad hūmānitātem pertinent habent quoddam commūne vinculum et quasi cognātiōne quādam inter sē continentur.

*14. Nam . . . māiōrēs . . . arborēs caedēbant, quam quās ferre cum armīs mīles posset.

*15. Ego vērō istōs ōtī, concordiae, lēgum, iūdiciōrum, lībertātis inimīcōs tantum abest ut ornem, ut efficī nōn possit quīn eōs tam ōderim quam rem pūblicam dīligō.

16. Equidem tantum absum ab istā sententiā, ut nōn modo nōn arbitrer subsidium senectūtis in eōrum, quī cōnsultum veniunt, multitūdine esse pōnendum, sed tamquam portum aliquem exspectem istam, quam tū timēs, sōlitūdinem.

(For 17–18 see Lessons XXXII, XXXIV, and XXXVI.)

17. Omnia, patrēs cōnscrīptī, quae nunc vetustissima crēduntur, nova fuēre; plēbēiī magistrātūs post patriciōs, Latīnī post plēbēiōs, cēterārum Italiae gentium post Latīnōs. Inveterāscet hoc quoque, et quod hodiē exemplīs tuēmur, inter exempla erit.

*18. Quī profectō sī nihil . . . litterīs adiuvārentur, numquam sē ad eārum studium contulissent. Quod sī nōn hic tantus fructus ostenderētur et sī ex hīs studiīs dēlectātiō sōla peterētur, tamen, ut

opīnor, hanc animī remissiōnem hūmānissimam ac līberalissimam
iūdicārētis.

19. 'Convīvia cum patre nōn inībat.'   Quippe, quī nē in oppidum
quidem, nisi perrārō, venīret.

20. Lūcius quidem frāter ēius, utpote quī peregrē dēpugnārit, familiam
dūcit.

EXERCISE 2

1. In the works of Plautus young men are often afraid that their wrongdoing may be found-out.   2. There are some who do not fear the enemy
but seem to be afraid that enough grain cannot be brought to the army.
3. Terentia is afraid that Cicero has not received (her) previous letter.
4. Cato eagerly learnt Greek literature, just as if he desired to satisfy a
great thirst.   5. Far from honoring men who are enemies of liberty, Cicero
always hates them.

EXERCISE 3

ANSWER IN LATIN:

1. Quid apud Plautum dīcit adulēscēns?   2. Quid timēbant Rōmānī,
antequam fortius pugnāre coepērunt?   3. Quid verētur Scaevola ut
Crassō concēdere possit?   4. Quid verēbantur paucī ex mīlitibus Caesaris?
5. Quid mīlitēs timēbant ut supportārī posset?   6. Quid veritus est
Labiēnus?   7. Quid verēbātur Terentia?   8. Quōmodo Antōnium
salūtāvērunt Anagnīnī?   9. Quōmodo Catō sē ex vītā discēdere dīcit?
10. Quandō Catō litterās Graecās arripuit?   11. Quid habent omnēs artēs
quae ad hūmānitātem pertinent?   12. Quantae fuērunt arborēs quās apud
Līvium caedēbantur?   13. Utrum lībertātis inimīcōs ornat an ōdit
Cicerō?   14. Quid tamquam portus apud Cicerōnem exspectātur?   15.
Quid posteā id erit quod Claudius prīnceps exemplīs tuētur?   16. Sī ex
litterīs dēlectātiōnem sōlam peterēs, quālem hanc animī remissiōnem esse
iūdicārēs?

THE GERUND AND THE GERUNDIVE.
THEIR USE TO EXPRESS PURPOSE. DATIVE OF THE AGENT

Sect. 143. The gerund

THE gerund is a verbal noun and is *active* in meaning. It has no nominative and is not used in the plural. Where a nominative is needed, the infinitive should be used.

The gerund may govern a case like a verb and it may be modified by an adverb.

	I	II	III (*a*)
Gen.	amandī	monendī	regendī
Dat.	amandō	monendō	regendō
Acc.	amandum	monendum	regendum
Abl.	amandō	monendō	regendō
	loving	advising	ruling

	III (*b*)	IV	*Deponent* (III)
Gen.	capiendī	audiendī	ūtendī
Dat.	capiendō	audiendō	ūtendō
Acc.	capiendum	audiendum	ūtendum
Abl.	capiendō	audiendō	ūtendō
	taking	hearing	using

Pārendō discimus imperāre. By obeying we learn to command.

Since *pāreō* takes the dative, the noun *imperātōrī* could be added, and the adverb *libenter* would also be appropriate.

Imperātōrī libenter pārendō discimus imperāre.
By obeying the general willingly we learn to command.

Though the gerund may govern a direct object in the accusative, it is better to use the gerundive unless the object is a neuter pronoun or adjective, e.g. *multa*, many things. See Section 146 on Purpose.

Sect. 144. The gerundive

The gerundive is a verbal adjective and is *passive* in meaning.

I	II	III (a)
amandus, -a, -um	**monendus, -a, -um**	**regendus, -a, -um**
III (b)	IV	*Deponent* (III)
capiendus, -a, -um	**audiendus, -a, -um**	**ūtendus, -a, -um**

In the nominative the gerundive expresses the idea of obligation or necessity.

Vir amandus.
A man to be loved, a man who ought to be loved.

When it is combined with the verb *sum*, it forms the passive periphrastic construction mentioned in Lesson XIII.

Hic vir amandus est.   This man ought to be loved.
Dēlenda est Carthāgō.   Carthage must be destroyed.

In the main clause of an indirect statement the gerundive is of course used in the accusative. It may also be used in the oblique cases as a passive participle.

Frūmentō dandō sociīs subvēnimus.
We helped our allies by giving them grain (lit. by grain being given).

The gerundive can be used in the nominative if the verb is transitive; but if the verb is intransitive, it must be used impersonally in the neuter nominative.

Imperātōrī pārendum est.
One must obey the general (lit. it must be obeyed to the general, i.e. obedience must be shown to him).

Sect. 145. The dative of the agent

The dative of the agent is used when the gerundive expresses obligation or necessity.

Hic vir tibi amandus est.
You ought to love this man (lit. this man ought to be loved by you).

Carthāgō Rōmānīs dēlenda est.
The Romans must destroy Carthage (lit. Carthage must be destroyed by the Romans).

But if the verb itself takes the dative, the agent may be expressed by *ā* or *ab* with the ablative.

Imperātōrī ā tē pārendum est.
You must obey the general.

Sect. 146. Purpose expressed by the gerund and gerundive

The preposition *ad* may be used with the accusative of the gerund or the gerundive to express purpose. Another construction is *causā* or *gratiā* preceded by the genitive.

Lēgātī ad pācem petendam vēnērunt.
Lēgātī pācis petendae causā vēnērunt.
The envoys came to seek peace.

The use of the gerundive in *ad pācem petendam* is better than the use of the gerund. Here *petendam* is an adjective agreeing with *pācem*. It would also be possible to say:

Lēgātī vēnērunt ut pācem peterent. (See Lesson XXVI.)

The genitive or ablative of the gerund should be used instead of the gerundive if the object is a neuter pronoun or adjective. *Multa videndī causā* is better than *multōrum videndōrum causā*, since *multorum* might be either neuter or masculine.

Oppida videndī causā vēnērunt.
They came to see the towns.

Here also the gerund is better than the following use of the gerundive:

Oppidōrum videndōrum causā vēnērunt.

The awkward repetition of the genitive ending -*ōrum* can be avoided by the use of the gerund.

The genitive of the gerund or gerundive may be used with certain adjectives.

Multa discendī studiōsus.
Enthusiastic to learn many things (devoted to learning).
Pācis petendae cupidus.   Eager to seek peace.

See Lesson XL on the Objective Genitive.

Certain verbs like *cūrō* may be used with the gerundive.

Castra mūnienda cūrāvit.
He had the camp fortified (lit. he took care that it should be fortified).

VOCABULARY

cārus, -a, -um, dear.

cūnctor, 1, *deponent*, delay.

dēcidō, -ere, dēcidī, 3, fall down.

digitus, -ī, *m.*, finger.

dīmittō, -ere, dīmīsī, dīmissum, 3, send away, let go.

domō, -āre, domuī, domitum, 1, tame, conquer.

facultās, -ātis, *f.*, opportunity, ability, supply.

iniūria, -ae, *f.*, wrong, injury, injustice.

iungō, -ere, iūnxī, iūnctum, 3, join.

misceō, -ēre, miscuī, mixtum, 2, mix, mix with (*with abl.*).

nancīscor, nancīscī, nactus sum, 3, *deponent*, get, obtain.

necessārius, -a, -um, necessary.

ōrō, 1, beg, pray.

pertimēscō, -ere, pertimuī, 3, fear (greatly).

praeferō, -ferre, -tulī, -lātum, *irreg.*, prefer (*with acc. and dat.*).

prōcēdō, -cēdere, -cessī, -cessum, 3, advance.

propter, *prep. with acc.*, on account of.

pulsō, 1, strike, beat.

pūniō, -īre, pūnīvī, pūnītum, 4, punish.

quīlibet, quaelibet, quidlibet, *pron.*, anyone you like; *adj.*, quīlibet, quaelibet, quodlibet.

rēgnō, 1, reign, rule.

retineō, -ēre, retinuī, retentum, 2, retain, keep.

sānctus, -a, -um, holy, sacred.

semel, *numeral*, once.

sepeliō, -īre, sepelīvī, sepultum, 4, bury.

solvō, -ere, solvī, solūtum, 3, loose, set free; set sail (*sc.* navem).

temperō, 1, regulate; be moderate; (*with ā and abl.*), refrain from.

venia, -ae, *f.*, pardon.

vestis, -is, *f.*, clothing.

NOTES

1. restituō, -ere, restituī, restitū-tum, 3, restore.

   rem, i.e. rem pūblicam.

3. pūnctum, -ī, *n.* (*lit.* puncture, point) vote, applause.

   lēctor, -ōris, *m.*, reader.

   pariter, *adv.*, equally, at the same time.

6. trīduum, -ī, *n.*, three days.

   Vesontiō, -ōnis, a town of the Sequani in Gaul, now Besançon.

9. tellūs, -ūris, *f.*, earth, ground, land.

10. perpetuus, -a, -um, continuous, perpetual. *An adverb might have been used with* dormiō, *e.g.* in aeternum, forever.

    dormienda, *gerundive agreeing with* nox, we must sleep through (one night). *Since* dormiō *is intransitive, the impersonal construction*, dormiendum est, *would be usual.*

12. ut fit, as often happens.

    gremium, -ī (-iī), *n.*, lap.

excutiō, -ere, excussī, excussum, 3, shake out, shake off.

13. attonitus, -a, -um, astonished, amazed.

    putet; *the subject is* puella, *to whom* suā *refers, i.e.* fac (puella) putet tē esse suā formā attonitum.

    Tyrius, -a, -um, Tyrian, from Tyre in Phoenicia; = purple.

    amictus, -ūs, *m.*, clothing; *cf.* vestis, *f.*

    Cōus, -a, -um, Coan, from the island of Cos.

    Cōā, *abl. f. sing., sc.* veste; Cōa, *n. pl.*, Coan clothes.

    decēre, *here used personally*, are becoming; decet *is impers.*, it is becoming.

14. auferō, auferre, abstulī, ablā-tum, *irreg.*, carry off.

    bustum, -ī, *n.*, tomb (*here pl.*).

    tumulō, 1, bury (*poet.*); *cf.* sepeliō.

15. Pliny is writing about the

Christians. No. 16 contains
part of Trajan's reply.

praeeō, -īre, *irreg.,* go before
(*here* = say first, dictate).

16. **conquīrō, -ere,** 3, search for.
dēferō, -ferre, *irreg., here* =
indict, accuse.
arguō, -ere, 3, prove, accuse
(*here* = prove guilty).
manifestus, -a, -um, clear, evident.
supplicō, 1, pray to, worship
(*with dat.*).
paenitentia, -ae, *f.,* repentance.

17. **avidus, -a, -um,** greedy.
quam sī, than if (you were to ...).
Libya, -ae, *f.,* Libya, Africa.
Gādēs, -ium, *f. pl.,* Gades (=
Cadiz) in Spain.

18. **Licinī,** *voc. of* **Licinius.**
altum, -ī, *n.,* the deep (the sea).
urgeō, 2, here = press out to (sea).
procella, -ae, *f.,* storm.

cautus, -a, -um, cautious (*here
used adverbially*).
horrēscō, -ere, 3, become frightened (*here with acc.* = fear).
premō, 3, *here* = hug (the shore).
inīquus, -a, -um, unfair (*here* =
unfriendly).

19. **aliunde,** *adv.,* from another place.

20. **Tullius** = Cicero, **Tullia** =
Cicero's daughter, **Cicerō** =
Cicero's son, Marcus.
anima, *f.,* soul (used as a term of
endearment).
mātrī = Terentiae, **sorōrī** =
Tulliae.
vestrum cōnsilium est, it is for
you to decide.
ille = Julius Caesar.
modestē, *adv.,* with moderation
(*i.e.* without violence).
in praesentia, for the present,
at this time.
istīc, *adv.,* there, *i.e.* in Rome.

Exercise 1

*1. Ūnus homō nōbīs cūnctandō restituit rem.

2. Summum crēde nefās animam praeferre pudōrī
et propter vītam vīvendī perdere causās.

*3. Omne tulit pūnctum quī miscuit ūtile dulcī
lēctōrem dēlectandō pariterque monendō.

4. Hīs cōnstitūtīs rēbus nactus idōneam ad nāvigandum tempestātem
tertiā ferē vigiliā solvit.

*5. Neque hominēs inimīcō animō, datā facultāte per prōvinciam iti-
neris faciendī, temperātūrōs ab iniūriā ... exīstimābat.

6. Cum triduī viam prōcessisset, nuntiātum est eī Ariovistum cum suīs
omnibus cōpiīs ad occupandum Vesontiōnem ... contendere.

7. Potest enim hoc dīcī, bellī genus esse ita necessārium ut sit gerendum,
nōn esse ita magnum ut sit pertimēscendum.

*8. Ōrandum est ut sit mēns sāna in corpore sānō.

9. Nunc est bibendum, nunc pede līberō
pulsanda tellūs.

*10. Sōlēs occidere et redīre possunt;
nōbīs cum semel occidit brevis lūx,
nox est perpetua ūna dormienda.

11. Quī mihi tē, Cērinthe, diēs dedit, hic mihi sānctus
atque inter fēstōs semper habendus erit.

*12. Utque fit, in gremium pulvis sī forte puellae
dēciderit, digitīs excutiendus erit;
et sī nūllus erit pulvis, tamen excute nūllum;
quaelibet officiō causa sit apta tuō.

*13. Sed tē, cuicumque est retinendae cūra puellae,
     attonitum formā fac putet esse suā.
     Sīve erit in Tyriīs, Tyriōs laudābis amictūs;
     sīve erit in Cōā, Cōa decere putā.

  14. . . . Quoniam concordēs ēgimus annōs,
     auferat hōra duōs eadem, nec coniugis umquam
     busta meae videam, neu sim tumulandus ab illā.

*15. Quī negābant esse sē Christiānōs aut fuisse, cum praeeunte mē deōs
     appellārent . . . dīmittendōs esse putāvī.

  16. Conquīrendī nōn sunt; sī dēferantur et arguantur, pūniendī sunt,
     ita tamen ut, quī negāverit sē Christiānum esse idque rē ipsā
     manifestum fēcerit, id est supplicandō dīs nostrīs, . . . veniam
     ex paenitentiā impetret.

*17. Lātius rēgnēs avidum domandō
     spīritum quam sī Libyam remōtīs
     Gādibus iungās . . .

  18. Rēctius vīvēs, Licinī, neque altum
     semper urgendō, neque, dum procellās
     cautus horrēscis, nimium premendō
     lītus inīquum.

  19. Nam quod semper movētur aeternum est; quod autem mōtum
     adfert alicui quodque ipsum agitātur aliunde, quandō fīnem habet
     mōtūs, vīvendī fīnem habeat necesse est. Sōlum igitur quod sēsē
     movet, quia numquam dēseritur ā sē, numquam . . . movērī . . .
     dēsinit.

*20. Tullius Terentiae et pater Tulliae, duābus animīs suīs, et Cicerō
     mātrī optimae, suāvissimae sorōrī S.P.D.
     Sī vōs valētis, nōs valēmus. Vestrum iam cōnsilium est, nōn sōlum
     meum, quid sit vōbīs faciendum. Sī ille Rōmam modestē ventūrus
     est, rēctē in praesentia domī esse potestis. . . . Vōs, meae cārissimae
     animae, quam saepissimē ad mē scrībite et vōs quid agātis et quid
     istīc agātur.

Exercise 2

1. When Hannibal had come to Italy, Q. Fabius Maximus delayed in
order to save the republic. 2. Horace writes what is both useful and
delightful in order to advise and please the reader. 3. Men who-are-
unfriendly will hurt the Romans, if Caesar gives them an opportunity
of going through the province. 4. Juvenal says you must pray that you
may have a healthy mind and a healthy body. 5. You will get possession
of a greater kingdom by taming a greedy mind than if you rule Africa
and Spain.

Exercise 3

Answer in Latin:

1. Quōmodo rempūblicam restituit Fabius? 2. Quid nefās est perdere, ut
vīvās? 3. Quōmodo ūtile dulcī miscuit poēta? 4. Quālem tempestātem

nactus est Caesar?   5. Quis ad occupandum Vesontiōnem contendēbat?
6. Potest-ne dīcī hoc bellī genus esse pertimēscendum?   7. Quid nōbīs
ōrandum est?   8. Quid Cleopatrā victā Rōmānīs faciendum erat?   9.
Quandō nōbīs, nisi Catullus errat, in aeternum dormiendum est?   10.
Quī diēs Sulpiciae sānctus habendus est?   11. Quid iuvenī faciendum
erit, sī pulvis in gremium puellae dēciderit?   12. Quid iuvenis excutiet, si
nūllus pulvis erit?   13. Quid semper efficiēs ut puella putet, sī eam
retinēre volēs?   14. Quālēs amictūs laudābis, sī puella in Tyriīs erit?
15. Quid ōrat Philēmōn, nē sit ā Baucide sepeliendus?   16. Quōs hominēs dīmittendōs esse putāvit Plīnius?   17. Dīxit-ne Trāiānus Christiānōs
esse conquīrendōs?   18. Quōmodo is veniam impetrāre potuit, quī sē
Christiānum esse negāvit?   19. Quid domāre dēbēs, ut lātius rēgnēs?
20. Quōmodo rēctius vīvet Licinius, sī bene monet Horātius?   21. Quid
aeternum est?   22. Quōrum cōnsilium est quid sit faciendum?

THE SUPINE. ITS USE TO EXPRESS PURPOSE.
THE FUTURE INFINITIVE PASSIVE.
ALTERNATIVE USE OF *futūrum esse (fore) ut.*
USE OF THE ABLATIVE OF THE SUPINE.
HISTORICAL INFINITIVE

Sect. 147. The supine

THE supine is a verbal noun of the fourth declension and is used in the accusative and the ablative case.

Conj.:	I	II	III (*a*)	III (*b*)	IV
Acc.	**amātum**	**monitum**	**rēctum**	**captum**	**audītum**

The ablative ends in -*ū*, but it is not common. It is found, for example, in verbs of saying and hearing, e.g. *dictū, audītū.*

Sect. 148. Use of the supine to express purpose

The accusative is used to express purpose after verbs of motion, especially *veniō* and *eō.*

Lēgātī pācem petītum vēnērunt.
The envoys came to seek peace.

Here *pācem* is the object of *petītum*; it never agrees with the supine, as it does with the gerundive in *ad pācem petendam.*

Sect. 149. The future infinitive passive

Since there is no regular form for the future infinitive passive, the supine has to be used after a verb of motion. This verb is *īrī*, the present infinitive passive of *eō*, 'I go', which is used impersonally.

Thus *petītum īrī* means that '(someone) is going to seek', 'there is a movement towards seeking'. The object of *petītum* is in the accusative case and does not agree with it.

Dīxit pācem petītum īrī.
He said that peace would be sought, lit. that there was a movement (*īrī*) to seek (*petītum*) peace (*pācem*).

M. Tullius Cicero, Vatican Museum, Rome

Atq; sic asumus homunib; erudttsssumsq; accepimus.
ceterarū rerū studia et doctrina apceptsoc arte
constare; poetā natura ipsā ualere; oc mtsuribus
excttart; et quasi diuino qdā spū inflart; Quare suo
ure nr ille ennius scos appellat poetas; qd quasi deorm
aliq dono atq; munere comendati nob eē uideantur;

Cicero, *Pro Archia*, 8. 18, manuscript in minuscule writing at
Brussels, No. 5352 (Gemblacensis), twelfth century.

Atque sīc ā summīs hominibus ērudītissimīsque accēpimus, cēterārum rērum studia et (? ex) doctrīnā et praeceptīs et arte cōnstāre;
poētam nātūrā ipsā valēre et mentis vīribus excitārī et quasi dīvīnō
quōdam spīritū īnflārī. Quārē suō iūre noster ille Ennius 'sānctōs'
appellat poētās, quod quasi deōrum aliquō dōnō atque mūnere
commendātī nōbīs esse videantur.

(Here Cicero says that poets are inspired.)

Sect. 150. Alternative use of futūrum esse ut

The future infinitive passive can be avoided by the use of the future infinitive of *sum*, *futūrum esse* or *fore*, followed by *ut* with the subjunctive.

Secondary sequence:

Dīxit futūrum esse ut pāx peterētur.
He said that peace would be sought (lit. it would happen that peace would be sought.)

Primary sequence:

Dīcit fore ut pāx petātur.
He says that peace will be sought.

This alternative construction is not necessary, if a verb like *petō* is used, because this has a supine. But some verbs have no supine; with these *fore ut* must be used, since without the supine the future infinitive passive cannot be formed.

This construction is useful with verbs like *spērō*, 'I hope', which are followed by the accusative and future infinitive.

Spērat fore ut sapiās.
He hopes that you will be wise.

Sapiō is a verb without a supine.

Sect. 151. Use of the ablative of the supine

This is generally used with adjectives like *facilis*, 'easy', *difficilis*, 'difficult'.

Difficile est dictū.
It is difficult to say (lit. difficult in the saying).
Facile est factū.
It is easy to do (lit. easy in the doing).

But the ablative of the supine is not at all important and many verbs do not make use of this form.

Sect. 152. The historical infinitive

Sometimes the historians use an infinitive as the main verb, especially if they are describing some lively action. This must not be confused with indirect statement; the subject is always in the nominative and not in the accusative, and the infinitive represents the imperfect indicative, e.g. *fors omnia regere*, 'chance ruled everything'.

VOCABULARY

accūsō, 1, accuse.
adipīscor, adipīscī, adeptus sum, 3, *deponent*, get, obtain.
auxilium, -ī, (-iī), *n.*, help; *pl.*, auxiliary troops.
dēmōnstrō, 1, point out, show, prove.
fore (futūrum esse) ut (*with subjve.*), it will happen that (*may be used instead of the fut. infin. pass.*).
grātulor, 1, *deponent*, congratulate, (*with dat.*).
invīsus, -a, -um, hated, hateful.
iūs, iūris, *n.*, right, justice, law.
mundus, -ī, *m.*, the universe, world.
nātālis, -e, belonging to one's birth, natal; *noun, m.* (*sc.* **diēs**), birthday.
nocturnus, -a, -um, by night, nightly.

perficiō, -ficere, -fēcī, -fectum, 3, accomplish, complete; **perfectus,** *part.*, perfect.
pugna, -ae, *f.*, battle.
senātus, -ūs, *m.*, senate.
spoliō, 1, strip, despoil, rob (*with acc. and abl.*).
supersum, -esse, *irreg.*, be over, remain.
timor, -ōris, *m.*, fear.
trānseō, -īre, -iī, -itum, *irreg.*, go across, cross.
vēnor, 1, *deponent*, hunt.
victōria, -ae, *f.*, victory.
voluptās, -ātis, *f.*, pleasure, delight.
vultus (voltus), -ūs, *m.*, face, expression.

NOTES

1. **nemus, -oris,** *n.*, grove, wood.
4. **cōnāta, -ōrum,** *n. pl.*, undertaking, attempt.
5. **vitrum, -ī,** *n.*, glass (*here* = woad, a plant used for a blue dye).
   īnficiō, -ere, 3, dye.
   caeruleus, -a, -um, blue.
   hōc, *abl. neut. sing. used adverbially*, in this respect, on this account, by so much (*with comp.*).
   horridus, -a, -um, rough, horrid (*here* = horrible, dreadful).
   aspectus, -ūs, appearance; *cf.* **aspiciō,** supine **aspectum.**
6. **Vercingetorīx, -īgis,** *m.*, leader of the Gallic revolt against Caesar in 52 B.C.
7. **altē,** *adv. of* **altus,** high.
   migrō, 1, depart, migrate.
9. **in spem veniō,** *lit.* come into the hope, hope (that).
   postulātum, -ī, *n.* (*usually pl.*), demand, request.
   pertinācia, -ae, *f.*, obstinacy.
10. **Theophrastus, -ī,** *m.*, Greek philosopher who became head of the Peripatetic School at

Athens after Aristotle's death in 322 B.C.
accūsāsse = **accūsāvisse.**
longinquus, -a, -um, distant, long, lasting.
ērudiō, -īre, 4, teach; *here perhaps* = embellish (with learning).
11. **interpretor**, 1, *deponent*, explain, interpret.
12. **nihil** = not at all.
   Palātium, -ī, *n.*, the Palatine, one of the seven hills of Rome.
   vigiliae, -ārum, *f.* (*pl. of* **vigilia,** watch), watchmen, sentries (= **vigilēs**).
   concursus, -ūs, *m.*, concourse, assembly.
   mūnītissimus, -a, -um, *superlative of* **mūnītus,** fortified.
   habeō, 2, *here* = hold a meeting (of the senate).
13. **quid,** anything; *cf.* **si quid.**
14. **repetō, -ere,** 3, repeat, recall.
   fastus, -ūs, *m.*, arrogance, pride.
   fleō, -ēre, flēvī, flētum, 2, weep.

16. **commendō,** 1, commend, recommend.

quō ... modo, in what way, how.

18. See note on Lesson XXXVII, Ex. 1, No. 17.

suppleō, -ēre, 2, fill up, make complete.

agitō, 1, drive (here = consider, deliberate upon).

prīmōrēs, -um, *m.*, chiefs.

Gallia Comāta, *f.*, Transalpine Gaul (*lit.* having long hair).

expetō, -ere, 3, seek after, desire.

super (*with abl.*), about; cf. **dē** (*with abl.*).

19. **beātōs,** *sc.* **eōs esse.**

beātissimōs, *sc.* **eōs esse putō.**

utrumque, *sc.* **datum est.**

20. **colendī,** *sc.* **agrī.**

mulceō, -ēre, mulsī, mulsum, 2, soothe.

dēbilis, -e, weak, feeble.

pinna, -ae, *f.*, = **penna,** wing.

irritus (inr-), -a, -um, vain, useless, without effect.

EXERCISE 1

1. Vēnātum Aenēās ūnāque miserrima Dīdō in nemus īre parant.

*2. Aeduī, cum sē suaque ab eīs dēfendere nōn possent, lēgātōs ad Caesarem mittunt rogātum auxilium.

3. Bellō Helvētiōrum cōnfectō tōtīus ferē Galliae lēgātī ... ad Caesarem grātulātum convēnērunt.

*4. (Orgetorīx) perfacile factū illīs probat cōnāta perficere, proptereā quod ipse suae cīvitātis imperium obtentūrus esset.

5. Omnēs vērō sē Britannī vitrō īnficiunt, quod caeruleum efficit colōrem, atque hōc horridiōrēs sunt in pugnā aspectū.

*6. Vercingetorīx ... vēnisse tempus victōriae dēmōnstrat: fugere in prōvinciam Rōmānōs ... Sī ... relictīs impedīmentīs suae salūtī cōnsulant, et ūsū rērum necessāriārum et dignitāte spoliātum īrī.

*7. Videō tē altē spectāre et velle in caelum migrāre. Spērō fore ut contingat id nōbīs.

*8. Locūtus est ... Dīviciācus: ... Futūrum esse paucīs annīs utī omnēs ex Galliae fīnibus pellerentur atque omnēs Germānī Rhēnum trānsīrent.

9. Caesar ... magnam ... in spem veniēbat ... cognitīs suīs postulātīs, fore ut (Ariovistus) pertināciā dēsisteret.

10. Theophrastus ... accūsāsse nātūram dīcitur ... : quōrum (= hominum) sī aetās potuisset esse longinquior, futūrum fuisse ut omnibus perfectīs artibus omnī doctrīnā hominum vīta ērudīrētur.

*11. Multī ad deōs manūs tollere, plūrēs nusquam iam deōs ūllōs aeternamque illam et novissimam noctem mundō interpretābantur.

(For 12–20 see Lesson XXXVIII.)

*12. Nihil-ne tē nocturnum praesidium Palātī, nihil urbis vigiliae, nihil timor populī, nihil concursus bonōrum omnium, nihil hic mūnītissimus habendī senātūs locus, nihil hōrum ōra voltūsque mōvērunt?[1]

---

[1] This is a good example of Anaphora. The various units of a sentence are connected by a word which is repeated at the beginning of each unit; here *nihil* is used six times.

*13. Nīl āctum crēdēns, cum quid superesset agendum.
 14. Unde tuōs prīmum repetam, mea Cynthia, fastūs?
      Quod mihi dās flendī, Cynthia, prīncipium?
 15. Invīsus nātālis adest, quī rūre molestō
      et sine Cērinthō tristis agendus erit.
 16. Discite, quae faciem commendet cūra, puellae,
      et quō sit vōbīs forma tuenda modo.
*17. Neque enim sunt istī audiendī, quī virtūtem dūram et quasi ferream
      esse . . . volunt.
*18. Cum dē supplendō senātū agitārētur prīmōrēsque Galliae, quae
      Comāta appellātur, . . . iūs adipīscendōrum in urbe honōrum
      expeterent, multus eā super rē variusque rūmor.
 19. Equidem beātōs putō, quibus deōrum mūnere datum est aut facere
      scrībenda aut scrībere legenda, beātissimōs vērō, quibus utrumque.
 20. Rūra quoque oblectant animōs studiumque colendī;
      quaelibet huic cūrae cēdere cūra potest.
    Cum semel haec animum coepit mulcēre voluptās,
      dēbilibus pinnīs irritus exit Amor.

EXERCISE 2

1. The Gauls came to Caesar to ask for support. 2. This is easy to say but difficult to do. 3. Vercingetorix thought that the Romans would soon be conquered. 4. You always hoped that this would happen to you. 5. Does the guard of the city not move you at all, nor the anger of the people, nor the sad faces of all the good-citizens?

EXERCISE 3

ANSWER IN LATIN:

1. Cūr Aenēās et Dīdō in silvam īre voluērunt? 2. Cūr Aeduī lēgātōs ad Caesarem mīsērunt? 3. Cūr tōtīus ferē Galliae lēgātī ad Caesarem convēnērunt? 4. Quid perfacile est factū? 5. Quid faciunt Britannī, ut in pugnā horridī sint aspectū? 6. Quibus rēbus Rōmānōs spoliātum īrī dīxit Vercingetorīx? 7. Quid dē Germānīs dīxit Dīviciācus? 8. Quid Caesar dē Ariovistō spērābat? 9. Quid multī apud Plīnium faciēbant? 10. Quid āctum esse crēdēbat Caesar, sī quid agendum superesset? 11. Cūr invīsus est Sulpiciae diēs nātālis? 12. Quid puellās discere iubet Ovidius? 13. Quī hominēs nōn sunt audiendī? 14. Quī hominēs Claudiō prīncipe iūs adipīscendōrum in urbe honōrum petēbant? 15. Quōs hominēs beātōs esse putat Plīnius? 16. Quid facit Amor, cum agrī colendī studium iuvenum animōs dēlectāre coepit?

THE OBJECTIVE GENITIVE USED WITH NOUNS AND
ADJECTIVES. GENITIVE WITH VERBS OF REMEMBERING
AND FORGETTING. GENITIVE OF VALUE. GENITIVE
WITH VERBS OF ACCUSING AND CONDEMNING.
GENITIVE WITH IMPERSONAL VERBS

Sect. 153. The objective genitive used with nouns and adjectives

(*a*) AN objective genitive is in the same relation to its governing noun as an object is to a verb. Whenever English uses a phrase like 'desire *for* praise', 'love *of* country', 'fear *of* death', Latin uses an objective genitive.

Laudis cupiditās, desire for praise.
Amor patriae, love of country.
Nūllus est tibi mortis timor.
You have no fear of death.

If a verb were used instead of *timor*, *mortis* would be in the accusative.

Mortem nōn timēs. You do not fear death.

But sometimes the noun is related to a verb that governs the dative.

Litterārum studium, enthusiasm for literature.

If a verb were used instead of *studium*, *litterārum* would be in the dative.

Litterīs studēs. You are devoted to literature.

(*b*) This genitive may also be used with adjectives related to certain verbs, such as those of desiring, knowing, or remembering.

Laudis cupidus, eager for (desirous of) praise.
Litterārum studiōsus, devoted to literature.
Tuī memor, mindful of you.

Sect. 154. The genitive with verbs of remembering and forgetting

The genitive completes the sense of verbs like *meminī*, 'I

remember', *oblīvīscor*, 'I forget'. Just as the adjective *memor* is used with the genitive, so it is possible to say:

Tuī meminit.   He remembers (is mindful of) you.

Meī oblīvīscitur.   He forgets (is forgetful of) me.

But *meminī* may take the accusative of persons and sometimes of things. For *nostrī* and *vestrī*, the objective genitives of *nōs* and *vōs*, see Lesson XIV.

Sect. 155. The genitive of value

The genitive may be used with verbs of 'valuing', such as *aestimō*, 'I estimate', 'I value', 'I reckon', or *faciō* or *habeō*. *Magnī, maximī, parvī, minimī, nihilī*, are common examples of this genitive.

Tē maximī aestimō.   I value you very highly.

Illum nihilī facis.

You set no value on him (lit. you value him at nothing).

The following sections may be omitted at the discretion of the instructor.

Sect. 156. The genitive with verbs of accusing and condemning

Verbs like *accūsō*, 'I accuse', *condemnō*, 'I condemn', are used with a genitive which expresses the charge.

Prōditiōnis eum { **accūsant.**   They accuse him of treachery.

condemnant.   They condemn him for treachery.

The punishment is sometimes expressed by the genitive, but generally by the ablative.

Morte { **condemnātus est.**   He was condemned to death.

multātus est.   He was punished by (with) death.

Sect. 157. The genitive with impersonal verbs

Impersonal verbs like *pudet, paenitet, miseret*, which express 'shame', 'repentance', and 'pity', take the accusative of the person and the genitive of the thing.

Mē pudet inertiae.

I am ashamed of my idleness (lit. it shames me).

Interest, 'it concerns', takes the genitive of the person; but with *rēfert* and *interest* the ablative singular of the possessive pronouns (*meā, tuā, nostrā, vestrā*) is used instead of the genitive of the personal pronouns *ego, tū, nōs,* and *vōs.* These verbs may be followed by an infinitive (or an *ut* clause or an indirect question).

Hoc tuā et omnium cīvium interest.
This concerns you and all the citizens.
Nostrā rēfert hoc facere.
It is to our interest to do this.

Here *tuā* and *nostrā* agree with the noun *rē.* The *rē-* in *rēfert* was regarded as the ablative of *rēs,* and the use of this ablative was extended to *interest,* which has the same meaning as *rēfert.*

VOCABULARY

aestimō, 1, value, reckon.
condemnō, 1, condemn.
conloquor (coll-), -loquī, -locūtus sum, 3, *deponent,* converse, confer.
damnum, -ī, *n.,* loss, damage.
dēsīderium, -ī, (-iī), *n.,* longing, desire (for something once possessed).
exsilium, -ī (-iī), *n.,* exile.
fraus, fraudis, *f.,* deceit, fraud.
fruor, fruī, fructus sum, 3, *deponent,* enjoy (*with abl.*).
Homērus, -ī, *m.,* Homer, the early Greek poet to whom the *Iliad* and *Odyssey* are attributed.
ignōminia, -ae, *f.,* disgrace.
imāgō, -inis, *f.,* image, picture.
immemor, -oris, unmindful, forgetful (*with gen.*).
innocēns, -entis, innocent, guiltless.
interest, *impers.,* it is to the interest of, it concerns (*with gen. or ablatives like* **meā**).
libīdō, -inis, *f.,* desire, lust.

memor, -oris, mindful of (*with gen.*).
oblīvīscor, oblīvīscī, oblītus sum, 3, *deponent,* forget (*with gen.*).
paenitet, *impers.,* repent, grieve, *lit.* it repents, grieves someone (*with acc. and gen.*).
paulō, *adv.,* a little, by a little (*with comp.*).
piget, *impers.,* dislike, *lit.* it irks, troubles (*with acc. and gen. or inf.*).
potentia, -ae, *f.,* power.
pudet, *impers.,* be ashamed of, *lit.* it causes shame (*with acc. and gen.*).
respōnsum, -ī, *n.,* reply, answer.
sinō, -ere, sīvī, 3, allow.
solum, -ī, *n.,* soil, earth, land.
suāvis, -e, sweet, pleasant.
taedet, *impers.,* be weary of, *lit.* it wearies (*with acc. and gen.*).
tendō, -ere, tetendī, tentum, 3, stretch, stretch out.
ulterior, -ius, farther.
ūrō, -ere, ussī, ustum, 3, burn.

NOTES

1. This refers to the souls of the dead in *Aeneid* 6.
   amōre, *abl.,* in their love of, because of their love; *cf.* **ob amōrem.**
2. **moveō,** 2, *here* = stir. The subject is Narcissus.
3. *Here Tacitus uses the dative instead*

of the ablative of the agent, **ā sapientibus.**
novissima = last.
exuō, -ere, exuī, exūtum, put off (clothes), cast off, shed.
4. **Tullius** = Cicero, **Tīrō** = his secretary, **Cicerō** = his son, **frāter** = his brother Quintus.

plānē, *adv.,* plainly, clearly.

5. **Elissa** = Dido.
   artūs, *m. pl.,* limbs.

8. **Orpheus,** the mythical singer of Thrace who tried to bring his wife Eurydice back from the Lower World (Ovid, *Met.* 10).
   Mūsaeus, Greek poet in the time of Orpheus, mentioned in *Aeneid* 6.
   Hēsiodus, -ī, *m.,* Hesiod. *See* **Ascraeus** *in* Lesson VI.
   quantī, *gen. of value,* at what value? how high?

9. **minimī,** *gen. of value,* at a very small value, very little.

10. **floccī,** *gen. of value,* of no account, (*with* **faciō**) care not a straw for (*lit.* a flock of wool).

11. **bonō,** *abl. neut. sing. from* **bonum.**
    At enim (*introducing an objection*), but you will say.
    dolōre, *abl., sc.* **fruitur.**
    nihilī, *gen. of value,* at no value, at nothing.

12. **quantō opere,** how greatly, how much.
    distineō, -ēre, 2, keep apart.

13. **bellātum** (*sc. est*), *perf. pass. impers. from* **bellō,** wage war, fight.
    Actium, where Antony and the

Egyptian queen Cleopatra were defeated at sea by Octavian (Augustus) in 31 B.C.
cōnferō, -ferre, *irreg., here* = confer, grant (*with* **ad** *and acc.*).
ingenia, *neut. pl.,* intellects = men of genius.
cessēre (= **cessērunt**), *perf. of* **cēdō,** depart, pass away.

14. **cum . . . tum** = both . . . and.
15. **infāmia, -ae,** *f.,* disgrace, infamy.
16. **centēsimus, -a, -um,** hundredth.
17. **ambitus, -ūs,** *m.,* unlawful canvassing for office (*here* = bribery).
18. **exardēscō, -ere, exarsī, exarsum,** 3, take fire, be inflamed.
    capitis, *gen. of* **caput,** head, *expressing the punishment (with* **condemnō** = condemn to death).
19. The subject is the Emperor Domitian.
    capitālis (poena), capital punishment (= death or loss of civil rights); *here the punishment is expressed by the ablative.*
20. **verbera, -um,** *n. pl.,* lashes, flogging.
    multō, 1, punish (*with acc. and abl. of the punishment*).

Exercise 1

*1. Tendēbantque manūs rīpae ulterioris amōre.

*2. Iste ego sum: sēnsī, nec mē mea fallit imāgō;
   ūror amōre meī, flammās moveōque ferōque.

3. Etiam sapientibus cupīdō glōriae novissima exuitur.

*4. Tullius Tīrōnī suō S.P.D. et Cicerō meus et frāter et frātris f(ilius).
   Paulō facilius putāvī posse mē ferre dēsīderium tuī, sed plānē nōn ferō.

5.   . . . Nec mē meminisse pigēbit Elissae,
   dum memor ipse meī, dum spīritus hōs regit artūs.

*6. Nescioquā nātāle solum dulcēdine captōs
   dūcit et immemorēs nōn sinit esse suī.

7. Vīvōrum meminī, nec tamen Epicūrī licet oblīvīscī.

*8. Ut vērō conloquī cum Orpheō, Mūsaeō, Homērō, Hēsiodō liceat,
   quantī tandem aestimātis?

9. Voluptātem . . . virtūs minimī facit.

10. Ego, quae tū loquere, floccī nōn faciō, senex.

*11. Uterque (Iuppiter et Epicūrus) summō bonō fruitur, id est voluptāte.

'At enim hic etiam dolōre.' At eum nihilī facit; ait enim sē, sī
ūrātur, 'Quam hoc suāve!' dictūrum.

12. (Caesar) ipse Dīviciācum . . . docet quantō opere reīpūblicae com-
mūnisque salūtis intersit manūs hostium distinērī.

*13. Postquam bellātum (est) apud Actium atque omnem potentiam ad
ūnum cōnferrī pācis interfuit, magna illa ingenia cessēre.

*14. Cum tuā et meā maximē interest tē valēre, tum multīs est cūrae.

15. Sunt hominēs, quōs libīdinis īnfāmiaeque suae neque pudeat neque
taedeat.

16. Num igitur, sī ad centēsimum annum vīxisset, senectūtis eum suae
paenitēret?

*17. Accūsātī sunt ab iīs, quī erant ipsī ambitūs condemnātī.

18. Cūius (= Sōcratis) respōnsō iūdicēs sīc exarsērunt, ut capitis
hominem innocentissimum condemnārent.

19. Epaphrodītum . . . capitālī poenā condemnāvit.

*20. Vitia autem hominum atque fraudēs damnīs, ignōminiīs, vinclīs,
verberibus, exsiliīs, morte multantur.[1]

EXERCISE 2

1. Vergil says that the souls of the dead stretch out their hands in their
longing (love) for the farther shore. 2. Cicero thought he could bear his
longing for Tiro, but he could not bear it. 3. The soil of our fatherland,
which captures us with a wonderful charm, allows no one to forget it.
4. Socrates valued it highly that he might be allowed to talk to Homer
after death. 5. When (the battle) had been fought near Actium, it was to
the interest of all the citizens that power should be given to Augustus.

EXERCISE 3

ANSWER IN LATIN:

1. Quid cupiēbant animae, quae in rīpā flūminis manūs tendentēs stābant?
2. Cūius amōre ūritur Narcissus? 3. Quid etiam ā sapientibus nōn facile
exuitur? 4. Cūius dēsīderium ferre nōn potest Cicerō? 5. Cūius
fēminae meminerit Aenēās, dum suī memor erit? 6. Quid nōs suī immemorēs esse nōn sinit? 7. Parvī-ne aestimat Sōcratēs, ut cum Homērō
conloquī liceat? 8. Utrum maximī an minimī voluptātem facit virtūs?
9. Quid nihilī facit Epicūrus? 10. Quid Epicūrus ait sē, sī ūrātur,
dictūrum? 11. Quid Caesar dīcit interesse reīpūblicae? 12. Quid
Antōniō Cleopatrāque apud Actium victīs pācis interfuit? 13. Quid suā
interesse dīcit Cicerō? 14. Cūius reī condemnātī erant eī quī aliōs accūsā-
bant? 15. Quem capitis condemnāvērunt iūdicēs? 16. Quālī poenā condemnātus est Epaphrodītus? 17. Quid morte multātur?

---

[1] *Morte multantur* is an example of a Ciceronian clausula or rhythmical
ending. Here a cretic ($-\cup-$) is followed by a trochee ($-\cup$). Sometimes a paeon
($-\cup\cup\cup$) is substituted for the cretic, e.g., *esse videātur*; sometimes the cretic is
followed by two trochees or by a second cretic.

LESSON XLI

SUBJUNCTIVE WITH VERBS OF PREVENTING AND
DOUBTING. USE OF *quōminus* WITH *impediō* AND OF
quīn, WHICH FOLLOWS A NEGATIVE, WITH *nōn dubitō*.
BUT *prohibeō* MAY TAKE THE INFINITIVE.
COMMANDS AND QUESTIONS IN INDIRECT STATEMENT

Sect. 158. Subjunctive with verbs of preventing

VERBS like *impediō* or *dēterreō*, 'I hinder, prevent', are followed by
the subjunctive, introduced either by *nē*, *quōminus* (lit. by which the
less), or *quīn* (lit. by which not). Either *quōminus* or *nē* may be
used, if the main verb is affirmative, and *quīn* or *quōminus*, if the
main verb is negative. Note that *quīn* (= *quī nōn*, *quō nōn*) *contains*
a negative and always *follows* a negative.

> **Nēmō impedit quōminus hoc faciās.**
> No one prevents you from doing this (by which the less you
> may do it, so that you may not do it).

Since *nēmō* is negative, *quīn* could have been used instead of
quōminus.

> **Tē deterruit nē hoc facerēs.**
> He prevented you from doing this.

But *prohibeō*, 'I prevent', is often used with the infinitive, and this
is the normal construction with *vetō*, 'I forbid'.

> **Tē hoc facere prohibuit.**
> **Tē hoc facere vetuit.**
> He prevented you from doing this (lit. to do it).
> He forbade you to do this.

The subjunctive after *impediō* forms part of a noun clause of
Indirect Command. *Nē hoc faciās*, 'you are *not* to do this', combined with *impediō*, 'I am preventing you', becomes *impediō nē
hoc faciās*; this makes it clear why *nē*, *quōminus*, and *quīn* are all
negative.

Sect. 159. Subjunctive with verbs of doubting

After *nōn dubitō*, 'I do not doubt', or *nōn dubium est*, 'there is no doubt', *quīn* is used to introduce a clause with the verb in the subjunctive.

Nōn dubitō quīn hoc fēcerīs.
I do not doubt that you did this.
Nōn dubium erat quīn hoc fēcissēs.
There was no doubt that you had done this.

The main verb must either be preceded by a negative or must be interrogative.

Quis dubitat? Who doubts? (i.e. no one doubts).

Another common expression is *dubitārī nōn potest*, 'it cannot be doubted', i.e. 'no one can doubt'.

When *dubitō* means 'I hesitate to', it may take an infinitive.

Hoc facere dubitō.   I hesitate to do this.

And when *dubitō* means 'I am doubtful, uncertain', it may introduce an indirect question.

Dubitō num hoc vērum sit.   I doubt whether this is true.

Sometimes *quīn* is used instead of *ut nōn* in a result clause.

Nōn fierī potest quīn hoc fēcerīs (= **ut hoc nōn fēcerīs**).

If the main verb were affirmative, this would be:

Fierī potest ut hoc fēcerīs.
It is possible that you have done this.

The conjunction *quīn* was originally the old ablative form *quī* combined with -*ne*, and it meant 'why not?' It still has this meaning.

Quīn hoc facis?   Do this (why not do it?).

The following sections may be omitted at the discretion of the instructor.

Sect. 160. Commands in indirect statement

The main clause of an indirect statement is in the accusative and infinitive, but an indirect command is expressed by the subjunctive, which stands alone and is not combined with *ut*. But if it is a negative command, *nē* must be added.

The subjunctive in an indirect command represents an imperative in direct speech.

Direct statement:

> **'Adsunt hostēs', inquit; 'ad mē properāte, cīvēs, nōlite fugere.'**
>
> 'The enemy are at hand', he said; 'hasten to me, citizens, do not run away.'

In indirect statement, *adsunt* becomes the infinitive *adesse*, but the imperative *properāte* becomes the imperfect subjunctive *properārent* in secondary sequence after the verb *dīxit*. *Nōlīte fugere* changes to *nē fugerent*.

Indirect statement:

> **(Dīxit) adesse hostēs; cīvēs ad sē properārent; nē fugerent.**
>
> (He said that) the enemy were at hand; let the citizens hasten to him and not run away.

Properārent implies a verb of commanding, understood from *dīxit*. In a substantive clause of purpose the wording would be: *imperāvit ut cīvēs properārent*.

Sect. 161. Questions in indirect statement

(*a*) *Real questions*

Real questions, which expect an answer, are put in the subjunctive in indirect statement.

Direct statement:

> **Quid vultis?** What do you want?

Indirect statement (in secondary sequence):

> **Quid vellent?** What did they want?

This corresponds to *rogāvit quid vellent* (he asked what they wanted), but the verb of asking is not expressed; it is understood from the main verb of saying (e.g. *dīxit*), which introduces the indirect statement.

(*b*) *Deliberative questions*

Deliberative questions in direct statement are in the subjunctive and they remain in the subjunctive in indirect statement.

Direct statement:

Quid faciam? What am I to do?

Indirect statement (in secondary sequence):

Quid faceret? What was he to do?

This corresponds to *rogāvit quid faceret* (he asked what he was to do), but here again the verb of asking is understood from the main verb of saying (e.g. *dīxit*). The phrase *rogāvit quid faceret* is ambiguous, as it might also mean 'he asked what he was doing'.

(c) Rhetorical questions

Rhetorical questions, which do not expect an answer, are put in the accusative and infinitive, since they are really statements and not questions.

Direct statement:

Num sociōrum oblīvīscī possum? Can I forget my allies?

Indirect statement (in secondary sequence):

Num sē sociōrum oblīvīscī posse?
Could he forget his allies? (This really means 'he said he could not forget them'.)

But it is not always clear whether a question is real or rhetorical.

Pronouns in indirect statement

In indirect statement personal pronouns, demonstrative pronouns, and possessive adjectives must be changed to suit the point of view of the speaker.

Direct statement		Indirect statement
I will do *this* **(Ego) hoc faciam**	becomes	He said that he would do *that* **Dīxit sē illud factūrum esse**
You have come **(Vōs) vēnistis**	,,	He said that *they* had come **Dīxit illōs vēnisse**

ego	becomes	**sē**	**tū**	becomes	**ille (illum)**
nōs	,,	**sē**	**vōs**	,,	**illī (illōs)**
meus	,,	**suus**	**tuus**	,,	**illīus**
noster	,,	**suus**	**vester**	,,	**illōrum**
hic	,,	**ille (is)**	**hīc**	,,	**ibi**
nunc	,,	**tunc**	**hūc**	,,	**illūc**
hodiē	,,	**illō diē**			

VOCABULARY

barbarus, -a, -um, foreign, barbarous; a foreigner, native.

cōnsentiō, -sentīre, -sēnsī, -sēnsum, 4, agree (*here* = conspire).

continentia, -ae, *f.,* moderation, temperance.

dēspiciō, -spicere, -spexī, -spectum, 3, despise.

dēterreō, -terrēre, -terruī, -territum, 2, deter, prevent, hinder.

dubitō, 1, doubt; **nōn d. quin** (*with subjve.*), I don't doubt that.

dubium, *neut. of* **dubius,** doubtful; **nōn d. est quin** (*with subjve.*), there is no doubt that.

fierī potest ut (*with subjve.*), it is possible that; *neg.,* **nōn f. p. quin.**

furor, -ōris, *m.,* fury, madness.

hiems, hiemis, *f.,* winter.

honestās, -ātis, *f.,* honesty, integrity, reputation.

incohō, 1, begin.

incommodum, -ī, *n.,* inconvenience, misfortune.

magnopere (= **magnō opere**), *adv.,* greatly, very much.

memoria, -ae, *f.,* memory.

modō, *abl. of* **modus,** way; with **nūllō** = by no means.

prīstinus, -a, -um, former, original.

quin (= **quī nōn, quō nōn**) *used* (*with subjve.*) *after a negative and verbs like* **impediō.**

quōminus (= **quō minus**), *used after verbs like* **impediō.**

reminiscor, reminīscī, 3, remember (*with gen. or acc.*).

sōlum, only; **nōn sōlum,** not only.

summa, -ae, *f.,* main part, sum, total.

ultimus, -a, -um, last, farthest.

ūtilitās, -ātis, *f.,* usefulness, expediency, profit.

vetō, -āre, vetuī, vetitum, 1, forbid (*with inf.*).

vetus, -eris, old.

vulnerō, 1, wound.

NOTES

2. **ūsque,** continuously (*with* **ad** *and acc.*).

3. **Suessiōnēs** is the object of **dēterrēre.**
   hīs = **Belgīs,** Belgians.

4. **coniciō, -ere,** 3, throw.

5. **plūrimum possent** = were the most powerful.

7. **contendō** (*with* **cum** *and abl.*), *here =* conflict with, fight against.

12. **quin** *here is equivalent to* **ut nōn.**

13. **quin** *here is like* **quī nōn,** who was not (wounded).

14. **Trēverī, -ōrum,** *m.,* a people in Belgic Gaul on the Moselle.
   intermittō (*with* **tempus**), **-mittere, -mīsī, -missum,** 3, leave off, interrupt (*here* = did not cease at any time).
   quin = **quō nōn** (on which not), when they did not (send), without (sending).

15. **adiūtor, -ōris,** *m.,* helper (*here* perhaps = as their advocate).

16. **Dīvicō, -ōnis,** *m.,* a leader of the Helvetii.

agō cum, see note on Lesson XXXIV, Ex. 1, No. 18.

persequor, -sequī, 3, *deponent,* follow up, pursue.

perseverō, 1, persist.

17. **imprōvīsō,** *adv.,* unexpectedly.
   pāgus, -ī, *m.,* canton.
   adorior, -orīrī, -ortus sum, 4, *deponent,* attack.
   suae refers to Caesar, *the subject of* **tribueret.**
   tribuō, *here* = attribute (this) to.
   ipsōs refers to **Dīvicō,** *the subject of the main verb* **ēgit,** and to the rest of the Helvetians.

18. *In indirect statement* (*after* **respondit**) **hoc tempus,** this time, *would generally be changed to* **illud tempus,** that time.
   ēgressum = **ēgressum esse.**
   quid sibi vellet? what did the Roman army mean? what was its aim, purpose?
   Here **suās** *does not refer to the subject of* **venīret,** *the verb in the dependent clause, but looks*

back to **Ariovistus,** *the subject of* **respondit. Cūr veniret** *is equivalent to* **rogāvit cūr venīret,** he asked why the Roman army came into his lands.

possessiō, -ōnis, *f.,* *here pl.,* possessions, lands.

20. **hūius** refers to **Verrēs,** the corrupt governor of Sicily, who was attacked in Cicero's *Verrine Orations.*

praetor = **Verrēs,** who was a propraetor, a governor of praetorian rank.

illīus refers to Marcellus, who conquered Syracuse in 212 B.C.

cohors, cohortis, *f.,* cohort, the tenth part of a legion (*here* = the staff or retinue of a governor).

impūrus, -a, -um, impure, infamous, vile.

invictus, -a, -um, unconquered, invincible.

Syrācūsae, -ārum, *f.,* Syracuse in Sicily.

EXERCISE 1

*1. Plūra nē dīcam, tuae mē . . . lacrimae impediunt vestraeque, iūdicēs, nōn sōlum meae.

*2. Hāc igitur fortūnā fruī licet senibus, nec aetās impedit quōminus . . . agrī colendī studia teneāmus ūsque ad ultimum tempus senectūtis.

3. (Rēmī . . . dīxērunt) . . . tantum . . . esse eōrum omnium furōrem, ut nē Suessiōnēs quidem . . . dēterrēre potuerint quīn cum hīs consentīrent.

4. Germānī retinērī nōn poterant quīn in nostrōs tēla conicerent.

*5. (Orgetorīx dīxit) nōn esse dubium, quīn tōtīus Galliae plūrimum Helvētiī possent.

6. Tum vērō (Caesar) dubitandum nōn existimāvit quīn ad eōs proficīscerētur.

*7. Dubitandum nōn est quīn numquam possit ūtilitās cum honestāte contendere.

*8. Dubium . . . illī nōn erat, quid futūrum esset.

9. Gallī . . . flūmen trānsīre . . . nōn dubitant.

*10. At barbarī . . . nostrōs nāvibus ēgredī prohibēbant.

*11. Vītae summa brevis spem nōs vetat incohāre longam.

12. Fierī nūllō modō poterat quīn Cleomenī parcerētur.

13. Nēmō fuit . . . mīlitum, quīn vulnerārētur.

14. Trēverī vērō . . . tōtīus hiemis nūllum tempus intermīsērunt, quīn trāns Rhēnum lēgātōs mitterent.

15. (Q. Cicerō respondet) . . . sī ab armīs discēdere velint, sē adiūtōre ūtantur lēgātōsque ad Caesarem mittant.

*16. (Dīvicō ita cum Caesare ēgit) . . . sīn bellō persequī persevērāret, reminīscerētur et veteris incommodī populī Rōmānī et prīstinae virtūtis Helvētiōrum.

17. (Dīvicō ita cum Caesare ēgit) quod imprōvīsō ūnum pāgum adortus esset, . . . nē ob eam rem aut suae magnopere virtūtī tribueret aut ipsōs dēspiceret.

*18. (Ariovistus respondit) . . . Numquam ante hoc tempus exercitum populī Rōmānī Galliae prōvinciae fīnibus ēgressum. Quid sibi vellet? Cūr in suās possessiōnēs venīret?

*19. (Caesar respondit) . . . Quod sī veteris incommodī oblīvīscī vellet, num etiam recentium iniūriārum memoriam (sē) dēpōnere posse?

(For 20 see Lesson XXXVI, footnote 2, on antithesis.)

20. Conferte hanc pācem cum illō bellō, hūius praetōris adventum cum illīus imperātōris victōriā, hūius cohortem impūram cum illīus exercitū invictō, hūius libīdinēs cum illīus continentiā; ab illō quī cēpit conditās, ab hōc quī cōnstitūtās accepit captās dīcētis Syrācūsās.[1]

EXERCISE 2

1. Cicero does not believe that age prevents old men from keeping their interest in agriculture. 2. The Remi could not prevent the Suessiones from conspiring with the Belgians. 3. There was no doubt that the Helvetians could fight well. 4. Divico tells Caesar that the Romans have attacked one part of his army unexpectedly; do not (he says) despise those soldiers, but remember the great bravery of the Helvetians. 5. Ariovistus replied that the Romans had gone out of the province. Why (he asked) had they come into his territory?

EXERCISE 3

1. Quid Cicerōnem impedit nē plūra dīcat? 2. Quid ad ultimum senectūtis tempus tenēre possumus? 3. Quī hominēs retinērī nōn poterant quīn tēla conicerent? 4. Quid nōn esse dubium putāvit Orgetorīx? 5. Quid dubitandum nōn exīstimāvit Caesar? 6. Potest-ne dubitārī quīn ūtilitas cum honestāte numquam contendat? 7. Quid Gallī facere nōn dubitant? 8. Quid barbarī prohibēbant? 9. Quid vīta brevis nōs facere vetat? 10. Cui parcendum erat? 11. Quot mīlitēs nōn vulnerātī sunt? 12. Quid per tōtam hiemem faciēbant Trēverī? 13. Quid Cicerō Gallīs imperat ut faciant? 14. Quid Dīvicō Caesarem monuit ut faceret? 15. Quid Dīvicō Caesarem monuit nē faceret? 16. Quid Ariovistus dē exercitū populī Rōmānī Caesarem rogāvit? 17. Quid Caesar negāvit sē dēpōnere posse? 18. Quam urbem cēpit Marcellus, accēpit Verrēs?

---

[1] The order of words in *captās dīcētis Syrācūsās* is known as *hyperbaton*, which means 'going over' the verb (Latin *transgressio*), so that the verb is not in the usual position at the end of the sentence. This makes a rhythmical ending or *clausula*.

THE ROMAN CALENDAR

BEFORE Julius Caesar reformed the calendar (46 B.C.), the Roman year had 355 days. After this reform the year had 365 days and the number of days in each month was the same as it is today. The first day of each month was the Calends (*Kalendae*). The Nones (*Nōnae*) were the seventh of March, May, July, and October and the fifth day of the other months.

The Ides (*Īdūs*) were the fifteenth of March, May, July, October, and the thirteenth day of the other months.

> March, July, October, May
> Make Nones the seventh, Ides the fifteenth day.

Thus the month was divided into three parts, and a date was so many days before the Nones, or so many days before the Ides, or so many days before the Calends of the following month. But the Romans counted the first day as well as the last day of a series. March 4 would be four days (not three days) before the Nones of March on the 7th (subtract 4 from 7 plus 1). March 12 would be four days before the Ides on the 15th (subtract 12 from 15 plus 1). March 29 would be four days before the Calends of April (subtract 29 from 31 plus 2; the figure here is 2 because April 1 and not March 31 is the last day of the series).

Kalendae, *Nōnae*, and *Īdūs* are all feminine, but *mēnsis*, a month, is masculine. Thus *Īdūs Martiae* = the Ides of March, but *mēnsis Martius* = March.

MARCH

1. Kalendīs Martiīs (*ablative*, on the Calends).
2. a.d. VI Nōn. Mart. = ante diem sextum Nōnās Martiās, i.e. diē sextō ante Nōnās Martiās.
3. ,, V ,,
4. ,, IV ,,
5. ,, III ,,
6. prid. ,, = pridiē Nōnās Martiās, the day before the Nones.
7. Nōnīs Martiīs (*ablative*, on the Nones).
8. a.d. VIII Īd. Mart. = ante diem octāvum Īdūs Martiās.
9. ,, VII ,,
10. ,, VI ,,
11. ,, V ,,

12. a.d. IV Īd. Mart.
13. „   III   „
14. prid.   „   = pridiē Īdūs Martiās.
15. Īdibus Martiīs (*ablative*, on the Ides).
16. a.d. XVII Kal. Aprīlīs = ante diem septimum decimum Kalendās
                              Aprīlīs (-ēs).

17. „   XVI   „
18. „   XV   „
19. „   XIV   „
20. „   XIII   „
21. „   XII   „
22. „   XI   „
23. „   X   „
24. „   IX   „
25. „   VIII   „
26. „   VII   „
27. „   VI   „
28. „   V   „
29. „   IV   „
30. „   III   „
31. prid.   „   = pridiē Kalendās Aprīlīs (-ēs).

To find the Roman equivalent for 44 B.C., subtract 44 from 754 (since 753 B.C. is the traditional date of the founding of the City of Rome). 44 B.C. = A.U.C. 710 (A.U.C. = *annō urbis conditae*). Julius Caesar died on March 15 (the Ides of March), 44 B.C.

LATIN METERS

LATIN verse is based on the quantity of the syllable. See Sections 3 and 4 of the Introduction on 'Syllables' and 'Quantity of Syllables'. Elision is also important. A final vowel is elided when the next word begins with a vowel or with *h*; and a final *m* with the preceding vowel is suppressed in the same way.

1. *The dactylic hexameter*

This was used by Vergil in the *Aeneid*, by Ovid in the *Metamorphoses*, and by Lucretius, Lucan, and Juvenal.

Each line is divided into six feet, and each foot is either a dactyl (– ‿‿) or a spondee (– –). The first four feet may be either dactyls or spondees, the fifth should be a dactyl, though there are exceptions to this rule, and the last foot should be a spondee, though the final syllable of a line may be short or long. It is usual to have a break between words (known as a *caesura*) in the middle of the third or the fourth foot. The effect would be ugly if the end of a word always corresponded with the end of a foot.

Each line must conform to the following pattern:

$$1 \quad\quad 2 \quad\quad 3 \quad\quad 4 \quad\quad 5 \quad\quad 6$$
$$– \underset{\smile\smile}{} \mid – \underset{\smile\smile}{} \mid – \underset{\smile\smile}{} \mid – \underset{\smile\smile}{} \mid – \smile\smile \mid – \smile$$

Ārmă vǐ|rūmquě că|nō ‖ Trōi|āē quī | prīmŭs ăb | ōrīs
(Verg. *Aen.* i. 1).

In this line there are three dactyls and three spondees and there is a strong caesura in both the third and the fourth foot. When there a break between words after the first short syllable of a dactyl, as there is in the second foot of this line, that is known as a weak caesura.

In a dactyl or spondee the *ictus* or beat comes on the first syllable of the foot (Árma vi|rúmque ca|nó Troi|áe qui | prímus ab | óris), but in all Latin meters the quantity of the syllables must also be correct. The first syllable of a dactyl must really be long, either because it contains a long vowel or diphthong or because the vowel is followed by two consonants.

In English verse quantity is not considered, but the *ictus* must fall naturally on the right syllable. The following line from Longfellow's *Evangeline* imitates the classical hexameter:

This is the forest primeval, the murmuring pines and the hemlocks.

Here there are five dactyls and one spondee, but the effect depends on the beat's falling on the first syllable of each foot.

Thís is the | fórest pri|méval the | múrmuring | pínes and the | hémlocks.

But if 'forest', for example, were a Latin word, the first syllable would be short and it could not stand as the first part of a dactyl. Sometimes in Latin poetry there is a conflict between the *ictus* of the verse and the natural accent of the word. Thus in the first line of the *Aeneid*, which was quoted above, the accent of both *canō* and *Trōiae* is on the first syllable, but the *ictus* of the verse is on the second.

2. *The elegiac couplet*

This was used by Catullus, by the elegiac poets Tibullus, Propertius, and Ovid, and later by Martial in his epigrams.

The first line is a hexameter of six feet, the second is a pentameter of five feet, consisting of two and a half feet followed by two and a half. Thus the pentameter is like the hexameter, but has lost a syllable in the middle and at the end of the line.

Just as the fifth foot of a hexameter should be a dactyl, so the second half of the pentameter must contain two dactyls. These are followed by a single syllable, which may be long or short. There must be a complete break between words in the middle of the pentameter.

$$- \cup\cup \mid - \cup\cup \mid - \mid\mid \cup\cup \mid - \cup\cup \mid - \cup\cup \mid - \triangledown$$
$$- \cup\cup \mid - \cup\cup \mid - \mid\mid - \cup\cup \mid - \cup\cup \mid \triangledown$$

Sīt prŏcŭl | ōmnĕ nĕ|fās; || ŭt ă|mērĭs ă|mābĭlĭs | ēstō;
quōd tĭbĭ | nōn făcĭ|ēs || sōlăvĕ | fōrmă dă|bĭt.

(Ovid, *Ars. Am.* ii. 107–8. Lesson XXVI. 1. 3.)

Here the hexameter has five dactyls and one spondee. The pentameter has four dactyls and two incomplete feet.

This meter can be imitated in English. Here is an example from Clough's *Amours de Voyage*:

Só go | fórth to the | wórld || to the | góod re|pórt and the | évil!
Gó, little | bóok! thy | tále, || ís it not | évil and | góod?

The hexameter has three spondees and three dactyls, and the pentameter has three dactyls, one spondee, and two incomplete feet, but here everything depends on the *ictus* and not on the quantity of the syllables.

3. *The hendecasyllabic or Phalaecean meter*

This meter was used by Catullus and Martial. It has eleven syllables; *hendeka* is Greek for 'eleven' and the meter is associated with the name of Phalaecus. The first foot is a spondee, though occasionally Catullus uses a trochee; a dactyl forms the second foot, and this is followed by three trochees.

$$- \cup \mid - \cup\cup \mid - \cup \mid - \cup \mid - \cup$$

Vīvā|mūs, mĕă | Lēsbĭ|(a) ātqu(e) ă|mēmŭs
(Catullus 5. 1. Lesson XXV. 1. 7).

There is a humorous imitation of this meter written by Tennyson:

Ó you | chórus of | índo|lént re|víewers,
Irresponsible, indolent reviewers,
Look, I come to the test, a tiny poem
All composed in a metre of Catullus.

Compare Swinburne:

In the month of the long decline of roses . . .

4. *The Sapphic strophe*

This takes its name from Sappho, the Greek poetess of Lesbos. It is used twenty-five times by Horace in the *Odes* and twice by Catullus. The first three lines of each strophe are the same. The feet consist of four trochees and one dactyl which comes in the middle, but Sappho's second trochee was changed by the Romans to a spondee. There is usually a strong caesura in the middle of the third foot, but sometimes a weak caesura occurs after the first short syllable of the dactyl. The fourth line is short and consists of a dactyl followed by a trochee or spondee.

(1, 2, 3) $- \cup \mid - - \mid - \mid\mid \cup\cup \mid - \cup \mid - \cup$ (Lesser Sapphic of eleven syllables)

(4) $- \cup\cup \mid - \cup$ (Adonic of five syllables)

Aūrĕ|ām quīs|quīs || mĕdĭ|ōcrĭ|tātĕm
dīlĭ|gīt tū|tūs || cărĕt | ōbsŏ|lētī
sōrdĭ|būs tē|ctī, || cărĕt | īnvĭ|dēndā
sōbrĭŭs | aūlā.
(Horace, *Odes* ii. 10. 5–8. Lesson XXXII. 1. 17.)

It is difficult to give this effect in English, but here is an example from Swinburne:

Áll the | níght sleep | cáme not u|pón my | éyelids,
Shéd not | déw, nor | shóok nor un|clósed a | féather,
Yét with | líps shut | clóse and with | éyes of | íron
Stóod and be|héld me.

5. *The Alcaic strophe*

This takes its name from Alcaeus, the Greek poet of Lesbos. It is used by Horace thirty-seven times in the *Odes* and occurs more often than any other strophe. It consists of four lines; the first two are the same and have a caesura after the fifth syllable. The original Greek meter consisted of trochees and dactyls, but Horace lengthened the fifth syllable in the first three lines. The third line has a slow movement and the fourth is rapid and contains two dactyls.

The syllable at the beginning of the first three lines is usually regarded as outside the system. This is known as an *anacrusis*, an unaccented syllable prefixed to a verse; generally it is long, but sometimes it is short.

(1, 2)   ⌄ | – ⌣ | – – || – ⌣⌣ | – ⌣ | ⌄   (Greater Alcaic of eleven syllables)

(3)   ⌄ | – ⌣ | – – | – ⌣ | – ⌣̲   (nine-syllable Alcaic)

(4)   – ⌣⌣ | – ⌣⌣ | – ⌣ | – ⌣̲   (Lesser Alcaic of ten syllables)

Aē|quām mĕ|mēntō || rēbŭs ĭn | ārdŭ|īs
sēr|vārĕ | mēntēm, || nōn sĕcŭs | ĭn bŏ|nīs
ăb | īnsŏ|lēntī | tēmpĕ|rātăm
lāetĭtĭ|ā, mŏrĭ|tūrĕ | Dēllī.[1]
(Horace, *Odes* ii. 3. 1–4. Lesson XXXI. 1. 10. 1–2.)

Tennyson's lines about Milton create the grand effect of the Alcaic strophe in English.

O | míghty-|móuth'd in||véntor of | hármo|níes,
O | skíll'd to | síng of || Tíme or E|térni|tý,
God-|gífted | órgan-|vóice of | Éngland,
Mílton, a | náme to re|sóund for | áges.

6. *The Asclepiadic meters*

There are five of these meters and they make use of four different lines based on the trochee and the dactyl.

(i) *Lesser Asclepiad*

– – | – ⌣⌣ | – || – ⌣⌣ | – ⌣ | ⌄ (twelve syllables)

Ēxē|gī mŏnŭ|mēnt(um) || āerĕ pĕ|rēnnĭ|ŭs
(Horace, *Odes* iii. 30. 1. Lesson XIX. 1. 2.)

(ii) *Glyconic*

– – | – ⌣⌣ | – ⌣ | ⌄ (eight syllables)

(iii) *Pherecratic*

– – | – ⌣⌣ | – | ⌄ (seven syllables)

[1] (2–4) Nor less (to preserve a mind) free from excessive joy in prosperity, since you will die, Dellius . . . .

(iv) *Greater Asclepiad*

$--\ |\ -\cup\cup\ |\ -\ ||\ -\cup\cup\ |\ -\ ||\ -\cup\cup\ |\ -\cup\ |\ \circ$ (sixteen syllables)

Tū nē | quaēsĭĕ|rĭs || (scīrĕ nĕ|fās) || quēm mĭhĭ, | quēm tĭ|bĭ
(Horace, *Odes* i. 11. 1. Lesson XXVIII. 1. 12.)

The Lesser Asclepiad is combined with the Glyconic or Pherecratic to make the three Asclepiadic strophes.

(i) *First strophe*, a Glyconic followed by a Lesser Asclepiad

(1) Īllĭ | rōbŭr ĕt | āēs trĭ|plēx
(2) cĭrcā | pēctŭs ĕ|rāt, || quī frăgĭ|lēm trŭ|cī . . .
(Horace, *Odes* i. 3. 9–10. Lesson XVII. 1 (B), 6.)

(ii) *Second strophe*, three Lesser Asclepiads followed by a Glyconic

(3) Mīscē | stūltĭtĭ|ăm || cōnsĭlĭ|īs brĕ|vĕm:
(4) dūlc(e) ēst | dēsĭpĕ|r(e) īn lŏ|cō.
(Horace, *Odes* iv. 12. 27–28. Lesson XXI. 1. 9.)

(iii) *Third strophe*, two Lesser Asclepiads, one Pherecratic, and one Glyconic

(1) O fōns | Bāndŭsĭ|āe, || splēndĭdĭ|ōr vĭ|trō . . .
(3) crās dō|nābĕrĭs | hāe|dō,
(4) cuī frōns | tūrgĭdă | cōrnĭ|bŭs.[1]
(Horace, *Odes* i. 5. 1 and 3–4. Lesson XIX. 1. 1.)

7. *The trochaic septenarius or trochaic tetrameter catalectic*

This meter is based on the trochee ($-\cup$) and has seven and a half feet. Normally resolutions are allowed in the even feet, but in the comedies of Plautus and Terence a tribrach ($\cup\cup\cup$), spondee ($--$), dactyl ($-\cup\cup$), or anapaest ($\cup\cup-$) may be used in any of the first six feet and a tribrach in the seventh. In a trochee the *ictus* is always on the first syllable ($\stackrel{\prime}{-}\cup$).

Crās ă|mēt quī | nūmqu(am) ă|māvīt | quīqu(e) ă|māvīt | crās ă|mĕt.
(*Pervigilium Veneris*, 1.)

This line has four trochees, three spondees, and one half-foot. The final *am* of *numquam* and the final *e* of *quīque* are elided before the following vowels. The meter is used by Tennyson in *Locksley Hall*:

Cómrades, | léave me | hére a | líttle, | whíle as | yét 'tis | éarly | mórn.

This gives the effect of seven trochees and one half-foot.

A tetrameter consists of four double-feet. 'Catalectic' means that a syllable is missing at the end.

[1] (3–4) Tomorrow you will be presented with a kid, whose forehead (is) swollen with horns.

8. *The iambic senarius or iambic trimeter*

This meter is based on the iambus and has six feet. In the pure iambic trimeter (of three double-feet) each foot must be an iambus. The *ictus* is always on the second syllable of each iambus (◡ ´). Generally the iambic trimeter allows certain resolutions, especially in the first, third, and fifth feet; a spondee or a tribrach and sometimes a dactyl or an anapaest are substituted for an iambus, but the sixth foot must not be changed. This meter is used in the comedies of Plautus and Terence, who are very free in their use of resolutions, but the last foot is always an iambus, and a trochee (– ◡) must never be used. The caesura is in the third or fourth foot. This is the scheme for the trimeter in Horace's *Epodes*.

```
◡ –    | ◡ –    | ◡ ||  –  | ◡ –    | ◡ – | ◡ ◑
◡ ◡◡  | ◡ ◡◡  | ◡   ◡◡ |◡ ◡◡  |
– –    |        | –    – |        | | – – |
– ◡◡            –  ◡◡
◡◡ –           (◡◡ –)           (◡◡ –)
```

Here is an example from Catullus of a pure iambic trimeter:

Phăsēl|lŭs īl|lĕ ‖ quēm | vĭdē|tĭs, hō|spĭtēs . . .[1]

(Catullus 4. 1).

But the following line from Terence contains four resolutions:

hŏmō | s(um); hūmā|nī ‖ nīl | ā m(e) ălĭ|ēnūm | pŭtō.[2]

(Terence, *Heaut. Tim.* 77.)

English blank verse is iambic, but it has five feet instead of six. Compare the first line of Milton's *Paradise Lost*.

Of mán's | first dís|obé|dience ánd | the frúit.

9. *The Choliambic meter*

This is used by Catullus and is known as the *Scazon* or limping meter, because it seems to start as an iambic line of six feet but to end abruptly with a trochee.

```
◡ ´ | ◡ ´ | ◡ ´ | ◡ ´ | ◡ ´ | ´ ◡
```

Since trochees should not be used in iambic meters, it can also be regarded as a trochaic line with a syllable missing in the fifth foot.

```
◡ | ´ ◡ | ´ ◡ | ´ ◡ | ´ ◡ | ´ | ´ ◡
```

Ō | quĭd sŏ|lūtĭs | ēst bĕ|ātĭ|ūs | cūrīs . . .

(Catullus, 31. 7. Lesson XIX. 1. 17).

O | whát 's more | bléssed | thán to | háve our | cáres | bánished?

[1] That yacht which you see, my friends.
[2] I am a man; I think nothing that concerns mankind is alien to me.

10. Horace uses nineteen different meters in the *Odes* and *Epodes*. In addition to the Alcaic, Sapphic, and Asclepiadic meters there are several others represented in this book, for example:

(i) *First Archilochian strophe*

A dactylic hexameter is followed by a lesser Archilochian, consisting of two dactyls and a long syllable.

Dīffū|gērĕ nĭ|vēs, || rĕdĕ|ūnt iām | grāmĭnă | cāmpīs
     ārbŏrĭ|būsquĕ cŏ|māē.

(Horace, *Odes* iv. 7. 1–2. Lesson XXXI. 1. 2.)

(ii) *Fourth Archilochian strophe*

A greater Archilochian, consisting of four feet of a dactylic hexameter and three trochees, followed by an iambic trimeter catalectic.

Pāllĭdă | mōrs āe|quō || pūl|sāt pĕdĕ | paupĕ|rūm tă|bērnās
     rēgūm|quĕ tūr|rīs. || Ō | bĕā|tĕ Sē|stī . . .

(Horace, *Odes* i. 4. 13–14. Lesson XVII. 1. 6).

(iii) *Iambic strophe*

An iambic trimeter is followed by an iambic dimeter of four feet.

Bĕā|tŭs īl|lĕ || quī | prŏcūl | nĕgō|tĭīs,
     ūt prī|scă gēns | mōrtā|lĭŭm . . .

(Horace, *Epode* 2. 1–2. Lesson XVIII. 1 (B), 14).

APPENDIX 3

SUMMARY OF GRAMMATICAL TERMS

Parts of speech

THERE are eight parts of speech: Nouns or Substantives, Adjectives, Pronouns, Verbs, Adverbs, Prepositions, Conjunctions, and Interjections.

A *Noun* is the name of a person, place, or thing, e.g. *Rōma*, 'Rome'. It may be concrete, e.g. *mōns*, 'a mountain', or abstract, e.g. *fidēs*, 'faith'. (It is not preceded by an article like *the* or *a* in English.)

An *Adjective* describes the qualities of a noun, e.g. *vir bonus*, 'a good man'.

A *Pronoun* is used instead of a noun, e.g. *ille*, 'that (man)'.

A *Verb* describes an action or a state, e.g. *hoc facit*, 'he does this'; *est hortus*, 'there is a garden'.

An *Adverb* qualifies a verb or an adjective or adverb, e.g. *hoc bene facit*, 'he does this well'.

A *Preposition* governs a noun, e.g. *in Ītaliā habitat*, 'he lives in Italy'.

A *Conjunction* connects words or sentences, e.g. *ubi vēnī, tē vīdī*, 'when I came, I saw you'.

An *Interjection* expresses emotion, e.g. *heu*, 'alas'.

A *Numeral*, which expresses a number, is usually an adjective, e.g. *ūnus*, 'one', or an adverb, e.g. *bis*, 'twice'.

Inflection. Inflection is the variation which words undergo to express gender, number, case, person, tense, mood, and voice.

Nouns, adjectives, pronouns, and verbs can be inflected, but apart from the comparison of adverbs, the other four parts of speech do not show inflection.

Declension. Declension is a term applied to the inflection of nouns, adjectives, and pronouns. This involves a change in Gender, Number, or Case.

Gender. There are three Genders: Masculine, Feminine, and Neuter.

Number. There are two Numbers: Singular, used for one person or thing, and Plural, used for more than one.

Case. There are six Cases, which are the different forms taken by a noun, adjective, or pronoun.

The *Nominative* is the subject of the verb, e.g. *pater vēnit*, 'the father came'.

The *Genitive* usually indicates possession, e.g. *patris fīlius*, 'the father's son'.

The *Dative* is usually the indirect object of the verb, e.g. *dōnum fīliō dat*, 'he gives a present to his son'.

The *Accusative* is the direct object of the verb, e.g. *fīlium videt*, 'he sees his son'.

The *Ablative* is often translated by the prepositions 'by', 'with', or 'from', e.g. *ab oppidō discēdit*, 'he goes away from the town'.

The *Vocative* is used when someone is addressed, e.g. *Marce, venī*, 'come, Marcus'.

Originally there was a *Locative* case; this survives in forms like *Rōmae*, 'at Rome'.

The Declensions. There is a second use of the word Declension. This expresses the inflectional class of a noun, e.g. a noun of the first declension. There are five declensions of nouns, and adjectives use the forms of the first three declensions.

Conjugation. Conjugation is a term applied to the inflection of verbs.

Person. Verbs have three Persons: First, Second, and Third, corresponding to the pronouns I or We, You, and He or They.

Number. Verbs have two Numbers: Singular and Plural.

Tense. Verbs have six Tenses: the Present, Imperfect, Future, Perfect, Pluperfect, and Future Perfect.

Mood. Verbs have three Moods: the Indicative, Imperative, and Subjunctive. These are known as finite moods. The *Indicative* mood states a fact, the *Imperative* mood expresses a command, and the *Subjunctive* mood is used in commands and conditions and in certain dependent clauses, where it is often translated by the auxiliary words 'may', 'might', 'would', 'should'.

The Conjugations. The word Conjugation is also used to describe the class to which a verb belongs, e.g. a verb of the first conjugation. There are four Conjugations of Regular verbs and also verbs that are Irregular.

Voice. There are two Voices: Active and Passive. The Active voice shows what the subject of the verb does. The Passive voice shows what is done to the subject, e.g. *missus est*, 'he was sent'.

Deponent verbs. A Deponent verb is passive in form but active in meeting, e.g. *ūtitur*, 'he uses'.

Transitive verbs. A Transitive verb governs an object, e.g. *litterās mittō*, 'I send a letter'. An Intransitive verb does not govern an object, e.g. *veniō*, 'I come'.

The following parts of a verb are not limited by person and mood. The *Infinitive* is a verbal substantive, e.g. *ōrāre*, 'to pray (= prayer)'; it may be present, future, or perfect, e.g. *facere, factūrus esse, fēcisse*, 'to do', 'to be about to do', 'to have done'. The *Participle* is a verbal adjective; it may be present, future, or perfect, e.g. *mittēns, missūrus, missus* (passive), 'sending', 'about to send', 'having been sent'.

The *Gerund* is a verbal substantive and is active, e.g. *labōrandō* (abl.), 'by working'. The *Gerundive* is a verbal adjective and is passive, e.g. *amandus est*, 'he must be loved'. The *Supine* is a verbal substantive. The accusative is used to express purpose, e.g. *auxilium rogātum venit*, 'he comes to ask for help', and the ablative is used with certain adjectives, e.g. *difficile est dictū*, 'it is difficult to say'.

Note on consonants (see Introduction, Sect. 1)

Consonants are either voiced or voiceless: *b, d, g, l, r, m, n, z*, consonantal *i* and *v* are voiced; *p, t, c* (with *k* and *q*), *f, h, s, x* are voiceless.

Labials are pronounced at the lips, linguals or dentals at the tongue and teeth, and palatals or gutturals at the tongue and the hard or the soft palate.

The consonants may be arranged as follows:

	Labials	*Dentals*	*Palatals and gutturals*
Stops			
(*a*) voiced	b	d	g
(*b*) voiceless	p	t	c (k, q)
(*c*) aspirates	ph	th	ch
Nasals	m	n	n (*before* c, g, q)
Liquids		l, r	
Fricatives and sibilants	f	s, z	
Semi-vowels	v		*consonantal* i

x (= *cs*) and *z* are double consonants and *h* is a breathing.

APPENDIX 4

THE following extracts from Chapters 5 and 6 of St. Matthew's Gospel show the kind of Latin that was written by St. Jerome (*c.* A.D. 348–420). This is much nearer to English and French than the classical Latin of Cicero. For example, instead of using the accusative and infinitive after a verb of saying, St. Jerome writes *dīcō quoniam*, followed by the indicative. This is similar to 'I say that . . .' in English and 'je dis que . . .' in French.

NOTES

caelum, -i, *n.,* heaven; *here pl.,* the heavens.

cōnsōlō, 1, comfort; *here passive.* **cōnsōlor,** *deponent, is more common.*

ēsuriō, 4, be hungry, hunger.

sitiō, 4, be thirsty; (*with acc.*) thirst for, long for.

saturō, 1, fill, satisfy.

misericors, -cordis, merciful.

cōnsequor, 3, *deponent,* obtain.

mundus, -a, -um, *here* = pure.

cor, cordis, *n.,* heart.

pācificus, -a, -um, peace-making, peace-maker.

persecūtiō, -ōnis, *f., here* = persecution.

maledīcō, maledīxī, 3, (*with dat.*) speak ill of, revile.

persequor, persecūtus sum, 3, *deponent, here* = persecute.

adversum = **adversus,** *prep. with acc.,* against.

mentior, 4, *deponent,* lie, speak falsely.

exultō = **exsultō,** 1, exult, rejoice exceedingly.

mercēs, -ēdis, *f.,* pay, reward.

cōpiōsus, -a, -um, plentiful.

sānctificō, 1, make holy, sanctify.

sīcut, as, like.

supersubstantiālis, -e, necessary to support life. *This is a rare adjective; in the English translation of the Lord's Prayer the word daily is used* (*Latin* **cottīdiānus, -a, -um**).

dīmittō, 3, send away; *here* = remit, forgive (debts), *with acc. and dat.*

dēbitum, -ī, *n.,* debt.

dēbitor, -ōris, *m.,* debtor.

indūcō, 3, lead into.

tentātiō, -ōnis, *f., here* = temptation.

āmēn, *adv.,* so be it, amen.

mammōna, -ae, *m.,* riches, mammon.

ideō, *adv.,* for that reason, therefore.

dīcō, *here used with* **nē** *and subjunctive, as if it were a verb of commanding or asking.*

sollicitus, -a, -um, anxious; **sollicitī sitis** (be anxious about) *is used with an indirect question,* **quid mandūcētis,** *which is a deliberative subjunctive* = what you are to eat.

animae, *dat.; compare* **corporī.**

mandūcō, 1, eat, *lit.* chew.

induō, 3, put on (clothing); *here passive in a middle sense* = put on yourselves, wear.

esca, -ae, *f.,* food.

vestimentum, -ī, *n.,* clothing.

volātilis, -e, flying; **volātile,** *n.,* a fowl, a bird.

serō, 3, sow.

metō, 3, reap.

congregō, 1, collect.

horreum, -ī, *n.,* barn.

pāscō, 3, feed.

magis *seems redundant, since* **plūris** (*gen. of value*) *is also a comparative.*

illīs, *abl. of comparison.*

cōnsīderō, 1, consider; *this is followed by the accusative* **lilia** *and by* **quōmodo crēscunt.** *In Classical Latin this would be an indirect question with the verb in the subjunctive* (**quōmodo lilia crēscant**).

lilium, -ī (-iī), *n.,* lily.

crēscō, 3, grow.

neō, 2, spin.

dīcō, *followed by* **quoniam** *and the indicative, is used instead of the accusative and infinitive; in post-classical Latin* **quoniam** (since) *and* **quia** (because) *are used in this sense*

and mean that.

Salomōn, -ōnis, *m.,* Solomon, son of David.

cooperiō, -operīre, -operuī, -opertum, 4, cover; **coopertus** *here* = clothed, arrayed.

EXERCISE

1. Beātī pauperēs spīritū: quoniam ipsōrum est rēgnum caelōrum. Beātī mītēs: quoniam ipsī possidēbunt terram. Beātī, quī lūgent: quoniam ipsī cōnsōlābuntur. Beātī, quī ēsuriunt et sitiunt iūstitiam: quoniam ipsī saturābuntur. Beātī misericordēs: quoniam ipsī misericordiam cōnsequentur. Beātī mundō corde: quoniam ipsī Deum vidēbunt. Beātī pācificī: quoniam fīliī Deī vocābuntur. Beātī, quī persecūtiōnem patiuntur propter iūstitiam: quoniam ipsōrum est rēgnum caelōrum. Beātī estis cum maledīxerint vōbīs, et persecūtī vōs fuerint, et dīxerint omne malum adversum vōs mentientēs, propter mē: Gaudēte, et exultāte, quoniam mercēs vestra copiōsa est in caelīs.

2. Sīc ergō vōs ōrābitis: Pater noster, quī es in caelīs: sanctificētur nōmen tuum. Adveniat rēgnum tuum. Fīat voluntās tua, sīcut in caelō, et in terrā. Pānem nostrum supersubstantiālem dā nōbīs hodiē. Et dīmitte nōbīs dēbita nostra, sīcut et nōs dīmittimus dēbitōribus nostrīs. Et nē nōs indūcās in tentātiōnem. Sed līberā nōs ā malō. Āmēn.

3. Nōn potestis Deō servīre, et mammōnae. Ideō dīcō vōbis, nē sollicitī sītis animae vestrae quid mandūcētis, neque corporī vestrō quid induāminī. Nonne anima plūs est quam esca, et corpus plūs quam vestīmentum? Respicite volātilia caelī, quoniam nōn serunt, neque metunt, neque congregant in horrea: et pater vester caelestis pāscit illa. Nonne vōs magis plūris estis illīs? . . . Cōnsīderāte līlia agrī quōmodo crēscunt: nōn labōrant, neque nent. Dīcō autem vōbīs, quoniam nec Salomōn in omnī glōriā suā coopertus est sīcut ūnum ex istīs.

APPENDIX 5

REVIEW OF
IMPORTANT CONSTRUCTIONS

Lesson

Lesson		
I	(1) Agricola in silvā est.	The farmer is in the forest.
II	(2) Dōnum fīliae dat.	He gives a present to (his) daughter.
III	(3) Hortus est dominō.	The master has a garden.
	(4) Frūmentum ad Graeciam (in Ītaliam, Rōmam) portant.	They carry grain to Greece (into Italy, to Rome).
IV	(5) In īnsulā Crētā habitat.	He lives on the island of Crete.
V	(6) Taurum gladiō vulnerat.	He wounds the bull with a sword.
VI	(7) Cum gaudiō, magnō gaudiō (magnō cum gaudiō).	With joy, with great joy.
VII	(8) Ab amīcīs amāmur.	We are loved by our friends.
VIII	(9) Cōpiae nostrae ē castrīs (dē locīs altīs, ab oppidō, Rōmā) properābant.	Our troops hastened out of the camp (down from the high places, away from the town, away from Rome).
IX	(10) Rōmam cum amīcō vēnī.	I have come to Rome with a friend.
X	(11) Hōc annō vēnimus.	We came this year.
	(12) Quattuor annīs venīēmus.	We shall come within four years.
XI	(13) Nōlī venīre.	Do not come.
XIV	(14) Ego et tū vēnimus.	You and I came.
	(15) Gallī sē suaque Rōmānīs dēdidērunt.	The Gauls surrendered themselves and their (possessions) to the Romans.
XV	(16) Catullus erat poēta quī Lesbiam amābat.	Catullus was the poet who loved Lesbia.
	(17) Is est quī hoc fēcit.	He is the man who did this.
	(18) Quodcumque iubēs, id faciō.	I do whatever you order.
XVI	(19) Magna pars mīlitum.	A large part of the soldiers.
	(20) Quattuor ē mīlitibus.	Four of the soldiers.
XVII	(21) Rōmae, Athēnīs, Tarentī, Philippīs, Carthāgine (Carthāginī), Curibus.	At Rome, Athens, Tarentum, Philippi, Carthage, Cures.
XVIII	(22) Hī virī mōribus sunt similēs.	These men are similar in character.
	(23) Dux magnō honōre dignus.	A general worthy of great honor.

Lesson

XIX	(24) Ō mātre pulchrā fīlia pulchrior.	O daughter fairer than your mother fair.
	(25) Quam maximus.	As great as possible.
	(26) Vir magnā sapientiā.	A man of great wisdom.
	(27) Mūrus decem pedum.	A wall of ten feet (ten feet high).
XX	(28) Multō mē sapientior est.	He is far wiser than I.
	(29) Gallīs amīcī sumus.	We are friendly to the Gauls.
XXI	(30) Labōrāre est ōrāre.	To work is to pray (work is prayer).
	(31) Tē hoc facere oportet.	You ought to do this (it is necessary for you to do this).
	(32) Sapientis est vēra dīcere.	It is the part of a wise (man) to tell the truth.
	(33) Hoc facere possum (dēbeō, sciō).	I can (ought to, know how to) do this.
	(34) Labōrāre mālō quam otiōsus esse.	I would rather work than be at leisure (I prefer to work).
	(35) Cīvis Rōmānus esse cupit.	He wants to be a Roman citizen.
XXII	(36) Ubi (postquam, simul ac) Rōmānōs vīdērunt, lēgātōs ad Caesarem mīsērunt.	When (after, as soon as) they saw (had seen) the Romans, they sent envoys to Caesar.
	(37) Dum nostrī iter faciunt, lēgātī ad Caesarem vēnērunt.	While our men were marching, the envoys came to Caesar.
	(38) Caesar exspectāvit dum lēgātī ad castra vēnērunt.	Caesar waited until the envoys came to the camp.
	(39) Quamquam Caesar diū exspectāvit, lēgātī ad castra non vēnērunt.	Although Caesar waited a long time, the envoys did not come to the camp.
	(40) Caesar, quod lēgātī ad castra nōn vēnerant, legiōnēs ēdūxit.	Because the envoys had not come to the camp, Caesar led out his legions.
XXIII	(41) Mīles clāmāns discessit.	The soldier went away shouting.
	(42) Pugnantium clāmōrem audīvī.	I heard the shout(s) of those who were fighting.
	(43) Hōc audītō discessit.	When he had heard this, he went away.
	(44) Tē audiente carmen recitāvit.	He recited the poem while you were listening.
XXIV	(45) Dīxit tē in Ītaliā esse.	He said that you were in Italy.
	(46) Dīxit tē in Ītaliā fuisse.	He said that you had been in Italy.
	(47) Dīxit tē in Ītaliā futūrum esse.	He said that you would be in Italy.
	(48) Negat sē umquam in Ītaliā fuisse.	He says that he was never in Italy.
	(49) Spērat sē in Ītaliā futūrum esse.	He hopes that he will be in Italy.
XXV	(50) Caveat emptor.	Let the buyer beware.
	(51) Nē hoc faciāmus.	Let us not do this.

Lesson

(52) Quid faciam?   What am I to do?

(53) Utinam tē mox videam.   May I see you soon!

XXVI   (54) Hodiē vēnī ut tē videam.   I have come today in order to see you.

(55) Herī vēnī, ut tē vidērem.   I came yesterday in order to see you.

(56) Herī discessī nē quis mē vidēret.   I went away yesterday in order that no one might see me.

(57) Lēgātum mīsit, quī haec nuntiāret.   He sent an envoy to announce this (these things).

(58) Lēgātum mīsit, quō celerius haec nuntiāret.   He sent an envoy in order to announce this more quickly.

(59) Tē rogō ut hoc faciās.   I ask you to do this.

(60) Tibi imperō ut veniās.   I order you to come.

(61) Tē venīre iubeō.   I order you to come.

(62) Lēgātī Caesarem ōrābant ut sē ex perīculō servāret.   The envoys begged Caesar to save them from danger.

XXVII   (63) Utinam adessēs.   I wish you were here (now).

(64) Utinam herī vēnissēs.   I wish you had come yesterday.

(65) Nōn est tam stultus ut hoc faciat.   He is not so foolish as to do this.

(66) Tanta fuit mīlitum virtūs ut nēmō vāllum relinqueret.   So great was the courage of the soldiers that no one left the rampart.

(67) Effēcit ut manērent.   He made them stay (brought it about that they stayed).

(68) Fac domī maneās.   See that you stay at home.

(69) Hoc faciās necesse est.   You must do this.

(70) Accidit ut domī manērēs.   It happened that you stayed at home.

(71) Nē haec fēcerīs.   Do not do this.

XXVIII   (72) Nōnne haec fēcistī?   You did this, didn't you?

(73) Num haec fēcistī?   You didn't do this, did you?

(74) Utrum haec fēcistī, annōn?   Did you do this, or not?

(75) Tē rogō quid faciās.   I ask you what you are doing.

(76) Tē rogō num haec fēcerīs.   I ask you whether you did this.

(77) Tē rogāvī quid facerēs.   I asked you what you were doing.

(78) Tē rogāvī num haec fēcissēs.   I asked you whether you had done this.

(79) Tē rogō quid crās factūrus sīs.   I ask you what you will do tomorrow.

(80) Tē rogō utrum haec fēcerīs necne.   I ask you whether you have done this or not.

(81) Sīve iubēs seu vetās, hoc faciō.   I am doing this, whether you order or forbid it.

XXIX   (82) Duōrum frātrum alter Rōmae, alter Athēnīs habitat.   One of the two brothers lives in Rome, the other in Athens.

(83) Aliī Rōmae, aliī Athēnīs habitant.   Some live in Rome, others in Athens.

Lesson

XXIX (84) Aliī alia dīcunt.　　Some say one thing and some another.

(85) Quattuor annōs Athēnīs habitābat.　　He lived at Athens for four years.

(86) Abhinc quattuor annōs Athēnās vēnit.　　He came to Athens four years ago.

XXX (87) Īdem est quī anteā fuit.　　He is the same as he was before.

(88) Rōmam vēnistī nec quisquam tē vīdit.　　You came to Rome and no one saw you.

(89) Suum quisque dōnum capiat.　　Let each man take his own gift.

(90) Optimus quisque.　　All the best men.

(91) Tālis es quālis anteā fuistī.　　You are the same kind of man as you were before (your character is such as it always was).

(92) Is est quī haec faciat.　　He is the sort of man to do this (who would do this).

(93) Nēmo est quī haec faciat.　　There is no one who would do this.

(94) Dignus est quī amētur.　　He deserves to be loved.

XXXI (95) Dīxit Gallōs cum Germānīs, quī trāns Rhēnum incolerent, bellum gerere.　　He said that the Gauls waged war with the Germans who lived across the Rhine.

XXXII (96) Rōmānī castrīs potītī sunt.　　The Romans got possession of the camp.

(97) Mortis metū līberantur.　　They are freed from the fear of death.

XXXIII (98) Cum Rōmam veniam (vēnerō), tē vidēbō.　　When I come to Rome, I shall see you.

(99) Cum Rōmam vēnī, tum Athēnās abiistī.　　Just at the time when I came to Rome, you went away to Athens.

(100) Cum Rōmam vēneram, tē vidēbam.　　Whenever I came to Rome, I used to see you.

(101) Cum hoc vīdissem, Athēnās abiī.　　When I had seen this, I went away to Athens.

(102) Cum Rōmae habitēs, mox tē vidēbō.　　Since you are living in Rome, I shall see you soon.

(103) Cum Rōmae habitēs, (tamen) tē nōn vidēbō.　　Although you are living in Rome, I shall not see you.

XXXIV (104) Sī hoc facis, peccās.　　If you are doing this, you are doing wrong.

(105) Sī hoc fēcistī, peccāvistī.　　If you did this, you did wrong.

(106) Sī hoc fēceris (faciēs), peccābis.　　If you do this, you will do wrong.

(107) Sī hoc faciās, peccēs.　　If you were to do this, you would do wrong.

(108) Sī hoc facerēs, peccārēs.　　If you were doing this (now), you would be doing wrong.

(109) Sī hoc fēcissēs, peccāvissēs.　　If you had done this (then), you would have done wrong.

Lesson

XXXV (110) Tibi persuādētur.

You are persuaded.

(111) Hoc magnō ūsuī nostrīs fuit.

This was of great use to our men.

XXXVI (112) Caesar exspectāvit dum lēgātī ad castra venīrent.

Caesar waited for the envoys to come to the camp.

(113) Antequam lēgātī ad castra venīrent, legiōnēs ēdūxit.

He led out his legions before the envoys could come to the camp.

(114) Caesar lēgātōs laudāvit, quod ad castra vēnissent.

Caesar praised the envoys because (as he said) they had come to the camp (on the ground that they had come).

(115) Caesar lēgātōs laudāvit, nōn quod ad castra vēnissent, sed quia legiōnēs exspectābat.

Caesar praised the envoys, not because they had come to the camp, but because he was waiting for his legions.

(116) Lēgātōs laudāvit, quippe quī sociī fidēlēs essent.

He praised the envoys since (inasmuch as) they were faithful allies.

(117) Lūdant, dum (dummodo) labōrent.

Let them play, provided that they work.

(118) Quamvīs ad castra vēnissent, (tamen) Caesarem nōn vīdērunt.

Although they had come to the camp, (yet) they did not see Caesar.

(119) Caesar, quī diū exspectāvisset, tamen abīre cōnstituit.

Although Caesar had waited for a long time, (yet) he determined to go away.

XXXVII (120) Vereor nē hoc faciās.

I fear that (lest) you will do this.

(121) Vereor ut (= nē nōn) hoc faciās.

I fear that you will not do this.

(122) Hoc ita fēcit ut iusseram.

He did this just as I had ordered.

(123) Hoc fēcit quasi iussissem.

He did this just as if I had ordered it.

(124) Prūdentior es quam quī hoc faciās.

You are too wise to do this (wiser than one who would do it).

(125) Tantum abest ut hoc faciās ut abīre velīs.

Far from doing this you want to go away.

XXXVIII (126) Hic vir tibi amandus est.

You ought to love this man.

(127) Imperātōrī ā tē pārendum est.

You must obey the general.

(128) Lēgātī ad pācem petendam (pācis petendae causā) vēnērunt.

The envoys came to seek peace.

(129) Oppida videndī causā vēnērunt.

They came to see the towns.

XXXIX (130) Lēgātī pācem petītum vēnērunt.

The envoys came to seek peace.

(131) Dīxit pācem petītum īrī.

He said that peace would be sought.

(132) Dīxit futūrum esse ut pāx peterētur.

He said that peace would be sought.

Lesson

XXXIX (133) Spērat fore ut sapiās. — He hopes that you will be wise.

(134) Difficile est dictū. — It is difficult to say.

XL (135) Nūllus est tibi mortis timor. — You have no fear of death.

(136) Meī oblīvīscitur. — He forgets me.

(137) Tē maximī aestimō. — I value you very highly.

(138) Prōditiōnis eum accūsant. — They accuse him of treachery.

(139) Morte condemnātus est. — He was condemned to death.

(140) Mē pudet inertiae. — I am ashamed of my idleness.

(141) Hoc tuā et omnium cīvium interest. — This concerns you and all the citizens.

XLI (142) Nēmō impedit quōminus hoc faciās. — No one prevents you from doing this.

(143) Tē dēterruit nē hoc facerēs. — He prevented you from doing this.

(144) Tē hoc facere prohibuit. — He prevented you from doing this.

(145) Nōn dubitō quīn hoc fēcerīs. — I do not doubt that you did this.

(146) Nōn dubium erat quīn hoc fēcissēs. — There was no doubt that you had done this.

(147) Fierī potest ut hoc fēcerīs. — It is possible that you have done this.

(148) Nōn fierī potest quīn hoc fēcerīs. — It is impossible that you have not done this.

(149) (Dīxit) adesse hostēs; cīvēs ad sē properārent; nē fugerent. — (He said that) the enemy were at hand; let the citizens hasten to him and not run away.

(150) (Dīxit) ... Quid vellent? — What did they want? (he asked what they wanted).

APPENDIX 6
REVIEW OF GRAMMAR

1. Nouns

First declension			Second declension		
silva,			**hortus,**		**dōnum,**
f., wood, forest			*m.*, garden		*n.*, gift

S. Nom.	silva		hortus		dōnum
Gen.	silvae	*fīlia, f.,* daugh-	hortī		dōnī
Dat.	silvae	ter, has *fīliā-*	hortō	The vocative	dōnō
Acc.	silvam	*bus* in the	hortum	singular	dōnum
Abl.	silvā	dative and	hortō	masculine	dōnō
P. Nom.	silvae	ablative plural	hortī	ends in *e,*	dōna
Gen.	silvārum	instead of	hortōrum	e.g. *Mārce*	dōnōrum
Dat.	silvīs	*fīliīs* (see	hortīs	from *Mārcus*	dōnīs
Acc.	silvās	*fīlius*)	hortōs		dōna
Abl.	silvīs		hortīs		dōnīs

Some Greek nouns retain Greek forms, e.g. *Daphnē,* gen. *Daphnēs.*

ager,		**puer,**	**fīlius,**	**praemium,**
m., field		*m.*, boy	*m.*, son	*n.*, reward
S. Nom.	ager	puer	fīlius	praemium
Gen.	agrī	puerī	fīlī (-iī)	praemī (-iī)
Dat.	agrō	puerō	fīliō	praemiō
Acc.	agrum	puerum	fīlium	praemium
Abl.	agrō	puerō	fīliō	praemiō
			(*Voc.* fīlī)	
P. Nom.	agrī	puerī	fīliī	praemia
Gen.	agrōrum	puerōrum	fīliōrum	praemiōrum
Dat.	agrīs	puerīs	fīliīs	praemiīs
Acc.	agrōs	puerōs	fīliōs	praemia
Abl.	agrīs	puerīs	fīliīs	praemiīs

Third declension, consonant stems

	prīnceps,	**mīles,**	**dux,**	**cōnsul,**	**pater,**
	m., chief	*m.*, soldier	*m.*, leader	*m.*, consul	*m.*, father
S. Nom.	prīnceps	mīles	dux	cōnsul	pater
Gen.	prīncipis	mīlitis	ducis	cōnsulis	patris
Dat.	prīncipī	mīlitī	ducī	cōnsulī	patrī
Acc.	prīncipem	mīlitem	ducem	cōnsulem	patrem
Abl.	prīncipe	mīlite	duce	cōnsule	patre
P. Nom.	prīncipēs	mīlitēs	ducēs	cōnsulēs	patrēs
Gen.	prīncipum	mīlitum	ducum	cōnsulum	patrum
Dat.	prīncipibus	mīlitibus	ducibus	cōnsulibus	patribus
Acc.	prīncipēs	mīlitēs	ducēs	cōnsulēs	patrēs
Abl.	prīncipibus	mīlitibus	ducibus	cōnsulibus	patribus

	amor,	**legiō,**	**caput,**	**nōmen,**
	m., love	*f.*, legion	*n.*, head	*n.*, name
S. Nom.	amor	legiō	caput	nōmen
Gen.	amōris	legiōnis	capitis	nōminis
Dat.	amōrī	legiōnī	capitī	nōminī
Acc.	amōrem	legiōnem	caput	nōmen
Abl.	amōre	legiōne	capite	nōmine
P. Nom.	amōrēs	legiōnēs	capita	nōmina
Gen.	amōrum	legiōnum	capitum	nōminum
Dat.	amōribus	legiōnibus	capitibus	nōminibus
Acc.	amōrēs	legiōnēs	capita	nōmina
Abl.	amōribus	legiōnibus	capitibus	nōminibus

Third declension, -i-stems

	cīvis,	**nūbēs,**	**urbs,**	**nox,**
	m. and f., citizen	*f.*, cloud	*f.*, city	*f.*, night
S. Nom.	cīvis	nūbēs	urbs	nox
Gen.	cīvis	nūbis	urbis	noctis
Dat.	cīvī	nūbī	urbī	noctī
Acc.	cīvem	nūbem	urbem	noctem
Abl.	cīve	nūbe	urbe	nocte
P. Nom.	civēs	nūbēs	urbēs	noctēs
Gen.	cīvium	nūbium	urbium	noctium
Dat.	cīvibus	nūbibus	urbibus	noctibus
Acc.	cīvīs, -ēs	nūbīs, -ēs	urbīs, -ēs	noctīs, -ēs
Abl.	cīvibus	nūbibus	urbibus	noctibus

Neuter -i-stems

Irregular nouns

	mare,	**animal,**	**senex,**	**vis,**	**iter,**
	n., sea	*n.*, animal	*m.*, old man	*f.*, force, *pl.*, strength	*n.*, journey, march
S. Nom.	mare	animal	senex	vīs	iter
Gen.	maris	animālis	senis	(vīs)	itineris
Dat.	marī	animālī	senī	(vī)	itinerī
Acc.	mare	animal	senem	vim	iter
Abl.	marī	animālī	sene	vī	itinere
P. Nom.	maria	animālia	senēs	vīrēs	itinera
Gen.	. .	animālium	senum	vīrium	itinerum
Dat.	maribus	animālibus	senibus	vīribus	itineribus
Acc.	maria	animālia	senēs	vīrīs, -ēs	itinera
Abl.	maribus	animālibus	senibus	vīribus	itineribus

Fourth declension

Fifth declension

	gradus,	**genū,**	**domus,**	**rēs,**
	m., step	*n.*, knee	*f.*, home	*f.*, thing
S. Nom.	gradus	genū	domus	rēs

Gen.	gradūs	genūs	domūs (domī, at home)	reī
Dat.	graduī	genū	domuī (domō)	reī
Acc.	gradum	genū	domum	rem
Abl.	gradū	genū	domō (domū)	rē
P. Nom.	gradūs	genua	domūs	rēs
Gen.	graduum	genuum	domuum (domōrum)	rērum
Dat.	gradibus	genibus	domibus	rēbus
Acc.	gradūs	genua	domōs (domūs)	rēs
Abl.	gradibus	genibus	domibus	rēbus

Locative case

First declension: Rōmae, at Rome.   Athēnīs, at Athens.
Second declension: Tarentī, at Tarentum.   domī, at home.
    Philippīs, at Philippi.
Third declension: Carthāginī, Carthāgine, at Carthage.   rūrī, in
    the country.   Curibus, at Cures.

2. Adjectives

First and second declensions

bonus, good   **liber,** free

	M.	*F.*	*N.*	*M.*	*F.*	*N.*
S. Nom.	bonus	bona	bonum	līber	lībera	līberum
Gen.	bonī	bonae	bonī	līberī	līberae	līberī
Dat.	bonō	bonae	bonō	līberō	līberae	līberō
Acc.	bonum	bonam	bonum	līberum	līberam	līberum
Abl.	bonō	bonā	bonō	līberō	līberā	līberō
(*Voc.* bone)						
P. Nom.	bonī	bonae	bona	līberī	līberae	lībera
Gen.	bonōrum	bonārum	bonōrum	līberōrum	līberārum	līberōrum
Dat.	bonīs	bonīs	bonīs	līberīs	līberīs	līberīs
Acc.	bonōs	bonās	bona	līberōs	līberās	lībera
Abl.	bonīs	bonīs	bonīs	līberīs	līberīs	līberīs

pulcher, beautiful

	M.	*F.*	*N.*
S. Nom.	pulcher	pulchra	pulchrum
Gen.	pulchrī	pulchrae	pulchrī
Dat.	pulchrō	pulchrae	pulchrō
Acc.	pulchrum	pulchram	pulchrum
Abl.	pulchrō	pulchrā	pulchrō
P. Nom.	pulchrī	pulchrae	pulchra
Gen.	pulchrōrum	pulchrārum	pulchrōrum
Dat.	pulchrīs	pulchrīs	pulchrīs
Acc.	pulchrōs	pulchrās	pulchra
Abl.	pulchrīs	pulchrīs	pulchrīs

Third declension (*including present participles*)

	omnis, all			**ācer,** keen, sharp		
	M., F.		*N.*	*M.*	*F.*	*N.*
S. Nom.	omnis		omne	ācer	ācris	ācre
Gen.		omnis			ācris	
Dat.		omnī			ācrī	
Acc.	omnem		omne		ācrem	ācre
Abl.		omnī			ācrī	
P. Nom.	omnēs		omnia		ācrēs	ācria
Gen.		omnium			ācrium	
Dat.		omnibus			ācribus	
Acc.	omnīs, -ēs		omnia		ācrīs, -ēs	ācria
Abl.		omnibus			ācribus	

	fēlīx, happy			**amāns,** loving		
	M., F.		*N.*	*M., F.*		*N.*
S. Nom.	fēlīx		fēlīx	amāns		amāns
Gen.		fēlīcis			amantis	
Dat.		fēlīcī			amantī	
Acc.	fēlīcem		fēlīx	amantem		amāns
Abl.		fēlīcī			amantī, -e	
P. Nom.	fēlīcēs		fēlīcia	amantēs		amantia
Gen.		fēlīcium			amantium	
Dat.		fēlīcibus			amantibus	
Acc.	fēlīcīs, -ēs		fēlīcia	amantīs, -ēs		amantia
Abl.		fēlīcibus			amantibus	

Comparison of adjectives

Positive		Comparative		Superlative	
dūrus	hard	dūrior	harder	dūrissimus	hardest
longus	long	longior		longissimus	
brevis	short	brevior		brevissimus	
audāx	bold	audācior		audācissimus	
ācer	keen	ācrior		ācerrimus	
pulcher	beautiful	pulchrior		pulcherrimus	
miser	miserable	miserior		miserrimus	
similis	like	similior		simillimus	

Irregular comparison

bonus	good	melior	better	optimus	best
malus	bad	pēior	worse	pessimus	worst
magnus	great	māior	greater	maximus	greatest
parvus	small	minor	smaller	minimus	smallest
multus	much	plūs	more	plūrimus	most

Comparatives and superlatives corresponding to adverbs

extrā	outside	exterior	outer	extrēmus	outermost
īnfrā	below	īnferior	lower	īnfimus	lowest

suprā	above	superior	higher	suprēmus	highest
				summus	
post	after	posterior	latter	postrēmus	last
intrā	within	interior	inner	intimus	inmost
prae	before	prior	former	prīmus	first
prope	near	propior	nearer	proximus	next
ultrā	beyond	ulterior	farther	ultimus	farthest
idōneus	fit	magis idōneus		maximē idōneus	
dubius	doubtful	magis dubius		maximē dubius	

Declension of the comparative

		melior, better			plūs, more		
		M., F.		*N.*	*M., F.*		*N.*
S. Nom.	melior			melius	..		plūs
Gen.		meliōris			..		plūris
Dat.		meliōrī			..		..
Acc.	meliōrem			melius	..		plūs
Abl.		meliōre			..		plūre
P. Nom.	meliōrēs			meliōra	plūrēs		plūra
Gen.		meliōrum				plūrium	
Dat.		meliōribus				plūribus	
Acc.	meliōrēs (-īs)			meliōra	plūrēs (-īs)		plūra
Abl.		meliōribus				plūribus	

Adjectives with genitive singular in -īus and dative in -ī

ūnus, -a, -um	one	alius, alia, aliud	another
tōtus, -a, -um	whole	alter, altera, alterum	the other (of two)
sōlus, -a, -um	alone	uter, utra, utrum	which (of two)
ūllus, -a, -um	any	neuter, neutra, neutrum	neither
nūllus, -a, -um	no, none	uterque, utraque, utrumque	both, each (of two)

	M.	*F.*	*N.*	*M.*	*F.*	*N.*
Nom.	ūnuṣ	ūna	ūnum	alter	altera	alterum
Gen.		ūnīus			alterīus	
Dat.		ūnī			alterī	
Acc.	ūnum	ūnam	ūnum	alterum	alteram	alterum
Abl.	ūnō	ūnā	ūnō	alterō	alterā	alterō

Nom.	alius	alia	aliud	
Gen.		..		The genitive *alterīus* is used instead
Dat.		aliī		of *alīus*.
Acc.	alium	aliam	aliud	The plural of these adjectives is like
Abl.	aliō	aliā	aliō	the plural of *bonus*.

3. Adverbs

First and second declensions (ending in -ē, sometimes in -ō)

dignus   worthy   dignē   worthily

Third declension (ending in -ter or in -e)

fortis	brave	fortiter	bravely
facilis	easy	facile	easily

Comparison of adverbs

fortiter bravely   **fortius** more bravely   **fortissimē** most bravely

Irregular comparison

bene	well	melius	better	optimē	best
male	badly	pēius	worse	pessimē	worst
magnopere	greatly	magis	more	maximē	most, especially
parum	too little	minus	less	minimē	least
multum	much	plūs	more	plūrimum	most
diū	for a long time	diūtius		diūtissimē	
saepe	often	saepius		saepissimē	
prope	near	propius		proximē	
..		prius	before	prīmum	first

4. Pronouns

Personal pronouns: **ego,** I,   **tū,** you,   **nōs,** we,   **vōs,** you (pl.)

Nom.	ego	tū	nōs	vōs
Gen.	meī	tuī	nostrum, nostrī	vestrum, vestrī
Dat.	mihi	tibi	nōbīs	vōbīs
Acc.	mē	tē	nōs	vōs
Abl.	mē	tē	nōbīs	vōbīs

Possessive adjectives

1st person:	meus, mea, meum	my, mine
	noster, nostra, nostrum	our, ours
2nd person:	tuus, tua, tuum	your, yours (sing.)
	vester, vestra, vestrum	your, yours (pl.)
3rd person:	suus, sua, suum	his, her, its, their (reflexive)

Demonstrative pronouns

hic, this (near me); **ille,** that (over there); **is,** this, that, he, she, it; also **iste,** that (near you)

	M.	F.	N.	M.	F.	N.
S. Nom.	hic	haec	hoc	ille	illa	illud
Gen.		hūius			illīus	
Dat.		huic			illī	
Acc.	hunc	hanc	hoc	illum	illam	illud
Abl.	hōc	hāc	hōc	illō	illā	illō

P. Nom.	hī	hae	haec	illī	illae	illa
Gen.	hōrum	hārum	hōrum	illōrum	illārum	illōrum
Dat.		hīs			illīs	
Acc.	hōs	hās	haec	illōs	illās	illa
Abl.		hīs			illīs	

The pronoun **idem**, the same

S. Nom.	is	ea	id	īdem	eadem	idem
Gen.		ēius			ēiusdem	
Dat.		eī			eīdem	
Acc.	eum	eam	id	eundem	eandem	idem
Abl.	eō	eā	eō	eōdem	eādem	eōdem
P. Nom.	eī (iī)	eae	ea	eīdem	eaedem	eadem
Gen.	eōrum	eārum	eōrum	eōrundem	eārundem	eōrundem
Dat.		eīs (iīs)			eīsdem	
Acc.	eōs	eās	ea	eōsdem	eāsdem	eadem
Abl.		eīs (iīs)			eīsdem	

Emphatic and reflexive pronouns
ipse, self (myself, yourself, himself)

S. Nom.	ipse	ipsa	ipsum	*P.*	ipsī	ipsae	ipsa
Gen.		ipsīus			ipsōrum	ipsārum	ipsōrum
Dat.		ipsī				ipsīs	
Acc.	ipsum	ipsam	ipsum		ipsōs	ipsās	ipsa
Abl.	ipsō	ipsā	ipsō			ipsīs	

sē, sēsē, himself, herself, itself, themselves

Gen.	suī	*Acc.*	sē
Dat.	sibi	*Abl.*	sē

Relative pronoun: **quī,** who

S. Nom.	quī	quae	quod	*P.*	quī	quae	quae
Gen.		cūius			quōrum	quārum	quōrum
Dat.		cui				quibus	
Acc.	quem	quam	quod		quōs	quās	quae
Abl.	quō	quā	quō			quibus	

Interrogative pronoun: **quis,** who?, adjective **quī**

	M., F.		*N.*	
S. Nom.	quis		quid	The plural of *quis* and the adjective
Gen.		cūius		*quī* are declined like the relative.
Dat.		cui		
Acc.	quem		quid	Indefinite relative pronouns:
Abl.		quō		*quīcumque, quaecumque, quodcumque,*

whoever, whatever.
quisquis, quicquid, or *quidquid,*
whoever, whatever.

Indefinite pronouns

quis, anyone; *adjective,* **quī,** any

| *Nom.* | quis | quid | quī | qua (quae) | quod |

These are declined like the interrogative *quis* and the relative *quī,* but *qua* is often used instead of *quae.*

quisquam, any at all; *adjective* **ūllus, -a, -um**

(used after a negative or a virtual negative, in a question or in comparisons)

| *Nom.* | quisquam | quidquam (quicquam) | No plural |

In the ablative *ūllus* is used instead of *quisquam.*

Compare **nēmō,** no one; *adjective* **nūllus, -a, -um**

Nom	nēmō	In the genitive and ablative *nūllus* is used
Gen.	. .	instead of *nēmō.*
Dat.	nēminī	
Acc.	nēminem	
Abl.	. .	

quīvīs *or* **quīlibet,** anyone you like (pronoun or adjective)

| *Nom.* | quīvīs | quaevīs | quidvīs (quodvīs) |

aliquis, someone; *adjective,* **aliquī**

| *Nom.* | aliquis | aliquid | aliquī | aliqua | aliquod |

These are declined like *quis* and *quī.*
Compare *nōnnullī = nōn* and the plural of *nūllus,* 'some few'.

quīdam, a certain one (pronoun or adjective)

	S.			*P.*		
Nom.	quīdam	quaedam	quiddam	quīdam	quaedam	quaedam
		(quoddam, *adj.*)				
Gen.		cūiusdam		quōrun-dam	quārundam	quōrun-dam
Dat.		cuidam			quibusdam	
Acc.	quendam	quandam	quiddam	quōsdam	quāsdam	quaedam
Abl.	quōdam	quādam	quōdam		quibusdam	

nescio quis, somebody or other; *adjective,* **nescio quī**

quisque, each one (pronoun and adjective)

| *Nom.* | quisque | quaeque | quidque | quisque | quaeque | quodque |

This is frequently used after the adjective *suus* and nearly always in the singular.

5. *Prepositions*

Prepositions taking the accusative

| ad | to | ante | before |
| adversus | against | apud | at, near |

circā, circum	around	per	through
citrā, cis	this side	pōne	behind
contrā	against	post	after
ergā	towards	praeter	beyond
	(not used of place)	prope	near
extrā	outside	propter	on account of
īnfrā	below	secundum	next to
inter	among	suprā	above
intrā	inside	trāns	across
iuxtā	near	ultrā	on the farther side
ob	on account of	versus	towards
penes	in the power of		

Prepositions taking the ablative

ā, ab	away from, by	prae	in comparison with
absque	without, but for	prō	in front of, on behalf of, for
cōram	in the presence of	sine	without
cum	with	tenus	up to, as far as
dē	from, down from, concerning		
		clam	secretly ⎱ generally
ē, ex	out of	palam	openly ⎰ adverbs

Prepositions taking the accusative or the ablative

| in | into, in | sub | under |
| subter | beneath | super | above |

The accusative expresses *motion to*; the ablative, *rest in* a place.

6. Numerals

	Cardinals	Ordinals	Roman numerals
1	ūnus, -a, -um	prīmus, -a, -um	I
2	duo, duae, duo	secundus (alter)	II
3	trēs, tria	tertius	III
4	quattuor	quārtus	IIII, IV
5	quīnque	quīntus	V
6	sex	sextus	VI
7	septem	septimus	VII
8	octō	octāvus	VIII
9	novem	nōnus	VIIII, IX
10	decem	decimus	X
11	ūndecim	ūndecimus	XI
12	duodecim	duodecimus	XII
13	tredecim	tertius decimus	XIII
14	quattuordecim	quārtus decimus	XIIII, XIV
15	quīndecim	quīntus decimus	XV
16	sēdecim	sextus decimus	XVI
17	septendecim	septimus decimus	XVII
18	duodēvīgintī	duodēvīcēsimus	XVIII

19	ūndēvīgintī	ūndēvīcēsimus	XVIIII, XIX
20	vīgintī	vīcēsimus	XX
21	{ vīgintī ūnus / ūnus et vīgintī	vīcēsimus prīmus / ūnus et vīcēsimus	XXI
22	{ vīgintī duo / duo et vīgintī	vīcēsimus secundus / alter et vīcēsimus	XXII
30	trīgintā	trīcēsimus	XXX
40	quadrāgintā	quadrāgēsimus	XXXX, XL
50	quīnquāgintā	quīnquāgēsimus	L
60	sexāgintā	sexāgēsimus	LX
70	septuāgintā	septuāgēsimus	LXX
80	octōgintā	octōgēsimus	LXXX
90	nōnāgintā	nōnāgēsimus	LXXXX, XC
100	centum	centēsimus	C
200	ducentī, -ae, -a	ducentēsimus	CC
300	trecentī	trecentēsimus	CCC
400	quadringentī	quadringentēsimus	CCCC
500	quīngentī	quīngentēsimus	D
600	sescentī	sescentēsimus	DC
700	septingentī	septingentēsimus	DCC
800	octingentī	octingentēsimus	DCCC
900	nōngentī	nōngentēsimus	DCCCC, CM
1000	mīlle	mīllēsimus	M
2000	duo mīlia	bis mīllēsimus	MM

Ordinals ending in -*ēsimus* may also end in -*ēnsimus*.

Declension of numerals

For **ūnus** see Adjectives with genitive in **-īus**.

duo, two; **trēs,** three; *plural of* **mīlle**, a thousand

Nom.	duo	duae	duo	trēs	tria	mīlia
Gen.	duōrum	duārum	duōrum	trium		mīlium
Dat.	duōbus	duābus	duōbus	tribus		mīlibus
Acc.	duōs (duo)	duās	duo	trēs (trīs) tria		mīlia
Abl.	duōbus	duābus	duōbus	tribus		mīlibus

7. Verbs

The verb 'to be', **sum, esse, fuī,** *fut. part.* **futūrus**

	Present		Imperfect	Futur
Indicative	Subjunctive	Indicative	Subjunctive	
sum	sim	eram	essem	erō
es	sīs	erās	essēs	eris
est	sit	erat	esset	erit
sumus	sīmus	erāmus	essēmus	erimus
estis	sītis	erātis	essētis	eritis
sunt	sint	erant	essent	erunt

Perfect		Pluperfect		Future perfect
fuī	fuerim	fueram	fuissem	fuerō
fuistī	fuerīs	fuerās	fuissēs	fueris
fuit	fuerit	fuerat	fuisset	fuerit
fuimus	fuerīmus	fuerāmus	fuissēmus	fuerimus
fuistis	fuerītis	fuerātis	fuissētis	fueritis
fuērunt (-ēre)	fuerint	fuerant	fuissent	fuerint

Imperative

es (estō)   este (estōte)
estō   suntō

Infinitive

Pres. esse
Perf. fuisse
Fut. futūrus esse (fore)

Participle

Fut. futūrus, -a, -um

The four regular conjugations

First conjugation: **amō, amāre, amāvī, amātum,** love

Active

Present		Imperfect		Future
Indicative	Subjunctive	Indicative	Subjunctive	
amō	amem	amābam	amārem	amābō
amās	amēs	amābās	amārēs	amābis
amat	amet	amābat	amāret	amābit
amāmus	amēmus	amābāmus	amārēmus	amābimus
amātis	amētis	amābātis	amārētis	amābitis
amant	ament	amābant	amārent	amābunt

Perfect		Pluperfect		Future perfect
amāvī	amāverim	amāveram	amāvissem	amāverō
amāvistī	amāverīs	amāverās	amāvissēs	amāveris
amāvit	amāverit	amāverat	amāvisset	amāverit
amāvimus	amāverīmus	amāverāmus	amāvissēmus	amāverimus
amāvistis	amāverītis	amāverātis	amāvissētis	amāveritis
amāvērunt (-ēre)	amāverint	amāverant	amāvissent	amāverint

Imperative

amā (amātō)   amāte (amātōte)
amātō   amantō

Infinitive

Pres. amāre
Perf. amāvisse
Fut. amātūrus esse

Participles

Pres. amāns
Fut. amātūrus, -a, -um

Gerund

amandī, amandō, amandum, amandō

Supine

amātum, amātū

Passive

Present		Imperfect		Future
Indicative	Subjunctive	Indicative	Subjunctive	
amor	amer	amābar	amārer	amābor
amāris	amēris	amābāris	amārēris	amāberis
(-re)	(-re)	(-re)	(-re)	(-re)

amātur	amētur	amābātur	amārētur	amābitur
amāmur	amēmur	amābāmur	amārēmur	amābimur
amāminī	amēminī	amābāminī	amārēminī	amābiminī
amantur	amentur	amābantur	amārentur	amābuntur

Perfect		*Pluperfect*		*Future perfect*
amātus (-a, -um) sum	amātus sim	amātus eram	amātus essem	amātus erō
amātus es	amātus sīs	amātus erās	amātus essēs	amātus eris
amātus est	amātus sit	amātus erat	amātus esset	amātus erit
amātī (-ae, -a) sumus	amātī sīmus	amātī erāmus	amātī essēmus	amātī erimus
amātī estis	amātī sītis	amātī erātis	amātī essētis	amātī eritis
amātī sunt	amātī sint	amātī erant	amātī essent	amātī erunt

Imperative		*Infinitive*	*Participles*
amāre (amātor)	amāminī	*Pres.* amārī	*Perf.* amātus, -a, -um
amātor	amantor	*Perf.* amātus esse	*Gerundive (Future)*
		Fut. amātum īrī	amandus, -a, -um

Second conjugation: **moneō, monēre, monuī, monitum**, advise

Active

	Present		*Imperfect*		*Future*
Indicative	*Subjunctive*	*Indicative*	*Subjunctive*		
moneō	moneam	monēbam	monērem		monēbō
monēs	moneās	monēbās	monērēs		monēbis
monet	moneat	monēbat	monēret		monēbit
monēmus	moneāmus	monēbāmus	monērēmus		monēbimus
monētis	moneātis	monēbātis	monērētis		monēbitis
monent	moneant	monēbant	monērent		monēbunt

Perfect		*Pluperfect*		*Future perfect*
monuī	monuerim	monueram	monuissem	monuerō
monuistī	monuerīs	monuerās	monuissēs	monueris
monuit	monuerit	monuerat	monuisset	monuerit
monuimus	monuerīmus	monuerāmus	monuissēmus	monuerimus
monuistis	monuerītis	monuerātis	monuissētis	monueritis
monuērunt (-ēre)	monuerint	monuerant	monuissent	monuerint

Imperative		*Infinitive*	*Participles*
monē	monēte	*Pres.* monēre	*Pres.* monēns
(monētō)	(monētōte)	*Perf.* monuisse	*Fut.* monitūrus, -a,
monētō	monentō	*Fut.* monitūrus esse	-um

Gerund	*Supine*
monendī, monendō, monendum, monendō	monitum, monitū

Passive

Present		Imperfect		Future
Indicative	*Subjunctive*	*Indicative*	*Subjunctive*	
moneor	monear	monēbar	monērer	monēbor
monēris	moneāris	monēbāris	monērēris	monēberis
(-re)	(-re)	(-re)	(-re)	(-re)
monētur	moneātur	monēbātur	monērētur	monēbitur
monēmur	moneāmur	monēbāmur	monērēmur	monēbimur
monēminī	moneāminī	monēbāminī	monērēminī	monēbiminī
monentur	moneantur	monēbantur	monērentur	monēbuntur

Perfect		Pluperfect		Future perfect
monitus	monitus	monitus	monitus	monitus
sum	sim	eram	essem	erō
monitus	monitus	monitus	monitus	monitus
es	sīs	erās	essēs	eris
monitus	monitus	monitus	monitus	monitus
est	sit	erat	esset	erit
monitī	monitī	monitī	monitī	monitī
sumus	sīmus	erāmus	essēmus	erimus
monitī	monitī	monitī	monitī	monitī
estis	sītis	erātis	essētis	eritis
monitī	monitī	monitī	monitī	monitī
sunt	sint	erant	essent	erunt

Imperative		Infinitive	Participles
monēre	monēminī	*Pres.* monērī	*Perf.* monitus, -a, -um
(monētor)		*Perf.* monitus esse	*Gerundive*
monētor	monentur	*Fut.* monitum īrī	monendus, -a, -um

Third conjugation: **regō, regere, rēxī, rēctum,** rule

Active

Present		Imperfect		Future
Indicative	*Subjunctive*	*Indicative*	*Subjunctive*	
regō	regam	regēbam	regerem	regam
regis	regās	regēbās	regerēs	regēs
regit	regat	regēbat	regeret	reget
regimus	regāmus	regēbāmus	regerēmus	regēmus
regitis	regātis	regēbātis	regerētis	regētis
regunt	regant	regēbant	regerent	regent

Perfect		Pluperfect		Future perfect
rēxī	rēxerim	rēxeram	rēxissem	rēxerō
rēxistī	rēxerīs	rēxerās	rēxissēs	rēxeris
rēxit	rēxerit	rēxerat	rēxisset	rēxerit
rēximus	rēxerīmus	rēxerāmus	rēxissēmus	rēxerimus

rēxistis	rēxerītis	rēxerātis	rēxissētis	rēxeritis
rēxērunt (-ēre)	rēxerint	rēxerant	rēxissent	rēxerint

Imperative		Infinitive	Participles
rege	regite	*Pres.* regere	*Pres.* regēns
(regitō)	(regitōte)	*Perf.* rēxisse	*Fut.* rēctūrus, -a, -um
regitō	reguntō	*Fut.* rēctūrus esse	

Gerund	Supine
regendī, regendō, regendum, regendō	rēctum, rēctū

Passive

Present		Imperfect		Future
Indicative	*Subjunctive*	*Indicative*	*Subjunctive*	
regor	regar	regēbar	regerer	regar
regeris (-re)	regāris (-re)	regēbāris (-re)	regerēris (-re)	regēris (-re)
regitur	regātur	regēbātur	regerētur	regētur
regimur	regāmur	regēbāmur	regerēmur	regēmur
regiminī	regāminī	regēbāminī	regerēminī	regēminī
reguntur	regantur	regēbantur	regerentur	regentur

Perfect		Pluperfect		Future perfect
rēctus sum	rēctus sim	rēctus eram	rēctus essem	rēctus erō
rēctus es	rēctus sīs	rēctus erās	rēctus essēs	rēctus eris
rēctus est	rēctus sit	rēctus erat	rēctus esset	rēctus erit
rēctī sumus	rēctī sīmus	rēctī erāmus	rēctī essēmus	rēctī erimus
rēctī estis	rēctī sītis	rēctī erātis	rēctī essētis	rēctī eritis
rēctī sunt	rēctī sint	rēctī erant	rēctī essent	rēctī erunt

Imperative		Infinitive	Participles
regere (regitor)	regiminī	*Pres.* regī	*Perf.* rēctus, -a, -um
regitor	reguntor	*Perf.* rēctus esse	*Gerundive*
		Fut. rēctum īrī	regendus, -a, -um

Fourth conjugation: **audiō, audīre, audīvī, audītum,** hear

Active

Present		Imperfect		Future
Indicative	*Subjunctive*	*Indicative*	*Subjunctive*	
audiō	audiam	audiēbam	audīrem	audiam
audīs	audiās	audiēbās	audīrēs	audiēs
audit	audiat	audiēbat	audīret	audiet
audīmus	audiāmus	audiēbāmus	audīrēmus	audiēmus
audītis	audiātis	audiēbātis	audīrētis	audiētis
audiunt	audiant	audiēbant	audīrent	audient

Perfect		Pluperfect		Future perfect
audīvī	audīverim	audīveram	audīvissem	audīverō
audīvistī	audīverīs	audīverās	audīvissēs	audīveris
audīvit	audīverit	audīverat	audīvisset	audīverit
audīvimus	audīverīmus	audīverāmus	audīvissēmus	audīverimus
audīvistis	audīverītis	audīverātis	audīvissētis	audīveritis
audīvērunt	audīverint	audīverant	audīvissent	audīverint
(-ēre)				

Imperative		Infinitive	Participles	
audī	audīte	*Pres.* audīre	*Pres.* audiēns	
(audītō)	(audītōte)	*Perf.* audīvisse	*Fut.* audītūrus, -a,	
audītō	audiuntō	*Fut.* audītūrus esse	-um	

Gerund	Supine
audiendī, audiendō, audiendum, audiendō	audītum, audītū

Passive

Present		Imperfect		Future
Indicative	*Subjunctive*	*Indicative*	*Subjunctive*	
audior	audiar	audiēbar	audīrer	audiar
audīris	audiāris	audiēbāris	audīrēris	audiēris
(-re)	(-re)	(-re)	(-re)	(-re)
audītur	audiātur	audiēbātur	audīrētur	audiētur
audīmur	audiāmur	audiēbāmur	audīrēmur	audiēmur
audīminī	audiāminī	audiēbāminī	audīrēminī	audiēminī
audiuntur	audiantur	audiēbantur	audīrentur	audientur

Perfect		Pluperfect		Future perfect
audītus sum	audītus sim	audītus eram	audītus essem	audītus erō
audītus es	audītus sīs	audītus eras	audītus essēs	audītus eris
audītus est	audītus sit	audītus erat	audītus esset	audītus erit
audītī sumus	audītī sīmus	audītī erāmus	audītī essēmus	audītī erimus
audītī estis	audītī sītis	audītī erātis	audītī essētis	audītī eritis
audītī sunt	audītī sint	audītī erant	audītī essent	audītī erunt

Imperative		Infinitive	Participles	
audīre	audīminī	*Pres.* audīrī	*Perf.* audītus, -a, -um	
(audītor)		*Perf.* audītus esse	*Gerundive*	
audītor	audiuntor	*Fut.* audītum īrī	audiendus, -a, -um	

Third conjugation ending in **-iō, capiō, capere, cēpī, captum**, take

Active

Present		Imperfect		Future
Indicative	*Subjunctive*	*Indicative*	*Subjunctive*	
capiō	capiam	capiēbam	caperem	capiam
capis	capiās	capiēbās	caperēs	capiēs
capit	capiat	capiēbat	caperet	capiet

capimus	capiāmus	capiēbāmus	caperēmus	capiēmus
capitis	capiātis	capiēbātis	caperētis	capiētis
capiunt	capiant	capiēbant	caperent	capient

| *Perfect* | | *Pluperfect* | | *Future perfect* |
| cēpī | cēperim | cēperam | cēpissem | cēperō |

Imperative		*Infinitive*		*Participles*
cape	capite	*Pres.* capere		*Pres.* capiēns
(capitō)	(capitōte)	*Perf.* cēpisse		*Fut.* captūrus, -a, -um
capitō	capiuntō	*Fut.* captūrus esse		

| *Gerund* | *Supine* |
| capiendī, capiendō, capiendum, capiendō | captum, captū |

Passive

Present		*Imperfect*		*Future*
Indicative	*Subjunctive*	*Indicative*	*Subjunctive*	
capior	capiar	capiēbar	caperer	capiar
caperis	capiāris	capiēbāris	caperēris	capiēris
(-re)	(-re)	(-re)	(-re)	(-re)
capitur	capiātur	capiēbātur	caperētur	capiētur
capimur	capiāmur	capiēbāmur	caperēmur	capiēmur
capiminī	capiāminī	capiēbāminī	caperēminī	capiēminī
capiuntur	capiantur	capiēbantur	caperentur	capientur

| *Perfect* | | *Pluperfect* | | *Future perfect* |
| captus sum | captus sim | captus eram | captus essem | captus erō |

Imperative		*Infinitive*		*Participles*
capere	capimini	*Pres.* capī		*Perf.* captus, -a, -um
(capitor)		*Perf.* captus esse		*Gerundive*
capitor	capiuntor	*Fut.* captum īrī		capiendus, -a, -um

Deponent verbs

First conjugation	mīror, mīrārī, mīrātus sum	admire
Second conjugation	vereor, verērī, veritus sum	fear
Third conjugation	ūtor, ūtī, ūsus sum	use
Fourth conjugation	partior, partīrī, partītus sum	share

Indicative

Pres.	mīror	vereor	ūtor	partior
	mīrāris, etc.	verēris, etc.	ūteris, etc.	partīris, etc.
Imp.	mīrābar	verēbar	ūtēbar	partiēbar
Fut.	mīrābor	verēbor	ūtar	partiar
Perf.	mīrātus sum	veritus sum	ūsus sum	partītus sum
Plup.	mīrātus eram	veritus eram	ūsus eram	partītus eram
Fut. P.	mīrātus erō	veritus erō	ūsus erō	partītus erō

Subjunctive

Pres.	mīrer	verear	ūtar	partiar
Imp.	mīrārer	verērer	ūterer	partīrer
Perf.	mīrātus sim	veritus sim	ūsus sim	partītus sim
Plup.	mīrātus essem	veritus essem	ūsus essem	partītus essem

Imperative

mīrāre (mīrātor)   verēre (verētor)   ūtere (ūtitor)   partīre (partītor)

Infinitive

Pres.	mīrārī	verērī	ūtī	partīrī
Perf.	mīrātus esse	veritus esse	ūsus esse	partītus esse
Fut.	mīrātūrus esse	veritūrus esse	ūsūrus esse	partītūrus esse

Participles

Pres.	mīrāns	verēns	ūtēns	partiēns
Fut.	mīrātūrus	veritūrus	ūsūrus	partītūrus
Perf.	mīrātus	veritus	ūsus	partītus
Gerun- *dive*	mīrandus	verendus	ūtendus	partiendus

Deponent verbs governing the ablative case

fruor	fruī	frūctus sum	enjoy
fungor	fungī	fūnctus sum	perform
potior	potīrī	potītus sum	get possession of
ūtor	ūtī	ūsus sum	use
vēscor	vēscī	. .	feed on

Semi-deponent verbs

audeō	audēre	ausus sum	dare
fīdō	fīdere	fīsus sum	trust

(and the compound verbs, *cōnfīdō*, 'trust', and *diffīdō*, 'distrust')

gaudeō	gaudēre	gāvīsus sum	rejoice
soleō	solēre	solitus sum	be accustomed

Irregular verbs

possum, posse, potuī, . . , be able, can

Present		Imperfect		Future
Indicative	*Subjunctive*	*Indicative*	*Subjunctive*	
possum	possim	poteram	possem	poterō
potes	possīs	poterās	possēs	poteris
potest	possit	poterat	posset	poterit
possumus	possīmus	poterāmus	possēmus	poterimus
potestis	possītis	poterātis	possētis	poteritis
possunt	possint	poterant	possent	poterint

Perfect		Pluperfect		Future perfect
potuī	potuerim	potueram	potuissem	potuerō

Infinitive			Participle	
Pres. posse	*Perf.* potuisse		*Pres.* potēns (*adj.*), powerful	

volō, velle, voluī, . . . , be willing, wish

Present		Imperfect		Future
Indicative	*Subjunctive*	*Indicative*	*Subjunctive*	
volō	velim	volēbam	vellem	volam
vīs	velīs	volēbās	vellēs	volēs
vult	velit	volēbat	vellet	volet
volumus	velīmus	volēbāmus	vellēmus	volēmus
vultis	velītis	volēbātis	vellētis	volētis
volunt	velint	volebant	vellent	volent

Perfect		Pluperfect		Future perfect
voluī	voluerim	volueram	voluissem	voluerō

Imperative	Infinitive		Participle	
. .	*Pres.* velle		*Pres.* volēns	
. .	*Perf.* voluisse			

nōlō, nōlle, nōluī, . . . , be unwilling

Perfect		Imperfect		Future
Indicative	*Subjunctive*	*Indicative*	*Subjunctive*	
nōlō	nōlim	nōlēbam	nōllem	nōlam
nōn vīs	nōlīs	nōlēbās	nōllēs	nōlēs
nōn vult	nōlit	nōlēbat	nōllet	nōlet
nōlumus	nōlīmus	nōlēbāmus	nōllēmus	nōlēmus
nōn vultis	nōlītis	nōlēbātis	nōllētis	nōlētis
nōlunt	nōlint	nōlēbant	nōllent	nōlent

Perfect		Pluperfect		Future perfect
nōluī	nōluerim	nōlueram	nōluissem	nōluerō

Imperative	Infinitive		Participle	
nōlī nōlīte	*Pres.* nōlle		nōlēns	
(nōlītō)	*Perf.* nōluisse			

mālō, mālle, māluī, . . . , prefer

Present		Imperfect		Future
Indicative	*Subjunctive*	*Indicative*	*Subjunctive*	
mālō	mālim	mālēbam	māllem	mālam
māvīs	mālīs	mālēbās	māllēs	mālēs
māvult	mālit	mālēbat	māllet	mālet
mālumus	mālīmus	mālēbāmus	māllēmus	mālēmus
māvultis	mālītis	mālēbātis	māllētis	mālētis
mālunt	mālint	mālēbant	māllent	mālent

Perfect	Pluperfect	Future perfect
māluī māluerim	mālueram māluissem	māluerō

Imperative	Infinitive	Participle
. .	Pres. mālle	. .
. .	Perf. māluisse	. .

eō, īre, iī (īvī), itum, go

Present		Imperfect		Future
Indicative	Subjunctive	Indicative	Subjunctive	
eō	eam	ībam	īrem	ībō
īs	eās	ībās	īrēs	ībis
it	eat	ībat	īret	ībit
īmus	eāmus	ībāmus	īrēmus	ībimus
ītis	eātis	ībātis	īrētis	ībitis
eunt	eant	ībant	īrent	ībunt

Perfect	Pluperfect	Future perfect
iī (īvī) ierim (īverim)	ieram (īveram) īssem (īvissem)	ierō (īverō)

Imperative	Infinitive	Participles
ī īte	Pres. īre	Pres. iēns, gen. euntis
	Perf. īsse (īvisse)	Fut. itūrus
	Fut. itūrus esse	Gerundive
		eundum

Gerund

eundī, eundō, eundum, eundō

Supine

itum, itū

fīō, fierī, factus sum, become (the passive of faciō)

Present		Imperfect		Future
Indicative	Subjunctive	Indicative	Subjunctive	
fīō	fīam	fīēbam	fierem	fīam
fīs	fīās	fīēbās	fierēs	fīēs
fit	fīat	fīēbat	fieret	fīet
. .	fīāmus	fīēbāmus	fierēmus	fīēmus
. .	fīātis	fīēbātis	fierētis	fīētis
fīunt	fīant	fīēbant	fierent	fīent

Perfect	Pluperfect	Future perfect
factus sum factus sim	factus eram factus essem	factus erō

Imperative	Infinitive	Participles
Rare	Pres. fierī	Perf. factus
	Perf. factus esse	Gerundive
	Fut. factum īrī	faciendus

fero, ferre, tulī, lātum, bear

Active

Present		Imperfect		Future
Indicative	Subjunctive	Indicative	Subjunctive	
ferō	feram	ferēbam	ferrem	feram
fers	ferās	ferēbās	ferrēs	ferēs
fert	ferat	ferēbat	ferret	feret
ferimus	ferāmus	ferēbāmus	ferrēmus	ferēmus
fertis	ferātis	ferēbātis	ferrētis	ferētis
ferunt	ferant	ferēbant	ferrent	ferent

Perfect		Pluperfect		Future perfect
tulī	tulerim	tuleram	tulissem	tulerō

Imperative		Infinitive		Participles	
fer	ferte	Pres.	ferre	Pres.	ferēns
		Perf.	tulisse	Fut.	lātūrus
		Fut.	lātūrus esse		

Gerund	Supine
ferendī, ferendō, ferendum, ferendō	lātum, lātū

Passive

Present		Imperfect		Future
Indicative	Subjunctive	Indicative	Subjunctive	
feror	ferar	ferēbar	ferrer	ferar
ferris (-re)	ferāris (-re)	ferēbāris (-re)	ferrēris (-re)	ferēris (-re)
fertur	ferātur	ferēbātur	ferrētur	ferētur
ferimur	ferāmur	ferēbāmur	ferrēmur	ferēmur
feriminī	ferāminī	ferēbāminī	ferrēminī	ferēminī
feruntur	ferantur	ferēbantur	ferrentur	ferentur

Perfect		Pluperfect		Future perfect
lātus sum	lātus sim	lātus eram	lātus essem	lātus erō

Imperative		Infinitive		Participles	
ferre	feriminī	Pres.	ferrī	Perf.	lātus
		Perf.	lātus esse		Gerundive
		Fut.	lātum īrī		ferendus

meminī, meminisse, remember

Perfect		Pluperfect		Future perfect
Indicative	Subjunctive	Indicative	Subjunctive	
meminī	meminerim	memineram	meminissem	meminerō

Imperative		Infinitive
mementō	mementōte	meminisse

Meminī has no present tense, but the perfect has the meaning of the present. Compare *ōdī*, 'hate'.

QUOTATIONS FROM LATIN AUTHORS (LESSONS XI–XLI)

Auct. Pervig. Ven. = Author of the *Pervigilium Veneris*, second to fifth century.

August. = Gāius Iūlius Caesar Octaviānus Augustus, emperor 27 B.C.–A.D. 14.

Caes. = Gāius Iūlius Caesar, 102 (100)–44 B.C.

Cat. = Gāius Valerius Catullus, *c*. 84–*c*. 54 B.C.

Cic. = Marcus Tullius Cicerō, 106–43 B.C.

Claud. = Claudius Claudiānus, fl. A.D. 400.

Don. = Aelius Dōnātus, fl. A.D. 350.

Enn. = Quintus Ennius, 239–169 B.C.

Flor. = Lūcius Annaeus Flōrus, reign of Hadrian.

Had. = Hadrian (P. Aelius Hadriānus), emperor A.D. 117–38.

Hor. = Quintus Horātius Flaccus, 65–8 B.C.

Iuv. = Decimus Iūnius Iuvenālis, *c*. A.D. 60–*c*. 130.

Liv. = Titus Līvius, 59 B.C.–A.D. 17.

Luc. = Marcus Annaeus Lūcānus, A.D. 39–65.

Lucr. = Titus Lucrētius Cārus, 99 (94)–55 B.C.

Mart. = Marcus Valerius Martiālis, *c*. A.D. 40–*c*. 104.

Ov. = Publius Ovidius Nāso, 43 B.C.–*c*. A.D. 18.

Pers. = Aulus Persius Flaccus, A.D. 34–62.

Petr. = (? Gāius) Petrōnius, died A.D. 66.

Plaut. = Titus Maccius Plautus, 254–184 B.C.

Plin. mai. = Gāius Plīnius Secundus (māior), A.D. 23/4–79.

Plin. min. = Gāius Plīnius Caecilius Secundus (minor), A.D. 61/62–before 114.

Prop. = Sextus Propertius, *c*. 50–after 16 B.C.

Pub. Syr. = Publilius Syrus, fl. 44 B.C.

Quint. = Marcus Fabius Quīntiliānus, *c*. A.D. 35–before 100.

Rutil. Nam. = Rutilius Claudius Namatiānus, fl. A.D. 416.

Sall. = Gāius Sallustius Crispus, 86–*c*. 34 B.C.

Suet. = Gāius Suētōnius Tranquillus, *c*. A.D. 69–*c*. 140.

Sulpic. = Sulpicia, daughter of Servius Sulpicius Rufus (Tibullus 4. 7–12).

Tac. = Cornelius Tacitus, *c*. A.D. 55–after 115/17.

Ter. = Publius Terentius Āfer, *c*. 195–159 B.C.

Tib. = Albius Tibullus, *c*. 55/48–19 B.C.

Trai.   = Trajan (M. Ulpius Trāiārus), emperor A.D. 96–117.
Verg.   = Publius Vergilius Maro, 70–19 B.C.
Vulg.   = the Vulgate, revision and translation of the Latin Bible by
          St. Jerome (Hieronymus), *c.* A.D. 348–420.

Hymn   = Medieval or later Latin hymn.
Alcu.   = Alcuin, 8th century.
Ab.   = Peter Abelard, 11th/12th century.
Bern.   = Bernard of Cluny, 12th century.
Innoc.   = Pope Innocent III, 12th/13th century.
Cel.   = Thomas a Celano, 13th century.
Kemp.   = Thomas a Kempis, 14th/15th century.
Mant.   = Baptista Mantuānus, 15th/16th century.

METERS (see Appendix 2)

Hex.   = Dactylic hexameter.
El.   = Elegiac couplet (dactylic hexameter and pentameter).
Pent.   = Dactylic pentameter.
Phal.   = Phalaecean or hendecasyllabic.
Chol.   = Choliambic or Scazon.
Sapp.   = Sapphic strophe.
Alc.   = Alcaic strophe.
Ascl.   = Asclepiadic (Lesser, Greater, and three strophes).
Arch.   = Archilochian strophes.
Troch.   = Trochaic (especially the septenarius).
Iamb.   = Iambic (especially the trimeter).

Lesson XI, Ex. 1

(1) Cat. (Hex.)
(2) Ov. (Hex.)
(3) Cat. (Pent.)
(4) August. in Suet.
    (trans. from
    Greek)
(5) August. in Suet.
(6) Verg. (Hex.)
(7) Ov. (Hex.)
(8) Verg. (Hex.)
(9) Verg. (Hex.)
(10) Ov. (El.)
(11) Ov. (El.)
(12) Hymn (? Innoc.)
(13) Hymn (17th or
    18th cent.)

Lesson XII, Ex. 1 (A)

(1) Hor. (Hex.)
(2) Ov. (El.)
(3) Verg. (Hex.)
(4) Mart. (El., Hex.)
(5) Suet.
(6) Verg. (Hex.)

Lesson XIV, Ex. 1

(1) Ov. (Hex.) *et al.*
(2) Used by Shake-
    speare; cf. Suet.,
    Iul. 82.
(3) Hor. (Hex.)
(4) Verg. (Hex.)
(5) Verg. (Hex.)
(6) Ter. (Iamb.).

(7) Plin. min.
(8) Cic.
(9) Ter. (Iamb.)
(10) Verg. (Hex.)
(11) Ov. (El.)
(12) Ov. (El.)
(13) Verg. (Hex.)
(14) Prop. (Pent.)
(15) Hymn (Ab.)

Lesson XV, Ex. 1

(1) Claud. (El.)
(2) Verg. (Hex.)
(3) Hor. (Hex.)
(4) Mart. (El.)
(5) Verg. (Hex.)
(6) Ov. (Hex.)

(7) Iuv. (Hex.)
(8) Luc. (Hex.)
(9) Tac.
(10) Verg. (Hex.)
(11) Verg. (Hex.)

Lesson XVI, Ex. 1

(A)

(1) Vulg. (Psalms)
(2) Vulg. (St. John)
(3)
(4) Vulg. (Exodus)
(5) Vulg. (Psalms)
(6) Alcu.
(7) Petr.
(8) Hor. (Alc.)
(9) Hor. (Hex.)
(10) Attributed to Verg. by Don. (Pent.)
(11) (a) Hor. (Ascl.)
(b) Lucr. (Hex.)
(12) Cic.
(13) Cic.
(14) Luc. (Hex.)
(15) Hor. (Arch.)
(16) (a) Prop. (Pent.)
(b) Ov. (Pent.)
(17) Ov. (El.)
(18) Prop. (Pent.)
(19) Hor. (Hex.)
(20) Sulpic. (El.)
(21) Prop. (El.)
(22) Cic.
(23) Adapted from Plin. mai.
(24) Claud (El.)

(B)

(1) Petr.
(2) Adapted from Plin. mai.
(3) Iuv. (Hex.)
(4) Hor. (Ascl.)
(5) Ov. (El., Hex.)
(6) Iuv. (Hex.)
(7) Lucr. (Hex.)
(8) Kemp.

Lesson XVII, Ex. 1

(A)

(1) Cic.
(2) Tac.
(3) Verg. (Hex.)
(4) Cic.
(5) Cic.
(6) Hor. (Arch.)
(7) Lucr. (Hex.)
(8) Lucr. (Hex.)
(9) Ov. (El.)
(10) Ov. (Pent.)
(11) Ov. (El.)
(12) Verg. (Hex.)
(13) Ov. (El.)
(14) Cat. (El.)
(15) Ov. (El.)
(16) Verg. (Hex.)
(17) Verg. (Hex.)
(18) Plin. min.
(19) Cat. (Chol.)
(20) Hor. (Hex.)

(B)

(1) Verg. (Hex.)
(2) Verg. (Hex.)
(3) Caes.
(4) Ov. (El.)
(5) Hor. (Ascl.)

Lesson XVIII, Ex. 1

(A)

(1) Tac.
(2) Hor. (Sapp.)
(3) Hor. (Sapp.)
(4) Hor. (Alc.)
(5) Verg. (Hex.)
(6) Ter. (Iamb.)
(7) Ov. (Hex.)
(8) Verg. (Hex.)
(9) Hor. (Alc.)
(10) Ter. (Troch.)
(11) Verg. (Hex.)
(12) Hor. (Hex.)
(13) Verg. (Hex.)
(14) Enn. (Hex.)
(15) Verg. (Hex.)

(16) Lucr. (Hex.)
(17) Verg. (Hex.)
(18) Hor. (Hex.)
(19) Verg. (Hex.)
(20) Ov. (El., Hex.)
(21) Verg. (Hex.)
(22) Cic.
(23) Caes.
(24) Prop. (Pent.)
(25) Suet. on Hor.

(B)

(1) Mant. (Hex.)
(2) Lucr. (Hex.)
(3) Tac.
(4) Verg. (Hex.)
(5) Hor. (Hex.)
(6) Hor. (Ascl.)
(7) Ov. (El.)
(8) Hor. (Iamb.)
(9) Hymn (Cel.)
(10) Quint.

Lesson XIX, Ex. 1

(1) Hor. (Ascl.)
(2) Hor. (Ascl.)
(3) Ov. (Hex.)
(4) Cat. (El., Hex.)
(5) Hor. (Ascl.)
(6) Motto of the Jesuits
(7) Cic.
(8) Verg. (Hex.)
(9) Iuv. (Hex.)
(10) Caes.
(11) Cic.
(12) Iuv. (Hex.)
(13) Iuv. (Hex.)
(14) Cat. (Phal.)
(15) Iuv. (Hex.)
(16) Lucr. (Hex.)
(17) Cat. (Chol.)
(18) Plin. min.
(19) Tac.
(20) Ov. (Hex.)

Lesson XX, Ex. 1

(1) Plin. min.
(2) Hor. (Sapp.)

(3) Rutil. Nam. (Pent.)
(4) Caes.
(5) Cic.
(6) Hor. (Alc.)
(7) Caes.
(8) Verg. (Hex.)
(9) Quint.
(10) Cic.
(11) Don. (Life of Vergil)
(12) Cic.
(13) Cic.

Lesson XXI, Ex. 1

(1) Verg. (Hex.)
(2) Lucr. (Hex.)
(3) Mart. (El.)
(4) Mart. (Phal.)
(5) Mart. (El.)
(6) Mart. (El.)
(7) Cat. (El., Hex.)
(8) Cic.
(9) Hor. (Ascl.)
(10) Verg. (Hex.)
(11) Hor. (Hex.)
(12) Flor. and Had. (Troch.)
(13) Cic.
(14) Cic.
(15) Caes.
(16) Verg. (Hex.)
(17) Sall.
(18) Verg. (Hex.)
(19) Hor. (Alc.)
(20) Cat. (El.)

Lesson XXII, Ex. 1

(1) Tac.
(2) Pub. Syr. (Iamb.)
(3) Caes.
(4) Caes.
(5) Caes.
(6) Hor. (Ascl.)
(7) Caes.
(8) Caes.
(9) Ov. (El.)
(10) Ov. (El.)

(11) Iuv. (Hex.)
(12) Caes.

Lesson XXIII, Ex. 1

(1) Hor. (Sapp.)
(2) Verg. (Hex.)
(3) Ov. (El.)
(4) Cat. (Sapp.)
(5) [Tib.] (El.)
(6) Hor. (Alc.)
(7) Ov. (Hex.)
(8) Ov. (El.)
(9) Caes.
(10) Caes.
(11) Caes.
(12) Caes.
(13) Caes.
(14) Hor. (Hex.)
(15) Hor. (Hex.)
(16) Hor. (Alc.)
(17) Hor. (Alc.)
(18) Ov. (El., Hex.)
(19) Ov. (Hex.)

Lesson XXIV, Ex. 1

(1) Caes.
(2) Caes.
(3) Caes.
(4) Caes.
(5) Caes.
(6) Lucr. (Hex.)
(7) Cat. (Phal.)
(8) Mart. (El.)
(9) Hor. (Hex.)
(10) Ov. (Hex.)
(11) Hor. (Ascl.)
(12) Caes.
(13) Ov. (El.)

Lesson XXV, Ex. 1

(1) Verg. (Hex.)
(2) Auct. Pervig. Ven. (Troch.)
(3) Ov. (Pent.)
(4) Ov. (Pent.)
(5) Ov. (El.)
(6) Ov. (El.)

(7) Cat. (Phal.)
(8) Cat. (Chol.)
(9) Ov. (El.)
(10) Cat. (Phal.)
(11) Quint.
(12) Cic.
(13) Hor. (Sapp.)
(14) Ov. (El., Hex.)
(15) Hor. (Hex.)
(16) Hor. (Hex.)
(17) Verg. (Hex.)
(18) Iuv. (Hex.)
(19) Mart. (El., Hex.)
(20) Verg. (Hex.)
(21) Verg. (Hex.)
(22) Ov. (El.)
(23) Attributed to Don.
(24) Hymn (Bern.)
(25) Song (13th and 18th cent.)

Lesson XXVI, Ex. 1

(1) Caes.
(2) Caes.
(3) Ov. (El.)
(4) Ov. (El., Hex.)
(5) Caes.
(6) Caes.
(7) Ter. (Iamb.)
(8) Plin. min.
(9) Cic.
(10) Hor. (Arch.)
(11) Caes.
(12) Caes.
(13) Caes.
(14) Caes.
(15) Caes.
(16) Caes.
(17) Caes.
(18) Caes.
(19) Caes.

Lesson XXVII, Ex. 1

(1) Ov. (Hex.)
(2) Suet.
(3) Ov. (El.)

(4) Caes.
(5) Caes.
(6) Caes.
(7) Caes.
(8) Caes.
(9) Tac.
(10) Hor. (Hex.)
(11) Ov. (El.)
(12) Cic.
(13) Cic.
(14) Cic.
(15) Lucr. (Hex.)
(16) Caes.
(17) Caes.
(18) Cic.
(19) Tac.

Lesson XXVIII, Ex. 1

(1) Cat. (El.)
(2) Verg. (Hex.)
(3) Hor. (Hex.)
(4) Ov. (Pent.)
(5) Caes.
(6) Caes.
(7) Ov. (El.)
(8) Ov. (El.)
(9) Ov. (El., Hex.)
(10) Ov. (El.)
(11) Hor. (Alc.)
(12) Hor. (Ascl.)
(13) Hor. (Alc.)
(14) Tac.
(15) Cic.
(16) Cic.
(17) Pers.
(18) Caes.
(19) Lucr. (Hex.)
(20) Cic.

Lesson XXIX, Ex. 1

(1) Rutil. Nam. (El., Hex.)
(2) ? Adapted from Verg., *Moretum* (Hex.)
(3) Iuv. (Hex.)
(4) Caes.

(5) Caes.
(6) Caes.
(7) Caes.
(8) Prop. (El., Hex.)
(9) Cat. (Phal.)
(10) Pub. Syr. (Iamb.)
(11) (a) Prop. (El., Hex.)
    (b) Prop. (Pent.)
(12) Caes.
(13) Ov. (El.)
(14) Ov. (El.)
(15) Ov. (Pent.)
(16) Ov. (El.)
(17) Caes.
(18) Plin. min.
(19) Plin. min.
(20) Hor. (Sapp.)
(21) Quint.
(22) Ov. (El.)
(23) Trai. in Plin. min.

Lesson XXX, Ex. 1

(1) Verg. (Hex.)
(2) Prop. (El., Hex.)
(3) Ov. (El.)
(4) Hor. (Hex.)
(5) Sall.
(6) Ov. (El.)
(7) Motto of Scottish regiments
(8) Cic.
(9) Cic.
(10) Cic.
(11) Ov. (El., Hex.)
(12) Hor. (Ascl.)
(13) Hor. (Hex.)
(14) Plin. min.
(15) Tac.
(16) Cic.
(17) Tac.
(18) Cic.
(19) Cic.
(20) Ov. (El.)

Lesson XXXI, Ex. 1

(1) Cic.
(2) Hor. (Arch.)

(3) Iuv. (Hex.)
(4) Iuv. (Hex.)
(5) Cat. (Phal.)
(6) Tib. (El.)
(7) Ov. (El.)
(8) Hor. (Hex.)
(9) Auct. Pervig. Ven. (Troch.)
(10) Hor. (Alc.)
(11) Verg. (Hex.)
(12) Verg. (Hex.)
(13) Hor. (Hex.)
(14) Caes.
(15) Ov. (Hex.)
(16) Ov. (Hex.)
(17) Cic.
(18) Cic.
(19) Cic.
(20) Verg. (Hex.)

Lesson XXXII, Ex. 1

(1) Hor. (Alc.)
(2) Cat. (Phal.)
(3) Hor. (Hex.)
(4) Prop. (El.)
(5) Tac.
(6) Ov. (El.)
(7) Ov. (El.)
(8) Tac.
(9) Cic.
(10) Iuv. (Hex.)
(11) Hor. (Hex.)
(12) Lucr. (Hex.)
(13) Plin. min.
(14) Caes.
(15) Iuv. (Hex.)
(16) Hor. (Sapp.)
(17) Hor. (Sapp.)
(18) Verg. (Hex.)
(19) Cic.
(20) Had. (Iamb.)

Lesson XXXIII, Ex. 1

(1) Ov. (El.)
(2) Ov. (El.)
(3) Cat. (Phal.)
(4) Tib. (El.)

(5) Hor. (Hex.)
(6) Tac.
(7) Ov. (El.)
(8) Caes.
(9) Caes.
(10) Mart. (El.)
(11) Caes.
(12) Caes.
(13) Caes.
(14) Caes.
(15) Cic.
(16) Cic.
(17) Ov. (El., Hex.)
(18) Cic.
(19) Caes.
(20) Verg. (Hex.)

Lesson XXXIV, Ex. 1

(1) Iuv. (Hex.)
(2) Mart. (Chol.)
(3) Cic.
(4) Cic.
(5) Tac.
(6) Cic.
(7) Ov. (El.)
(8) Cat. (Phal.)
(9) Verg. (Hex.)
(10) Hor. (Hex.)
(11) Iuv. (Hex.)
(12) Verg. (Hex.)
(13) Hor. (Hex.)
(14) Lucr. (Hex.)
(15) Verg. (Hex.)
(16) Iuv. (Hex.)
(17) Tac.
(18) Caes.
(19) Caes.
(20) Plin. min.

Lesson XXXV, Ex. 1

(1) Cic.
(2) Lucr. (Hex.)
(3) Prop. (Pent.)
(4) Prop. (El., Hex.)
(5) Cat. (El.)
(6) Caes.
(7) Caes.

(8) Caes.
(9) Caes.
(10) Caes.
(11) Ov. (El.)
(12) Tac.
(13) Ov. (El.)
(14) Ov. (El.)
(15) Ov. (Hex.)
(16) Iuv. (Hex.)
(17) Ov. (El.)
(18) Verg. (Hex.)
(19) Cic.
(20) Cic.

Lesson XXXVI, Ex. 1

(1) Caes.
(2) Caes.
(3) Caes.
(4) Ter. (Troch.)
(5) Plaut. (Troch.)
(6) Cic.
(7) Liv.
(8) Cic.
(9) Caes.
(10) Cic.
(11) Tib. (El.)
(12) Accius in Cic.
(13) Ter. (Iamb.)
(14) Cic.
(15) Caes.
(16) Verg. (Hex.)
(17) Cic.
(18) Cic.
(19) Cic.
(20) Cic.

Lesson XXXVII, Ex. 1

(1) Plaut. (Troch.)
(2) Cic.
(3) Caes.
(4) Cic.
(5) Caes.
(6) Caes.
(7) Cic.
(8) Cic.
(9) Cic.
(10) Cic.

(11) Cic.
(12) Cic.
(13) Cic.
(14) Liv.
(15) Cic.
(16) Cic.
(17) Tac.
(18) Cic.
(19) Cic.
(20) Cic.

Lesson XXXVIII
Ex. 1

(1) Enn. (Hex.)
(2) Iuv. (Hex.)
(3) Hor. (Hex.)
(4) Caes.
(5) Caes.
(6) Caes.
(7) Cic.
(8) Iuv. (Hex.)
(9) Hor. (Alc.)
(10) Cat. (Phal.)
(11) [Tib.] (El.)
(12) Ov. (El.)
(13) Ov. (El.)
(14) Ov. (Hex.)
(15) Plin. min.
(16) Trai. in Plin. min.
(17) Hor. (Sapp.)
(18) Hor. (Sapp.)
(19) Cic.
(20) Cic.

Lesson XXXIX, Ex. 1

(1) Verg. (Hex.)
(2) Caes.
(3) Caes.
(4) Caes.
(5) Caes.
(6) Caes.
(7) Cic.
(8) Caes.
(9) Caes.
(10) Cic.
(11) Plin. min.
(12) Cic.

(13) Luc. (Hex.)
(14) Prop.
(15) Sulpic. (El.)
(16) Ov. (El.)
(17) Cic.
(18) Tac.
(19) Plin. min.
(20) Ov. (El.)

Lesson XL, Ex. 1

(1) Verg. (Hex.)
(2) Ov. (Hex.)
(3) Tac.
(4) Cic.
(5) Verg. (Hex.)
(6) Ov. (El.)
(7) Cic.
(8) Cic.

(9) Cic.
(10) Plaut. (Iamb.)
(11) Cic.
(12) Caes.
(13) Tac.
(14) Cic.
(15) Cic.
(16) Cic.
(17) Cic.
(18) Cic.
(19) Suet.
(20) Cic.

Lesson XLI, Ex. 1

(1) Cic.
(2) Cic.
(3) Caes.

(4) Caes.
(5) Caes.
(6) Caes.
(7) Cic.
(8) Caelius in Cic.
(9) Caes.
(10) Caes.
(11) Hor. (Arch.)
(12) Cic.
(13) Caes.
(14) Caes.
(15) Caes.
(16) Caes.
(17) Caes.
(18) Caes.
(19) Caes.
(20) Cic.

LATIN–ENGLISH VOCABULARY

This mainly contains words used in Exercise 1 and Exercise 3 of each Lesson. But some of the words in the sections on Grammar and the words appearing on the photographs have also been added.

ā, ab, *prep. with abl.*, from; by (agent).

abeō, -īre, -iī, -itum, *irreg.*, go away.

abhinc, ago (*usually with acc.*).

abhorreō, -horrēre, -horruī, 2, shrink from, be remote from, averse to (*with ā and abl.*).

abiciō, -icere, -iēcī, -iectum, 3, throw away, throw.

abnuō, -ere, abnuī, 3, deny, refuse.

absolvō, -solvere, -solvī, -solūtum, 3, acquit.

absum, abesse, āfuī, *irreg.*, be away; *with* longē, be far from.

absurdē, *adv.*, absurdly.

abūtor, -ūtī, -ūsus sum, 3, *deponent*, abuse (*with abl.*).

ac, *see* atque.

Acadēmīa, -ae, *f.*, University (a Greek word referring to Plato's Academy at Athens).

accēdō, -cēdere, -cessī, -cessum, 3, approach, be added.

accidō, -ere, accidī, 3, happen, occur; accidit ut (*with subjve.*), it happens, happened that.

accipiō, -ere, accēpī, acceptum, 3, receive.

accūsō, 1, accuse; (*with acc. and gen. of the charge*) accuse of.

ācer, ācris, ācre, keen, sharp.

aciēs, -eī, *f.*, line of battle.

acquiēscō, -ere, acquiēvī, acquiētum, 3, rest.

ācriter, *adv.*, keenly.

acuō, -ere, acuī, acūtum, 3, sharpen, improve.

ad, *prep. with acc.*, to; near.

addō, addere, addidī, additum, 3, add.

addūcō, -dūcere, -dūxī, -ductum, 3, lead to, induce.

adeō, -īre, -iī, -itum, *irreg.* go to, approach.

adeō, so, to such an extent.

adferō, -ferre, attulī, adlātum (all-), *irreg.*, bring to.

adfirmō, 1, affirm, declare.

adflīgō, -flīgere, -flīxī, -flictum, 3, shatter.

adigō, -igere, -ēgī, -āctum, 3, bring to; (of weapons) drive home, send to.

adipīscor, adipīscī, adeptus sum, 3, *deponent*, get, obtain.

aditus, -ūs, *m.*, approach, entrance.

adiungō, -iungere, -iūnxī, -iūnctum, 3, add, join (to).

adiūtor, -ōris, *m.*, helper.

adiuvō, -iuvāre, -iūvī, -iūtum, 1, help.

admīror, -ārī, admīrātus sum, 1, *deponent*, marvel at, wonder at; to be brought by anything into a state of desire or longing.

admodum, *adv.*, very.

adnuō (ann-), -ere, adnuī, adnūtum, 3, nod, give assent.

adorior, -orīrī, -ortus sum, 4, *deponent*, attack.

adprobō (app-), 1, approve of, prove, establish.

adripiō (arr-), -ripere, -ripuī, -reptum, 3, seize.

adsentātiō (ass-), -iōnis, *f.*, flattery.

adsum, adesse, adfuī, *irreg.*, be present.

adulēscēns, -entis, *m.*, youth, young man.

adulēscentia, -ae, *f.*, (the time of) youth.

adulēscentulus, -ī, *m.*, *diminutive of* adulescens, young man.

adveniō, -venīre, -vēnī, -ventum, 4, arrive, come.

adventus, -ūs, *m.,* arrival.
adversus, *adv.,* opposite; *prep. with acc.,* toward, against.
adversus, -a, -um, opposite, unfavorable; **rēs adversae** = adversity.
aedificō, 1, build.
Aeduus, -a, -um, Aeduan; *pl.,* **Aeduī (Haeduī), -ōrum,** *m.,* a tribe in Gaul between the Loire and the Saône.
aeger, -gra, -grum, sick.
Aeneadēs, -um, *m. pl.,* sons (descendants) of Aeneas.
Aeolius, -a, -um, Aeolian; refers to the Greek odes of Sappho and Alcaeus.
aequō, 1, make equal.
aequor, -oris, *n.,* sea.
aequus, -qua, -quum, equal, impartial.
aes, aeris, *n.,* bronze, copper.
aestās, -ātis, *f.,* summer.
aestimō, 1, value, reckon; *(with acc. and gen. of value)* value at.
aetās, -ātis, *f.,* life, age; an age, generation.
aeternus, -a, -um, eternal, immortal.
aetherius, -a, -um, ethereal, heavenly.
aevum, -ī, *n.,* life, age.
afferō, *see* **adferō.**
age, *imperat.,* come.
ager, agrī, *m.,* field.
agitō, 1, move, drive; consider, deliberate upon.
agmen, -inis, *n.,* column, army (on the march).
agō, agere, ēgī, āctum, 3, drive, do; *(with acc., e.g.* **annōs, vītam)** live; *(with* **cum** *and abl.)* negotiate, confer with.
agrestis, -e, rustic, of the country.
agricola, -ae, *m.,* farmer.
agricultūra, agrī cultūra, -ae, *f.,* agriculture.
ahēneus, aēneus, -a, -um, of copper or bronze.
āiō, *def.,* 3 *sing.* **ait,** say.
albus, -a, -um, white.
alcyonēs, *f. pl.,* halcyons, kingfishers.
ālea, -ae, *f.,* a game played with dice; *(with* **iacta est)** the die is cast.

algeō, algēre, alsī, 2, to be cold; to be neglected.
aliēnus, -a, -um, another's, not one's own; *(with* **ā** *and abl.)* incapable of, foreign to.
aliī . . . aliī, some . . . others.
aliquāndō, *adv.,* sometimes; now at last.
aliquī, -qua, -quod, some, any.
aliquis, aliquid, *pron.,* someone, something.
aliter, otherwise; used with **ac (atque),** than.
aliunde, *adv.,* from another place.
alius, alia, aliud, another.
almus, -a, -um, kindly, fostering.
alō, -ere, aluī, altum, 3, nourish, sustain.
alter, -era, -erum, the other (of two); **alter . . . alter** = the one . . . the other.
altitūdō, -inis, *f.,* height.
altum, -ī, *n.,* the deep (the sea).
altus, -a, -um, high, deep; *adv.,* **altē,** on high.
amābilis, -e, lovable.
amāns, -antis, loving; a lover.
ambitus, -ūs, *m.,* unlawful canvassing for office, bribery.
ambulō, 1, walk.
āmentia, -ae, *f.,* madness.
āmentum, -ī, *n.,* thong.
Americānus, -a, -um, may be used for American.
amīca, -ae, *f.,* friend.
amīcitia, -ae, *f.,* friendship.
amictus, -ūs, *m.,* clothing.
amīcus, -a, -um, friendly *(with dat.).*
amīcus, -ī, *m.,* friend.
amnis, -is, -ium, *m.,* stream, river.
amō, 1, love.
amor, -ōris, *m.,* love.
an, or *(introducing the second half of a double question).*
Anagninī, -ōrum, *m. pl.,* the people of Anagnia, a town in Latium.
ancora, -ae, *f.,* anchor.
Ancyrānus, -a, -um, *see* **monumentum.**
angulus, -ī, *m.,* corner.
angustiae, -ārum, *f.,* narrow pass, defile; difficulties.

angustus, -a, -um, narrow, contracted, difficult; **rēs angusta** = poverty.

anima, -ae, *f.,* soul; also used as a term of endearment.

animal, -ālis, -ium, *n.,* animal.

animō, see **in animō esse.**

animula, -ae, *f.,* *diminutive of* **anima,** soul.

animus, -ī, *m.,* mind; *sometimes used for* **anima,** soul.

annōn, or not (*in direct questions*).

annus, -ī, *m.,* year.

ante, *prep. with acc.,* before; *adv.,* before.

anteā, *adv.,* formerly, before.

antequam, *conj.,* before.

antīquus, -a, -um, old, ancient, former.

anxius, -a, -um, anxious.

aperiō, aperīre, aperuī, apertum, 4, open.

apis, -is, -ium (-um), *f.,* bee.

appellō, 1, call (by name), name.

appropinquō (adp-), 1, approach (*with* **ad** *and acc., or dat.*).

aptus, -a, -um, (*with* **ad** *and acc., or dat.*) fit, suitable.

apud, *prep. with acc.,* at, near, in the works of, in the house of.

aqua, -ae, *f.,* water.

aquila, -ae, *f.,* eagle; the eagle or standard of a Roman legion.

aquilus, -a, -um, dark.

Aquītānī, -ōrum, *m.,* the inhabitants of south-west Gaul, Aquitania.

āra, -ae, *f.,* altar.

arātor, -ōris, *m.,* ploughman.

arātrum, -trī, *n.,* plough.

arbiter, -trī, *m.,* judge.

arbitror, -ārī, arbitrātus sum, 1, *deponent,* think, consider.

arbor, -oris, *f.,* tree.

arcus, -ūs, *m.,* bow.

ardeō, -ēre, arsī, arsum, 2, burn, be on fire.

arduus, -a, -um, steep, difficult; **rēs arduae** = **rēs adversae.**

arguō, -ere, arguī, 3, prove, accuse; prove guilty.

arma, -ōrum, *n.,* arms.

armō, 1, arm.

arō, 1, plough.

arripiō, -ripere, -ripuī, -reptum, 3, seize, learn quickly.

ars, artis, -ium, *f.,* art; *pl.* the arts.

artificium, -ī (-iī), *n.,* handicraft.

artūs, -uum, *m. pl.,* limbs.

arx, arcis, -ium, *f.,* citadel.

as, assis, *m.,* the *as,* a Roman coin.

Ascraeus, -a, -um, of Ascra in Boeotia. This refers to the Greek poet Hesiod.

aspectus, -ūs, *m.,* appearance.

asperitās, -ātis, *f.,* harshness.

aspiciō, -ere, aspexī, aspectum, 3, look at, see.

assentior, -īrī, assēnsus sum, 4, *deponent,* agree with.

assiduus, -a, -um, continual, perpetual.

at, *conj.,* but, yet.

at enim (*introducing an objection*), but you will say.

atavus, -ī, *m.,* ancestor.

āter, -tra, -trum, black.

atomus, -ī, *f.,* atom (indivisible).

atque, ac, and.

attingō, -ere, attigī, 3, touch, reach, apply one's self to.

attonitus, -a, -um, astonished, amazed.

auctior, *comp. of* **auctus,** increased, greater.

auctor, -ōris, *m.,* author, originator; **sine auctōre** = anonymous.

auctōritās, -ātis, *f.,* authority, influence.

audācia, -ae, *f.,* boldness.

audāx, -ācis, bold.

audeō, -ēre, ausus sum, 2, *semideponent,* dare.

audiō, audīre, audīvī, audītum, 4, hear, listen to.

auditor, -ōris, *m.,* hearer.

auferō, auferre, abstulī, ablātum, *irreg.,* carry off.

augeō, -ēre, auxī, auctum, 2, increase.

aula, -ae, *f.,* hall, palace.

aura, -ae, *f.,* breeze.

aureus, -a, -um, golden.

auris, -is, -ium, *f.,* ear.

aurum, -ī, *n.,* gold.

aut, or; **aut . . . aut,** either . . . or.

autem, *conj.*, but, however, moreover.

autumnus, -ī, *m.*, autumn.

auxilium, -ī (-iī), *n.*, help; *pl.*, auxiliary troops.

avē atque valē, hail and farewell.

avidus, -a, -um, greedy; avidē, *adv.*, eagerly.

avis, -is, -ium, *f.*, bird.

avunculus, -ī, *m.*, uncle (mother's brother).

avus, -ī, *m.*, grandfather.

barbarus, -a, -um, foreign, barbarous; a foreigner, native.

bāsium, -ī (-iī), *n.*, kiss.

beātus, -a, -um, happy, blessed.

Belgae, -ārum, *m. pl.*, the Belgians in the north-east of Gaul.

bellātum est, *perf. pass. impers. from* bellō, wage war, fight.

Bellovacī, -ōrum, *m. pl.*, a tribe of the Belgae in Gaul.

bellum, -ī, *n.*, war.

bene, *adv.*, well.

beneficium, -ī (-iī), *n.*, kindness.

benevolentia, -ae, *f.*, goodwill.

benignus, -a, -um, kindly.

bibō, bibere, bibī, 3, drink.

bis, *adv.*, twice.

blandulus, -a, -um, *diminutive of* blandus.

blandus, -a, -um, pleasant, charming.

bona, -ōrum, *n. pl.*, good things, blessings, property.

bonus, -a, -um, good.

bōs, bovis, *m. and f.*, ox.

brevis, -e, short.

breviter, *adv.*, briefly.

Britannus, -a, -um, British; *pl.* the Britons.

bustum, -ī, *n.*, tomb.

cachinnus, -ī, *m.*, laughter.

cadō, -ere, cecidī, cāsum, 3, fall.

cadūcus, -a, -um, falling.

caecus, -a, -um, blind; hidden.

caedēs, -is, -ium (-um), *f.*, slaughter, murder.

caedō, -ere, cecīdī, caesum, 3, cut down, kill.

caelestis, -e, heavenly; *pl.*, the gods.

caelum, -ī, *n.*, sky, heaven.

caeruleus, -a, -um, blue.

calor, -ōris, *m.*, heat, fever.

campus, -ī, *m.*, plain.

candidus, -a, -um, white, dazzling white, beautiful.

canis, -is, -um, *m. and f.*, dog.

canō, canere, cecinī, 3, sing.

cantō, 1, sing.

capax, -ācis, capacious; (*with gen.*) capable of.

capiō, capere, cēpī, captum, 3, take, capture.

capitālis poena, *f.*, capital punishment (death or loss of civil rights).

caput, capitis, *n.*, head; capitis condemnō, sentence to death.

careō, -ēre, caruī, 2, be without, lack (*with abl.*).

carmen, -inis, *n.*, song.

carpō, -ere, carpsī, carptum, 3, gather, pluck; diem carpere, to pluck the blossom of the day; viam carpere, to take one's way.

carrus, -ī, *m.*, wagon.

cārus, -a, -um, dear.

castra, -ōrum, *n.*, camp (*pl. of* castrum, fort).

castus, -a, -um, chaste.

cāsus, -ūs, *m.*, fall, misfortune.

causa, -ae, *f.*, cause.

causā, for the sake of, *used with gen. of gerundive to express purpose.*

cautus, -a, -um, cautious.

caveō, -ēre, cāvī, cautum, 2, take care, beware (of) (*with acc.*).

cēdō, -ere, cessī, cessum, 3, withdraw; (*with dat.*) yield to; depart, pass away.

celer, -eris, -ere, swift; celeriter, *adv.*, swiftly.

celeritās, -ātis, *f.*, swiftness, speed.

Celtae, -ārum, *m.*, Celts, the inhabitants of Middle Gaul.

cēna, -ae, *f.*, dinner.

cēnō, 1, dine.

cēnseō, -ēre, cēnsuī, cēnsum, 2, think, propose.

cēnsor, -ōris, *m.*, censor; critic.

centēsimus, -a, -um, hundredth.

centum, *numeral*, a hundred.

certāmen, -inis, *n.*, contest, struggle.

certē, *adv.*, at any rate.

certior fīō, become more certain, be informed; **certiōrem faciō**, make someone more certain, inform (*with acc.*).

certus, -a, -um, certain, sure.

cervīx, -īcis, *f.*, *usually pl.*, neck.

cēterī, -ae, -a, the others, the rest, *cf. Eng.* etc. (et cētera).

charta, -ae, *f.*, paper, *cf. Magna Charta*; may be used for a map.

chelīdōn, -onis, *f.*, swallow.

Christiānus, -a, -um, Christian; **Christiānī, -ōrum**, *m. pl.*, the Christians.

cibus, -ī, *m.*, food.

cingō, -ere, cīnxī, cīnctum, 3, surround.

circā, *prep. with acc.*, around.

circensēs, *sc.* **lūdī**, the games in the Circus.

circiter, *adv.*, about.

circumveniō, -venīre, -vēnī, -ventum, 3, surround.

Cisalpīnus, -a, -um, Cisalpine (on the Italian side of the Alps).

cīvilis, -e, civil.

cīvis, -is, -ium, *m.* and *f.*, citizen.

cīvitās, -ātis, -um (-ium), *f.*, state; citizenship.

clāmō, 1, shout.

clārus, -a, -um, bright, clear, famous.

classis, -is, -ium, *f.*, fleet.

claudō, claudere, clausī, clausum, 3, shut.

clēmēns, -entis, gentle, merciful.

clināmen, -inis, *n.*, swerve (the swerve of atoms falling through space).

coepī (*used as perf. of* **incipiō**, begin), 3, *def.*, began.

coerceō, -ēre, coercuī, coercitum, 2, restrain, curb.

cognātiō, -ōnis, *f.*, relationship, association.

cognōscō, -ere, cognōvī, cognitum, 3, get to know, learn, understand.

cōgō, -ere, coēgī, coāctum, 3, collect, compel.

cohors, cohortis, -ium, *f.*, cohort, the tenth part of a legion; also the staff of the governor of a province.

collis, -is, -ium, *m.*, hill.

collocō, 1, place.

colloquium (conl-), -ī (-iī), *n.*, conference.

collum, -ī, *n.*, neck.

colō, colere, coluī, cultum, 3, worship, cultivate.

color, -ōris, *m.*, color.

coma, -ae, *f.*, hair, foliage (*poet.*).

comātus, -a, -um, having long hair; **Gallia Comāta**, *f.*, Transalpine Gaul.

comes, -itis, *m.* and *f.*, companion.

cōmis, -e, affable, kind, friendly.

commeātus, -ūs, *m.*, provisions, supplies (*sing. and pl.*).

commendō, 1, commend, recommend.

committō, -mittere, -mīsī, -missum, 3, entrust to (*with acc. and dat.*); (**proelium**) **committō**, engage in, join (battle).

commodē, *adv.*, properly, well, completely.

commodum, -ī, *n.*, advantage, profit.

commoror, 1, *deponent*, stay.

commoveō, -movēre, -mōvī, -mōtum, 2, move deeply.

commūnis, -e, common.

commūtātiō, -ōnis, *f.*, change.

comparō, 1, prepare, make ready.

complūres, -ium, *pl.*, several.

compōnō, -pōnere, -posuī, -positum, 3, put together, arrange.

compositus, -a, -um, composed, calm.

comprimō, -primere, -pressī, -pressum, 3, compress, crush.

cōnāta, -ōrum, *n. pl.*, undertaking, attempt.

concēdō, -cēdere, -cessī, -cessum, 3, withdraw, yield, grant, allow.

concidō, concidere, concidī, 3, fall down.

conciliō, 1, obtain, win over.

concordia, -ae, *f.*, concord, harmony.

concors, concordis, harmonious.

concursus, -ūs, *m.*, running together, concourse, assembly.

condemnō, 1, condemn; (*with acc. and gen. of the charge*) condemn for; (*with abl. of the punishment*) condemn to.

condiciō, -ōnis, *f.*, agreement, terms.

condō, condere, condidī, conditum, 3, found.

condūcō, -dūcere, -dūxī, -ductum, 3, collect, lead together.

cōnferō, -ferre, -tulī, -lātum, *irreg.*, collect, compare; *with* ad *and* acc., confer, grant.

cōnficiō, -ficere, -fēcī, -fectum, 3, complete, finish, exhaust; exercitum cōnficiō, raise an army.

cōnfīdō, -fīdere, -fīsus sum, 3, *semi-deponent*, trust (*with dat.*).

cōnfirmō, 1, confirm, establish, prove.

coniciō, -icere, -iēcī, -iectum, 3, throw.

coniūnx, coniugis, *f.*, wife; *sometimes m.*, husband.

coniūratiō, -ōnis, *f.*, conspiracy.

conloquium, *see* colloquium.

conloquor (coll-), -loquī, -locūtus sum, 3, *deponent*, converse, confer.

cōnor, -ārī, cōnātus sum, 1, *deponent*, try.

conquirō, -quirere, -quīsīvī, -quīsītum, 3, search for.

cōnscīscō, cōnscīscere, cōnscīvī, cōnscītum, 3, resolve upon; mortem sibi c., commit suicide.

cōnscrībō, -scrībere, -scrīpsī, -scrīptum, 3, write together, enroll; write; patrēs cōnscrīptī, senators.

cōnsensus, -ūs, *m.*, agreement.

cōnsentiō, -sentīre, -sēnsī, -sēnsum, 4, agree, conspire.

cōnsīderō, 1, consider, reflect.

cōnsīdō, cōnsīdere, cōnsēdī, cōnsessum, 3, sit down.

cōnsilium, -ī (-iī), *n.*, plan; (vestrum) cōnsilium est, it is for (you) to decide.

cōnsistō, -sistere, -stitī, -stitum, 3, halt, take one's stand.

cōnspectus, -ūs, *m.*, sight, view.

cōnspiciō, -spicere, -spexī, -spectum, 3, look at, catch sight of, observe.

cōnstāns, -antis, constant, steadfast.

cōnstantia, -ae, *f.*, constancy, steadfastness.

cōnstituō, cōnstituere, cōnstituī,

cōnstitūtum, 3, set up, determine, establish, settle; (*with inf.*) determine to.

cōnstitūtus, -a, -um, appointed.

cōnstō, -stāre, -stitī, 1, stand with, stand firm, endure; *with abl. or* ex *and abl.*, consist of, rest upon.

cōnsuētūdō, -inis, *f.*, custom.

cōnsul, -ulis, *m.*, consul, one of the two chief magistrates at Rome.

cōnsulāris, -e, consular; one who has been consul.

cōnsulō, -ere, cōnsuluī, cōnsultum, 3, consult; (*with dat.*) consult the interests of.

cōnsurgō, cōnsurgere, cōnsurrēxī, cōnsurrēctum, 3, stand up, arise together.

contemnō, -ere, contempsī, contemptum, 3, despise

contendō, -ere, contendī, contentum, 3, hasten, fight, struggle; assert, contend; *with* cum *and* abl., fight against.

continenter, *adv.*, continuously.

continentia, -ae, *f.*, moderation, temperance.

contineō, -ēre, continuī, contentum, 2, keep together, enclose, check.

contingō, -ere, contigī, 3, happen; contingit, *impers.*, it happens.

contrā, *adv.*, opposite, in opposition; *prep. with* acc., against.

convalēscō, -ere, convaluī, 3, recover, grow strong.

conveniō, -īre, convēnī, conventum, 4, meet, assemble.

convertō, convertere, convertī, conversum, 3, turn, direct (towards).

convincō, -vincere, -vīcī, -victum, 3, convict (of crime).

convīvium, -ī (-iī), *n.*, meal, banquet.

coorior, -orīrī, -ortus sum, 4, *deponent*, arise.

cōpia, -ae, *f.*, abundance, plenty; cōpiae, -ārum, *f. pl.*, troops; resources.

cōram, *prep. with* abl., in the presence of.

corpus, -oris, *n.*, body.

corpusculum, -ī, n., diminutive of corpus, a little body.

corrigō, -ere, corrēxī, corrēctum, 3, correct.

corvus, -ī, m., rook, raven.

Cōrycius, -a, -um, Corycian, from Cilicia.

cottīdiānus, -a, -um, daily.

Cōus, -a, -um, Coan, from the island of Cos; Cōa, n. pl., Coan clothes.

crās, adv., tomorrow.

crāstinus, -a, -um, tomorrow's.

crēdō, -ere, crēdidī, crēditum, 3, believe (with dat. of person).

creō, 1, create, appoint.

crēta, -ae, f., chalk.

crīmen, -inis, n., charge, accusation.

croceus, -a, -um, yellow (saffron-colored).

cruciō, 1, torture, torment.

culpa, -ae, f., fault.

culpō, 1, blame.

cultus, -ūs, m., civilization, culture.

cum, prep. with abl., with.

cum, conj., when, since, although.

cum . . . tum, both . . . and.

cuncti, -ae, -a, all, all together.

cūnctor, 1, deponent, delay.

cupiditās, -ātis, f., desire.

cupīdō, -inis, m., desire.

cupidus, -a, -um, eager; eager for (with gen.).

cupiō, -ere, cupīvī, cupītum, 3, desire, wish.

cūr, why.

cūra, -ae, f., care; Cura, Care personified.

cūrātē, adv., carefully.

cūriōsus, -a, -um, painstaking, careful.

cūrō, 1, attend to, care for, take care that (ut); also with acc. of gerundive.

currō, currere, cucurrī, cursum, 3, run.

currus, -ūs, m., chariot.

cursus, -ūs, m., running, course.

curtus, -a, -um, broken, short.

curvus, -a, -um, curved, winding.

custōdiō, custōdīre, custōdīvī, custōdītum, 4, guard.

custōs, -ōdis, m., guardian.

cutis, -is, f., skin.

cycnus, -ī, m., swan.

D.D.D. (= dat, dicat, dēdicat), gives, assigns, dedicates.

damnō, 1, condemn.

damnum, -ī, n., loss, damage.

Danaī, -ōrum, m., the Greeks in the Trojan War.

dē, prep. with abl., from, down from, about, concerning.

dea, -ae, f., goddess.

dēbellō, 1, overthrow, vanquish.

dēbeō, -ēre, dēbuī, dēbitum, 2, owe, ought; (with inf.) ought to.

dēbilis, -e, weak, feeble.

decānus, -ī, m., a dean (Late Latin).

dēcēdō, -ere, dēcessī, dēcessum, 3, retire, withdraw.

decem, numeral, ten.

dēcernō, -ere, dēcrēvī, dēcrētum, 3, decide, decree.

decet, impers., it befits, it suits; also used personally, e.g. (clothes) are becoming.

dēcidō, -ere, dēcidī, 3, fall down.

dēclāmātiō, -ōnis, f., declamation, exercise in speaking.

dēclīnō, 1, swerve; with acc. pl. cursūs, turn aside from the course.

decōrus, -a, -um, fitting, suitable, proper.

dēcurrō, -currere, -cucurrī, (-currī), -cursum, 3, run down.

decus, -oris, n., glory, pride.

dēdecus, -oris, n., disgrace.

dēditiō, -ōnis, f., surrender.

dēditus, -a, -um, devoted to (with dat.).

dēdō, dēdere, dēdidī, dēditum, 3, surrender.

dēdūcō, -dūcere, -dūxī, -ductum, 3, lead down, lead away.

dēfendō, -ere, dēfendī, dēfēnsum, 3, defend.

dēferō, -ferre, -tulī, -lātum, irreg., bring down, deliver; indict, accuse.

dēficiō, -ere, dēfēcī, dēfectum, 3, fail, be wanting; (with acc.) fail.

dēgō, -ere, dēgī, 3, spend, pass (time).

deinde, adv., then, next.

dēlectātiō, -ōnis, f., delight, pleasure.

dēlectō, 1, delight, please (with acc.).

dēleō, dēlēre, dēlēvī, dēlētum, 2, destroy.

dēliberō, 1, discuss, deliberate.

dēliciae, -ārum, f., delight, darling.

dēligō, 1, tie together, bind fast.

dēmēns, -entis, mad.

dēmittō, -ere, dēmīsī, dēmissum, 3, send down, lower.

dēmōnstrō, 1, point out, show, prove.

dēmum, adv., at last; (with is, ea, id) precisely, indeed.

dēnique, adv., at last, finally.

deorsum, adv., downwards.

dēpellō, -ere, dēpulī, dēpulsum, 3, drive away.

dēperdō, -perdere, -perdidī, -perditum, 3, lose.

dēpōnō, -ere, dēposuī, dēpositum, 3, lay aside.

dēportō, 1, bring home.

dēpugnō, 1, fight (violently).

dēscendō, -ere, dēscendī, dēscēnsum, 3, come down, descend.

dēscrībō, -scrībere, -scrīpsī, -scrīptum, 3, describe.

dēserō -ere, dēseruī, dēsertum, 3, desert, abandon.

dēsīderium, -ī (-iī), n., longing, desire (for something once possessed).

dēsīderō, 1, miss, long for.

dēsiliō, -īre, dēsiluī, 4, leap, jump down.

dēsinō, -ere, dēsiī, dēsitum, 3, cease.

dēsipiō, -ere, 3, be foolish.

dēsistō, -ere, dēstitī, 3, cease.

dēspiciō, -spicere, -spexī, -spectum, 3, despise.

dēspondeō, -ēre, dēspondī, dēspōnsum, 2, promise in marriage, betroth.

dēsum, dēesse, dēfuī, irreg., be lacking, fail (with dat.).

dēterior, -ius, worse.

dēterreō, -terrēre, -terruī, -territum, 3, deter, prevent, hinder (with nē or quōminus and subjve., or quīn after a negative).

dētrīmentum, -ī, n., loss; with capiō, suffer harm.

deus, -ī, pl. dī, deī, m., God.

dexter, -era, -erum, right, skillful, fitting.

dextra, -ae, f., (sc. manus) right hand; the right (side).

dīcō, dīcere, dīxī, dictum, 3, say, tell.

dictātor, -ōris, m., dictator, title used in emergencies and held by Julius Caesar.

diēs, diēī, m. and f., day; sometimes = time.

differō, differre, distulī, dīlātum, irreg., differ; inter sē differre, to differ from one another.

difficilis, -e, difficult.

difficultās, -ātis, f., difficulty.

diffīdō, -fīdere, -fīsus sum, 3, semi-deponent, distrust (with dat.).

diffugiō, -ere, diffūgī, 3, flee (in different directions), scatter.

digitus, -ī, m., finger.

dignitās, -ātis, f., dignity, rank.

dignus, -a, -um, worthy, (with abl.) worthy of.

dīligēns, -entis, diligent, careful; adv., dīligenter, carefully.

dīligō, -ere, dīlēxī, dīlēctum, 3, esteem, love.

dīlūcēscō, -ere, dīlūxī, 3, shine.

dīmittō, -ere, dīmīsī, dīmissum, 3, send away, let go.

dīmoveō, -movēre, -mōvī, -mōtum, 2, part, divide.

dīnumerō, 1, count, reckon up.

discēdō, -ere, discessī, discessum, 3, go away, depart.

discessus, -ūs, m., departure.

discō, -ere, didicī, 3, learn, learn (how).

discordia, -ae, f., discord, strife.

discutiō, -cutere, -cussī, -cussum, 3, scatter, dispel.

dispōnō, -pōnere, -posuī, -positum, 3, dispose, arrange.

dissipō, 1, scatter, disperse.

distineō, -tinēre, -tinuī, -tentum, 2, keep apart.

diū, adv., for a long time.

diurna, daily records (sc. acta).

diurnus, -a, -um, by day, daily.

diūturnus, -a, -um, long, lasting.

dīversus, -a, -um, in different directions, different.

dīvidō, -videre, -vīsī, -vīsum, 3, divide.

dīvīnitus, *adv.*, by divine power.
dīvīnus, -a, -um, divine.
dīvitiae, -ārum, *f.*, riches, wealth.
dīvus, -ī, divine, epithet for certain Roman emperors after their death; dīvī, -ōrum, *m.*, the gods (= dī).
dō, dare, dedī, datum, 1, give.
doceō, docēre, docuī, doctum, 2, teach.
doctrīna, -ae, *f.*, teaching, learning.
doctus, -a, -um, learned.
doleō, -ēre, doluī, 2, feel pain, grieve; (of a wound) hurt.
dolor, -ōris, *m.*, pain, grief.
dolus, -ī, *m.*, deceit, guile.
domina, -ae, *f.*, mistress of a house, lady; sweetheart.
dominātiō, -ōnis, *f.*, dominion, tyranny, despotism.
dominus, -ī, *m.*, master (of a house), owner; Annō Dominī, in the year of our Lord.
domō, -āre, domuī, domitum, 1, tame, conquer.
domus, -ūs, *f.*, home, house; domī, at home.
dōnec, *conj.*, until; *sometimes* = while.
dōnō, 1, present, give.
dōnum, -ī, *n.*, gift.
dormiō, -īre, dormīvī (-iī), dormītum, 4, sleep.
dōs, dōtis, -ium (-um), *f.*, dowry, endowment, talent; *pl.*, endowments.
druidēs, -um, *m.*, druids, the priestly class in Gaul.
dubitō, 1, doubt; nōn d. quīn (*with subjve.*), I don't doubt that; hesitate (*with inf.*).
dubium, *neut. of* dubius, doubtful; nōn dubium est quīn (*with subjve.*), there is no doubt that.
dūcō, dūcere, dūxī, ductum, 3, lead, conduct; consider, *also with* animō *and acc. and inf.*; *with* uxōrem, marry a wife.
ductus, -ūs, *m.*, leadership, command.
dulcēdō, -inis, *f.*, sweetness, charm.
dulcis, -e, sweet.
dum, *conj.*, while, until.
dummodo, dum, modo, *conj.*, provided that (*with subjve.*).

duo, -ae, -o, numeral, two.
dūrō, 1, endure, hold out.
dūrus, -a, -um, hard.
dux, ducis, *m.*, general, leader.
ē, *see* ex.
ecce, look, behold.
ēdiscō, -discere, -didicī, 3, learn (thoroughly).
ēdō, -ere, ēdidī, ēditum, 3, give forth, produce, publish; ēditus, -a, -um, sprung from, raised up, lofty.
ēdūcō, -dūcere, -dūxī, -ductum, 3, lead out.
efficiō, -ficere, -fēcī, -fectum, 3, effect, accomplish, bring it about that (ut).
effugiō, -fugere, -fūgī, 3, escape.
ēgelidus, -a, -um, warm, balmy (*opposite of* gelidus, cold).
egeō, -ēre, -eguī, 2, be in want of, need (*with abl.*).
egestās, -ātis, *f.*, need, want.
ego, *pers. pron.*, I.
egomet, *emphatic form of* ego.
ēgredior, ēgredī, ēgressus sum, 3, *deponent*, go out, depart.
ēgregius, -a, -um, excellent.
ēiciō, -icere, -iēcī, -iectum, 3, cast out, cast ashore.
elegīa, (elegeia), -ae, *f.*, elegy.
ēligō, -ere, ēlēgī, ēlēctum, 3, choose.
ēloquēns, -entis, eloquent.
Ēlysius, -a, -um, *adj. of* Ēlysium, -ī, *n.*, Elysium, the home of the blest.
ēmendō, 1, free from faults, correct.
ēmergō, -ere, ēmersī, ēmersum, 3, emerge, raise one's self up.
emō, emere, ēmī, emptum, 3, buy.
ēmolliō, -mollīre, -molliī, -mollītum, 4, soften, make mild.
emptor, -ōris, *m.*, buyer.
ēn, look, behold.
enim, *conj.*, for.
ēnsis, -is, -ium, *m.*, sword.
ēnumerō, 1, count.
eō, īre, iī, itum, *irreg.*, go.
eō, to that place.
eōdem, to the same place.
Epicūrēus, -a, -um, Epicurean; Epicūrēī, -ōrum, *m.*, Epicureans,

followers of the Epicurean philosophy.

epistula, -ae, *f.,* letter; also refers to the *Epistulae,* Ovid's *Heroides.*

eques, equitis, *m.,* horseman; *pl.,* cavalry.

equidem, *adv.,* indeed (*usually with the first person*).

equus, equi, *m.,* horse.

ergō, *adv.,* therefore.

errō, 1, wander, make a mistake, be wrong.

error, -ōris, *m.,* wandering, mistake, error.

ērudiō, -ire, -ivi, -itum, 4, teach; embellish, *e.g.* with learning.

ēruditus, -a, -um, learned.

ērumpō, -ere, ērūpi, ēruptum, 3, break out, burst forth.

erus, -i, *m.,* master (of a house).

ēsuriō, -ire, -itum, 4, be hungry.

et, *conj.,* and; also, even.

et . . . et, both . . . and.

etenim, *conj.,* for, and indeed.

etiam, *adv.,* also, even.

etiamsi, even if.

ēvādō, -ere, ēvāsi, ēvāsum, 3, go out, escape, turn out.

ēveniō, -ire, ēvēni, ēventum, 4, turn out, happen.

ēventus, -ūs, *m.,* result, end.

ex, ē, *prep. with abl.,* from, out of.

exārdēscō, -ere, exārsi, exārsum, 3, take fire, be inflamed.

excēdō, -ere, excessi, excessum, 3, go out, go away; **ē vitā excēdō,** die, depart from life.

excellēns, -entis, distinguished, excellent.

excipiō, -ere, excēpi, exceptum, 3, take, receive.

excitō, 1, arouse, awaken, excite.

excruciō, 1, torment greatly.

excūdō, -ere, excūdi, excūsum, 3, beat out, mould.

excutiō, -ere, excussi, excussum, 3, shake out, shake off.

exemplar, -āris, -ium, *n.,* model, copy.

exemplum, -i, *n.,* example, precedent.

exeō, -ire, -ii, -itum, *irreg.,* go out.

exerceō, -ēre, exercui, 2, keep

busy, drive on; (*with* **rūra**) work, till.

exercitus, -ūs, *m.,* army.

exigō, -ere, exēgi, exāctum, 3, complete, finish.

exiguus, -a, -um, small, short, scanty.

eximius, -a, -um, extraordinary, excellent.

exīstimō, 1, think, consider.

exitium, -i (-ii), *n.,* destruction.

exitus, -ūs, *m.,* departure, end, result.

exorior, -oriri, -ortus sum, 4, *deponent,* arise.

expediō, -ire, -ivi (-ii), -itum, 4, explain, relate (*poet.*).

expedit, *impers.,* it is expedient.

expellō, expellere, expuli, expulsum, 3, expel, drive out.

expendō, -ere, expendi, expēnsum, 3, weigh (on the scales).

expetō, -petere, -petivi, -petitum, 3, seek after, desire.

expleō, -plēre, -plēvi, -plētum, 2, fill up, satisfy.

explōrātor, -ōris, *m.,* scout.

expōnō, -pōnere, -posui, -positum, 3, put out, disembark; explain, expound.

exprimō, -primere, -pressi, -pressum, 3, press out, extort, wrest.

exsilium, -i (-ii), *n.,* exile.

exsistō, -sistere, -stiti, -stitum, 3, come forth, arise, exist.

exspectō, 1, wait for (*with acc.*), wait.

exstinguō, -ere, exstinxi, exstinctum, 3, extinguish, wipe out.

exstruō, -struere, -strūxi, -strūctum, 3, heap up, construct.

extrā, *prep. with acc.,* outside.

extrēmus, -a, -um, outermost, last.

exuō, -ere, exui, exūtum, 3, put off (clothes), cast off, shed.

faber, -ri, *m.,* smith, artisan; (*with* **fortūnae**) maker.

fābula, -ae, *f.,* story, tale.

fac, *imperat. of* **faciō,** see that, bring it about that (*with subjve.*).

faciēs, -ēi, *f.,* face.

facilis, -e, easy; **facile,** *adv.,* easily.

facilitās, -ātis, *f.,* affability.

facinus, -oris, *n.,* misdeed, outrage.
faciō, facere, fēcī, factum, 3, do, make; (*with acc. and gen. of value*) value at.
factiō, -ōnis, *f.,* faction, party.
facultās, -ātis, *f.,* opportunity, ability, supply.
fallō, -ere, fefellī, falsum, 3, deceive, escape the notice of.
fāma, ae, *f.,* fame, report, glory.
familia, -ae, *f.,* a household establishment; company.
fās, *n. indecl.,* right, divine law.
fastus, -ūs, *m.,* arrogance, pride.
fateor, -ērī, fassus sum, 2, *deponent,* confess.
fātum, -ī, *n.,* fate, destiny.
faveō, favēre, fāvī, fautum, 2, favor (*with dat.*).
fax, facis, *f.,* torch.
fēlīcitās, -ātis, *f.,* good luck, happiness; felicity.
fēlīx, -īcis, happy, lucky.
fēmina, -ae, *f.,* woman.
fenestra, -ae, *f.,* window.
fera, -ae, *f.,* wild beast.
ferē, nearly, almost, about.
ferō, ferre, tulī, lātum, *irreg.,* bear, bring.
ferreus, -a, -um, made of iron, hardhearted.
ferrum, -ī, *n.,* iron, sword.
ferus, -a, -um, wild, rude, uncivilized.
fessus, -a, -um, tired, weary.
festīnō, 1, hasten.
fēstus, -a, -um, festal, joyful; **fēstus diēs,** *m.,* festival, holiday.
fētus, -a, -um, pregnant; newly delivered.
fidēlis, -e, faithful; **fidēliter,** *adv.,* faithfully.
fidēs, -eī, *f.,* faith, belief, trust, loyalty.
fīdus, -a, -um, loyal, faithful.
fierī potest ut, it is possible that (*with subjve.*); *neg.,* **nōn f. p. quīn** (**ut nōn**).
fīgō, fīgere, fīxī, fīxum, 3, fix, pierce.
figūra, -ae, *f.,* figure, form.
fīlia, -ae, (*dat. and abl. pl.* **fīliābus**), *f.,* daughter.

fīlius, fīlī (-iī), *m.,* son.
fīniō, -īre, -fīnīvī (-iī), fīnītum, 4, put an end to, limit.
fīnis, -is, -ium, *m.,* end; *pl.,* boundaries, territory.
fīnitimus, -a, -um, neighboring to (*with dat.*); neighbor.
fīō, fierī, factus sum, *irreg.,* become, be made.
firmō, 1, make firm, strengthen.
firmus, -a, -um, firm, steadfast.
flamma, -ae, *f.,* flame.
flammāns, -antis, fiery, flaming.
fleō, -ēre, flēvī, flētum, 2, weep.
floccī, *gen. of value,* of no account; *with* **faciō,** care not a straw for (*lit.* a flock of wool).
flōs, -ōris, *m.,* flower.
flūmen, -inis, *n.,* river.
fluō, -ere, flūxī, 3, flow.
fluvius, -ī (-iī), *m.,* river.
foedus, -a, -um, disgraceful, foul.
folium, -ī (-iī), *n.,* leaf.
fōns, fontis, -ium, *m.,* spring, fountain.
fore (= **futūrum esse**), *fut. inf. of* **sum,** will be, would be.
fore (**futūrum esse**) **ut** (*with subjve.*), it will happen that (*may be used instead of the fut. infin. pass.*).
forīs, *adv.,* out of doors, outside, abroad; **forās** *with verb of motion.*
fōrma, -ae, *f.,* form, shape, beauty.
fōrmōsus, -a, -um, beautiful.
fors, *f.,* chance (*in nom. and abl.*).
forsan, perhaps.
forsitan, (*with subjve.*) perhaps.
fortasse, perhaps.
forte, *adv.,* by chance.
fortis, -e, brave.
fortuitus, -a, -um, accidental.
fortūna, -ae, *f.,* fortune.
fortūnātus, -a, -um, fortunate.
forum, -ī, *n.,* forum, market-place.
fragilis, -e, fragile.
frangō, frangere, frēgī, frāctum, 3, break.
frāter, -tris, *m.,* brother.
fraus, fraudis, -ium (-um), *f.,* deceit, fraud.
frētus, -a, -um, relying on (*with abl.*).
frondeō, -ēre, 2, put forth leaves.
frūctus, -ūs, *m.,* fruit, profit, reward.

frūgēs, frūgum, *f. pl.,* fruits (of the earth).

frūmentārius, -a, -um, of grain; (*with* **rēs**) grain supply.

frūmentum, -ī, *n.,* grain.

fruor, fruī, frūctus sum, 3, *deponent,* enjoy (*with abl.*).

fuga, -ae, *f.,* flight.

fugiō, fugere, fūgī, 3, flee; (*with acc.*) flee from.

fulvus, -a, -um, tawny.

fungor, fungī, fūnctus sum, 3, perform (*with abl.*).

furō, -ere, 3, be mad; play the fool.

furor, -ōris, *m.,* fury, madness.

Gallī, -ōrum, *m.,* the Gauls.

gaudeō, -ēre, gāvīsus sum, 2, *semi-deponent,* rejoice, delight in (*with abl.*).

gaudium, -ī (-iī), *n.,* joy.

gemellus, -ī, *m.,* *diminutive,* little twin.

geminus, -a, -um, twin, two.

genetrīx, -trīcis, *f.,* mother.

genitālis, -e, causing birth, generative.

gēns, gentis, -ium, *f.,* race, clan, people.

genū, -ūs, *n.,* knee.

genus, generis, *n.,* race, kind, sort.

Germanī, -ōrum, *m.,* the Germans.

gerō, gerere, gessī, gestum, 3, carry on, wage (war), perform.

gignō, gignere, genuī, genitum, 3, beget, produce.

gladius, -ī (-iī), *m.,* sword.

glōria, -ae, *f.,* glory.

glōrior, 1, *deponent,* boast.

glōriōsus, -a, -um, glorious.

gradus, -ūs, *m.,* step.

Graeculus, -a, -um, *diminutive of* **Graecus,** Greekling.

Graecus, -a, -um, Greek; **Graecī, -ōrum,** *m.,* the Greeks.

Grāius, Grāus, -a, -um (= **Graecus**), Greek.

grāmen, -inis, *n.,* grass.

grandis, -e, large.

grātia, -ae, *f.,* favor, charm, gratitude; *pl.,* thanks; **grātiās agō,** give thanks, thank (*with dat.*).

grātulor, -ārī, grātulātus sum, 1, *deponent,* congratulate (*with dat.*).

grātus, -a, -um, pleasing.

gravis, -e, heavy, serious.

gravitās, -ātis, *f.,* seriousness.

gravō, 1, weigh down.

gremium, -ī (-iī), *n.,* the lap.

grex, gregis, *m.,* herd, flock.

gurges, -itis, *m.,* gulf, waters, stream.

gutta, -ae, *f.,* drop.

habeō, habēre, habuī, habitum, 2, have.

habitō, 1, live, reside.

habitus, -ūs, *m.,* condition, appearance; dress.

hasta, -ae, *f.,* spear.

haud, not.

haud proinde . . . quam, not so much . . . as.

hauriō, -īre, hausī, haustum, 4, draw (water), drink in.

haustus, -ūs, *m.,* a drink, draught.

Helvetiī, *m. pl.,* the Helvetians. Their territory is now Switzerland.

Helvētius, -a, -um, Helvetian.

herba, -ae, *f.,* grass.

herī, *adv.,* yesterday.

hīberna, -ōrum, *n. pl.,* winter quarters.

hic, haec, hoc, *dem. pron.,* this (near me); the latter.

hīc, *adv.,* here.

hiems, hiemis, *f.,* winter.

hilaris, -e, cheerful, gay.

hīlum (*with* **neque**), *see* **nihilum (nīlum).**

hinc, *adv.,* from here, hence.

hōc, *abl. n. sing.,* in this respect; on this account, by so much (*with comp.*).

hodiē, *adv.,* today.

homo, -inis, *m.,* man, human being.

honestās, -ātis, *f.,* honesty, integrity, reputation.

honestus, -a, -um, honorable, virtuous.

honōs (honor), -ōris, *m.,* honor, repute, public office.

hōra, -ae, *f.,* hour.

horrendus, -a, -um, dreadful, horrible.

horrēscō, -ere, horruī, 3, become frightened; *(with acc.)* fear.
horridus, -a, -um, rough, horrid; horrible, dreadful.
hortor, -ārī, hortātus sum, 1, *deponent,* encourage *(with acc. and with* ut *and subjve.).*
hortus, -ī, m., garden.
hospes, -itis, m., host, guest.
hospitium, -ī (-iī), n., hospitality; inn, lodging.
hostis, -is, -ium, m., enemy (public enemy), *usually pl.,* **hostēs,** the enemy.
hūc, adv., to this place, hither.
hūmānitās, -ātis, f., humanity, kindliness, culture.
hūmānus, -a, -um, human, humane.
humus, -ī, f., earth, ground.

iaceō, iacēre, iacuī, 2, lie down.
iaciō, iacere, iēcī, iactum, 3, throw, cast.
iactō, 1, throw, toss, drive.
iactus, -ūs, m., throwing.
iaculum, -ī, n., javelin.
iam, adv., now, already.
iānua, -ae, f., door.
ibi, adv., there.
īdem, eadem, idem, pron., the same; *with* **quī, atque, ac,** the same as.
identidem, again and again.
idōneus, -a, -um, suitable.
igitur, conj., therefore.
ignis, -is, -ium, m., fire, a flame, lover *(poet.).*
ignōminia, -ae, f., disgrace.
ignōrō, 1, not to know, be ignorant of.
ignōtus, -a, -um, unknown.
Īlias, -adis, f., the *Iliad* of Homer.
ille, illa, illud, dem. pron., that (over there); the former.
illinc, adv., from that side, on that side.
illūc, to that place.
illūminātiō, -ōnis, f., light *(post-class.).*
imāgō, -inis, f., image, picture, phantom, shadow.
imber, -bris, -ium, m., rain.
imbuō, -ere, imbuī, imbūtum, 3, imbue, inspire, inure.

immātūrus, -a, -um, untimely.
immemor, -oris, unmindful, forgetful *(with gen.).*
immineō, 2, hang over, threaten, be near at hand.
immodicus, -a, -um, excessive.
immortālis, -e, immortal.
impedīmentum, -ī, n., hindrance; *(pl.)* baggage.
impediō, -īre, impedīvī, impedītum, 4, hinder, prevent *(with* **nē** *or* **quōminus** *and subjve., or* **quīn** *after a negative).*
imperātor, -ōris, m., general, commander-in-chief.
imperium, -ī (-iī), n., military power, dominion, empire.
imperō, 1, command *(with acc. of thing, dat. of person); with* **ut** *and subjve.*
impetrō, 1, gain a request, obtain (by asking).
impetus, -ūs, m., attack.
implōrō, 1, beg, entreat.
impōnō, -pōnere, -posuī, -positum, 3, place on, impose upon.
improbus, -a, -um, bad, wicked.
imprōvīsō, adv., unexpectedly.
impūne, adv., with impunity.
impūrus, -a, -um, impure, infamous, vile.
in, prep. with abl., in.
in, prep. with acc., into.
in aeternum, forever.
in animō esse *(with dat.),* have it in mind, intend.
in locō, at the right place or time.
in perpetuum, forever.
in praesentia, for the present, at this time.
in spem veniō, *lit.* come into the hope, hope (that).
inānis, -e, empty; **ināne, n.,** the void.
incendium, -ī (-iī), n., fire, conflagration.
incidō, -ere, incidī, incāsum, 3, fall into, meet, happen.
incīdō, -cīdere, -cīdī, -cīsum, 3, cut into, inscribe, engrave on.
incipiō, -cipere, -cēpī, -ceptum, 3, begin *(for perf. use* coepī).
incohō, 1, begin.

incolō, -ere, incoluī, 3, inhabit, live.
incommodum, -ī, n., inconvenience, misfortune.
incrēdibilis, -e, incredible, unbelievable.
inde, adv., then, thereupon, thence.
indignātiō, -ōnis, f., indignation.
indūcō, -dūcere, -dūxī, -ductum, 3, lead in, induce.
indulgēns, -entis, indulgent, kind.
indulgentia, -ae, f., indulgence, kindness.
inēluctābilis, -e, inevitable, unavoidable.
ineō, -ire, -iī, -itum, irreg., go into, enter.
ineptiō, -ire, 4, play the fool.
iners, -ertis, idle, inactive.
inertia, -ae, f., idleness.
infāmia, -ae, f., disgrace, infamy.
infandus, -a, -um, unspeakable.
infēlix, -icis, unlucky, unhappy.
inferiae, -ārum, f. pl., sacrifices (in honor of the dead).
infernī, -ōrum, m., see inferī.
inferō, -ferre, intulī, illātum, irreg., introduce, bring in.
inferus, -a, -um, lower; inferī, pl., the inhabitants of the lower world, the dead.
infēstus, -a, -um, hostile; rēs infēstae = rēs adversae.
inficiō, -ficere, -fēcī, -fectum, 3, dye.
inflō, 1, blow into, inflate; pass. with spiritū, be infused with.
influō, -fluere, -flūxī, 3, flow into.
infrā, prep. with acc., below.
infūsus, -a, -um, poured into.
ingenium, -ī (-iī), n., nature, ability, natural capacity, genius; pl., ingenia, intellects, men of genius.
ingēns, ingentis, huge.
ingenuus, -a, -um, free-born; worthy of a freeman; (with artēs) liberal.
inglōrius, -a, -um, inglorious, without glory.
inimīcus, -a, -um, unfriendly, hostile; an enemy (personal enemy).
inīquus, -a, -um, unfair, unfriendly.
initium, -ī (-iī), n., beginning.
iniūria, -ae, f., wrong, injury, injustice.

innocēns, -entis, innocent, guiltless.
innocentia, -ae, f., innocence, integrity.
inopia, -ae, f., lack, want.
inops, -opis, resourceless, needy, poor.
inpēnsa, impēnsa, -ae, f., cost, expense.
inquam, irreg., say; 3 pers. sing. inquit, he said (used after one or more words of a quotation).
insāniō, -ire, -īvī (-iī), -ītum, 4, be mad.
inscrībō, -scrībere, -scrīpsī, -scrīptum, 3, inscribe.
insistō, -ere, institī, 3, stand upon.
instituō, -ere, instituī, institūtum, 3, set up, establish, train.
institūtum, -ī, n., custom, practice.
insula, -ae, f., island.
insurgō, -surgere, -surrēxī, -surrēctum, 3, rise up.
integer, -gra, -grum, untouched, whole, blameless, pure.
integrātiō, -ōnis, f., a renewing.
intellegō, -ere, intellēxī, intellēctum, 3, understand.
inter, prep. with acc., between, among.
inter sē, among themselves, together.
intercēdō, -cedere, -cessī, -cessum, 3, come between, intervene.
intercipiō, -cipere, -cēpī, -ceptum, 3, cut off, intercept.
intereā, adv., meanwhile.
interest, impers., it is to the interest of, it concerns (with gen. or ablatives like meā).
interficiō, -ficere, -fēcī, -fectum, 3, kill (with acc.).
interim, adv., meanwhile.
intermittō, -mittere, -mīsī, -missum, 3, (with tempus) leave off, interrupt.
interpretor, 1, deponent, explain, interpret.
intersum, -esse, -fuī, irreg., be between, be present (at), take part in (with dat.).
intrā, prep. with acc., inside, within.
intus, adv., within.
inūtilis, -e, useless.
inveniō, -ire, invēnī, inventum, 4, find, find out.

inveterāscō, -ere, inveterāvī, 3,
grow old, become established.
invictus, -a, -um, unconquered, invincible.
invidendus, -a, -um, enviable, en-
vied.
invidus, -a, -um, envious, jealous.
invīsus, -a, -um, hated, hateful.
invītus, -a, -um, unwilling.
iocōsus, -a, -um, merry, humorous.
iocus, -ī, m., joke, jest.
ipse, ipsa, ipsum, emph. pron., himself, herself, itself.
īra, -ae, f., anger.
īrāscor, īrāscī, īrātus sum, 3,
deponent, be angry; (with dat.) be
angry with.
irreparābilis, -e, irretrievable, that
cannot be recovered.
irritus (inr-), -a, -um, vain, useless,
without effect.
is, ea, id, dem. pron., he, she, it.
iste, ista, istud, dem. pron., that
(near you, of yours).
istīc, adv., there.
ita, adv., thus, so; yes; ita . . . ut,
just as.
itaque, conj., and so, therefore.
iter, itineris, n., journey; iter faciō,
march.
iterum, adv., again.
Ītalicus, -a, -um, Italian.
Ītalus, -a, -um, Italian (= Ītalicus).
iubeō, iubēre, iussī, iussum, 2,
with inf., order, command (with
acc.).
iūcunditās, -ātis, f., charm, pleasantness.
iūcundus, -a, -um, delightful,
pleasant.
iūdex, -icis, m., judge.
iūdicium, -ī (-iī), n., trial, court,
judgment.
iūdicō, 1, judge, pass judgment,
decide.
iungō, -ere, iūnxī, iūnctum, 3, join.
iūrō, 1, swear; with per and acc., to
swear by.
iūs, iūris, n., right, justice, law.
iūstitia, -ae, f., justice.
iūstus, -a, -um, just, upright.
iuvat, 1, impers., it pleases (with inf.).
iuvenis, -is, -um, m., young man

(usually from twenty to forty years
old).
iuventūs, -ūtis, f., youth.
iuvō, -āre, iūvī, iūtum, 1, help,
please.
iūxtā, adv., close by; prep. with acc.,
near to.

labor, -ōris, m., work, toil.
labōrō, 1, work; with inf., strive to.
lacessō, -ere, lacessīvī, lacessītum, provoke.
lacrima, -ae, f., tear.
lacus, -ūs, m., lake, pond.
laedō, -ere, laesī, laesum, 3, hurt
(with acc.).
laetus, -a, -um, joyful, glad.
languēscō, -ere, languī, 3, become
faint, weak; droop.
lar, laris, m., home; larēs (pl.),
household gods.
lascīvus, -a, -um, wanton, playful.
lassus, -a, -um, weary.
lateō, latēre, latuī, 2, lie hid.
Latīnus, -a, -um, Latin (belonging
to Latium).
latitō, 1, lie hid.
latrō, -ōnis, m., robber, brigand.
lātus, -a, -um, broad; adv., lātē,
widely.
laudō, 1, praise.
laurus, -ī, f., laurel.
laus, laudis, f., praise, glory, worth.
Lāvīnius, -a, -um, of Lavinium, a
city founded by Aeneas in honor of
his Italian wife Lavinia.
lēctor, -ōris, m., reader.
lectus, -ī, m., bed.
lēgātus, -ī, m., envoy, ambassador; legion-commander, lieutenant-
general.
legiō, -ōnis, f., legion.
legō, legere, lēgī, lēctum, 3, read.
lēnitās, -ātis, f., gentleness, slowness.
lentē, adv., slowly.
lētum, -ī, n., death.
levis, -e, light.
levō, 1, lift up, raise; relieve.
lēx, lēgis, f., law.
libellus, -ī, m., diminutive of liber,
book.
libenter, adv., willingly.
liber, librī, m., book.

liber, -era, -erum, free; **liberī, -ōrum,** *m. pl.,* children.

līberālis, -e, befitting a freeman, noble, honorable, liberal.

līberātor, -ōris, *m.,* deliverer (used of Iupiter).

līberō, 1, set free; (*with abl.*) set free from.

lībertās, -ātis, *f.,* freedom, liberty.

libīdō, -inis, *f.,* desire, lust.

lībō, 1, pour out a libation.

lībra, -ae, *f.,* (the Roman) pound.

licet, -uit, 2, *impers.,* it is allowed, lawful (*with dat. and inf.*).

līma, -ae, *f.,* a file.

lingua, -ae, *f.,* tongue, language.

littera, -ae, *f.,* a letter (of the alphabet); **litterae, -ārum,** *f. pl.,* a letter (epistle) *or* literature.

litūra, -ae, *f.,* erasure, correction.

lītus, -oris, *n.,* shore.

locō, 1, place.

locus, -ī, *m., pl.* **loca, -ōrum,** *n.,* place.

longē, *adv.,* far, by far.

longinquus, -a, -um, distant, long, lasting.

longus, -a, -um, long.

loquor, loquī, locūtus sum, 3, *deponent,* speak, talk.

lūceō, lūcēre, lūxī, 2, shine.

lūcidus, -a, -um, bright.

lūdō, -ere, lūsī, lūsum, 3, play.

lūdus, -ī, *m.,* game.

lūgeō, -ēre, lūxī, 2, mourn.

lūmen, inis, *n.,* light; *pl.* (*poet.*), eyes.

lūna, -ae, *f.,* moon.

lupa, -ae, *f.,* (*fem. of* **lupus, -ī,** *m.*), she-wolf.

lūx, lūcis, *f.,* light.

lyricus, -a, -um, lyric.

māchinātiō, -ōnis, *f.,* engine, machine (*cf.* **māchina, -ae,** *f.*).

magis, *adv.,* more (in degree).

magister, magistrī, *m.,* master, teacher.

magistrātus, -ūs, *m.,* civil office, magistrate.

magnificus, -a, -um, magnificent, splendid.

magnitūdō, -inis, *f.,* greatness, size.

magnopere (= **magnō opere**), *adv.,* greatly, very much.

magnus, -a, -um, great.

māior, māius, greater.

mala, -ōrum, *n. pl.,* evils, wickedness.

malefactum (male factum), -ī, *n.,* evil deed, crime.

maleficium, -ī (-iī), *n.,* evil deed, harm, wrong.

mālō, mālle, māluī, *irreg.,* prefer.

malus, -a, -um, bad.

maneō, manēre, mānsī, mānsum, 2, remain; **manet,** it is established that, regarded as settled that.

mānēs, -ium, *m. pl.,* departed spirits.

manifestus, -a, -um, clear, evident.

manus, -ūs, *f.,* hand; band (of men).

mare, maris, *n.,* the sea.

margō, -inis, *m. and f.,* edge.

marmor, -oris, *n.,* marble.

māter, mātris, *f.,* mother.

māteria, -ae, *f.,* matter, materials, timber.

mātūrō, 1, hasten.

mātūrus, -a, -um, early, timely; *adv.* **mātūrē.**

Maurus, -a, -um, Moorish.

Māvortius, -a, -um, of Mars.

maximē, *adv.,* most (in degree), especially.

maximus, -a, -um, greatest.

mē miserum, alas (*lit.* miserable me).

meā, *see* **interest.**

meātus, -ūs, *m.,* motion.

medeor, -ērī, 2, *deponent,* heal, cure, relieve (*with dat.*).

medicīna, -ae, *f.,* medicine, remedy.

medicus, -ī, *m.,* doctor.

mediocritās, -ātis, *f.,* a middle state, the mean (Aristotle's *mesotēs*).

mediterrāneus, -a, -um, inland, remote from the sea.

medius, -a, -um, middle.

melior, melius, better; *adv.,* **melius,** better.

meminī, -isse, *imperat.* **mementō,** *irreg.,* remember; (*with inf.*) remember to.

memor, -oris, mindful of (*with gen.*).

memoria, -ae, *f.,* memory.

memoriā teneō, 2, remember.

mendāx, -ācis, f., lying, false.
mēns, mentis, -ium, f., mind.
mēnsis, -is, -ium (-um), m., month.
mercātor, -ōris, m., merchant,
    trader.
mereor, -ērī, meritus sum, 2, de-
    ponent, deserve; bene mereor dē
    (with abl.), deserve well of.
messis, -is, -ium, f., harvest.
metuō, -ere, metuī, 3, fear.
metus, -ūs, m., fear.
meus, mea, meum, my, mine.
mī = mihi, dat. of ego.
migrātiō, -ōnis, f., migration, re-
    moval.
migrō, 1, depart, migrate.
mīles, -itis, m., soldier.
mīlitia, -ae, f., warfare, military
    service.
mīlitō, 1, serve as a soldier.
mīlle, numeral, indecl. in sing.,
    thousand; pl. mīlia, thousands.
mināciter, adv., with threats.
minimē, adv., least; no, not at all.
minimī, gen. of value, at a very small
    value, very little.
minus, adv., less; (after sī) not at all.
mīror, -ārī, mīrātus sum, 1, de-
    ponent, marvel at, wonder at.
mīrum, an exclamation, how wonder-
    ful!
mīrus, -a, -um, wonderful.
misceō, -ēre, miscuī, mixtum, 2,
    mix, mix with (with abl.).
miser, -era, -erum, sad, wretched.
miseret, impers., feel pity for, lit. it
    distresses (with acc. and gen.).
miseror, 1, deponent, pity.
miserrimus, -a, -um, most wretched.
miserum, see mē miserum.
mītis, -e, gentle, mild.
mittō, mittere, mīsī, missum, 3,
    send.
moderātus, -a, -um, observing
    moderation, moderate.
modestē, adv., with moderation.
modo, only.
modo, see dummodo.
modo, see quō . . . modo.
modus, -ī, m., measure, limit, way;
    meter, rhythm; modō, abl. of
    modus, e.g. nullō modō, by no
    means.

moenia, -ium, n. pl., walls (of a city).
mōlēs, -is, -ium, f., mass.
molestus, -a, -um, troublesome.
mollis, -e, soft.
moneō, monēre, monuī, moni-
    tum, 2, advise, warn; with acc. and
    with ut and subjve.
mōns, montis, -ium, m., mountain.
mōnstrō, 1, show.
monumentum, -ī, n., monument;
    Monumentum Ancyrānum, n.,
    the Monumentum Ancyranum, con-
    taining an inscription in Latin and
    Greek, set up at Ancyra in Asia
    Minor. It is the official account of
    the achievements (rēs gestae) of
    Augustus.
mora, -ae, f., delay.
morbus, -ī, m., disease.
mōrēs, see mōs.
morior, morī, fut. part. moritūrus,
    3, deponent, die.
mors, mortis, f., death.
mortālis, -e, mortal.
mortuus, -a, -um, dead, dead man.
mōs, mōris, m., custom; (with
    pācis) law, rule; pl. mōrēs, morals,
    character.
mōtus, -ūs, m., motion; emotion,
    passion.
moveō, movēre, mōvī, mōtum, 2,
    move, stir.
mox, adv., soon.
mulceō, -ēre, mulsī, mulsum, 2,
    soothe.
mulier, -eris, f., woman.
multī, -ae, -a, many.
multitūdō, -inis, f., large number.
multō, adv., by far.
multō, 1, punish (with acc. and abl.
    of the punishment).
multus, -a, -um, much.
mundus, -ī, m., the universe, world.
mūniō, munīre, munīvī, munī-
    tum, 4, fortify; mūnītissimus,
    -a, -um, superlative of mūnītus.
mūnitiō, -ōnis, f., fortification.
mūnus, -eris, n., duty, function;
    gift.
murmur, -uris, n., murmur, sound.
mūs, mūris, -ium, m., mouse; used
    of an anticlimax in literature.
mūtō, 1, change.

nam, namque, for.
nancīscor, nancīscī, nactus (nānctus) sum, 3, *deponent*, get, obtain.
narcissus, -ī, *m.*, narcissus.
narrō, 1, *with dat. of pers.*, relate, tell.
nāscor, nāscī, nātus sum, 3, *deponent*, be born.
nāsus, -ī, *m.*, nose.
nātālis, -e, belonging to one's birth, natal; nātālis (*sc.* diēs), *m.*, birthday.
nātiō, -ōnis, *f.*, clan, people.
nātūra, -ae, *f.*, nature.
nātus, -ī, *m.*, son.
nauta, -ae, *m.*, sailor.
nāvigō, 1, sail.
nāvis, -is, -ium, *f.*, ship.
nāvita, -ae, *m.* (= nauta), sailor.
-ne, *enclitic*, asks a question.
-ne, *used instead of* utrum, whether.
nē, in order that . . . not, lest; *also used in negative command.*
nē . . . quidem, not even.
nec, neque, nor.
nec (neque) . . . nec (neque), neither . . . nor.
necessārius, -a, -um, necessary.
necesse est, *impers.* it is necessary, one must (*with subjve.*).
necne, or not (*in indirect questions*).
necō, 1, kill.
nefās, *n.*, *indecl.*, wrong, contrary to divine law.
neglegō, -ere, neglēxī, neglēctum, 3, neglect.
negō, 1, say no, deny, say that . . . not.
negōtium, -ī (-iī), *n.*, business.
nēmō, *acc.* nēminem, *dat.* nēminī, no one; *for gen. and abl. use* nūllus.
nemus, -oris, *n.*, grove, wood.
neque, *see* nec.
nesciō, -īre, nescīvī (-iī), 4, not to know, to be ignorant.
nescio quis, nescio quid, *pron.*, someone (I don't know who); *adj.*, nescio quī.
nēve (neu), and that . . . not, and lest.
nex, necis, *f.*, death.
niger, -gra, -grum, black.
nihil (nīl), *n.*, *indecl.*, nothing.
nihil, *adv.*, not at all.
nihilī, *gen. of value*, at no value, at nothing.

nihilum (nīlum, *poet.*) -ī, *m.*, nothing = nihil (nīl), *indecl.*
nīl = nihil, nothing.
nimis, *adv.*, too much; *with* nē quid, nothing in excess.
nimium, *adv.*, too much.
nisi, *conj.*, unless.
nisi, *after interrog. or neg. clause*, except, save only.
nitidus, -a, -um, shining.
nix, nivis, -ium, *f.*, snow.
nō, 1, swim.
nōbilis, -e, noble.
nocēns, -entis, guilty, guilty man.
noceō, -ēre, nocuī, nocitum, 2, hurt (*with dat.*).
nocturnus, -a, -um, by night, nightly.
nōdus, -ī, *m.*, knot, difficulty.
nōlō, nōlle, nōluī, *irreg.*, be unwilling.
nōmen, -inis, *n.*, name.
nōn, *adv.*, not.
nōn iam, *adv.*, no longer.
nōn modo . . . sed etiam, not only . . . but also.
nōnne, *introduces a question expecting the answer* Yes.
nōnus, -a, -um, ninth.
nōs, *pers. pron.*, we.
nōscō, nōscere, nōvī, nōtum, 3, come to know; *perf.* nōvī, know.
noster, nostra, nostrum, our, ours; nostrī, *m. pl.*, our men.
nōtus, -a, -um, well-known.
novae rēs, *f. pl.*, revolution.
novissimus, -a, -um, last; novissimum agmen, rear-guard.
novō, 1, make new, invent.
novus, -a, -um, new.
nox, noctis, -ium, *f.*, night.
nūbēs, -is, -ium, *f.*, cloud.
nūbō, -ere, nūpsī, nūptum, 3, marry (*with dat.*); *used of a woman.*
nūllus, -a, -um, no, none.
num, *introduces a question expecting the answer* No.
num, whether (*in single indirect questions*).
nūmen, -inis, *n.*, divinity, divine will.
numerus, -ī, *m.*, number; numerī, *m. pl.*, numbers, *i.e.* poetry.

numquam, never.
nunc, *adv.,* now.
nuntiō, 1, announce, report.
nuntius, -ī (-iī), *m.,* messenger.
nūper, *adv.,* recently.
nusquam, nowhere.
nūtrīx, -trīcis, *f.,* nurse.

Ō, *an exclamation used with the vocative or an accusative of exclamation.*
ob, *prep. with acc.,* on account of.
obēsus, -a, -um, fat.
obdūrō, 1, endure, hold out.
oblectō, 1, delight.
oblīvīscor, oblīvīscī, oblītus sum, 3, *deponent,* forget (*with gen.*).
obscūrus, -a, -um, obscure.
obses, -idis, *m. and f.,* hostage.
obsolētus, -a, -um, old, worn out.
obstipēscō, (obstupēscō) -ere, obstipuī, 3, be amazed.
obstō, -stāre, -stitī, 1, hinder, oppose (*with dat.*).
obstringō, -stringere, -strīnxī, -strictum, 3, bind, tie.
obtineō, -ēre, obtinuī, obtentum, 2, obtain, hold; maintain, prove.
obvius, -a, -um, in the way, so as to meet; **obviam eō** (*with dat.*), meet.
occīdō, occīdere, occīdī, occīsum, 3 (*compound of* **caedō**), kill.
occidō, -ere, occidī, occāsum, 3 (*compound of* **cadō**), sink (of the sun), perish.
occupō, 1, seize, occupy.
oceanus, -ī, *m.,* ocean.
ocellus, -ī, *m., diminutive of* **oculus,** eye.
oculus, -ī, *m.,* eye.
ōdī, ōdisse, *perf. with pres. meaning,* hate, dislike.
odium, -ī (-iī), *n.,* hatred, dislike.
Oebalius, -a, -um, Oebalian, *i.e.* Spartan.
officium, -ī (-iī), *n.,* duty.
olfaciō, -facere, -fēcī, -factum, 3, smell.
ōlim, *adv.,* once, once upon a time; *sometimes* = one day, hereafter.
ollī, *old form of* **illī,** *dat. sing. of* **ille.**
omittō, -ere, omīsī, omissum, 3, omit, lay aside, say nothing of.
omnīnō, *adv.,* altogether.

omnis, -e, all, every.
onus, -eris, *n.,* burden.
opīniō, -ōnis, *f.,* opinion, reputation.
opīnor, 1, *deponent,* suppose, think.
oportet, -uit, *impers.,* 2, it is necessary, one must, ought (*with inf.*).
oppidum, -ī, *n.,* town.
opprimō, -primere, -pressī, -pressum, 3, press down, suppress, overthrow.
oppugnō, 1, attack.
(ops), opis, *def., f.,* help; *pl.,* **opēs,** wealth, resources.
optābilis, -e, desirable.
optātior, -ius, more desired.
optimē, *adv.,* very well.
optimus, -a, -um, best.
optō, 1, desire, long for.
opus, operis, *n.,* work, task.
opus est (*with abl.*), there is need of.
ōra, -ae, *f.,* shore, region.
ōrātiō, -ōnis, *f.,* speech; **ōrātiōnem habeō,** make a speech.
orbis, -is, -ium, *m.,* circle; the world (*usually with* **terrārum**).
orior, orīrī, ortus sum, 4, *deponent,* arise; *with abl.,* spring from, be born.
ornātus, -ūs, *m.,* adornment, ornament, dress.
ornō, 1, equip, adorn, honor.
ōrō, 1, beg, pray, *with acc. and with* **ut** *and subjve.*; **causās ōrō,** plead causes.
ōs, ōris, *n.,* face, mouth.
os, ossis, *n.,* bone.
ōsculum, -ī, *n.,* kiss.
ostendō, -ere, ostendī, ostentum, 3, show.
ōtiōsus, -a, -um, at leisure.
ōtium, ī- (-iī), *n.,* leisure, rest.
ovis, -is, -ium, *f.,* sheep.

pācō, 1, pacify, make peaceful.
Paelignus, -a, -um, of the Paelignī; Ovid was born in the Paelignian city of Sulmo.
paene, almost.
paenitentia, -ae, *f.,* repentance.
paenitet, *impers.,* repent, grieve, *lit.,* it repents, grieves someone (*with acc. and gen.*).

pāgus, -ī, *m.*, country district, canton.
pallidus, -a, -um, pale.
pānis, -is, -ium (-um), *m.*, bread.
papāver, -eris, *n.*, poppy.
pār, paris, equal (*with dat.*).
parcō, -ere, pepercī, *fut. part.*
parsūrus, 3, spare (*with dat.*).
parēns, -entis, *m. and f.*, parent.
pāreō, -ēre, paruī, 2, obey (*with dat.*).
pariēs, -ietis, *m.*, wall (of a house).
pariter, *adv.*, equally, at the same time.
parmula, -ae, *f.*, a (small) shield.
parō, 1, get ready, prepare; (*with inf.*) prepare to.
parricidium, -ī (-iī), *n.*, parricide, murder of one's father or parents.
pars, partis, -ium, *f.*, part.
parturiō, -īre, 4, to be in labor.
parum, *adv.*, too little.
parvulus, -a, -um, *diminutive of* parvus, little.
parvus, -a, -um, little, small.
pāscuum, -ī, *n.*, pasture (*usually pl.*).
passer, -eris, *m.*, sparrow.
passus, -ūs, *m.*, pace; mille passūs, a thousand paces, a mile.
pastor, -ōris, *m.*, shepherd.
pateō, -ēre, patuī, 2, lie open, be manifest; patet, *impers.*, it is clear (that).
pater, -tris, *m.*, father.
paternus, -a, -um, of one's father.
patientia, -ae, *f.*, patience.
patior, patī, passus sum, 3, *deponent*, suffer, endure; allow.
patrēs cōnscrīptī, *m. pl.*, senators.
patria, -ae, *f.*, country, fatherland.
patricius, -a, -um, patrician (belonging to the patricians).
patrius, -a, -um, of one's father or fathers.
paucī, -ae, -a, few, a few.
paulō, *adv.*, a little, by a little (*with comp.*).
pauper, -eris, poor, a poor man.
paupertās, -ātis, *f.*, poverty.
pāx, pācis, *f.*, peace.
peccō, 1, do wrong, sin.
pectus, -oris, *n.*, breast, heart; mind.
pecūnia, -ae, *f.*, money.

pēior, -ius, worse.
pelagus, -ī, *n.*, sea.
pellō, -ere, pepulī, pulsum, 3, drive, repel, banish.
Penātēs, -ium, *m. pl.*, household gods, the Penates.
penna, -ae, *f.*, wing.
per, *prep. with acc.*, through.
percurrō, -currere, -cucurrī (-currī), -cursum, 3, run through, mention (cursorily).
perdō, -ere, perdidī, perditum, 3, destroy, ruin, lose.
peregrē, *adv.*, abroad.
peregrīnor, 1, *deponent*, go abroad.
peregrīnus, -a, -um, foreign.
perennis, -e, lasting, enduring.
pereō, -īre, periī, *irreg.*, perish.
perfacilis, -e, very easy.
perfectus, -a, -um, perfect.
perferō, -ferre, -tulī, -lātum, *irreg.* carry through, announce, endure.
perficiō, -ficere, -fēcī, -fectum, 3, accomplish, complete.
perfringō, -fringere, -frēgī, -fractum, 3, break through, violate.
perfugium, -ī (-iī), *n.*, refuge.
pergō, -ere, perrēxī, perrēctum, 3, proceed, go on, continue.
periclum, *see* periculum.
periculum, -ī, *n.*, danger, risk.
permaneō, -manēre, -mānsī, mānsum, 2, remain, last, persist.
perniciōsus, -a, -um, destructive, ruinous, pernicious.
pernoctō, 1, pass the night.
perpetuum, *see* in perpetuum.
perpetuus, -a, -um, continuous, perpetual.
perrārō, *adv.*, very seldom.
persequor, -sequī, -secūtus sum, 3, *deponent*, follow up, pursue.
Persēs, -ae, *m.*, a Persian; *pl.* Persae, -ārum, the Persians.
persevērō, 1, persist.
persuādeō, -ēre, persuāsī, persuāsum, 2, persuade (*with dat.*); *with* ut *and subjve.*
pertimēscō, -ere, pertimuī, 3, fear (greatly).
pertinācia, -ae, *f.*, obstinacy.
pertineō, -ēre, pertinuī, 2, reach, concern (*with* ad *and acc.*).

perveniō, -īre, pervēnī, perven-tum, 4, *with* ad *and acc.*, arrive at.

pervincō, -vincere, -vīcī, -victum, 3, conquer, prevail.

pēs, pedis, *m.*, foot.

pessimus, -a, -um, worst, very bad.

petō, -ere, petīvi (-iī), petītum, 3, seek, aim at, ask for; *with* ā *and abl.*, ask, request (someone); *also with* ut *and subjve.*

phalanx, -angis, *f.*, phalanx.

philosophus, -ī, *m.*, philosopher.

pietās, -ātis, *f.*, piety, love, loyalty (dutiful conduct towards the gods or one's parents).

piget, *impers.*, dislike, *lit.* it irks, troubles (*with acc. and gen. or inf.*).

pīla, -ae, *f.*, pillar.

pīlum, -ī, *n.*, javelin.

pinguis, -e, fat.

pinna, -ae, *f.* = **penna,** wing.

pistrilla, -ae, *f.*, (*diminutive*) mill.

pius, -a, -um, pious, devout, devoted.

plācābilis, -e, easily appeased.

placeō, -ere, placuī, placitum, 2, please (*with dat.*).

placet, -uit, 2, *impers.*, it pleases, seems good (*with dat. and inf.*).

placidē, *adv.*, peacefully, calmly.

plācō, 1, appease, reconcile.

plānē, *adv.*, plainly, clearly.

plēbēius, -a, -um, plebeian (belonging to the common people).

plēbs, -bis, *f.*, the common people.

plēnus, -a, -um, full (*with gen.*).

plērīque, *pl.* (*rare in sing.*), very many, most.

plūrimus, -a, -um, most, very much; *adv.*, **plūrimum; plūrimum possum,** to be the most powerful.

plūs, *n.*, more; **plūrēs, -a,** more, many.

pluvia, -ae, *f.*, rain.

poena, -ae, *f.*, punishment.

Poenī, -ōrum, *m. pl.*, Carthaginians.

poēta, -ae, *m.*, poet.

polliceor, -ērī, pollicitus sum, 2, *deponent*, promise.

pōmum, -ī, *n.*, fruit, apple.

pōnō, pōnere, posuī, positum, 3, place, lay aside.

pōns, pontis, *m.*, bridge.

popīna, -ae, *f.*, cook-shop.

populus, -ī, *m.*, people.

porcus, -ī, *m.*, pig, hog.

porta, -ae, *f.*, gate, city-gate.

portō, 1, carry.

portus, -ūs, *m.*, harbor.

poscō, -ere, poposcī, 3, demand, request.

possessiō, -ōnis, *f.*, possession, occupation; *pl.*, possessions, lands.

possideō, -ēre, possēdī, possessum, 2, possess.

possum, posse, potuī, *irreg.*, be able, can.

post, *prep. with acc.*, after, behind.

posteā, *adv.*, afterwards.

posterus, -a, -um, next; **posterī,** *m. pl.*, posterity.

postmodo, *poet. for* **posteā,** afterwards.

postquam, *conj.*, after.

postulātum, -ī, *n.*, *usually pl.*, demand, request.

pote = **potest,** he/it can.

potēns, -entis, powerful; (*with gen.*) master of.

potentia, -ae, *f.*, power.

potior, -īrī, potītus sum, 3, *deponent*, get possession of (*with abl.*, *sometimes with gen.*).

potissimum, *adv.*, preferably, especially.

potius, rather.

prae, *prep. with abl.*, before, in front of; compared with; for, because of.

praebeō, praebēre, praebuī, praebitum, 2, offer, supply.

praecānus, -a, -um, grey before one's time.

praecēdō, -cēdere, -cessī, -cessum, 3, surpass.

praeceptum, -ī, *n.*, rule, precept.

praecipiō, -cipere, -cēpī, -ceptum, 3, advise, instruct.

praecipuē, *adv.*, especially.

praeclārus, -a, -um, distinguished, famous.

praeditus, -a, -um, endowed with (*with abl.*).

praedor, 1, *deponent*, plunder.

praeeō, -īre, -iī, -itum, *irreg.*, go before; say first, dictate.

praeferō, -ferre, -tulī, -lātum, *irreg.*, prefer (*with acc. and dat.*).

praeficiō, -ficere, -fēcī, -fectum, 3, place in command of (*with acc. and dat.*).

praemium, praemī (-iī), *n.*, reward.

praeparō, 1, prepare beforehand.

praesēns, -entis, present, in person.

praesentia, *see* in praesentia.

praesentiō, -sentīre, -sēnsī, -sēnsum, 4, feel, perceive beforehand.

praesidium, -ī (-iī), *n.*, guard, protection.

praestāns, -antis, superior, excellent.

praestō, -stāre, -stitī, 1, be superior (to), surpass; perform, show.

praesum, praeesse, praefuī, *irreg.*, be in command of (*with dat.*).

praeter, *prep. with acc.*, beyond.

praetereō, -īre, -iī, -itum, *irreg.*, go past, pass by, pass away.

praetor, -ōris, *m.*, praetor; prō-praetor, a provincial governor of praetorian rank.

prātum, -ī, *n.*, meadow.

prāvus, -a, -um, bad, depraved.

precor, -ārī, precātus sum, 1, *deponent*, pray, beg, request.

premō, -ere, pressī, pressum, 3, press, press hard on, repress; suppress (a manuscript), hug (the shore).

prima lūx (lūcis), *f.*, daylight, dawn.

primōrēs, -um, *m.*, chiefs.

primum, *adv.*, first.

primus, -a, -um, first.

princeps = primus, first.

princeps, prīncipis, *m.*, chief; the title of the Roman emperors.

prīncipātus, -ūs, *m.*, principate, reign; chieftainship.

prīncipium, -ī (-iī), *n.*, beginning; *pl.* first beginnings, atoms.

priscus, -a, -um, old, ancient.

pristinus, -a, -um, former, original.

prius, *adv.*, before, formerly, previously.

priusquam, *conj.*, before.

privātus, -a, -um, private, a private person, not holding office.

prō, *prep. with abl.*, on behalf of, for, instead of.

prō cōnsule = prōcōnsul, -is, *m.*, a proconsul, governor of a province (after the consulship).

probitās, -ātis, *f.*, goodness, honesty.

probō, 1, approve.

prōcēdō, -cēdere, -cessī, -cessum, 3, advance.

procella, -ae, *f.*, storm.

procul, *adv.*, far, far away; (*with abl.*) far from.

prōdō, -ere, prōdidī, prōditum, 3, betray, give forth, hand down.

proelium, -ī (-iī), *n.*, battle.

profānus, -a, -um, profane, uninitiated.

profectō, *adv.*, assuredly, certainly.

prōferō, -ferre, -tulī, -lātum, *irreg.*, bring forth, bring to light, invent.

prōficiō, -ere, prōfēcī, prōfectum, 3, make progress.

proficīscor, -iscī, profectus sum, 3, *deponent*, set out.

profugus, -a, -um, exiled, an exile.

profundus, -a, -um, deep, profound.

prohibeō, -ēre, prohibuī, prohibitum, 2, keep off, restrain, prevent, prevent from (*with inf.*).

prōicio, -icere, -iēcī, -iectum, 3, throw forward.

proinde, *see* haud proinde.

prōmittō, -ere, prōmīsī, prōmissum, 3, promise.

prōmoveō, -movēre, -mōvī, -mōtum, 2, move forward.

prope, *prep. with acc.*, near.

prope, *adv.*, almost.

properō, 1, hasten, hurry.

propior, propius, nearer.

propius, *adv.*, nearer.

prōpōnō, -pōnere, -posuī, -positum, 3, propose, put forward, offer.

proprius, -a, -um, one's own; proprium est, it is characteristic of, *with gen.*

propter, *prep. with acc.*, on account of.

proptereā quod, because.

prōsternō, -sternere, -strāvī, -strātum, 3, overthrow, destroy.

prōvehō, -vehere, -vexī, -vectum, 3, carry forward, advance.

prōvincia, -ae, *f.*, province; *also* = the Roman province in the south of France, Gallia Narbonensis.

prōvocō, 1, challenge.

proximus, -a, -um, next, the nearest (*with dat.*).

prūdēns, -entis, prudent, sensible.
prūdentia, -ae, *f.,* knowledge, intelligence, prudence, discretion.
pruīna, -ae, *f.,* frost.
pudet, *impers.,* be ashamed of, *lit.,* it causes shame (*with acc. and gen.*).
pudor, -ōris, *m.,* modesty, sense of shame.
puella, -ae, *f.,* girl.
puer, puerī, *m.,* boy.
pugna, -ae, *f.,* battle.
pugnātum est, *pass. impers.,* a battle was fought.
pugnō, 1, fight.
pulcher, -chra, -chrum, beautiful.
pulsō, 1, strike, beat.
pulvīnus, -ī, *n.,* cushion.
pulvis, -eris, *m.,* dust.
pūnctum, -ī, *n.,* puncture, point; vote, applause.
Pūnicus, -a, -um, Punic, Carthaginian. There were three Punic Wars, 264–241 B.C., 218–202 B.C., 149–146 B.C.
pūniō, -īre, punīvī, punītum, 4, punish.
purpureus, -a, -um, purple.
pūrus, -a, -um, pure, chaste.
puter, -tris, -tre, crumbling.
putō, 1, think.

quā, where.
quadrīgae, -ārum, *f. pl.,* four-horse team, chariot, car.
quadrupedāns, -antis, galloping (on four feet).
quaerō, -ere, quaesīvī (-iī), quaesītum, 3, seek, ask, inquire (*with ā and abl.*).
quaesō (*old form of* **quaerō**), 3, pray, beg (*used parenthetically*).
quālis, -e, of what kind?
quālis, -e, as (*after* **talis,** such).
quam, than, *after a comparative;* how (*with adjectives and adverbs*); as (*with* **tam,** so).
quam (*with superl.*), as . . . as possible; **quam plūrimī,** as many as possible.
quam quī, quam ut, *used with subjve. after a comparative.*
quamquam, *conj.,* although.
quamvīs, *conj.,* although (*with*

subjve.); *also with adjectives (lit.* as you will, as much as you will).
quandō, *interrog. adv.,* when?
quantī, *gen. of value,* at what value?, how high?
quantō, *adv.,* (by) how much (*with comparative*).
quantō opere, *adv.,* how greatly, how much.
quantum est (*with gen.*), as many as there are of, *i.e.* all.
quantus, -a, -um, how great?; as (*after* **tantus,** so great).
quārē, why.
quasi, as if, as it were; just as if (*with subjve.*).
quatiō, -ere, 3, shake.
quattuor, *numeral,* four.
-que, *enclitic* (*attached to the second of two words*), and.
queror, querī, questus sum, 3, *deponent,* complain.
quī, quae, quod, *rel. pron.,* who, which; *with subjve. in clauses of characteristic, e.g.,* **sunt quī,** there are some who.
quī, quae, quod, *interrog. adj.,* which?, what?
quia, *conj.,* because.
quīcumque, quaecumque, quodcumque, *indef. rel. pron.,* whoever, whatever.
quid, *n.* of **quis,** what?; also = why?
quīdam, quaedam, quiddam, *pron.,* a certain; *adj.,* **quīdam, quaedam, quoddam.**
quidem, indeed; **nē . . . quidem,** not even.
quiēs, -ētis, *f.,* rest, sleep.
quiēscō, -ere, quiēvī, quiētum, 3, rest, keep quiet.
quīlibet, quaelibet, quidlibet, *pron.,* anyone you like; *adj.,* **quīlibet, quaelibet, quodlibet.**
quīn (= **quī nōn, quō nōn**), *used* (*with subjve.*) *after a negative and verbs like* **impediō.**
quīndecim, *numeral,* fifteen.
quīnque, *numeral,* five.
quippe, *adv. and conj.,* certainly, to be sure; *with relative* **quī,** seeing that, since.
Quirītēs, -ium, *m. pl.,* citizens; the

citizens of Rome in their civil capacity (originally the inhabitants of the Sabine town of Curēs).

quis, quid, *interrog. pron.,* who? what?

quis, quid, *pron.,* anyone, anything; *used after* **sī, nisi, num,** *and* **nē.**

quisquam, quidquam, *pron.,* anyone (*after a negative*); *for abl. use* **ūllus.**

quisque, quaeque, quidque, *pron.,* each; *adj.,* **quisque, quaeque, quodque.**

quisquis, quicquid (quidquid), *indef. rel. pron.,* whoever, whatever.

quīvīs, quaevīs, quidvīs, *pron.,* anyone you like; *adj.,* **quīvīs, quaevīs, quodvīs.**

quō, *interrog. adv.,* where? to what place?

quō (= **ut eō**), in order that (*with a comparative*).

quod, *conj.,* because; the fact that.

quod sī, *conj.,* but if.

quōminus (= **quō minus**), *used after verbs like* **impediō.**

quōmodo, quō . . . modo, *interrog. adv.,* in what way, how?

quondam, once, formerly.

quoniam, *conj.,* since.

quoque, *adv.,* also, too.

quot, *indecl. adj.,* how many?; as (*after* **tot,** so many).

quotus, -a, -um, which in number?; *e.g.* **quota hōra est,** what time is it?

quousque, *adv.,* how long?

radius, -ī (-iī), *m.,* rod (for measuring); ray (of the sun).

rapidus, -a, -um, rapid.

rapiō, -ere, rapuī, raptum, 3, seize, snatch, hurry away.

rārus, -a, -um, rare, scarce.

ratiō, -ōnis, *f.,* reason, reckoning, plan.

ratis, -is, -ium, *f.,* raft; (*poet.*) bark, boat.

raucus, -a, -um, harsh.

recēns, -entis, recent, new.

recipiō, -ere, recēpī, receptum, 3, take back, recover; **sē recipere,** retreat, recover (oneself).

recitō, 1, read out, recite.

recordor, -ārī, recordātus sum, 1, *deponent,* recollect, remember.

rēctus, -a, -um, right, correct; **rēctē,** *adv.,* rightly.

reddō, reddere, reddidī, redditum, 3, give back.

redeō, -īre, rediī, *irreg.,* return.

redintegrō, 1, renew.

referō, -ferre, rettulī, relātum, *irreg.,* bring back, report.

rēfert, *impers.,* it concerns (*with ablatives like* **meā**).

rēgīna, -ae, *f.,* queen.

rēgnō, 1, reign, rule.

rēgnum, -ī, *n.,* kingdom, kingship.

regō, regere, rēxī, rēctum, 3, rule.

rēligiō, -ōnis, *f.,* religion, religious scruple; *also in pl.*

relinquō, relinquere, relīquī, relictum, 3, leave behind, leave, abandon.

reliquus, -a, -um, remaining, rest of.

relūceō, -ēre, relūxī, 2, shine.

remaneō, -manēre, -mānsī, -mānsum, 2, stay behind, remain.

Rēmī, -ōrum, *m.,* a tribe in Gaul near the modern Rheims.

reminīscor, reminīscī, 3, remember (*with gen. or acc.*).

remissiō, -ōnis, *f.,* relaxation.

remittō, -mittere, -mīsī, -missum, 3, send back.

removeō, -ēre, remōvī, remōtum, 2, remove, move back.

renovō, 1, renew.

reor, ratus sum, 2, *deponent,* think.

repente, *adv.,* suddenly.

reperiō, reperīre, repperī, repertum, 4, find.

repetō, -petere, -petīvī, -petitum, 3, repeat, recall.

repōnō, -ere, reposuī, repositum, 3, lay aside (replace).

reprehendō, -ere, reprehendī, reprehēnsum, 3, blame, rebuke.

requīrō, -quīrere, -quīsīvī (-iī), -quīsītum, 3, ask, ask for, search for.

rēs, reī, *f.,* thing, circumstance; **rem gerō,** conduct a campaign; *pl.,* activity, business; **rēs agō,** keep busy; **rēs gestae,** achievements.

rēs pūblica (rēspūblica), reī pūblicae, *f.*, republic, state.
rescindō, -ere, rescidī, rescissum,
3, break down.
reservō, 1, keep back, retain.
resolvō, -solvere, -solvī, -solūtum,
3, unbind, loose.
respiciō, -ere, respexī, respectum,
3, look back.
respondeō, -ēre, respondī, respōnsum, 2, reply, answer.
respōnsum, -ī, *n.*, reply, answer.
restituō, -ere, restituī, restitūtum,
3, restore.
restō, -stāre, -stitī, 1, stand firm,
remain.
retineō, -ēre, retinuī, retentum,
2, retain, keep.
reverentia, -ae, *f.*, reverence.
revertor, -vertī, 3, *deponent*, return;
perf. usually active, revertī.
rēx, rēgis, *m.*, king.
rideō, ridēre, risī, risum, 2, laugh,
smile at.
ridiculus, -a, -um, laughable, funny,
ridiculous.
riguus, -a, -um, that waters, running.
ripa, -ae, *f.*, bank.
rivus, -ī, *m.*, stream.
rōbur, -oris, *n.*, oak; strength.
rogō, 1, ask; *with acc. and with* ut *and
subjve.*
rogus, -ī, *m.*, funeral pile.
Rōmānus, -a, -um, Roman; Rōmānī, -ōrum, *m. pl.*, Romans.
rota, -ae, *f.*, wheel; *poet. for* currus,
a car.
rotundus, -a, -um, round.
rūmor, -ōris, *m.*, rumor, talk.
rūre = rūrī, *loc.*, in the country.
rūs, rūris, *n.*, country (*opp. to* the
city); *pl.* (*poet.*) fields.
rūsticānus, -a, -um, rustic.
rūsticor, 1, *deponent*, live in the
country.

Sabbatum, -ī, *n.*, the Sabbath.
Sabīnus, -a, -um, Sabine. The
Sabines lived in central Italy,
north-east of Rome.
saeculum, -ī, *n.*, generation, age,

century; nec nostrī saeculī, not
in accordance with the spirit of our
age.
saepe, *adv.*, often.
saevus, -a, -um, fierce, cruel.
sagitta, -ae, *f.*, arrow.
sal, salis, *m.*, salt, wit.
salūs, -ūtis *f.*, safety, welfare.
salūtem *acc. of* salūs, *used at the
beginning of a letter*, (sends) greetings (to). S. = Salūtem, S.D. =
Salūtem dicit, S.P.D. (*or* S.D.P.)
= Salūtem plūrimam dicit.
salūtō, 1, greet, pay one's respects to.
salvē (*imperat. of* salveō, am well),
greetings, good-day, *lit.* be well.
salvus, -a, -um, sound in health,
safe and sound.
sānctus, -a, -um, holy, sacred.
sānus, -a, -um, healthy, sane.
sapientia, -ae, *f.*, wisdom.
sapiēns, -entis, wise.
sapiō, sapere, 3, be wise, have sense.
sat = satis.
satis, *adv.*, enough.
satisfaciō, -facere, -fēcī, -factum,
3, satisfy (*with dat.*).
satura, -ae, *f.*, satire.
Sāturnius, -a, -um, of Saturn, an
ancient king of Latium and afterwards the god of agriculture.
saxum, -ī, *n.*, rock, stone.
scelerātus, -a, -um, wicked.
scelus, -eris, *n.*, crime.
schola, -ae, *f.*, school.
scientia, -ae, *f.*, knowledge, skill.
sciō, scīre, scīvī, 4, know, know
(how).
scitor, -ārī, 1, *deponent*, ask (*poet.*).
scrībō, scrībere, scrīpsī, scrīptum,
3, write.
scriptor, -ōris, *m.*, writer.
sculpō, sculpere, sculpsī, sculptum, 3, carve.
scūtum, -ī, *n.*, shield.
Scythicus, -a, -um, Scythian.
sē (sēsē), suī, *reflex. pron.*, himself,
herself, itself, themselves.
sēcēdō, -cēdere, -cessī, -cessum,
3, withdraw.
secundus, -a, -um, second, favorable; rēs secundae, prosperity,
good fortune.

sēcūritās, -ātis, f., freedom from care; safety.

sed, conj., but.

sedeō, sedēre, sēdī, sessum, 2, sit, be seated.

sēdēs, -is, -um, f., seat.

sēditiō, -ōnis, f., sedition, mutiny, insurrection.

sēgnis, -e, lazy, slack.

sella, -ae, f., chair.

semel, numeral, once.

semper, adv., always.

senātor, -ōris, m., senator.

senātus, -ūs, m., senate; senātum habeō, hold a meeting of the senate.

senecta, -ae, f., old age (= senectūs).

senectūs, -ūtis, f., old age.

senex, senis, m., old man.

senior, -ōris, comp. of senex, older man, elderly.

sententia, -ae, f., opinion.

sentiō, -īre, sēnsī, sēnsum, 4, feel, perceive, think.

sepeliō, -īre, sepelīvī, sepultum, 4, bury.

septem, numeral, seven.

septentriōnēs, -um, m. pl., the seven stars of the Great Bear, i.e. the north.

septimus, -a, -um, seventh.

sepulcrum, -ī, n., grave, tomb.

Sēquanus, -a, -um; pl., Sēquanī, a tribe in Gaul.

sequor, sequī, secūtus sum, 3, deponent, follow.

serēnus, -a, -um, serene, calm.

sērus, -a, -um, late; sērō, adv., late, too late.

serviō, -īre, -servīvī, servītum, 4, serve (with dat.).

servitūs, -ūtis, f., slavery.

servō, 1, save, preserve, keep.

servus, -ī, m., slave, servant.

sevērus, -a, -um, strict, severe.

sex, numeral, six.

sī, conj., if.

sīc, adv., thus.

sīdus, -eris, n., star.

signum, -ī, n., sign, standard, statue, seal.

sileō, -ēre, siluī, 2, be silent.

silva, -ae, f., wood, forest.

similis, -e, like, similar.

simplex, -icis, simple, frank, honest.

simul ac (atque), conj., as soon as.

sīn, conj., but if.

sine, prep. with abl., without.

singulāris, -e, singular, remarkable.

singulī, -ae, -a, pl., one to each, single.

sinō, -ere, sīvī, 3, allow.

sitis, -is, acc. -im, f., thirst.

sīve . . . sīve (seu), whether (= if) . . . or.

sōbrius, -a, -um, sober, moderate, prudent, cautious.

socius, -ī (-iī), m., ally, companion.

sōl, sōlis, m., sun.

sōlācium, -ī (-iī), n., comfort, solace.

soleō, -ēre, solitus sum, 2, semideponent, be accustomed.

sōlitūdō, -inis, f., loneliness, desert.

solitus, -a, -um, customary, usual.

sollicitus, -a, -um, anxious.

solum, -ī, n., soil, earth, land.

sōlum, adv., only; nōn sōlum, not only.

sōlus, -a, -um, alone, only.

solvō, -ere, solvī, solūtum, 3, loose, set free; set sail (sc. nāvem); solūtus, -a, -um, set free.

somnus, -ī, m., sleep.

sonitus, -ūs, m., sound.

sonus, -ī, m., sound.

sordēs, -is, -ium, f., dirt, squalor (especially in pl.).

soror, -ōris, f., sister.

sors, sortis, -ium, f., lot, casting of lots, fate.

spatium, -ī (-iī), n., room, space, length of time.

speciēs, -eī, f., appearance, form.

spectō, 1, look at (with acc.), watch.

speculum, -ī, n., mirror.

spērō, 1, hope.

spēs, -eī, f., hope; promise.

spīritus, -ūs, m., breath, spirit; (Late Latin) the Holy Ghost.

spīrō, 1, breathe.

splendidus, -a, -um, bright, splendid; splendidē, adv., nobly.

spoliō, 1, strip, despoil, rob (with acc. and abl.).

sponte suā, of its own accord.

statim, adv., immediately.

statūra, -ae, f., height.

status, -a, -um, appointed, regular.

stella, -ae, f., star.

sterilis, -e, barren; (with gen.) destitute of.

stō, stāre, stetī, statum, 1, stand.

Stoicus, -a, -um, Stoic; Stoicī, -ōrum, m., the Stoics, followers of the Stoic philosophy.

strēnuus, -a, -um, busy, strenuous.

strepitō, 1, make a noise, chatter (poet.), = strepō.

strepō, -ere, strepuī, 3, make a noise.

stringō, -ere, strīnxī, strictum, 3, draw tight, draw (a sword).

studeō, -ēre, studuī, 2, be eager for, favor (with dat.).

studiōsus, -a, -um, eager for, fond of (with gen.).

studium, -ī (-iī), n., enthusiasm, study, partiality.

stultitia, -ae, f., folly.

stultus, -a, -um, foolish.

suādeō, -ēre, suāsī, suāsum, 2, advise, urge.

suāvis, -e, sweet, pleasant.

sub, prep. with acc. (for motion) or abl., under.

subiciō, -icere, -iēcī, -iectum, 3, put under, subdue (conquer).

subitō, adv., suddenly.

sublīmis, -e, high, exalted, sublime.

subsidium, -ī (-iī), n., support, assistance.

subsīdō, -sīdere, -sēdī, -sessum, 3, sink down, settle down.

subveniō, -venīre, -vēnī, ventum, 4, come to the help of (with dat.).

succīdō, -ere, succīdī, succīsum, 3, cut down.

Suessiōnēs, -um, m. pl., a tribe in Gaul near the modern Soissons.

sum, esse, fuī, fut. part. futūrus, irreg., to be.

summa, -ae, f., main part, sum, total.

summus, -a, -um, highest, greatest.

sūmō, -ere, sūmpsī, sūmptum, 3, take, assume, exact (punishment).

supellex, supellectilis, f., furniture; also the furniture of the mind.

super, prep. with acc. or abl., over;

with abl. also = about, cf. dē with abl.

superbus, -a, -um, proud.

superior, -ius, higher, previous.

superō, 1, overcome.

superstes, -itis, surviving.

superstitiō, -ōnis, f., superstition.

supersum, -esse, -fuī, irreg., be over, remain.

superveniō, 4, come upon, arrive.

suppleō, -ēre, supplēvī, supplē-tum, 3, fill up, make complete.

supplicātiō, -ōnis, f., public prayer or thanksgiving.

suppliciter, adv., humbly.

supplicō, 1, pray to, worship (with dat.).

supportō, 1, bring up.

supprimō, -primere, -pressī, -pres-sum, 3, suppress, check.

suprā, prep. with acc., above.

suprēmus, -a, -um, highest, last.

surgō, surgere, surrēxī, surrē-ctum, 3, stand up, rise.

sustineō, -ēre, sustinuī, susten-tum, 2, hold out against, withstand.

suus, -a, -um, his own, her own, its own, their own.

tabella, -ae, f., writing-tablet; pl., letter.

taberna, -ae, f., hut, cottage, shop, tavern.

taceō, -ēre, tacuī, tacitum, 2, be silent.

taedet, impers., be weary of, lit. it wearies (with acc. and gen.).

tālis, -e, such, of such a character.

tam, so (with adjectives).

tam . . . quam, as much . . . as.

tamen, however, yet.

tamquam, adv., just as, as if, as it were; tamquam sī, just as if (with subjve.).

tandem, adv., at last, finally; (in interrog. clauses) pray, now, then.

tangō, -ere, tetigī, tactum, 3, touch.

tantum, adv., only, merely.

tantum, so much.

tantum abest ut . . . ut . . . (with two subjunctives), far from . . ., lit. so far is it absent that . . . that . . .

tantus, -a, -um, so great.
taratantara, the sound made by a trumpet.
taurus, -ī, m., bull.
tēctum, -ī, n., roof, house.
tegmen, -minis, n., covering.
tegō, -ere, tēxī, tēctum, 3, cover.
tellūs, -ūris, f., earth, ground, land.
tēlum, -ī, n., weapon, javelin.
temnō, -ere, tempsī, temptum, 3, despise (see contemno).
temperantia, -ae, f., moderation, temperance.
temperō, 1, regulate, be moderate; (with ā and abl.) refrain from.
tempestās, -ātis, f., storm, weather.
templum, -ī, ʉ., temple; pl., sanctuaries, high places.
temptō, 1, attempt, try; (with inf.) try to.
tempus, -oris, n., time.
tendō, -ere, tetendī, tentum, 3, stretch, stretch out.
tenebrae, -ārum, f. pl., darkness.
tenebricōsus, -a, -um, shadowy.
teneō, tenēre, tenuī, 2, hold, keep.
tepor, -ōris, m., warmth.
ter, three times.
tergum, -ī, n., back.
terminus, -ī, m., limit, end.
terra, -ae, f., earth, land; pl. the whole earth, e.g. orbis terrārum, the world.
terreō, -ēre, terruī, territum, 2, terrify.
terribilis, -e, terrible.
terror, -ōris, m., terror, fright.
tertius, -a, -um, third.
testis, -is, -ium, m. and f., witness.
theātrum, -ī, n., theatre.
timeō, -ēre, timuī, 2, fear.
timidus, -a, -um, afraid, fearful.
timor, -ōris, m., fear.
tollō, -ere, sustulī, sublātum, irreg., lift, remove, take away.
torreō, -ēre, torruī. tostum, 2, scorch, burn.
tot, so many.
totiens, so often.
tōtus, -a, -um, whole.
trādō, trādere, trādidī, trāditum, 3, hand over, hand down, relate, transmit to posterity.

trādūcō, -dūcere, -dūxī, -ductum, 3, lead across.
trāgula, -ae, f., javelin.
trāiciō, -icere, -iēcī, -iectum, 3, throw across; with acc., cross.
trāns, prep. with acc., across.
trānseō, -īre, -iī, -itum, irreg., go across, cross.
trānsigō, -igere, -ēgī, -āctum, 3, finish, complete.
trēs, tria, numeral, three.
Trēverī, -ōrum, m. pl., a tribe in Gaul on the Moselle.
tribuō, -ere, tribuī, tribūtum, 3, allot, grant, attribute.
triduum, -ī, n., three days.
triplex, -icis, triple.
tristis, -e, sad.
triumphō, 1, triumph.
Trōiānus, -a, -um, Trojan.
trucīdō, 1, kill, slaughter.
trux, trucis, rough, harsh.
tū, pers. pron., you (sing.).
tuā, see interest.
tuba, -ae, f., trumpet.
tueor, -ērī, 2, deponent, look at, guard, protect.
tum, tunc, adv., then.
tumidus, -a, -um, swelling, rising high.
tumulō, 1, bury (poet.).
tumulus, -ī, m., mound; tomb, monument.
turba, -ae, f., crowd, throng.
turpis, -e, base, disgraceful.
turris, -is, -ium, acc. -im (-em), f., tower.
tūtus, -a, -um, safe.
tuus, tua, tuum, your, yours (sing.).
Tyrius, -a, -um, Tyrian, from Tyre in Phoenicia; purple.

ubi, adv., where?
ubi, conj., where, when.
ūllus, -a, -um, any (after a negative).
ulterior, -ius, farther.
ultimus, -a, -um, last, farthest.
ultiō, -ōnis, f., taking vengeance, punishment.
ultor, -ōris, m., avenger.
umbra, -ae, f., shade, shadow; ghost (poet.).
umquam, adv., ever.

ūnā, *adv.*, together.
unda, -ae, *f.*, wave, water.
unde, *interrog. adv.*, from where?
whence?
ūndēvīgintī, *numeral*, nineteen.
undique, from all sides, everywhere.
ungula, -ae, *f.*, hoof.
unguentum, -ī, *n.*, perfume.
ūnicē, *adv.*, especially.
ūnus, -a, -um, *numeral*, one.
urbs, urbis, -ium, *f.*, city.
urgeō, -ēre, ursī, 2, press hard.
ūrō, -ere, ussī, ustum, 3, burn.
usquam, *adv.*, anywhere.
usque, always; (*with* ad *and acc.*)
continuously.
ūsus, -ūs, *m.*, use, experience, custom, utility, need.
ut, in order that, so that; as; when;
like; how; *after* vereor (= nē
nōn), lest . . . not.
ut ita dīcam, so to speak.
uter, utra, utrum, *interrog. pron.*,
which of two?
uterque, utraque, utrumque, both,
each (of two).
utī = ut.
ūtilis, -e, useful.
ūtilitās, -ātis, *f.*, usefulness, expediency, profit.
utinam, would that (*introduces a wish
in the subjve.*); *neg.* nē *or* utinam
nē.
ūtor, ūtī, ūsus sum, 3, *deponent*, use
(*with abl.*).
utpote (*with* quī *and subjve.*), seeing
that, since.
utrīque, *pl. of* uterque, both sides.
utrum . . . an . . . (necne), whether
. . . or . . . (or not) (*in double indirect
questions*).
utrum . . . an . . . (annōn) (*in double
direct questions*).
uxor, -ōris, *f.*, wife.

vacca, -ae, *f.*, cow.
vacuus, -a, -um, empty; empty-
handed.
vagulus, -a, -um, *diminutive of*
vagus.
vagus, -a, -um, wandering.
valdē, *adv.*, exceedingly, very.
valē (*imperat. of* valeō, be strong,

healthy), farewell, good-bye (*used
at the end of a letter*).
valeō, -ēre, valuī, 2, be strong, well
(in health).
valetūdō, -inis, *f.*, health, good or
bad health.
vallēs (vallis), -is, -ium, *f.*, valley.
vāllum, -ī, *n.*, rampart.
varius, -a, -um, various, varied.
vātēs, -is, -um, *m.*, poet.
vehō, vehere, vexī, vectum, 3, carry.
vel, -ve, or, even; vel . . . vel,
either . . . or.
vēlōx, -ōcis, swift.
velut, velutī, *adv.*, even as, like.
venia, -ae, *f.*, pardon.
veniō, venīre, vēnī, ventum, 4, come.
vēnor, 1, *deponent*, hunt.
ventus, -ī, *m.*, wind.
venustus, -a, -um, lovely, charming,
graceful.
vēr, vēris, *n.*, spring.
verbera, -um, *n. pl.*, lashes, flogging.
verberō, 1, beat, flog.
verbum, -ī, *n.*, word.
vērē, *adv.*, truly.
vereor, -ērī, veritus sum, 2, *deponent*, fear, revere; fear that (*with*
nē *and subjve.*), that not (*with* ut).
vergō, -ere, 3, turn, bend.
vēritās, -ātis, *f.*, truth, truthfulness.
vērō, *adv.*, indeed.
versō, 1, turn, turn over (*i.e.* read).
versus, -ūs, *m.*, a verse, line (in
poetry).
vertō, -ere, vertī, versum, 3, turn,
change.
vērum, *conj.*, but in truth, but.
vērus, -a, -um, true; vērum, *n.* the
truth; *also* vēra, *n. pl.*
vēscor, vēscī, 3, *deponent*, feed on
(*with abl.*).
vesper, -eris, *m.*, evening.
vespillo, -ōnis, *m.*, corpse-bearer
(*perhaps* undertaker). *Rare word
used by Martial.*
vester, vestra, vestrum, your,
yours (*pl.*).
vēstīgium, -ī (-iī), *n.*, footstep, footprint.
vestis, -is, -ium, *f.*, clothing.
vetō, -āre, vetuī, vetitum, 1, forbid
(*with inf.*).

vetus, -eris, old.
vetustus, -a, -um, old.
vexō, 1, molest, trouble.
via, -ae, f., road.
viātor, -ōris, m., traveller.
victor, -ōris, m., victor, conqueror; victorious.
victōria, -ae, f., victory.
victrīx, -īcis, fem. of victor, victorious.
videō, vidēre, vīdī, vīsum, 2, see.
videor, vidērī, vīsus sum, 2, seem (with dat. of person); vidētur, impers., it seems good.
viduus, -a, -um, widowed; sometimes unmarried.
vigeō, -ēre, viguī, 2, be vigorous, flourish.
vigilia, -ae, f., watch.
vigiliae, -ārum, f. (pl. of vigilia, watch), watchmen, sentries.
vigilō, 1, watch, be wakeful.
vigintī, numeral, twenty.
villa, -ae, f., country-house, villa, farm.
vinciō, -īre, vīnxī, vīnctum, 4, bind.
vincō, vincere, vīcī, victum, 3, conquer.
vinculum (vinclum), -ī, n., bond, fetter; pl., prison.
vindex, -icis, m., deliverer, liberator, avenger.
vindicō, 1, claim; with in lībertātem, set free.
vīnum, -ī, n., wine.

vir, virī, m., man, husband (a man in the best sense of the word).
virgō, -inis, f., maiden.
viridis, -e, green.
virtūs, -ūtis, f., virtue, courage, excellence.
vīs, (vīs), vīrium, f., force; pl., strength; vim faciō, use force.
viscera, -um, n. pl., the inner parts (of the body), flesh.
vīsō, -ere, vīsī, vīsum, 3, look at, view, go to see.
vīta, -ae, f., life; vītam agō, live.
vitiōsus, -a, -um, faulty, bad.
vitium, -ī (-iī), n., fault, defect.
vitrum, -ī, n., glass; woad.
vīvidus, -a, -um, lively.
vīvō, vīvere, vīxī, vīctum, 3, live.
vīvus, -a, -um, living.
vocō, 1, call, summon, name.
volō, velle, voluī, irreg., be willing, wish; quid sibi vult? what does he mean, what is his purpose?
volō, 1, fly.
volūbilis, -e, rolling, turning.
voluntās, -ātis, f., will, wish, choice.
voluptās, -ātis, f., pleasure, delight.
vōs, pers. pron., you (pl.).
vōsmet = vos.
vōx, vōcis, f., voice.
vulnerō, 1, wound.
vulnus, -eris, n., wound.
vultus (voltus), -ūs, m., face, expression.

Zephyrus, -ī, m., west wind.

ENGLISH–LATIN VOCABULARY

This contains words used in Exercise 2 of each Lesson

able, be able, can, possum, posse, potuī, *irreg.*
about, dē, *prep. with abl.*
about to . . ., *use fut. part.*
above, suprā, *prep. with acc.*
accustomed, be accustomed, soleō, -ēre, solitus sum, 2, *semi-deponent.*
achievements, rēs gestae, *f. pl.*
across, trāns, *prep. with acc.*
adversity, rēs adversae, *f. pl.*
advise, moneō, monēre, monuī, monitum, 2.
afraid, be afraid, *see* **fear.**
after, post, *prep. with acc.*
after, postquam, *conj.* (Lesson XXII).
afterwards, posteā, *adv.*
age, life, aetās, -ātis, *f.*
agriculture, agricultūra, agrī cultūra, -ae, *f.*
alike, *see* **like.**
all, every, omnis, -e; *usually pl.* omnēs, -ia.
all, *i.e.* **entirely (whole),** tōtus, -a, -um.
allow, sinō, -ere, sīvī, 3, *with inf.*
allowed, it is allowed, licet, licuit, *impers.*, 2 *(with dat. and inf.).*
ally, companion, socius, -ī, -iī, *m.*
alone, only, sōlus, -a, -um.
already, now, iam, *adv.*
altar, āra, -ae, *f.*
although, quamquam, *with indic.* (Lesson XXII), cum, *with subjve.* (Lesson XXXIII), quamvis, *with subjve.* (Lesson XXXVI).
always, semper.
am (are, is), *see* **be.**
American, *use* Americānus, -a, -um.
and, et, -que, *conj.*
anger, īra, -ae, *f.*
angry, be angry, īrāscor, -īrāscī, īrātus sum, 3, *deponent, with dat.*
announce, nuntiō, 1.
another, alius, alia, aliud.
any *(after a negative),* ūllus, -a, -um.

anyone, anything, quis, quid *(after sī, nisi, num, nē).*
anyone, anything, *(after a negative),* quisquam, quidquam (quicquam); **nor anything,** nec quidquam; **not . . . anything, nothing,** nihil.
appearance, speciēs, -eī, *f.*
appeased, easily appeased, plācābilis, -e.
apple (fruit), pōmum, -ī, *n.*
appointed, cōnstitūtus, -a, -um.
approach, adpropinquō (app-), 1, *with dat.*
approve of, probō, 1.
are (you) to, am (I) to, *express by deliberative subjve.*
arms, arma, -ōrum, *n. pl.*
army, exercitus, -ūs, *m.*
arrive (at), perveniō, -īre, pervēnī, perventum, 4, *with* ad *and acc.*
as, ut (Lesson XXII).
as, (such) as, quālis, -e *(after* tālis, -e).
as, (the same) as, quī, atque, ac *(after* īdem).
as soon as, simul ac, simul atque (Lesson XXII).
Ascra, of, Ascraeus, -a, -um.
ask, ask for, rogō, 1, *with acc.*
ask, inquire, quaerō, -ere, quaesīvī, quaesītum, 3, *with* ā *and abl.*
ask, request, petō, -ere, petīvī, petītum, 3, *with* ā *and abl.*
assemble, conveniō, -īre, convēnī, conventum, 4.
at the house of, apud, *prep. with acc.*
attack, oppugnō, 1; adorior, -orīrī, -ortus sum, 4, *deponent.*
away, be away, absum, abesse, āfuī, *irreg.*

baggage, impedīmenta, -ōrum, *n.*
battle, fight a battle, *see* **fight.**
be, to be, sum, esse, fuī, *irreg.*
bear, *see* **bring.**

beat, flog, verberō, 1.
beautiful, pulcher, -chra, -chrum.
because, quod, quia, *with indic.
or subjve*. (Lessons XXII and
XXXVI).
because (as they say), quod, *with
subjve.*
become, fīō, fierī, factus sum, *irreg.*
bee, apis, -is, -ium, *f.*
before, ante, *prep. with acc.*
before, anteā, *adv.*
before, antequam, priusquam, *with
indic. or subjve.* (Lessons XXII and
XXXVI).
behind, after, post, *prep. with acc.*
believe, crēdō, -ere, crēdidī, crēditum, 3, *with dat.*
below, infrā, *prep. with acc.*
better, melior, melius.
better, *adv.*, melius.
between, inter, *prep. with acc.*
bird, avis, -is, -ium, *f.*
black, āter, -tra, -trum; niger, -gra,
-grum.
blame, culpō, 1.
body, corpus, -oris, *n.*
book, liber, -brī, *m.*
born, be born, nāscor, nāscī, nātus
sum, 3, *deponent.*
both, each (of two), uterque, utraque, utrumque.
both . . . and, et . . . et.
boy, puer, puerī, *m.*
brave, fortis, -e.
bravery, courage, excellence, virtūs, -ūtis, *f.*
bring, bear, ferō, ferre, tulī, lātum,
irreg.
Briton, British, Britannus, -a, -um;
the Britons, Britannī.
build, aedificō, 1.
business, rēs, rērum, *f. pl.*
busy, keep busy, rēs agō.
but, sed.
buy, emō, emere, ēmī, emptum, 3.
by, ā, ab, *prep. with abl. (agent).*

call (by name), name, appellō, 1.
call, summon, name, vocō, 1.
camp, castra, -ōrum, *n. pl.*
can, *see* able.
capture, take, capiō, capere, cēpī,
captum, 3.

car, *see* chariot.
care, Care *personified*, cūra, -ae, *f.*
carry, portō, 1.
Carthaginians, Poenī, -ōrum, *m. pl.*
carve, sculpō, sculpere, sculpsī,
sculptum, 3.
cause, causa, -ae, *f.*
cause (*e.g.* hatred), *see* move.
cavalry, *see* horseman.
certain, a certain, quīdam, quaedam, quiddam.
chair, sella, -ae, *f.*
chalk, crēta, -ae, *f.*
change, mūtō, 1.
changed, mūtātus, -a, -um.
charm, dulcēdō, -inis, *f.*
charm, *see* capture.
chariot, currus, -ūs, *abl.* -ū, *m.*
children, līberī, -ōrum, *m. pl. of*
līber.
Christians, Christiānī, -ōrum, *m. pl.*
Cisalpine, Cisalpīnus, -a, -um.
citizen, cīvis, -is, -ium, *m. and f.*
city, urbs, urbis, -ium, *f.*
close by, near, iuxtā, *adv. and prep.
with acc.*
collect, bring together, cōnferō,
-ferre, contulī, collātum, *irreg.*
collect, compel, cōgō, -ere, coēgī,
coāctum, 3.
collect, lead together, condūcō,
dūcere, -dūxī, -ductum, 3.
come, veniō, venīre, vēnī, ventum, 4.
command, iubeō, -ēre, iussī, iussum,
2, *with inf.*; imperō, 1, *with dat. and
ut with subjve.*
companion, comes, -itis, *m. and f.*
conquer, defeat, vincō, vincere, vīcī,
victum, 3.
conspire, agree, cōnsentiō, -sentīre,
-sēnsī, -sēnsum, 4.
constancy, steadfastness, cōnstantia, -ae, *f.*
consul, cōnsul, -sulis, *m.*
consular, one who has been consul, cōnsulāris, *m.*
correctly, rightly, rēctē.
could, *see* able.
country (fatherland), patria, -ae, *f.*
country, the country, rūs, ruris, *n.*
country, of the, rustic, agrestis, -e.
courage, *see* bravery, constancy.
cow, vacca, -ae, *f.*

create, creō, 1.
crime, scelus, -eris, n.
cure, heal, medeor, -ērī, 2, deponent, with dat.

daughter, fīlia, -ae, f.
dawn, prīma lūx (lūcis), f.
dead, dead man, mortuus, -a, -um.
death, Death, mors, mortis, f.
defeat, see conquer.
defend, dēfendō, -ere, dēfendī, dēfēnsum, 3.
delay, cūnctor, 1, deponent.
delightful, see sweet.
deliver (from), līberō, 1, with abl.
demand, poscō, -ere, poposcī, 3.
describe, dēscrībō, -ere, dēscrīpsī, dēscrīptum, 3.
desire, cupiō, -ere, cupīvī, cupītum, 3.
despise, dēspiciō, -spicere, -spexī, -spectum, 3.
destroy, dēleō, dēlēre, dēlēvī, dēlētum, 2.
die, morior, morī, fut. part. moritūrus, 3, deponent.
difficult, difficilis, -e.
dine, cēnō, 1.
dinner, cēna, -ae, f.
divide, dīvidō, -videre, -vīsī, -vīsum, 3.
divine, dīvīnus, -a, -um.
do, make, faciō, facere, fēcī, factum, 3; to do (in the doing), factū.
doctor, medicus, -ī, m.
door, iānua, -ae, f.
doubt, there is no doubt that, non dubium est, with quīn and subjve.
drive, agō, agere, ēgī, āctum, 3.
drive out, expel, expellō, expellere, expulī, expulsum, 3.

each, quisque, quaeque, quidque.
eagerly, avidē, adv.
early, mātūrē, adv.
easily, facile, adv.
easy, facilis, -e.
eight, octō.
emperor, chief, prīnceps, -cipis, m.
enemy (public enemy), hostis, -is, -ium, m., usually pl.
enemy (personal enemy), inimīcus, -ī, m.
enough, satis.
envoy, lēgātus, -ī, m.

escape, effugiō, -ere, effūgī, 3.
even, also, etiam, adv.
everything, omnia, n. pl. of omnis.
example, exemplum, -ī, n.
excess, in excess, too much, nimis.
expedient, see useful.

face, faciēs, -eī, f.
face, expression, vultus (voltus), -ūs, m.
fall, cadō, cadere, cecidī, cāsum, 3.
far, by far, multō (with comparative).
far (with absum), longē, adv.
far from . . ., tantum abest ut . . . ut . . . with two subjves. (Lesson XXXVII).
farmer, agricola, -ae, m.
farther, ulterior, -ius.
fate, destiny, fātum, -ī, n.
fatherland, see country.
fathers, of one's, patrius, -a, -um.
fault, vitium, -ī, -iī, n.
faulty, vitiōsus, -a, -um.
fear, be afraid, timeō, -ēre, timuī, 2; vereor, -ērī, veritus sum, 2, deponent; fear that (lest), nē with subjve.; fear that (lest) not, ut (nē nōn) with subjve.
festival, holiday, fēstus diēs (-eī), m.
field, ager, agrī, m.
fifteen, quīndecim.
fight, pugnō, 1; (fight) with, cum with abl.; (a battle) was fought, pugnātum est, impers.
finally, at last, tandem, adv.
find, reperiō, reperīre, repperī, repertum, 4.
find, find out, inveniō, -īre, invēnī, inventum, 4.
finish, complete, cōnficiō, -ere, cōnfēcī, cōnfectum, 3.
fire, ignis, -is, -ium, m.
first, the first (to), prīmus, -a, -um.
five, quīnque.
flame, flamma, -ae, f.
flee, fugiō, -ere, fūgī, 3.
fly, volō, 1.
follow, sequor, sequī, secūtus sum, 3, deponent.
food, cibus, -ī, m.
foolish, stultus, -a, -um.
for, enim (second word in sentence), nam.

for a long time, *see* long time.
forces, troops, cōpiae, -ārum, *f. pl.*
forest, silva, -ae, *f.*
forget, oblīvīscor, -vīscī, oblītus sum,
    3, *deponent, with gen.*
form, fōrma, -ae, *f.*
former, the, ille, illa, illud, *dem.
    pron.*
formerly, before, prius, *adv.*
fortify, mūniō, mūnīre, mūnīvī,
    mūnītum, 4.
fortunate, fortūnātus, -a, -um.
fortune, fortūna, -ae, *f.*
forty, quadrāgintā.
free, līber, -era, -erum.
free from, be free from, *see*
    lack.
friend, amīcus, -ī, *m.*
friendly, amīcus, -a, -um.
friendship, amīcitia, -ae, *f.*
from, ā, ab, *prep. with abl.*
from, out of, ē, ex, *prep. with abl.*
from, (prevent) from, quōminus
    or nē *with subjve., or* quīn *after a
    neg.*

garden, hortus, -ī, *m.*
Gauls, Gallī, -ōrum, *m.*
general, commander-in-chief, im-
    perātor, -ōris, *m.*
general, leader, dux, ducis, *m.*
general, legion-commander, lēgā-
    tus, -i, *m.*
Germans, Germānī, -ōrum, *m.*
get possession of, potior, -īrī, potītus
    sum, 4, *deponent, with abl., some-
    times gen.*
ghost (*poet.*), shade, umbra, -ae, *f.*
gift, dōnum, -ī, *n.*
girl, puella, -ae, *f.*
give, dō, dare, dedī, datum, 1.
give back, reddō, reddere, reddidī,
    redditum, 3.
glory, praise, worth, laus, laudis, *f.*
go, eō, īre, iī, itum, *irreg.*
go away, discēdō, -ere, discessī,
    discessum, 3; abeō, -īre, -iī, -itum,
    irreg.
go out, exeō, -īre, -iī, -itum, *irreg.*,
    ēgredior, ēgredī, ēgressus sum, 3,
    deponent.
go past, praetereō, -īre, -iī, -itum,
    irreg.

god, deus, -ī, *pl.* dī, deī, *m.*
golden, aureus, -a, -um.
good, bonus, -a, -um.
good (citizens), bonī, -ōrum, *m.
    pl.*
good, the good, bonum, -ī, *n.*
grain, frūmentum, -ī, *n.*
great, magnus, -a, um.
greater, māior, māius.
greatest, maximus, -a, -um.
greedy, avidus, -a, -um.
Greek, Graecus, -a, -um.
Greeks, Graecī, -ōrum, *m. pl.*
guard, protection, praesidium, -ī,
    -iī, *n.*

hand, manus, -ūs, *f.*
hand (to), hand over, hand down,
    trādō, -ere, trādidī, trāditum, 3.
happen, contingō, -ere, contigī, 3;
    would happen (*fut. inf.*), *use* fore ut
    with subjve.
happy, beātus, -a, -um; fēlīx, fēlīcis.
harmonious, concors, -cordis.
harshness, asperitās, -ātis, *f.*
hasten, properō, 1.
hate, dislike, ōdī, ōdisse, *perf. with
    pres. meaning.*
hatred, dislike, odium, -ī, -iī, *n.*
have, has, habeō, habēre, habuī,
    habitum, 2; *or use* sum *with dat. of
    possession.*
he, she, it, (*with* quī) he who, is, ea,
    id, *dem. pron.*
healthy, sānus, -a, -um.
hear, listen to, audiō, audīre, audīvī,
    audītum, 4.
Helvetians, Helvētiī, -ōrum, *m. pl.*
her, *see* he.
here, hīc.
herself, *see* himself.
hide, lie hid, lateō, -ēre, latuī, 2.
high, altus, -a, -um.
highest, greatest, summus, -a, -um;
    suprēmus, -a, -um.
highly, magnī, *gen. of value with*
    aestimō.
him, *see* he; *sometimes* = himself.
himself, herself, itself, ipse, ipsa,
    ipsum, *emph. pron.*
himself, herself, itself, them-
    selves, sē (*acc., abl.*) suī (*gen.*),
    sibi (*dat.*), *reflex. pron.*

his (her, its, their) own, suus, -a, -um, *poss. adj.*
hold, teneō, tenēre, tenuī, 2.
home, domus, -ūs (*acc. pl.* -ōs), *f.*; at home, domī.
honor, adorn, ornō, 1.
honorable, virtuous, honestus, -a, -um.
hope, hope for, spērō, 1.
horse, equus, -ī, *m.*
horseman, (*pl.*) cavalry, eques, equitis, *m.*
hostage, obses, -idis, *m. and f.*
hour, hōra, -ae, *f.*
hurry, hasten, properō, 1.
hurt, feel pain, doleō, -ēre, doluī, 2.
hurt, harm, noceō, -ēre, nocuī, nocitum, 2, *with dat.*
husband, vir, virī, *m.*
hymn, *see* song.

I (me), ego, *pers. pron.*
if, sī.
if . . . not, unless, nisi.
immediately, statim.
immortal, immortālis, -e; aeternus, -a, -um.
impartial, equal, aequus, -qua, -quum.
in, in, *prep. with abl.*
in order that, in order to, to (*purpose*), ut *with subjve.*; quō *with sub ve. before a comparative*; ad *with acc. or* causā *with gen. of gerundive or gerund; acc. of supine after verbs of motion.*
in order that . . . not, not to . . ., nē *with subjve.*
in such a way, ita.
in the works of, apud, *with acc.*
integrity, innocence, innocentia, -ae, *f.*
intelligence, mind, mēns, mentis, *f.*
intelligence, prudence, prūdentia, -ae, *f.*
interest, enthusiasm, study, studium, -ī, -iī, *n.*; (interest) in, *use gen.*
interest, it is to the interest (of), interest, *impers., with gen. or ablatives like* meā.
into, in, *prep. with acc.*
is, *see* am.

island, īnsula, -ae, *f.*
it, *see* he.
it (= itself), *see* himself.
Italian, Ītalicus, -a, -um.
its own, *see* his own.

javelin, pīlum, -ī, *n.*; tēlum, -ī, *n.*
just as if, tamquam sī, quasi.

keep, save, servō, 1.
keep, hold, *see* hold.
kill, occīdō, -ere, occīdī, occīsum, 3; necō, 1.
kill oneself (resolve upon death), mortem sibi cōnscīscere (cōnscīscō, cōnscīscere, cōnscīvī, cōnscītum), 3.
kind of man who, is quī (*with subjve.*).
kindness, beneficium, -ī, -iī, *n.*
kindness, indulgence, indulgentia, -ae, *f.*
king, rēx, rēgis, *m.*
kingdom, rēgnum, -ī, *n.*
know, sciō, -īre, scīvī, 4; nōvī, *perf. of* nōscō, -ere, nōvī, nōtum, 3, come to know; not know, nesciō, -īre, nescīvī, 4; ignōrō, 1.

lack, be without, careō, -ēre, caruī, 2, *with abl.*
language, tongue, lingua, -ae, *f.*
last, at last, tandem.
last, remain, persist, permaneō, -ēre, permānsī, permānsum, 2.
latter, the, hic, haec, hoc, *dem. pron.*
laugh, rīdeō, -ēre, rīsī, rīsum, 2.
law, lēx, lēgis, *f.*
lazy, slack, segnis, -e.
lead, dūcō, dūcere, dūxī, ductum, 3,
leader, dux, ducis, *m.*
learn, discō, -ere, didicī, 3.
leave behind, leave, relinquō, relinquere, relīquī, relictum, 3.
legion, legiō, -ōnis, *f.*
let, should, *express by jussive subjve.*
letter (epistle), litterae, -ārum, *f. pl.*; epistula, -ae, *f.*
liberty, lībertās, -ātis, *f.*
lift up, levō, 1.
light, lūmen, -inis, *n.*; lūx, lūcis, *f.*
like, similar, similis, -e, *with dat.*

like, *see* wish.
listen-to, hear, audiō, audīre, audīvī, audītum, 4.
literature, litterae, -ārum, *f. pl.*
live, reside, habitō, 1.
live, be alive, vīvō, vīvere, vīxī, vīctum, 3.
live, (*with acc.*, *e.g.* annōs, vītam) agō, agere, ēgī, āctum, 3.
long, longus, -a, -um.
long time, for a long time, diū.
longing, dēsīderium, -ī, -iī, *n.*; (longing) for, *use gen.*
longing, love, *see* love.
look at, watch, spectō, 1, *with acc.*
loss, damnum, -ī, *n.*
lot, sors, sortis, *f.*
lovable, amābilis, -e.
love, amō, 1.
love, amor, -ōris, *m.*
lover, loving, amāns, -antis.
lyric, lyricus, -a, -um.

make, *see* do.
make a noise, strepō, -ere, strepuī, 3.
make a speech, ōrātiōnem habeō, 2.
man, human being, homo, -inis, *m.*
man, husband (a man in the best sense of the word), vir, virī, *m.*
man (who), *see* he.
many, multī, -ae, -a.
map (paper), charta, -ae, *f.*
march, iter faciō, facere, fēcī, factum, 3.
marvel, wonder at, admīror, -ārī, admīrātus sum, 1, *deponent.*
master (of a house), dominus, -ī, *m.*
master, teacher, magister, -trī, *m.*
me, *see* I.
mean, the mean, middle state, mediocritās, -ātis, *f.*
merchant, mercātor, -ōris, *m.*
messenger, nuntius, -ī, -iī, *m.*
mile, a thousand paces, mīlle passūs; two miles, duo mīlia passuum.
mind, intellect, mēns, mentis, -ium, *f.*
mind, spirit, animus, -ī, *m.*
miss, long for, dēsīderō, 1.
month, mēnsis, -is, -ium, *m.*
monument, monumentum, -ī, *m.*
moon, lūna, -ae, *f.*

morals, character, mōrēs, -um, *m.*, *pl. of* mōs, mōris, custom.
mountain, mōns, montis, -ium, *m.*
move, moveō, movēre, mōvī, mōtum, 2.
must, one must, it is necessary, oportet, -uit, *impers.*, 2, *with inf.*; necesse est, *impers.*, *with subjve.*; *also expressed by gerundive* (Lesson XXXVIII).

narcissus, narcissus, -ī, *m.*
nature, nātūra, -ae, *f.*
near, prope, *with acc.*; *sometimes* ad, apud, *with acc.*
nearer, propius.
neighborhood, neighboring (to), fīnitimus, -a, -um.
neither . . . nor, nec (neque) . . . nec (neque).
never, numquam.
ninth, nōnus, -a, -um.
no . . ., there is no . . ., . . . is lacking, dēsum, *irreg.*
no doubt, *see* doubt.
no longer, nōn iam.
no one, nēmō, *acc.* nēminem.
noise, *see* make a noise.
nose, nāsus, -ī, *m.*
not, nōn.
not at all . . . nor, nihil . . . nihil.
not, do not (*negative command*), nōlī (nōlīte) *with inf.*; nē *with perf. subjve.*; nē *with subjve. in indirect command.*
not only . . . but also, nōn modo . . . sed etiam.
nothing, nihil, *n.*, *indecl.*; nihilum, -ī, *n.*
now, nunc.

ode, *see* song.
of, *after a numeral*, ē, ex, *with abl.*
often, saepe, *adv.*
old man, senex, senis, *m.*
on, in, *prep. with abl.*
on account of, ob, *prep. with acc.*; propter, *prep. with acc.*
once, once upon a time, ōlim, *adv.*
one, ūnus, -a, -um.
one (of two), *see* other.
one who has been consul, *see* consular.
onto, *see* into.

open, aperiō, aperīre, aperuī, apertum, 4.
opportunity (ability), facultās, -ātis, f.
or, or not, see **whether.**
order, see **in order that.**
other, the other (of two), alter, -era, -erum; **one . . . the other,** alter . . . alter.
other, see **another.**
others, see **some.**
ought, owe, dēbeō, -ēre, dēbuī, dēbitum, 2.
our, our own, ours, noster, -tra, -trum, poss. adj.
our men, nostrī, m. pl. of noster.
over, super, prep. with acc.
overcome, superō, 1.
own, see **his own.**

pain, grief, dolor, -ōris, m.; **cause pain = be for a pain** (dat.).
part, pars, partis, f.
part, the part of, expressed by the genitive.
peace, pāx, pācis, f.; **make peace,** pācem faciō.
people, populus, -ī, m.
peoples, races, clans, pl. of gēns, gentis, -ium, f.; nātiō, -ōnis, f.
perfume, unguentum, -ī, n.
persuade, persuādeō, -ēre, persuāsī, persuāsum, 2, with dat.
philosopher, philosophus, -ī, m.
pig, porcus, -ī, m.
place, locus, -ī, m.; pl. loca, -ōrum, n.
place in command (of), praeficio, -ficere, -fēcī, -fectum, 3, with acc. and dat.
please, placeō, -ēre, placuī, placitum, 2, with dat.
please, delight, dēlectō, 1, with acc.
plenty, cōpia, -ae, f.
plough, arō, 1.
poem, see **song.**
poet, poēta, -ae, m.
poor, needy, inops, -opis.
possess, possideō, -ēre, possēdī, possessum, 2.
possession, see **get possession of.**
poverty, paupertās, -ātis, f.
power, potentia, -ae, f.
praise, laudō, 1.

pray, beg, ōrō, 1.
prefer, mālō, mālle, māluī, irreg.
prevent, hinder, prevent (from), impediō, -īre, impedīvī, impedītum, 4; dēterreō, -ēre, dēterruī, dēterritum, 2, with quōminus or nē and subjve., or quīn after a neg.; prohibeō, -ēre, prohibuī, prohibitum, 2, may take inf.
previous (higher), superior, -ius.
previously, before, anteā, adv.
progress, make progress, prōficiō, -ere, prōfēcī, prōfectum, 3.
promise, polliceor, -ērī, pollicitus sum, 2, deponent; prōmittō, -ere, prōmīsī, prōmissum, 3.
promise, hope, spēs, -eī, f.
prosperity, rēs secundae, f. pl.
provided that, dummodo, dum, modo, with subjve.
province, prōvincia, -ae, f.
publish, give forth, ēdō, -ere, ēdidī, ēditum, 3.

queen, rēgīna, -ae, f.

race, kind, genus, generis, n.
rampart, vāllum, -ī, n.
read, legō, legere, lēgī, lēctum, 3.
receive, accipiō, -ere, accēpī, acceptum, 3.
recently, nūper, adv.
recognize, see **understand** (cognōscō).
recollect, remember, recordor, -ārī, recordātus sum, 1, deponent; **recollection,** use infin.
remain, maneō, -ēre, mānsī, mānsum, 2.
remarkable, singular, singulāris, -e.
remember, reminīscor, reminīscī, 3, with gen. (or acc.); recordor, -ārī, recordātus sum, 1, deponent.
Remi, Rēmī, -ōrum, m.
reply, answer, respondeō, -ēre, respondī, respōnsum, 2.
report, announce, nuntiō, 1.
republic, rēs pūblica (rēspūblica), reī pūblicae, f.
rest (of), reliquus, -a, -um.
retreat, sē recipere (recipiō, -ere, recēpī, receptum, 3).

return, redeō, -īre, rediī, *irreg.*
reward, praemium, -ī, -iī, *n.*
rhythms, *pl. of* modus, -ī, *m.*
river, flūmen, -inis, *n.*; fluvius, -iī, *m.*
road, via, -ae, *f.*
Roman, Rōmānus, -a, -um.
Romans, Rōmānī, -ōrum, *m. pl.*
rule, govern, regō, regere, rēxī, rēctum, 3.
rule (as emperor), imperō, 1.

Sabine, Sabīnus, -a, -um.
sad, tristis, -e.
sad, wretched, miser, -era, -erum.
safe, tūtus, -a, -um.
sail, nāvigō, 1.
sailor, nauta, -ae, *f.*
same, the same, īdem, eadem, idem; the same . . . as, īdem qui, īdem atque (ac).
sanctuary, *see* temple.
satisfy (fill up), expleō, -plēre, -plēvī, -plētum, 2.
save, *see* keep.
say, tell, dīcō, -ere, dīxī, dictum, 3; to say (in the saying), dictū.
say (*in quotations*), inquam, 3 *sing.* inquit, *irreg.*
school, schola, -ae, *f.*
scorch, torreō, -ēre, torruī, tostum, 2.
sea, mare, maris, *n.*
seal, sign, standard, signum, -ī, *n.*
see, videō, vidēre, vīdī, vīsum, 2.
see that, bring it about that, fac, *imperat. of* faciō, *with subjve.*
seek, seek for, petō, petere, petīvī (-iī), petītum, 3.
seem, videor, vidērī, vīsus sum, 2.
senate, senātus, -ūs, *m.*
senator, senātor, -ōris, *m.*
send, mittō, mittere, mīsī, missum, 3.
serene, calm, serēnus, -a, -um.
servant, slave, servus, -ī, *m.*
set out, proficīscor, -īscī, profectus sum, 3, *deponent.*
set up, determine, cōnstituō, cōnstituere, cōnstituī, cōnstitūtum, 3.
seven, septem.
sheep, ovis, -is, -ium, *f.*
shepherd, pastor, -ōris, *m.*

shore, lītus, -oris, *n.*
show, mōnstrō, 1.
shut, claudō, claudere, clausī, clausum, 3.
since, cum, *with subjve.* (Lesson XXXIII); quoniam, *with indic.* (Lesson XXII).
sing, canō, canere, cecinī, 3.
sink down, subsīdō, -sīdere, -sēdī, -sessum, 3.
sister, soror, -ōris, *f.*
sit, be seated, sedeō, sedēre, sēdī, sessum, 2.
sit down, cōnsīdō, cōnsīdere, cōnsēdī, cōnsessum, 3.
sky, caelum, -ī, *n.*
slaughter, caedēs, -is, -ium, *f.*
small, parvus, -a, -um.
smell, olfaciō, -facere, -fēcī, -factum, 3.
so (*with adjectives*), tam.
soil, solum, -ī, *n.*
soldier, mīles, -itis, *m.*
some . . . others, aliī . . . aliī.
some who, *see* there are (some) who.
someone, aliquis, -qua, -quid.
something, *see* someone.
son, fīlius, -ī, -iī, *m.*
song, carmen, -inis, *n.*
soon, mox.
soul, anima, -ae, *f.*
spare, parcō, -ere, pepercī, parsum, 3, *with dat.*
speak, *see* say.
speech, ōrātiō, -ōnis, *f.*
spirit, breath, spīritus, -ūs, *m.*
spirit, mind, animus, -ī, *m.*
spring, vēr, vēris, *n.*
stand, stō, stāre, stetī, statum, 1.
stand up, surgō, surgere, surrēxī, surrēctum, 3.
star, stella, -ae, *f.*
state, cīvitās, -ātis, *f.*
Stoics, Stoicī, -ōrum, *m.*
story, fābula, -ae, *f.*
strengthen, make firm, firmō, 1.
stretch, stretch out, tendō, -ere, tetendī, tentum, 3.
such (the kind of man) . . . as, tālis, -e . . . quālis, -e.
Suessiones, Suessiōnēs, -um, *m.*
summer, aestās, -ātis, *f.*

sun, sōl, sōlis, *m.*
support, assistance, subsidium, -ī, -iī, *n.*
suppress, press, premō, -ere, pressī, pressum, 3.
sustain, nourish, alō, -ere, aluī, altum, 3.
sweet, dulcis, -e.
swim, nō, 1.
sword, gladius, -ī, -iī, *m.*

take, capiō, capere, cēpī, captum, 3.
talk to (with), loquor, loquī, locūtus sum, 3, *deponent, with cum and abl.*
tame, conquer, domō, -āre, domuī, domitum, 1.
tavern, taberna, -ae, *f.*
teach, doceō, docēre, docuī, doctum, 2.
tell, relate, narrō, 1 (*with dat. of pers.*).
tell, *see* **say.**
temple, templum, -ī, *n.*
ten, decem.
tenth, decimus, -a, -um.
territory, boundaries, *pl. of* fīnis, -is, -ium, *m.*, **end.**
terrify, terreō, -ēre, terruī, territum, 2.
than, quam, *or use abl. of comparison.*
that, so that, ut *with subjve.*; *negative* ut nōn.
that (over there), ille, illa, illud, *dem. pron.*
the man (who), *see* **he.**
theatre, theātrum, -ī, *n.*
their own, *see* **his own.**
them, *see* **he.**
themselves, *see* **himself.**
then, tum, tunc.
there are (some) who, sunt quī (*with subjve.*).
thing, rēs, reī, *f.*
things, *often expressed by neut. pl.*, *e.g.* ea, *n. pl. of* is.
think, putō, 1; existimō, 1; arbitror, -ārī, arbitrātus sum, 1, *deponent.*
think, feel, perceive, sentiō, -īre, sēnsī, sēnsum, 4.
think, propose, cēnseō, -ēre, cēnsuī, cēnsum, 2.
thirst, sitis, -is, *acc.* -im, *f.*
this, hic, haec, hoc, *dem. pron.*

those, *see* **he** (= is), **that** (= ille).
through, per, *prep. with acc.*
throw, iaciō, -ere, iēcī, iactum, 3.
time, tempus, -oris, *n.*
time, for a long time, *see* **long time.**
to, ad, *with acc.*
to, not to, *see* **in order that.**
today, hodiē, *adv.*
tomorrow, crās, *adv.*
too much, nimis, nimium.
torment, torture, cruciō, 1.
tower, turris, -is, -ium, *f.*
town, oppidum, -ī, *n.*
tree, arbor, -oris, *f.*
Trojan, Trōiānus, -a, -um.
troops, forces, cōpiae, -ārum, *f. pl.*
truth, vēra, *n. pl. of* vērus, -a, -um; vērum, -ī, *n.*
turn out, happen, ēveniō, -īre, ēvēnī, ēventum, 4.
twice, bis.
two, duo, duae, duo.

uncle (mother's brother), avunculus, -ī, *m.*
understand, intellegō, -ere, intellēxī, intellēctum, 3.
understand, get to know, cognōscō, -ere, cognōvī, cognitum, 3.
undertaker, *use* vespillo, -ōnis, *m.*
unexpectedly, imprōvīsō.
unfriendly, inimīcus, -a, -um.
universe, mundus, -ī, *m.*
University, Acadēmīa, -ae, *f.*
unknown, ignōtus, -a, -um.
unlucky, infēlīx, -īcis.
until, dum, dōnec, *with indic. or subjve.* (Lessons XXII and XXXVI).
until (= **to**), in, *prep. with acc.*
untimely, immātūrus, -a, -um.
unwilling, invītus, -a, -um.
us, *see* **we.**
use, ūtor, ūtī, ūsus sum, 3, *deponent, with abl.*
useful, ūtilis, -e.

valley, vallēs (vallis), -is, -ium, *f.*
value, reckon, aestimō, 1.
victorious (*fem.*), victrīx, -īcis, *fem. of* victor.
villa, country-house, vīlla, -ae, *f.*

wagon, carrus, -ī, *m.*

wait, wait for, exspectō, 1, *with acc.*

walk, ambulō, 1.

walls (of a city), moenia, -ium, *n. pl.*

want, *see* **wish.**

war, bellum, -ī, *n.*

watch, look at, spectō, 1.

water, aqua, -ae, *f.*

we, nōs.

wealth, riches, dīvitiae, -ārum, *f. pl.*

well, bene.

were, will be, shall be, *see* **be.**

were to . . ., *see* Lesson XXXIV (Conditions).

what (that which), *see* **who.**

what?, *see* **which?, who?**

what kind of? quālis, -e.

when, ubi, *with indic.* (Lesson XXII); cum, *with indic. or subjve.* (Lesson XXXIII); *sometimes expressed by abl. abs.*

where, ubi, quā.

whether, num *(in indirect questions with subjve.).*

whether . . . or (or not), utrum (-ne) . . . an . . . (necne) *(in indirect questions with subjve.);* utrum (-ne) . . . an . . . (annōn) *(in direct questions).*

which?, what?, quī, quae, quod, *interrog. adj.*

which, *see* **who.**

while, dum, *with indic.* (Lesson XXII).

who, which, quī, quae, quod, *rel. pron.*

who?, what?, quis, quid, *interrog. pron.*

why?, cūr, quārē.

wife, uxor, -ōris, *f.*

willing, be willing, *see* **wish.**

wind, ventus, -ī, *m.*

window, fenestra, -ae, *f.*

wine, vīnum, -ī, *n.*

wing, penna, -ae, *f.*

winter quarters, hīberna, -ōrum, *n.pl.*

wisdom, sapientia, -ae, *f.*

wise, wise man, sapiēns, -entis.

wish, be willing, volō, velle, voluī, *irreg.*

wish that, I wish that, *see* **would that.**

with, cum, *prep. with abl.*

withdraw, retire, dēcēdō, -ere, dēcessī, dēcessum, 3.

without, sine, *with abl.*

woman, fēmina, -ae, *f.*; mulier, -eris, *f.*

wonderful, mīrus, -a, -um.

word, verbum, -ī, *n.*

works of, *see* **in the works of.**

world, orbis, -is, *m., with* terrārum.

worse, pēior, -ius; dēterior, -ius.

worship, cultivate, colō, colere, coluī, cultum, 3.

would that, I wish that, utinam, *with subjve.*

would, would have . . ., *see* Lesson XXXIV (Conditions).

wound, vulnus, -eris, *n.*

write, scrībō, scrībere, scrīpsī, scrīptum, 3.

wrongdoing, evil deed, malefactum (male factum), -ī, *n.*

year, annus, -ī, *m.*

yesterday, herī, *adv.*

yet *(after* **although),** tamen.

yield (to), cēdō, -ere, cessī, cessum, 3, *with dat.*

you, tū *(sing.),* vōs *(pl.), pers. pron.*

young man *(usually from twenty to forty years old),* iuvenis, -is, *m.*

young man, youth, adulēscēns, -entis, *m.*

your, yours, tuus, -a, -um, *poss. adj. (sing.);* vester, -tra, -trum, *poss. adj. (pl.).*

VOCABULARY OF
PERSONS AND PLACES

Actium, -ī (-iī), *n.,* a promontory in Epirus, where Antony and Cleopatra, the Egyptian queen, were defeated at sea by Octavian (Augustus) in 31 B.C.

Aenēās, -ae, *m.,* Aeneas, the hero of Vergil's *Aeneid.*

Āfrica, -ae, *f.,* Africa.

Agamemnōn, -onis, *m.,* Agamemnon, king of Mycenae, leader of the Greeks in the Trojan War.

Alcyonē, -ēs, *f.,* the wife of Ceyx, who threw herself into the sea and was changed into a halcyon or kingfisher (Ovid's *Metamorphoses*).

Alpēs, -ium, *f. pl.,* the Alps.

Alphēus, -ī, *m.,* Alpheus, a river in Greece.

America, -ae, *f.,* may be used for America.

Anglia, -ae, *f.,* England; **Nova Anglia,** New England.

Antōnius, -ī (-iī), *m.,* Marcus Antonius (Antony), whom Cicero attacked in his *Philippics.*

Apollō, -inis, *m.,* Apollo. *See* **Phoebus.**

Appius, -ī (-iī), *m.,* Appius, quoted by Sallust.

Apūlia, -ae, *f.,* Apulia (in the southeast of Italy).

Arar, -is, *m.,* a river in Gaul, the Arar, now the Saône.

Arethūsa, -ae, *f.,* Arethusa, a Greek nymph who was changed into a spring of water at Syracuse in Sicily (Ovid's *Metamorphoses*).

Ariovistus, -ī, *m.,* Ariovistus, leader of the Germans who fought against Caesar in Gaul.

Aristotelēs, -is, *m.,* Aristotle, Greek philosopher, founder of the Peripatetic School, 384–322 B.C.

Arria, -ae, *f.,* Arria, the wife of Paetus; she chose to die with her husband, when he was condemned to death in A.D. 42.

Asia, -ae, *f.,* Asia, part of Asia Minor.

Atalanta, -ae, *f.,* a girl in Ovid's *Metamorphoses,* famous for her speed in running, who was beaten by Hippomenes and married him.

Athēnae, -ārum, *f. pl.,* Athens.

Augustus, -ī, *m.,* Augustus, the first Emperor; *princeps* 27 B.C.–A.D. 14.

Bacchus, -ī, *m.,* Bacchus, the Greek Dionysus, god of wine.

Bandusia, -ae, *f.,* a spring mentioned by Horace in the *Odes.*

Baucis, -idis, *f.,* Baucis, the wife of Philemon in Ovid's *Metamorphoses.*

Bethlehem, *n. indecl.,* Bethlehem in Palestine, the birthplace of Christ.

Britannia, -ae, *f.,* Britain.

Brūtus, -ī, *m.,* Marcus Junius Brutus, one of the leaders of the conspiracy against Julius Caesar, 44 B.C.

C., *abbrev. for* **Gāius.**

Caesar, -aris, *m.,* Gaius Julius Caesar, Roman statesman, general, and author, 102 (100)–44 B.C., conquered Gaul between 58 and 51; defeated Pompey's armies at Pharsalus in Thessaly (48), Thapsus in Africa (46), Munda in Spain (45), and won the battle of Zela in Asia Minor (47). Author of the *Gallic War* and the *Civil War.*

Canada, -ae, *f.,* may be used for Canada.

Cannae, -ārum, *f. pl.,* Cannae, a village in Apulia where Hannibal defeated the Romans in 216 B.C.

Cantabrigia, -ae, *f.,* Cambridge in England and in Massachusetts.

Carthāgō, -inis, *f.,* Carthage.

Cassius, -ī (-iī), *m.,* Gaius Cassius Longinus, one of the leaders of the conspiracy against Julius Caesar, 44 B.C.

Casticus, -ī, *m.,* Casticus, a member of the Sequani in Gaul.

Catilīna, -ae, *m.,* Catiline, whose conspiracy was exposed by Cicero in 63 B.C.

Catō, -ōnis, *m.* (1) M. Porcius Cato the elder (Censorius), 234–149 B.C., famous as a strict judge of morals; (2) M. Porcius Cato the younger (Uticensis), 95–46 B.C., the enemy of Caesar, who killed himself after the battle of Thapsus.

Catullus, -ī, *m.,* Gaius Valerius Catullus, Roman lyric and elegiac poet, *c.* 84–*c.* 54 B.C.

Cerēs, -eris, *f.,* Ceres, the Greek Demeter, goddess of the fruits of the earth.

Cērinthus, -ī, *m.,* Cerinthus, to whom Sulpicia wrote love poetry.

Cēÿx, -ÿcis, *m.,* Ceyx, who suffered shipwreck and was changed into a kingfisher (Ovid's *Metamorphoses*).

Chloē, -ēs, *f.,* Chloe, a woman mentioned by Martial.

Christus, -ī, *m.,* Christ (*lit.* the Anointed).

Cicerō, -ōnis, *m.,* (1) Marcus Tullius Cicero, 106–43 B.C. (*see* **Tullius**); (2) Marcus Tullius Cicero, Cicero's son, born in 65 B.C.; (3) Quintus Tullius Cicero, 102–43 B.C., Cicero's brother.

Cilicia, -ae, *f.,* Cilicia, a province in Asia Minor where Cicero was governor.

Cinara, -ae, *f.,* Cinara, a lady mentioned by Horace, who seems to have been a real person.

Claudius, -ī (-iī), *m.,* the Emperor Claudius, *princeps* A.D. 41–54.

Cleomenēs, -is, *m.,* Cleomenes, a Syracusan mentioned in Cicero's *Verrine Orations.*

Cn., *abbrev. for* **Gnaeus.**

Corinna, -ae, *f.,* a lady mentioned in Ovid's love poetry, probably not a real person.

Corinthus, -ī, *f.,* Corinth, in Greece.

Cornēlius, *see* **Tacitus.**

Corsica, -ae, *f.,* Corsica.

Crassus, -ī, *m.,* L. Licinius Crassus, the orator, one of the speakers in Cicero's *De Oratore.*

Crēta, -ae, *f.,* Crete.

Creūsa, -ae, *f.,* the wife of Aeneas at Troy.

Cupīdō, -inis, *m.,* Cupid, son of Venus.

Curēs, -ium, the chief town of the Sabines in Italy.

Cynthia, -ae, *f.,* a lady described in the love poetry of Propertius, probably Hostia.

Dacia, -ae, *f.,* Dacia, the modern Rumania, conquered by Trajan.

Daedalus, -ī, *m.,* mythical Athenian architect who built the Cretan labyrinth; he invented wings and escaped from Crete (Ovid's *Metamorphoses*).

Daphnē, -ēs, *f.,* Daphne, the daughter of the river-god Peneus, who was loved by Apollo and turned into a laurel tree (Ovid's *Metamorphoses*).

Dēlia, -ae, *f.,* a lady described in the love poetry of Tibullus, perhaps Plania.

Dēmocritus, -ī, *m.,* Democritus, Greek philosopher who introduced the atomic theory of Leucippus, *c.* 460–*c.* 370 B.C.

Dēmophoön, -ontis, *m.,* a son of Theseus, king of Athens, who deserted Phyllis (Ovid's *Heroides*).

Diaulus, -ī, *m.,* Diaulus, mentioned by Martial.

Dīdō, -ōnis, *f.,* Dido, queen of Carthage, who killed herself when Aeneas sailed for Italy (Vergil, *Aeneid* 4).

Dionȳsus, -ī, *m.,* *see* **Bacchus.**

Dīviciācus, -ī, *m.,* Diviciacus, a member of the Aedui in Gaul and friendly to Caesar.

Dīvicō, -ōnis, *m.,* a leader of the Helvetii.

Domitiānus, -ī, *m.,* the Emperor Domitian, *princeps* A.D. 81–96.

Dumnorīx, -īgis, *m.,* Dumnorix, an Aeduan.

Eborācum, -ī, *n.,* York (in England); **Novum Eborācum,** New York.

Elissa, -ae, *f.,* Dido, queen of Carthage.

Ennius, -ī (-iī), *m.,* Q. Ennius, early Roman epic poet, 239–169 B.C.

Epaphrodītus, -ī, *m.,* Epaphroditus, condemned to death by Domitian.

Ephesus, -ī, *f.,* Ephesus in Asia Minor.

Epicūrus, -ī, *m.,* Greek philosopher, founder of the Epicurean philosophy based on the theory of atoms, 342/1–271/70 B.C.

Eurōpa, -ae, *f.,* Europe.

Fabullus, -ī, *m.,* Fabullus, a friend of Catullus.

Flōrus, -ī, *m.,* Roman writer who lived in the time of Hadrian.

Gādēs, -ium, *f. pl.,* Gades (Cadiz) in Spain.

Gallia, -ae, *f.,* Gaul. Gallia Cisalpina was in the northern part of Italy, Gallia Transalpina was beyond the Alps. Gallia Narbonensis was the Roman province in the south of France; Caesar conquered the rest of Gaul north of this province.

Garumna, -ae, *m.,* the river Garonne.

Genāva, -ae, *f.,* Geneva.

Georgia, -ae, *f.,* may be used for Georgia.

Gracchī, -ōrum, *m. pl.,* Tiberius and Gaius Sempronius Gracchus, tribunes in 133 and 123 B.C., who lost their lives in trying to bring about reforms.

Graecia, -ae, *f.,* Greece.

Hadriānus, -ī, *m.,* the Emperor Hadrian, *princeps* A.D. 117–38.

Hannibal, -alis, *m.,* Hannibal, Carthaginian general in the Second Punic War.

Herculēs, -is, *m.,* Hercules, the Greek¹ Herakles, son of Jupiter and Alcmena, later the god of strength. The origin of his worship is described in Livy, Bk. 1, and Vergil, *Aen.* 8.

Hērō, -ūs, *f.,* Hero of Sestos, who was loved by Leander of Abydos (Ovid's *Heroides*).

Hēsiodus, -ī, *m.,* Hesiod, an early Greek poet who wrote the *Works*

and Days, a poem about farming. He came from Ascra in Boeotia. Vergil refers to him in the *Georgics.*

Hippomenēs, -ae, *m.,* the youth who raced against Atalanta (Ovid's *Metamorphoses*).

Hispānia, -ae, *f.,* Spain.

Homērus, -ī, *m.,* Homer, the early Greek poet to whom the *Iliad* and *Odyssey* are attributed.

Horātius, -ī (-iī), *m.,* Quintus Horatius Flaccus, poet, 65–8 B.C., author of *Odes, Satires,* and *Epistles.*

Īcarus, -ī, *m.,* Icarus, the son of Daedalus, who tried to fly but fell into the Aegean Sea (Ovid's *Metamorphoses*).

Īŏ, -ūs, *f.,* Io, the daughter of Inachus, king of Argos. She was loved by Jupiter and through fear of Juno was changed into a cow (Ovid's *Metamorphoses*).

Ītalia, -ae, *f.,* Italy.

Iūlius, -ī (-iī), *m.,* C. Iulius Caesar, *see* **Caesar.**

Iūnō, -ōnis, *f.,* Juno, the wife of Jupiter.

Iuppiter, Iovis, *m.,* Jupiter, the Italian sky-god, corresponding to the Greek Zeus, greatest of the Greek and Roman gods.

Iuvenālis, -is, *m.,* Decimus Iunius Iuvenalis, Juvenal, author of sixteen Satires, *c.* A.D. 60–130.

L., *abbrev. for* **Lūcius.**

Labiēnus, -ī, *m.,* T. Atius Labienus, one of Caesar's generals in Gaul.

Lalagē, -ēs, *f.,* a girl's name in Horace's *Odes* (from a Greek word meaning 'to prattle').

Latium, -ī (-iī), *n.,* Latium, a part of Italy which includes Rome.

Lēander, -rī, *m.,* Leander (in Ovid's *Heroides*), who swam the Hellespont to visit Hero.

Lentulus, -ī, *m.,* P. Cornelius Lentulus Sura, one of the conspirators supporting Catiline.

Lesbia, -ae, *f.,* a lady described in the love poetry of Catullus, probably Clodia. The name Lesbia suggests

Sappho, the Greek poetess of Lesbos (600 B.C.).

Leuconoë, -ēs, *f.,* Greek name of a girl in Horace's *Odes.*

Libya, -ae, *f.,* Libya, Africa.

Licinius, -ī (-iī), *m.,* Licinius Murena, consul in 23 B.C., addressed by Horace in the *Odes.*

Līvius, -ī (-iī), *m.,* Titus Livius, 59 B.C.–A.D. 17, historian of the Roman Republic. Only 35 of his 142 books survive.

Londinium, -ī (-iī), *n.,* London (in England); **Novum Londinium,** New London (in Connecticut).

Lūcānus, -ī, *m.,* M. Annaeus Lucanus, the poet Lucan, author of the *Pharsalia,* a poem about the war between Caesar and Pompey; he was condemned to death by Nero in A.D. 65.

Lūcius, a Roman praenomen.

Lucrētius, -ī (-iī), *m.,* T. Lucretius Carus, author of the *De Rerum Natura* on the philosophy of Epicurus, 99 (94)–55 B.C.

Lupercal, -ālis, *m.,* grotto on the Palatine Hill at Rome, sacred to Lycean Pan. His festival, the Lupercalia, was in February.

M., *abbrev. for* **Mārcus.**

Maecēnās, -ātis, *m.,* Maecenas, patron of Roman poets, addressed by Horace in the *Odes.*

Maeonidēs = Homērus, -ī, *m.,* Homer.

Mantua, -ae, *f.,* Mantua in north Italy; Vergil was born at Andes near Mantua.

Mārcus, -ī, *m.,* Marcus, a Roman praenomen or first name, as in M. Tullius Cicero.

Mars, Martis, *m.,* Mars, the Greek Ares, god of war.

Martiālis, -is, *m.,* M. Valerius Martialis, the Roman poet Martial, *c.* A.D. 40–*c.* 104.

Mēdēa, -ae, *f.,* daughter of the king of Colchis, who helped Jason and the Argonauts to get the golden fleece; when Jason rejected her, she killed her own children. This is described in the tragedy written by Euripides. *See also* Ovid's *Metamorphoses.*

Meliboeus, -ī, *m.,* a shepherd in Vergil's *Eclogues.*

Messalla, -ae, *m.,* M. Valerius Messalla, consul in 61 B.C.

Minerva, -ae, *f.,* goddess of wisdom, called Pallas Athene by the Greeks.

Misēnum, -ī, *n.,* a town and harbor in Campania, where the elder Pliny was admiral of the fleet. He died during the eruption of Mount Vesuvius in A.D. 79.

Mūsae, -ārum, *f.,* the nine Muses.

Mūsaeus, -ī, *m.,* Greek poet in the time of Orpheus, mentioned in *Aeneid* 6.

Narcissus, -ī, *m.,* a youth in Greek mythology who fell in love with himself and was changed into a narcissus (Ovid's *Metamorphoses*).

Nemesis, -is, *f.,* Nemesis, a lady mentioned in the poems of Tibullus. This is also the name of the Greek goddess of justice, who punishes human pride.

Numicius, -ī (-iī), *m.,* addressed by Horace in the *Epistles.*

Octāviānus, -ī, *m.,* C. Iulius Caesar Octavianus, grand-nephew and adopted son of Julius Caesar. He became the Emperor Augustus.

Opīmius, -ī (-iī), *m.,* L. Opimius, consul in 121 B.C.

Orgetorix, -īgis, *m.,* a Helvetian of noble rank.

Orpheus, -ī, *m.,* the mythical singer of Thrace who tried to bring his wife Eurydice back from the lower world (Ovid's *Metamorphoses*).

Ovidius, -ī (-iī), *m.,* Publius Ovidius Naso, Roman elegiac poet, 43 B.C.– *c.* A.D. 18, author of the *Amores, Heroides, Ars Amatoria, Remedia Amoris, Fasti, Tristia, Epistulae ex Ponto* in elegiac verse and of the *Metamorphoses,* a poem in hexameters about transformations.

Paetus, -ī, *m.,* Caecina Paetus, the husband of Arria.

Palātium, -ī (-iī), *n.,* the Palatine, one of the seven hills of Rome.

Parthenopē, -ēs, *f.,* the old name of Neapolis, Naples.

Phaëthōn, -ontis, *m.,* Phaëthon, the son of Apollo, who tried to drive the chariot of the sun (Ovid's *Metamorphoses*).

Philēmōn, -onis, *m.,* Philemon, an old man who prayed that he might never be separated from his wife. The gods turned them both into trees (Ovid's *Metamorphoses*).

Philippī, -ōrum, *m. pl.,* a town in Macedonia where Octavian and Antony defeated Brutus and Cassius in 42 B.C.

Phoebus, -ī, *m.,* Phoebus or Apollo, the god of the sun.

Phyllis, -idis, *f.,* Phyllis, a Thracian princess who was deserted by Demophoon (Ovid's *Heroides*).

Pīsō, -ōnis, *m.,* M. Piso, consul in 61 B.C.

Plancus, -ī, *m.,* L. Munatius Plancus, consul in 42 B.C., mentioned in Horace's *Odes*.

Platō, Platōn, -ōnis, *m.,* the Greek philosopher Plato, founder of the Academic philosophy *c.* 429–347 B.C.

Plautus, -ī, *m.,* T. Maccius Plautus, author of Comedies, 254–184 B.C.

Plīnius, -ī (-iī), *m.,* C. Plinius Caecilius Secundus, the younger Pliny, A.D. 61/62–before 114, author of *Letters,* especially letters to the Emperor Trajan (Book 10). Also C. Plinius Secundus, the elder Pliny, A.D. 23/24–79, author of the *Historia Naturalis* (*see* **Misenum**).

Pompēius, -ēī, *m.,* Gnaeus Pompeius Magnus, Roman statesman and general, rival of Julius Caesar, 106–48 B.C.

Postumus, -ī, *m.,* addressed by Martial in an epigram.

Priamus, -ī, *m.,* Priam, king of Troy, in Vergil's *Aeneid.*

Procris, *f.,* Procris, the wife of Cephalus. In this legend she

thought he was in love with 'Aura', when he was really addressing *aura* (the breeze). He mistook her for a wild beast and shot her in the forest (Ovid's *Metamorphoses*).

Propertius, -ī (-iī), *m.,* Sextus Propertius, Roman elegiac poet, *c.* 50– *c.* 16 B.C.

Prōtesilāus, -ī, *m.,* the first Greek to be killed in the Trojan War.

Pȳramus, -ī, *m.,* Pyramus, lover of Thisbe in a Babylonian story told by Ovid in the *Metamorphoses* and used by Shakespeare in *A Midsummer Night's Dream.*

Pȳthagorās, -ae, *m.,* Pythagoras, Greek philosopher about 550 B.C., founder of the Pythagorean philosophy.

Q., *abbrev. for* **Quīntus.**

Quīntiliānus, -ī, *m.,* M. Fabius Quintilianus, Quintilian, author of twelve books on the Training of the Orator, *c.* A.D. 35–before 100.

Quīntilius Vārus, -ī, *m.,* a general whose legions were defeated by the Germans in A.D. 9 while Augustus was emperor.

Quīntus, -i, *m.,* Quintus, a Roman praenomen; e.g. Cicero's brother, Q. Tullius Cicero.

Rhēnus, -ī, *m.,* the river Rhine.

Rhodanùs, -ī, *m.,* the river Rhone.

Rōma, -ae, *f.,* Rome.

Rōmulus, -ī, *m.,* Romulus, the first Roman king. The tradition is that there were kings at Rome from 753 to 510 B.C.

Rubicō, -ōnis, *m.,* the Rubicon, a river which was the boundary between Cisalpine Gaul and Italy.

Sabidius, -ī (-iī), *m.,* addressed by Martial in an epigram.

Sardinia, -ae, *f.,* Sardinia.

Sicilia, -ae, *f.,* Sicily.

Sirmio, -ōnis, *m.,* a peninsula on the Lacus Benacus in north Italy where Catullus had a home, now Sirmione.

Sōcratēs, -is, *m.,* Socrates, famous

Greek philosopher, 469–399 B.C., who appears in the works of Plato.

Sōracte, -is, *n.,* a mountain in Etruria mentioned in Horace's *Odes.*

Suētōnius, -ī (-iī), *m.,* C. Suetonius Tranquillus, who published the lives of the Caesars (Julius to Domitian) about A.D. 120.

Sulmō, -ōnis, *m.,* Sulmona, Ovid's birthplace in Italy in the land of the Paeligni.

Syrācūsae, -ārum, *f. pl.,* Syracuse in Sicily.

Syria, -ae, *f.,* Syria.

T., *abbrev. for* **Titus.**

Tacitus, -ī, *m.,* Cornelius Tacitus, the historian, author of the *Annals* and *Histories, c.* A.D. 55–*c.* 117.

Tamesis, -is, *m.,* the river Thames in England and in Connecticut.

Tarentum, -ī, *n.,* Tarentum, in south Italy.

Tarquinius, -ī (-iī), *m.,* Tarquinius Superbus, Tarquin the Proud, the last Roman king.

Terentia, -ae, *f.,* the wife of M. Tullius Cicero.

Terentius, -ī (-iī), *m.,* P. Terentius Afer, *c.* 195–159 B.C., author of Comedies.

Theophrastus, -ī, *m.,* Greek philosopher who became head of the Peripatetic School at Athens after Aristotle's death in 322 B.C.

Thisbē, -ēs, *f.,* a girl loved by Pyramus (Ovid's *Metamorphoses*).

Thrasea, -ae, *m.,* Thrasea Paetus, Stoic philosopher put to death by Nero in A.D. 66. His death occurs in the last surviving chapter of the *Annals* of Tacitus.

Thūlē, -ēs, *f.,* an island in the extreme north of Europe.

Tiberius, -ī (-iī), the Emperor Tiberius, *princeps* A.D. 14–37.

Tibullus, -ī, *m.,* Albius Tibullus, Roman elegiac poet, *c.* 55–19 B.C.

Tībur, -uris, *n.,* a town in Latium, now Tivoli.

Tīrō, -ōnis, *m.,* Cicero's secretary.

Titus, -ī, *m.,* the Emperor Titus, *princeps* A.D. 79–81.

Tomis, -is, *f.,* a town on the Black Sea, to which Ovid was banished in A.D. 8.

Trāiānus, -ī, *m.,* the Emperor Trajan; *princeps* A.D. 98–117.

Trasimēnus, -ī, *m.* (*used with* **lacus, -ūs,** lake), Lake Trasimene in Etruria where Hannibal defeated the Romans in 217 B.C.

Trōia, -ae, *f.,* Troy.

Tullia, -ae, *f.,* the daughter of M. Tullius Cicero.

Tullius, -ī (-iī), *m.,* Marcus Tullius Cicero, 106–43 B.C., statesman and orator, consul 63 B.C.; author of speeches, works on rhetoric and philosophy, and letters.

Ulubrae, -ārum, *f. pl.,* Ulubrae, a small town in Latium, now Cisterna.

Varius, -ī (-iī), *m.,* T. Varius, a tragic poet, contemporary with Vergil and Horace.

Vārus, -ī, *m.,* P. Attius Varus, Pompeian commander in Africa (Caesar's *Civil War*). *See also* **Quintilius Varus.**

Venus, Veneris, *f.,* Venus, the Greek Aphrodite, goddess of love.

Vercingetorix, -īgis, *m.,* leader of the Gallic revolt against Caesar in 52 B.C.

Vergilius, -ī (-iī), *m.,* Publius Vergilius Maro, Roman epic poet, 70–19 B.C., author of the *Eclogues, Georgics,* and *Aeneid.*

Vērōna, -ae, *f.,* birthplace of Catullus in north Italy (Cisalpine Gaul).

Verrēs, -is, *m.,* Verres, the corrupt governor of Sicily, who was attacked in Cicero's *Verrine Orations.*

Vesontiō, -ōnis, *f.,* a town of the Sequani in Gaul, now Besançon.

Vespasiānus, -ī, *m.,* the Emperor Vespasian, *princeps* A.D. 69–79.

Vesuvius, -ī (-iī), *m.,* a volcano in Campania, Italy.

Virginia, -ae, *f.,* may be used for Virginia.

INDEX

The numbers refer to sections